CHURCH AND POLITICS IN LATIN AMERICA

LATIN AMERICAN STUDIES SERIES

General Editors: Philip O'Brien and Peter Flynn

The series is a new initiative designed to give a comprehensive analysis of some of the many complex problems facing contemporary Latin America and individual Latin American countries.

published

Christian Anglade and Carlos Fortin (*editors*)
THE STATE AND CAPITAL ACCUMULATION IN LATIN AMERICA
Volume 1: Brazil, Chile, Mexico
Volume 2: Argentina, Bolivia, Colombia, Ecuador, Peru, Uruguay, Venezuela

David Booth and Bernardo Sorj (*editors*)
MILITARY REFORMISM AND SOCIAL CLASSES: The Peruvian Experience, 1968–80

Rhys Jenkins
TRANSNATIONAL CORPORATIONS AND INDUSTRIAL TRANSFORMATION IN LATIN AMERICA
TRANSNATIONAL CORPORATIONS AND THE LATIN AMERICAN AUTOMOBILE INDUSTRY

Dermot Keogh (*editor*)
CHURCH AND POLITICS IN LATIN AMERICA

David Slater
TERRITORY AND STATE POWER IN LATIN AMERICA: The Peruvian Case

forthcoming

Jean Carrière, Jacqueline Roddick and Nigel Howarth (*editors*) POLITICS, INDUSTRIAL RELATIONS AND THE LABOUR MOVEMENT IN LATIN AMERICA, 1860–1980 (*four volumes*)

Joe Foweraker
CLASS DOMINATION AND THE AUTHORITARIAN STATE: A Political Economy of Latin America

Church and Politics in Latin America

Edited by
Dermot Keogh
Department of Modern History
University College, Cork

Foreword by Graham Greene

MACMILLAN

First published 1990

Published by
THE MACMILLAN PRESS LTD
Houndmills, Basingstoke, Hampshire RG21 2XS
and London
Companies and representatives
throughout the world.

Printed in Hong Kong

British Library Cataloguing in Publication Data
Church and politics in Latin America.—
Latin American studies series).
1. Latin America. Christian Church.
Relations with state
I. Keogh, Dermott II. Series
322' . 1'098
ISBN 0–333–44534–1

Contents

Notes on the Contributors

Rodolfo Cardenal is a member of the Jesuit community in San Salvador. He is professor of history at the University of José Simeon Cañas, San Salvador. He is the author of *El poder eclesiástico en El Salvador* and *Historia de una esperanza. Vida de Rutilio Grande.*

Margaret E. Crahan is Luce Professor of religion, power and political process, Occidental College, Los Angeles, California. She is the author of a number of studies on religion and politics in Cuba and Nicaragua.

Conor Cruise O'Brien is a diplomat, historian, political scientist, literary critic and politician. Seconded from the Irish foreign service to the United Nations, he was UN representative in the Congo when Katanga tried to secede. He was an academic in Ghana and New York and later a member of the Dáil and an Irish government minister from 1973 until 1977. He was editor-in-chief of *The Observer* in London from 1978 until 1981. Among the many books which Dr Cruise O'Brien has written are: *Maria Cross – Imaginative Patterns in a group of Catholic Writers* and *To Katanga and Back.*

Graham Greene, the distinguished novelist, has had a long association with Latin America. His novel, *The Power and the Glory*, explored the theme of Church and politics in Mexico. More recently, Graham Greene has written *Getting to know the General – the Story of the Involvement.* This is based on his five-year friendship with Omar Torrijos, who ruled Panama from 1968 until 1981. The book also contains an essay on Nicaragua where he has been a frequent visitor in recent years.

Peter Hebblethwaite is Vatican affairs writer for the *National Catholic Reporter*. He joined the Jesuits at seventeen, studied philosophy in France and took a first in French and German at Oxford. He read theology at Heythrop College. In 1965 he went to Rome to report the final session of Vatican II. He was made editor of *The Month* in 1967. He left the Jesuits in 1974. His books include *In the Vatican*, *The Runaway Church*, *Christian-Marxist Dialogue and Beyond*, *The Year of Three Popes*, and *John XXIII, Pope of the Council*, for which he was given a major award in the USA. He is working on a biography of Paul VI. He is a journalist.

François Houtart is professor of sociology at Louvain-la-Neuve, Belgium and director of the Centre Tircontinental. He was an adviser to the Latin American bishops at the Second Vatican Council. Fr Houtart is the author of over twenty books on religion in the third world, many of which were written in collaboration with Professor G. Lemercinier. He has worked as a consultant on socio-religious problems in South America, Africa and Asia.

Dermot Keogh is a lecturer in the Department of Modern History, University College, Cork. He is the author of *The Vatican, the Bishops and Irish Politics, 1919–1939*; *The Rise of the Irish Working Class; Romero: El Salvador's Martyr*; *Ireland and Europe: a study in diplomacy, 1919–1948*, and editor of *Central America: Human Rights and US Foreign Policy*.

Daniel H. Levine is professor of political science at the University of Michigan, Ann Arbor. He is the author of many publications, including *Religion and Politics in Latin America: the Catholic Church in Venezuela and Colombia*, and *Conflict and Political Change in Venezuela*. He is the editor of two volumes of essays: *Churches and Politics in Latin America*, and *Religion and Political Conflict in Latin America*.

Soledad Loaeza-Lajous is a professor at the Colegio de Mexico where she teaches European and Latin American political history. She has written extensively on Church–State relations in Mexico.

Enda McDonagh is professor of moral theology, Pontifical University, Maynooth. He was a visiting fellow at the University of Cambridge in 1978, and Husking Professor of Theology, University of Notre Dame, Indiana, in 1979–81. He is a consultant editor to *Concilium, The Furrow* and *Irish Theological Quarterly*. He is the author of, among others, *Between Chaos and New Creation*, *The Making of Disciples, The Demands of Simple Justice, Social Ethics and the Christian*, and edited *Irish Challenges to Theology*.

Fr Leonard Martin is professor of systematic and pastoral theology in the Institute de Teología e Pastoral, Fortaleza-Ce., Brazil. He has worked in Latin America since 1974 as a missionary and as an academic. His ministerial experience includes assistance to the emerging base Christian communities in Goiás and in Cear, and youth ministry in Rio de Janeiro. In July 1983, he was one of the invited *assesores* at the Fifth National Congress of Base Christian Communities in Canindé, Ceará. More recently, Fr Martin, who is a member of the Redemptorist order, has worked as a visiting professor in Kimmage Manor Faculty of Missionary Theology, Dublin. His current research interests include Brazilian ecclesiology and the pastoral challenges posed by the variety of popular religions.

Emilio Mignone was born in 1922 in Argentina. He is a lawyer and a specialist in political science and human rights. He is President of the Centro de Estudios Legales y Sociales (CELS) in Buenos Aires. He played a central role as a lawyer in opposition to the military during the 1970s in his country. Dr Mignone is the author of *Iglesia y Dictadura – El papel de la Iglesia a la luz de sus relaciones con el régimen militar* which has been translated into English as *Witness to the Truth – The Complicity of Church and Dictatorship in Argentina*.

Emile Poulat is a sociologist and historian. He is a director of research at the Centre Nationale de la Recherche Scientifique in Paris, and director of studies at the École des Hautes Études en Sciences Sociales. He was a former director of Groupe de Sociologie des Religions and founder of the journal, *Archives de Sociologie des religions*. He is the author of over twenty books and has been a visiting professor at universities in Canada and Mexico.

Patrick Rice has worked in Latin America for the past twenty-five years as a priest and human rights organiser. He 'disappeared' in Argentina in 1976, was discovered in jail after vigorous inquiries by Irish diplomats and was expelled from the country by the military. He was a founder member of Federación Latino-Americana de Asociaciones de Familiares de Detenidos-Desaparecidos. He was director of FEDEFAM in Caracas until 1987 when he returned to Buenos Aires to work with human rights organisations.

Brian H. Smith is the author of *The Church and Politics in Chile: Challenges to Modern Catholicism*.

Jon Sobrino is a member of the Jesuit community in San Salvador. He is professor of philosophy and theology at the Centre for Theological Reflection, University of José Simeon Cañas, San Salvador. He is the author of *Christology at the Crossroads* and *The True Church and the Poor*.

Italo López Vallecillos is one of El Salvador's most distinguished poets and writers. He was director general of Editorial Universitaria Centroamericana (EDUCA) and professor at the Universidad de El Salvador and at the Universidad de Costa Rica. He is the author of *Biografía del Hombre Triste, Puro Asombro, El Periodismo en El Salvador*, and *Gerardo Barrios y su Tiempo*. His poetry has been translated into Italian, French and English. He died in exile in 1985.

Preface

This volume on the Catholic Church and politics in Latin America has been collected and edited over a two-year period. It is the first issue in book form of a journal entitled *Latin America – a Research Review*. I am very grateful to the Irish department of foreign affairs for making a generous financial contribution to cover the translation and other costs incurred in the preparation of this book.

The then minister of state for Development Co-operation, Mr Jim O'Keeffe, was very supportive of this project, as were his successors, Mr George Birmingham and Mr Sean Calleary. I would like to thank Billy Hawkes, Martin Greene and Robin Henry of the Development Co-operation Division. Patricia Cullen, now in the Anglo-Irish Division, was also most helpful.

The department of foreign affairs has been well disposed towards the academic study of international relations in the universities and has been strongly represented at the annual Jean Donovan Conference since it began in 1983.

The Irish Catholic Development Organisation, Trócaire, has also been very generous and has helped make the Jean Donovan Conference possible on an annual basis. Brian McKeown, Tony Meade, Sally O'Neill and Veronica Canning have been very helpful.

A number of the contributors to this volume have lectured at that conference: Professors Jon Sobrino, François Houtart, Dan Levine, Enda McDonagh have made important contributions.

Most of the articles in this book were specially prepared for this volume. Contributors worked very hard to get their material in on time. I am very grateful to all for their thoroughness.

I am grateful to Emile Poulat, François Houtart, Conor Cruise O'Brien and Jon Sobrino for allowing me to include essays which had already been published elsewhere. Their inclusion has added substantially to this volume.

When I set out to edit this series of essays, I had hoped to cover a number of topics which do not unfortunately appear in the volume. In an ideal world, it would have been possible to wait indefinitely for all contributions to be finished, but that did not prove possible.

Mary Harris of Clare Hall, Cambridge, worked with me on this volume during the summer of 1987. She translated most of the substantial contribution by Rodolfo Cardenal and helped with the editing. I am very grateful to her for the hard work which was very much appreciated.

A special word of thanks to Professor Joseph Lee of the Department of Modern History, University College, Cork, who has been very supportive of efforts to develop the study of international relations and Latin American History in the College, together with his very efficient staff. I am also grateful to the Director of Adult Education, Mr Seán Murphy and his staff, who have run the Jean Donovan Conference.

My thanks to Professor Philip O'Brien of the Latin American Institute, Glasgow, and Simon Winder, editor of the Macmillan Latin American series, who commissioned this work and waited patiently for its completion.

A number of academics and specialists on Latin America have contributed – directly and indirectly – to the compilation of this volume. Fr Ernest Bartell, Executive Director of the Kellogg Institute, put me in touch with two of the contributors. Anibal Romero, Professor at the Simon Bolivar University, Caracas, was also very helpful. I would also like to thank Dr Miriam Hood, Hugh O'Shaughnessy and Carlos Diaz Sosa for their advice.

This book could not have been produced without the encouragement and hard work of many academic colleagues and friends in Europe, the United States and Latin America.

I am grateful to my colleagues at University College, Cork, Dr Terence O'Reilly and Dr Matthew MacNamara, who translated the contributions from Spanish and French respectively. Fr Leonard Martin and Fr Raphael Gallagher assisted with the translation and helped ensure the accuracy of the theological vocabulary used in two of the contributions. Professor Pat Hannon of Maynooth also provided helpful advice in the preparation of this volume.

Fr Jim McLaughlin, who has worked for twenty-five years in Latin America as a Catholic missionary, helped in the translation and checked many Latin American phrases.

My thanks to Fr James Torrens, SJ, of Santa Clara University, California, and Seán Dunne for their translation and adaptation of the poem by Italo López Vallecillos which the poet's daughter, Silvia López, kindly allowed me include in this volume.

Three postgraduate students, Marita Foster, Josephine Vaughan and Sheila Crowley, also helped in the preparation of this volume. I am very grateful to them for their hard work.

Orla de Barra and Veronica Fraser typed the drafts of the chapters of this book and prepared the final version for publication.

My thanks to Patrick and Fatima Rice for their help and hospitality on my visits to Latin America.

This book has been relatively difficult to structure. Graham Greene who has had a lifelong association with Latin America, has written a foreword reflecting the changes that have taken place in Catholicism since he became a member of the Church. The other chapters have fallen into four broad divisions. Part I provides an overview of the Latin American Church and traces its development in a transnational context. Both Emile Poulat and Daniel Levine have provided analyses of basic trends while the role of the Vatican and the development of the Latin American Bishops Conference (CELAM) are examined by Peter Hebblethwaite and François Houtart respectively. All the contributors in this part focus on the role of the Vatican. Jon Sobrino looks at the Special Rome Synod from a Latin American perspective.

Part II contains two theological perspectives on the response of the Catholic Church to the growth of political violence in Latin America. Jon Sobrino, who lives in El Salvador, prepared the chapter included here for a Jean Donovan memorial lecture. Enda McDonagh, the distinguished Irish theologian, prepared a contribution which presents a series of reflections on liberation theology under the heading 'Liberation and New Creation – a theological conversation'.

Part III focuses on the theme of politics and the gospel in Central America. Conor Cruise O'Brien has contributed a very interesting article on Nicaragua for which he was awarded the Sidney Hillman Award in New York in May 1987. The Jesuit historian, Rodolfo Cardenal – a member of a very prominent Nicaraguan family – has written on Costa Rica, Honduras, Guatemala and El Salvador, and these chapters are followed by the poem by the Salvadorean poet, Italo Lopez Vallecillos: appropriately it is a reflection on the martyrdom of the Archbishop of San Salvador, Mgr Oscar Arnulfo Romero.

Part IV examines the historical experience of the Catholic Church when confronted by revolution and counter-revolution in Latin America. Margaret Crahan looks at the chequered role of the Church in Fidel Castro's Cuba. Soledad Loaeza-Lajous examines the theme of continuity and change in the Mexican Catholic Church. The recent historical experience of the Church in Brazilian society is examined by Leonard Martin – an Irish theologian who is teaching in the country. Brian Smith presents an analysis of the Church and politics in Chile and Andrea O'Brien sketches the changing role of the Catholic Church in Latin America's longest surviving dictatorship of Alfredo Stroessner's Paraguay. Emilio Mignone looks critically at the role of the Catholic Church in Argentina during the 'dirty war' and Patrick Rice has written a chapter on the response of the Catholic Church in Latin America to the phenomenon of the 'disappeared'.

Unfortunately, this book was not able to accommodate essays on all the Latin American countries. While there are no chapters on Venezuela, Colombia, Peru, Bolivia, Ecuador, Uruguay and Panama, Daniel Levine and Emile Poulat have made references to some of these countries in the overviews. In some cases, contributors failed to deliver. But it is hoped that over twenty chapters have covered in a comprehensive way most of the important themes on the subject of Church and Politics in Latin America.

I wish to thank all the contributors who have been drawn from Europe, the United States and Latin America.

Finally, there is no agreement in the literature on Latin America on the correct term for Basic Christian Communities: Base Communities, Basic Communities, Basic Ecclesial Communities, Ecclesial Communities, etc., have been used by different scholars. In Spanish, the term used most often is Comunidad Eclesial de Base (CEB) which can be translated as base Christian community. The same term is also used in Portuguese: Comunidade Eclesial de Base. It has been decided to standardise usage and adopt base Christian community (CEB) throughout the book.

Dermot Keogh
Department of Modern History
University College, Cork

Foreword: The Social Challenge of the Gospel

Graham Greene

This illuminating volume dealing with the development of a Latin American Catholicism, involving liberation theology and base Christian communities, made at least one old man lie back in his chair and remember what the Church was like when he joined it with some reluctance nearly sixty years ago, and contemplate the immensity of the changes. It was typical of the time that the Church was known to most people in England, with a good deal of reason, as the Roman Catholic Church. To some extent, by joining it I became a foreigner in my own country – not a bad thing to be for one who wanted to be a novelist, for a foreigner sees his surroundings with fresh eyes. But to be a foreigner entailed, too, certain assumptions for which I cared much less. The chief one was that as a Roman Catholic I must, it was generally assumed, belong politically to the Right. Ten years passed and it was still assumed that as a Roman Catholic I was expected to be a supporter of Franco by the vast majority who had not read my books.

And yet, changes *had* begun in the late 1930s and in my first reading of Sobrino's excellent essay on the Church in Central America I wondered whether Father Gutiérrez, whom he quotes, was not putting the change a little late when he wrote 'the history of the Church in Latin America divides into before and after Monsignor Romero'. After all, Dom Helder Câmara, former archbishop of Olinda and Recifé had already taken the dangerous option for the poor in Brazil. (He is not mentioned by Fr Martin in his chapter on conflict in the Brazilian Catholic Church, perhaps because he has confined himself to the later period 1968 to 1979.) Again there was a hint in Mexico as early as 1937 of what might become the future base Christian communities. As a result of religious persecution, the Church had been a good deal cleansed of Romanism – even drastically cleansed as I had seen in Tabasco where no church and no priest remained, and hardly less so in Chiapas where no priest was allowed to enter a church. The secret Masses held in private houses might have been described as middle class, but when on Sundays the Indians came down from the mountains and tried to celebrate the Mass, as far as they remembered it, without a priest, surely the base communities were already beginning.

But reading further I realise that I had misunderstood Father Gutiérrez. Archbishop Romero's martyrdom (the first archbishop murdered at the altar since Becket), followed by a too carefully moderate condemnation of his murder by Pope John Paul II, was certainly, as he described it, the watershed between the sporadic beginnings of the Latin-American Church and its steady growth as we see it today, strengthened by the very blatancy of the support given to the death squads in El Salvador and Guatemala and the Contras in Nicaragua by the US government, which has shocked many members of the American hierarchy. The White House has made sure that nothing will ever be the same again.

The Church of the poor and the base communities show their strength not only against the US government, the death squads and the Contras, but against the very Romanesque views of Cardinal Ratzinger, the great opponent of liberation theology, and perhaps the understandable suspicions of Pope John Paul II.

I write 'understandable' because I cannot help feeling that the Pope's experience of Poland in the 1950s may have led to the unfortunate attitude he manifested in his recent visit to Nicaragua. He seemed to see a false parallel between a government which contained three Catholic priests in the key positions of Health and Education, Foreign Affairs and Culture to the Pax movement, which was a deliberate attempt by a foreign power to divide the Church. I visited Poland in 1955 for a month, after the Pax movement had been established, and I enjoyed, if that is the right word, two very alcoholic sessions with Boleslaw Piaseki, the fascist leader who had fought bravely against both the Germans and the Russians, and to the astonishment of the Poles had returned alive from his imprisonment in Moscow, with permission to start a Catholic publishing firm and the sole right to manufacture rosaries, crucifixes etc., the paraphernalia of the Faith. The Archbishop was under house arrest and a few priests joined the Pax movement, but their churches stood nearly empty on a Sunday, when all other churches seemed crammed to overflowing. The Pax movement, foreign born, faded out, but the movement which gave birth to liberation theology, the base Christian communities, the option for the poor, was native born and had nothing in common with Pax.

Attacked by the US government and persecuted in El Salvador, Chile, Paraguay and Guatemala, the Catholic Church in the American continent, as this book demonstrates, has taken on a new and vigorous life, which in time may, one hopes, eventually convert even the Curia and persuade its members to return again to the teaching of John XXIII rather than follow the path of Cardinal Ratzinger and CELAM, so well analysed here in the chapter by François Houtart.

Part One
The Vatican and the Latin American Catholic Church

1 The Path of Latin American Catholicism

Emile Poulat

Between Europe and America lies an ocean, the Atlantic, which, depending on your point of view, either separates or unites them. Is it preferable to note the banality of the statement, or to stress the reality of the distance? Words disappear, realities persist. In Europe, since the beginning of the century, national traits have become more marked, and yet at the same time the continent has developed a particular identity. Even through the very wars which ravaged her, she has built a community with an historic destiny based on her economic and political predominance in the world, her cultural and colonial expansion, and the forms taken by the 'social question' and the 'religious question'. Western Catholicism as we know it, which is far from constituting the whole of the Latin Church, or even the whole of the Roman Catholic Church, is the product of this history. From Leo XIII onwards, it has been more and more marked by Catholic Action and by the Catholic social movement under names and in forms which have varied in time and in place.

What was the situation on the other side of the Atlantic? It is not too much to say that Latin American Catholicism much more than North American Catholicism, has developed in its own particular way. Like Europe it manifests national particularities underlying an unquestionable continental singularity. Latin America presents itself to us as a complex history, a religious mosaic, an ecclesiastical continent. Our astonishment in the face of its current evolution is no more than the measure of our ignorance.

Until one has examined the question in detail, any reference to the diversity of a country or of a region is no more than the enunciation of a truism. This is at least the case in our own time, when, having long believed in the universal vocation of our classic and western reason, we have progressively discovered in the resistance that this culture met, and indeed provoked, the multiplicity of indigenous cultures. The period of conquering expansion has been succeeded by that of jealous independence when everybody seeks to preserve his identity and to rediscover his authenticity.

This rhetorical evocation of a duality of cultures is too simple however. The opposition, which is real, should not blind us to either the links of interdependence (or of unequal dependence as some people say) which have been maintained or established, or the internal phenomena which reproduce internally that which they denounce externally. One must analyse rather than idealise. And in the particular case of Latin America at the hour of its independence, centrifugal forces had been powerful enough to produce an efflorescence of independent states, sometimes miniscule, as in Central America or in the Caribbean, and not a vast federation of states. This differentiates those countries from the United States, and even from Mexico.

The multiple factors which contributed to this situation were not wholly decisive. The same factors produced different effects in different places, and the comparative study of their historical combination has still to be undertaken. Three facts are worthy of notice in this regard.

Firstly, a discordance between history and culture. The geography is clear: there are two continents, North and South America joined by the isthmus of Central America, and seaward of this isthmus, the Caribbean zone. Linguistically, it is more complex. Attempts can be made to divide it into four parallel strips: French, English, Spanish and Portuguese, with a little bit of Dutch. Culturally, language and reality, words and things, are not easily reconciled. What is called Latin America occupies some of North America (Mexico has not forgotten the amputation of its territory by the United States of America). It excludes and then reintegrates, as they acquire their independence, certain territories which remained for a long time under foreign rule (the Guianas, and the islands of the West Indies, 20 territories in all). It is massively Hispanophone, yet at the same time includes a large Lusophone country, Brazil, a small Francophone country, Haiti, and for some time now, former English and Dutch continental or island possessions.

Secondly, in the last century in certain regions a significant European emigration of Spanish, Italian, German or Slav origin has joined the Creole descendents of the colonial period.

Thirdly, a relatively recent and always unsuccessful attempt to overcome state and national particularisms. While the Monroe declaration 'America for the Americans' dates from 1823, it was only in 1890 that the first international American Conference opened in Washington. This led to the foundation of the international union of American Republics which in 1948 at Bogotá, became the Organisation of American States (OAS). This organisation originally included 21 countries including the United States (but not Canada which was then part of the British Empire), and Cuba, which was excluded in 1961 because of the orientation of the new regime.

Before the word *liberation* which today is the key word in Latin America even in theology, the magic word in the whole of the Americas was *independence*. With French support, the English colonies gave the initial example and the second centenary of the battle of Yorktown was celebrated in 1981. In 1804 Haiti, a French possession, followed that example but against France. The Spanish colonies, led by Argentina and Mexico, took advantage of the intervention of Napoleon in Spain, and liberated themselves successively between 1810 and 1825. The independence of Brazil was proclaimed in 1822 by the Regent who was the son of the King of Portugal, and he immediately assumed the title of Emperor. This, however, did not mean peace nor the end of violence and of misery.

FROM THE COLONIAL CHURCH TO THE COLLEGIAL CHURCH

It is essential to mention this historical heritage because, for a long time now, it has been a major influence on the Churches which have themselves heavily influenced the national history of the various countries. In short, Latin America is an overwhelmingly Catholic region of the world. In this regard a priest and a theologian may put the question: 'what quality of Catholicism?', while a historian or a sociologist may ask: 'what types of Catholicism?' It is important, therefore, to recall briefly some characteristics of this Catholicism:

1. At its origin and over nearly three centuries, there were colonial Churches marked by the predominance of the conquerors, the whites, and their creole descendants. They had to submit to Royal patronage (*patronato* in Spanish, *padroado* in Portuguese), in the tradition of the purest Regalism of which the contemporary French form was the gallican spirit.

2. From the beginning, there was the missionary role played by the religious orders, Franciscans, Dominicans, Augustinians and

Jesuits. Each of these orders had its own style and its own territories of evangelisation which sometimes constituted veritable centres of opposition to the civil or religious power.

3. At independence, white authority was replaced by mixed race authority without bringing about any change in the situation of the tribal Indians. In Mexico the insurrection was provoked by the call of two mixed-race priests, Hidalgo and Morelos, and took the form of *Virgen* against *Virgen*, the banner of the *Virgen morena* of Guadalupe against the banner of the white *Virgen* of Guadalajara. In Colombia, the first bishop, Juan Fernández de Sotomayor was the author of a popular Catechism (1814) which legitimised independence even when it involved war.

   Politically, an opposition developed between Conservatives and Liberals. The anti-clericalism of the Liberals brought the Church to seek the support of the Conservatives, and led to conflicts which were sometimes violent. This however never undermined the tradition of regalism and patronage inherited from the colonial period.

4. The difficult situation of the Church throughout the nineteenth century, brought about by its conflict with the Liberal bourgeoisie, did not break its hold on the popular masses. This positive relationship with the masses had its high points in the Ecuador of García Moreno and its low points in the Mexico of Benito Juárez or of Plutarco Elías Calles. The model Church was always that of Colombia followed by that of Chile. In Brazil, as in Haiti, the slave trade introduced powerful religious ferments of African origin which produced extraordinary syncretisms.

5. Rome, whose hostility to the dominant Liberalism and to the principle of regalism in so far as it survived never flinched, intended several articles of the Syllabus of Errors (1864) to apply directly to the Latin American situation. From then on, the Holy See developed a counter policy of intense Romanisation of the clergy, of education, of the liturgy and so on.

It was in these circumstances that Pius IX created in Rome in 1858 the Pontificio Collegio Pio Latinoamericano[1] (diocesan seminary) which was a nursery of future professors (in those places where professors were not members of religious orders) and of future bishops. In 1925 among its living past pupils, one could number the first Latin American Cardinal, the Archbishop of Rio de Janeiro and fifty-two bishops. In 1935 its student body was made up of 136 seminarians and 30 priests.

Leo XIII opened a new phase when he convoked a Plenary Council for Latin America in Rome in 1889 – this was the first and last of its kind. Its decrees were prepared by the Pope's theologians and canon lawyers. The experts who had accompanied the bishops were not admitted to the Council.[2]

After the Second World War the definitive institutional arrangements were made by Pius XII at the end of his pontificate. A general conference of the Latin American Episcopate – the first – met at Rio de Janeiro from 25 July to 4 August 1955. It decided on the setting up of a permanent organ of liaison and of co-operation between the episcopates of the participating countries. It was called the Latin American Episcopal Conference and was better known by the initials CELAM. Its first secretary general was a Brazilian priest of whom one was going to hear more, Dom Helder Câmara.[3] On the following 2 November, the Pope gave it his approval but found it necessary to institute in Rome on 19 April 1958 a Pontifical Commission for Latin America which was also known by the initials CAL. This is an organ of the Curia which has also a function of liaison and of co-operation. Alone of all the Congregations concerned with the problems of the geo-cultural area of Latin America, it remained the responsibility of the Secretariat of State until July 1969 when Paul VI attached it henceforth to the Congregation for the Bishops. At the same time, he assigned it another task, that of following the activities of CELAM and of the European and North American agencies which bring help both in personnel and in money to the churches of Latin America. In the meantime, in 1963, to remedy the problems of demarcation and of rivalry, he instituted an overall body, the General Council for Latin America composed of CAL, the presidency of CELAM, and representatives of two specific institutions, the CLAR, or the Latin American Conference of Religious (founded in Rome in 1958), and the International Union of Superiors and Superioresses of Orders or of Congregations.

If a comparison were possible between the OAS and CELAM it would doubtless be to the advantage of the latter. This is because of its openness and its efficiency. Openness, because it practises no exclusivity either geographically or politically. Efficiency, because despite the tensions which affect it, it is not a place of confrontation between national governments representing national interests. Its tensions only reflect the range of situations and of personal temperaments represented, and, in a more general way, internal disagreements in the Catholic Church as to the manner of approaching and treating the great contemporary problems even if such disagreements can be explained in sociological terms.

The OAS brings together 30 states, and CELAM 22 episcopal conferences. Despite appearances, divergence in membership ultimately involves only a few particular situations, those of the United States, of Cuba and of Puerto Rico. The Episcopal Conference of the Antilles covers a constellation of territories diverse in political status and in language, and of which the ones which became independent have joined the OAS: Jamaica, the Bahamas, Bermuda, Belize, Martinique, Guadeloupe, French Guiana, Trinidad, Barbados, Guyana, Surinam, Curaçao, Santa Lucia, Dominica, Grenada, the Virgin Islands.[4]

We should not let the picturesque side of this arrangement blind us to the serious purpose of linking this confetti of islands to a wide continental grouping. Who still remembers that 'Latin America' was first an ecclesiastical term as the learned *Dictionnaire de Théologie Catholique* explained in 1900, and that it was still in ecclesiastical use in 1947.[5] CELAM, the first institution of its kind, still remains a unique phenomenon.

It is a model of transnational organisation which has been imitated – in Europe (in 1965), in Africa, in Asia – but never reproduced. Both by its influence and for the number of people involved, it has no counterpart. In 1979 it counted more than 800 active bishops and of these 300 came from Brazil. At a future Council, these bishops will make up a quarter of the world's total (and represent 40 per cent of the world's Catholics in so far as such a figure is meaningful). How can this religious potential not represent, on the continent itself, a considerable investment of political capital?

AN ENTANGLEMENT OF RELATIONSHIPS AND OF TENSIONS

It is not surprising that a law of pre-established harmony is not the law that governs the movement of this great ensemble. It cannot be described in terms of the traditional problem of Church–State relations. In fact it renders these terms irrelevant. One has to picture it as a terrain of manoeuvres and observe the participants.

Between the Holy See and the Latin American episcopate, there is a relationship both of communion and of submission. This means that every conflict has to be resolved in a way which is more or less satisfactory for each of the parties involved and without anything irreparable being done in the meantime. Except in certain individual and exceptional cases rupture is out of the question. On the other hand, ruptures may occur in the relationships between the Holy See and different governments. Any extreme positions are also individual and exceptional ones, and it is clear that Rome does not favour them when they are spectacular. This is the case of progressives like Dom Helder Câmara in Brazil, or Méndez Arceo in Mexico, or of integralists such as Castro Mayer and Proença Sigaud in Brazil. Bishops belonging to the Brazilian 'right-wing' can ignore the position of their conference and bishops of the 'left-wing' of CELAM have no difficulty in organising periodical meetings which the new statute of CELAM intended to make impossible in the future. At Puebla in 1979, in order to avoid a division of the plenary assembly, they had circulated, and signed in a personal capacity, a letter of support for Monsignor Romero of El Salvador who has since been assassinated.

At difficult moments, the Holy See does not hesitate to support an episcopate even if it means conflict with a particular government. This has been seen in recent years in Chile, in Paraguay and in Brazil. Here again, its policy is to avoid extreme positions either in the country or in Rome. Nicaragua is a recent example. Rome requested the four priest Ministers to withdraw from the government, but when they refused to do so it did not treat the question as an urgent one. The nomination of Monsignor Lopez Trujillo of Colombia as secretary general and then president of CELAM has marked a shift of balance in CELAM and a return to more moderate or more conservative positions. This evolution, which corresponded to the wishes of the Holy See, was approved and encouraged by John Paul II. In his opinion, the influence of the Church in the life of a nation has to be brought to bear through the action of the responsible hierarchy more than through the inspiration of active minorities (the base Christian communities which I will discuss further on).

This has given rise to an improvement in the relationships between CAL, presided over at the time of writing by Cardinal Baggio, and CELAM whose tensions were a secret to no-one.

There has also been some friction between CELAM and the Brazilian Episcopal Conference which tended to consider interventions of the Council primarily as an interference in its own affairs. This is a delicate situation. On the one hand, CELAM had the support of Rome as was shown by several direct interventions. On the other hand, the Brazilian bishops gave free reign to their dynamism. In Rome, there was worry about an initiative which seemed to be having a snowball effect. This was the operation 'For a Society which would Overcome the Dominations'. This movement sought not only to overcome the dominations, and by this was meant capitalism and communism, it was also going beyond the frontiers of Brazil. While it was doctrinally blameless, being a modern version of the social doctrines of the Church, it was worrying by its extension. Its international action seemed to be putting the Holy See in the shade in a particular domain even if it was substituting for it.

2. Other pawns in the game are the nuncios whose double function is well known. Firstly, it is a diplomatic one with regard to the states which accredit them, and secondly, it is an apostolic one as delegates of the Holy See to the Catholic hierarchy of a particular country.

Nothing is more eloquent than a comparison of the situation in 1914 and at the present day. On the eve of the First World War there was no ambassador at the Vatican from a Latin American country, and only seven plenipotentiary ministers (from Argentina, Bolivia, Brazil, Chile, Colombia, Costa Rica and Peru). In Latin America, the Holy See had one second-class nunciature (Brazil), one internunciature (Chile) and five apostolic delegations of which four served more than one country. Today, each of the countries represented in CELAM sends an Ambassador and receives a nuncio with the exception of Mexico, because of its anticlerical ideology, and the Antilles because of their small size. This last mentioned area is served by an apostolic delegate. Following the model of its northern neighbour, but in quite a different spirit, Mexico is the only Latin American country which since the last century practises a strict separation of Church and State.

The role of the nuncios varies according to the person and according to the country, and it is not always unanimously appreciated. Each interest group – government, episcopate, clergy, army, ruling classes and basic communities – has its own criteria of appreciation. It is difficult to make a global judgement on the nuncios as a body. Some have had to deal with particularly delicate situations and have done so quite well. If the nuncio in Havana had fled when Fidel Castro came to power, he would never have been able to come back, and the Holy See would no longer be represented in Cuba.

3. Since its re-constitution in 1969, one of the two objectives assigned to the Pontifical Commission for Latin America (CAL) is the monitoring of the activity of European and North American Catholic aid agencies to Latin America. Even if CAL's archives were open, they would be found to be inadequate for the pre-1969 period. In other words, this is an area for which numerous data are available, but no general assessment, nor indeed any overall view. However, one can state without fear of contradiction that this aid – made up of so many personal sacrifices, intellectual efforts and financial donations – has been multilateral, appreciated to different degrees, always inferior to the needs, but nevertheless substantial.

On the intellectual level a new interest in Latin America seems to have been awakened in France and in Belgium after the Second World War, to mention only these two countries. This trend was seen in the increasing numbers of students of Latin American problems who registered at the Catholic University of Louvain, and in particular at the Centre for Socio-Religious Studies founded by M. François Houtart. This centre inspired the establishment of a series of similar centres and subsequently of an International Federation of Catholic Institutes of Social and Socio-religious Research (FERES). They also went to the Institut Catholique in Paris, and in particular to the Institut Supérieur de Pastorale Catechetique. In the other direction, the influence of certain individuals played an important role. Canon Boulard, a much sought-after expert in religious sociology, Fr Louis Joseph Lebret, a director of *Economie et Humanisme*[6] whom Colombia made responsible for its development plan (which at that time was judged to be communist), Fr Bigo, the Jesuit director of l'Action Populaire, and an indefatigable apostle of the social doctrines of the Church who is today more than 80 years old. Priests have occupied key positions: José Comblin, a Belgian, and a Professor at the major seminary at Recife (which is the diocese of Dom Helder Câmara), and expelled in 1972; Roger Vekemans, a

Belgian Jesuit, a sociologist in Chile and then in Colombia;[7] Dom Grégoire Lemercier, a Belgian Benedictine who founded a monastery at Cuernavaca (Mexico) and made it a centre for psychoanalysis; Alex Morelli, a French Dominican, and former prisoner in Dachau who went to Uruguay and then to Mexico as the continental assessor of Catholic worker action, and then as initiator of the movement 'Priests for the people', which became 'Eglise Solidaire';[8] Charles Antoine who, on his return to France, founded an information bulletin, DIAL, using his network of contacts,[9] and so on.

The encyclical *Fidei Donum* (1957) of Pope Pius XII gave a new impetus to this current. Henceforth the missionary congregations would be joined by the diocesan priests placed, at their request, and with the agreement of their bishops, at the disposal of bishops in the Third World for an agreed period. Even if this current seems today to have slowed down, and international statistics are not available,[10] it is difficult to over-estimate its importance. It was the breath of a new spirit at the service of the most deprived people in difficult situations.

This explains the number of priests, religious and nuns who according to reports in the public press were arrested, imprisoned, expelled, tortured or even assassinated. The creation by the French episcopate of the Comité Épiscopal France-Amérique Latine (CEFAL), which is the only one of its kind in existence, shows at any rate a special attention for this Catholic region of the world.

While other bodies also played a role, it is difficult to assess their relative importance. Two of them deserve special mention: a new form of Catholic Action (this took the place of an older form of Catholic Action on a Spanish or Italian model which had been favoured by the episcopates), the Young Catholic Workers (JOC), and Young Catholic Students (JEC), and the new Christian Democratic parties. Cardijn went to Latin America after the Second World War at a period when JOC was being set up internationally. At this point one can ask: why has experience shown that the Franco-Belgian model was ill-suited both to the Latin American and African countries? It is in fact a paradox that international JEC has its headquarters in Paris where the French JEC is not present, while international JOC has become divided.[11] As for the organisations which claim to be inspired by Christian Democracy, they find support in Rome in the World

Union of Christian Democracy (UMDC) or in its sister organisations which, like the international Jacques Maritain Institute in Rome, each have their own autonomy. There again one observes a paradox, but of another kind: this is the gap between the conservative reputation of the German CDU whose contribution is by far the most important, and the more advanced orientations (to different degrees admittedly) of Latin American movements.[12]

Finally, there is the role of the material furnished by the international specialised charitable organisations on a regular basis in contrast to the *ad hoc* interventions practised all over the world by the Secours Catholique in the wake of catastrophies. In Germany, in 1981, that was more than the total of the budget attributed by the Holy See to the Congregation for the Evangelisation of Peoples. In France, this charity is primarily the work of the Comité Catholique contre la faim et pour le développement (CCFD). It is the view of CCFD that food aid given is of little lasting benefit if it is not accompanied by an awakening of conscience (a lot of use has been made of the term *conscientisation*). This requires help in education which begins with elementary literacy, the improvement of conditions of life and of work (*micro-réalisations*), the training of teachers, the apprenticeship of techniques which are sometimes quite elementary. It can also involve, or it should involve, even more ambitious projects at a more advanced level. These are the formation of cultural animators, of social workers, of trade union officials, or even of executives and directors. One can imagine that to those who do not share their spirit such initiatives may appear to be of a highly questionable orientation and inspiration.[13] What we have here is the criticism described above in the case of Fr Vekemans, but working this time in the opposite direction. When you do away with politics in the name of religion, you will find it making its way back again very quickly.

4. Neither the action of the papal nuncios nor these other exogenous elements can substantially modify the situation. There remain therefore the great institutional forces: Church and State in the countries themselves and, at a distance, the Vatican. A common error would be to think that their actual conduct can be inferred from their stated principles. This conduct is determined by many other considerations and is the result of infinitely more

subtle mixtures. Similarly, it would be an error to explain this gap on the basis of tactical opportunism which would recall the famous and facile distinction between thesis and hypothesis, the latter authorising that which the former would prevent. The error of these two approaches consists in treating as a confrontation of ideas what is really a field of force and thus seeing the problem as a purely ideological one.

Already, at the legal level, one has to distinguish three situations of which no single one determines any of the others. Today all of the Latin American states with the exception of Mexico maintain diplomatic relations with the Holy See. Only nine of them have signed a concordat: Costa Rica, Guatemala, Haiti, Honduras, Nicaragua, El Salvador, Venezuela and Ecuador (between 1852 and 1862) and Colombia (1887). But in nearly all of them with three exceptions (Mexico, 1875, Brazil, 1889 and Chile, 1925, which proclaimed the separation of Church and State) Catholicism is the official or national religion, or indeed the state religion. But even in the case of these three exceptions, the same formula is far from corresponding to the same reality.

In Mexico, confirming the measures of Juarez, the 'Reform' confiscated the property of the Church, banished the congregations, forbade all exterior liturgical manifestations and laicised schools, hospitals and residences with the exception of the national domain of Our Lady of Guadalupe.[14] In an undramatic manner, after the major conflicts of the Calles period,[15] the Mexican State gradually came to ignore the Church, and the Mexican Church began to prosper in the shade of this official disinterest.[16] In Brazil, in 1889, under the influence of positivism and free masonry, the glorious revolution overthrew the Emperor Pedro II, proclaimed the republic and adopted a constitution modelled on that of the United States: the unfettered Church in the free State had to renounce state payment of the clergy, but kept its property. For its part, the young Brazilian republic maintained its relations with the Holy See, and in 1909 accepted the arbitration of the nuncio in its frontier conflict with Bolivia and with Peru. In Chile, where a sort of equilibrium was arrived at between Liberals and Catholics, the separation introduced in 1925 recognised the legal personality of the Church, continued religious instruction in state schools, and did not break off relations with the Vatican. In the vast Latin American ensemble, Mexico therefore stands apart with its strict and uncompromising secular line (much more vigorously practised

> than in France). It confined religion to the private life of the elites and to the daily life of the masses, but failed to recognise the extraordinary social power of the Catholic Church. The visit of John Paul II in 1979 illustrated this in a manner which stupefied the political class and had an immediate effect on programmes of research and teaching. The Colombian situation stands in total contrast to the Mexican one. Between them one can observe varieties of a living paradox from which indeed Mexico and Colombia themselves are not exempt. Apart from ethnic minorities (tribal indians or religious minorities), nation and religion coincide, even if the diversity of Catholicism there reaches a degree which its institutional unity and our cultural conditioning make it hard to imagine. In addition, after independence, the anticlerical Liberalism of the ruling classes in its *Kulturkampf* used three weapons in combination. These were the leaving vacant for long periods of a small number of episcopal sees which perpetuated the under-development of ecclesiastical organisation, the tradition of patronage inherited from the colonial period which guaranteed a certain influence over the Church; or an open struggle by means of laws of secularisation and of 'desamortisación',[17] which on occasion was pushed as far as violence, yet was ultimately always contained within limits which varied according to period and according to country.

Thus, one finds between Church and State all over Latin America, the experience of a conflict, sometimes grave, always cyclical, in which the evolution of relationships never culminates either in a definitive elimination or a perfect solution. The present situation is a perfect illustration of this model.

All one needs to do is to observe the critical places. In 1929, in Mexico, the Cristeros were not beaten by the regular army but abandoned by the Catholic hierarchy, then disarmed. They had gone too far or threatened to go too far. In 1946 Argentina adopted left-wing policies with the blessing of the Church. In 1954, the 'justicialist, humanist and Christian movement' of Perón – which was authoritarian and populist – provoked tension with the traditionally conservative episcopate without leading to a major crisis. It had legalised divorce and suppressed religious education in the schools. In 1948 in Colombia, the assassination of Francisco Gaitán – 'el caudillo del pueblo' – inaugurated an era of violence which brought about the reconciliation of the Conservatives and Liberals who up to then had been irreconcilable adversaries. This era also saw the Conservatives and Liberals successfully appeal to the Church in the face of popular revolt and social peril, and it increased tensions within the Catholic organisations.[18] In 1959, the establishment in Cuba of the Castro regime which was rapidly forced to radicalise itself, did not prevent the maintenance of relations with the Church and the adaptation of the Church to the new state of things in spite of the severe measures taken against her. Since 1964 in Chile, the Church has lived with three successive regimes, a Christian democratic one (Frei), a regime of popular unity (Allende) and the military junta (Pinochet) to the point of being judged by their adversaries to be linked to each one of them.[19] When the Church, however, judged in the context of increasing repression that the soldiers had gone too far in 1976, it took under its responsibility a 'Vicariate of Solidarity'.[20] This proposed itself as a place of refuge, a space of liberty, an agent of mediation, a reserve force, while sections of the Catholics were being radicalised either in the name of the Junta or in the name of the Revolution.[21]

FROM A COLLEGIAL CHURCH TO A POPULAR CHURCH?

In conjunction with the visit of Paul VI, the Episcopal Conference of Medellín in 1968 had awoken extraordinary hopes and correspondingly strong fears. The conviction was then widespread that the forces of progress were going to be triumphant on the continent. In fact the opposite happened and one saw a multiplication of *coups d'état* and of military regimes. Subsequently, a new element played a considerable role in the links between the Church and various States. This was in the form of manpower, or demonstrations, or organisations, leading to an increased commitment of Catholic militants, of priests, religious and nuns; the endless dialectic of repression and protestation.[22]

In this situation, the classic issues of conflict (for example Canon Law opposed to Civil Law in the regulation of marriage, the defence of the rights of the Church and of its immunities) are displaced by those issues of attacks on the rights of man and the support of the people who denounce these attacks. Some bishops, few in number however and isolated, did not hesitate to take up advanced political positions. One can mention Monsignor Valencia Cano (Buonaventura, Colombia), who had been called 'el obispo rojo'.[23] More numerous were those whose progressive outlook affirmed itself vigorously in the social questions. Brazil is a striking example of this. But even the most conservative bishops had often been carried further than they would have been by their natural inclination. That was the situation in Argentina.[24]

All this might have led to the assumption that there was a prearranged connivance between the Catholic hierarchy and the military regimes, for were not the last-mentioned destroying the abhorred Liberalism at the hands of which the Church had suffered so much and which she had denounced so constantly? In reality, however, this Church, clerical and authoritarian from the top to the bottom, had always had its base in the people, in the mass of the population, and not in the army.

Now, by the action at the base of its clergy, of its congregations, and of its organisations, the episcopate found itself caught between the people and the army. Moreover, from being initially an institutional one – the clash of two powers – the conflict assumed an unexpected ideological dimension.

On the one hand, priests and militants radicalised their positions, increased their commitments and multiplied their movements. The group Golconde in Colombia, the National Office of Social Investigations (ONIS) in Peru, priests for the third world in Argentina, and, especially spreading from Chile where it was to find its continental dimension, Christians for Socialism (CpS). In Brazil, they may have joined the socialist party (Partido do Trabalho); elsewhere they engaged in revolutionary action and in combat. Thus was created the need for a theoretical expression which would translate their experience and their hopes better than the traditional social doctrine of the Church. This would be the theology of liberation, so typically Latin American,[25] since the African theologians had interested themselves more in a theology of authenticity.[26]

On the other hand, the military regimes had of course to look beyond the particular circumstances which had brought them to power and beyond mere pragmatism in their exercise of this power. They needed a doctrine which would give them legitimacy in their own eyes and provide a foundation for their policy. This was going to be the doctrine of national security against revolutionary subversion and international communism.[27] It was a kind of theology in so far as it referred to Christian principles and in so far as it invoked the defence of Christian civilisation. It was also a theology in so far as it could claim to enjoy the support of and to be in harmony with integralism and traditional Catholicism.[28]

Situated between these groups, the bishops have chosen much less an *aggiornamento* of the social doctrine of the Church than a development of its principles in a direction which had hitherto not been chosen. This goes against liberal individualism and communist collectivism, and stresses the primacy of the human person, or in the language of our times, the defence of the rights of man.

Let there be no mistake about it, in speaking the language of their time which awakened deep echoes in public opinion, Paul VI and then John Paul II and the episcopate following them practised a discourse of a modern kind but one which was less new in its content than people imagined generally. This discourse did not imply any conversion to Liberalism. On the contrary, it permitted the Church, through renunciation of certain out-dated polemical formulations which were no longer understood, to reaffirm great Christian principles of the right of peoples (*jus gentium*) which alone were capable of founding a more humane society. The bishops of Latin America thus found themselves caught in a field of contrary forces and submitted to antagonistic pressures. What divided them was not disagreement on these principles, but above all, the manner of interpreting them and applying them, and especially their concrete realisation on the ground in acts, interventions, forms of behaviour, in the play of relationships and of solidarities and even in the style of daily life. At the practical level, this gives the impression of a gap between action and words. Nevertheless, one must note the large spectrum of particular or of collective actions which refer to the same theological heritage – a 'post-conciliar', or the exception of some singular cases which do not draw upon it. It is not sufficient, or it is no longer sufficient, if one supposes this reality as having once existed, for the Pope just to speak and have the bishops follow him as one man. One can give an example of this. In 1977 Pope Paul VI, receiving the credentials of the new Argentinian ambassador, warned him against the extension of violence and violations of the rights of man in his country. The Argentinian episcopate waited several months before publicly expressing an opinion. In 1978, during his Brazilian tour, the Pope gave a similar warning. The Brazilian episcopate immediately relayed these words, and denounced the insecurity and marginalisation of the ordinary people: 'The Church does not wish for the peace of cemeteries'.

Neither does the fact that the bishops do speak out mean that they are heard and followed by a unanimous people. They do not even try to keep up the appearance of having this power. They are no longer able to wield it and the means which were available to them previously in this regard are no longer relevant to the situation. And how could they produce this consensus when they themselves are protagonists in the fundamental issues which divide Latin American society, when they themselves are a living example of its contradictions?

To be surprised by this one must have oneself broken the circle. Convinced that the Christian order which is threatened by subversion must be defended, the military men act with a clear conscience, but are obliged to invoke the necessity of order in the face of the bishops who speak to them of the exigencies of Christianity. Confronted with the terrible dilemma of a double fidelity to the Church and to the Revolution, the movement Christians for Socialism has had the painful experience of this duality of discourse where political language alternates with religious language, and where their juxtaposition underlines the lack of articulation and of synthesis.[29] It is not easy to maintain the cohesion of traditional models in a totally new situation. Neither is it easy to escape their influence by taking precipitate decisions. When one does this one finds oneself with the obligation of negotiating and of managing a reality which one has neither eliminated nor overcome.

Thus, the institutionalisation of the Latin American church, thanks to CELAM, has given to the member Churches a capacity of intervention and a consciousness of a unity which transcends national frontiers and which are without precedent on the sub-continent. But it has not brought unanimity to them. Its very centre of gravity has been displaced. Medellín (1968) had pushed the pendulum towards the Left; Puebla (1979) and John Paul II have pushed it in the other direction. That is what has been called the recentring and colombianisation of CELAM.

On a political level, two experiences have deeply affected Latin American Catholicism: the Cuban revolution and military reaction. These have created the conditions of a religious spread from the extreme Left to the extreme Right. They have also blurred the traditional spheres of influence of political parties, Conservatives and Liberals under such names or under others, and facilitated a certain breakthrough of Christian democracy (in Chile, Venezuela, Costa Rica, and to a lesser degree in Ecuador, Peru and El Salvador). Finally, they have encouraged the participation of the clergy in revolutionary movements in a militant or even military role.

At the same time, Latin American Catholicism cannot be reduced to this spectrum of political positions. It is characterised now, as always, by its socio-historic stratifications that one could also call socio-economic. It ranges from the Christianity of conquest that is maintained by the Indian tribes who speak only their own language and who ensure their own religious organisation by means of the institution of *mayor domo* (elected each year) to the private Christianity, purely an affair of conscience, of family and of tradition found among the upper classes. In between them, one finds the Christianity of the rural populations which mobilised the Cristeros or that which forms of Catholic Action tried to inspire. The consideration of such cultural distances poses more than purely pastoral problems. It has inspired both attempts to re-evaluate popular religion and many efforts to promote social awareness. This gives rise to a complex theological situation in which, by the force of things, even if it does not wish it, all theology becomes political. The dominant official theology can be qualified as post-conciliar. Its key word is *opening* and its slogan 'communion and participation' (López Trujillo). In practice it still largely leaves in peace a pre-conciliar theology which often remains that of the catechism. But above all, it is judged insufficient by two groups which count on the development of a *popular Church*. These are the numerous basic Christian communities, especially in Brazil, for whom the essential principle is not *opening* but *descent*, towards the poor and the deprived and towards the movements of revolutionary action which seek *liberation*. At the very moment when in certain books this theology of liberation seemed to have said its last word, on the ground, it considerably increased its influence. It inspires as much fear as enthusiasm and some people see it as the first heresy of Latin America. Recent events in Nicaragua and El Salvador show the degree to which in Latin America a Church of solidarity can be a divided Church.

NOTES

1. The following year saw the creation of the *Pontificio Collegio Americano del Nord* and approval for the Pontifical French Seminary created in 1853. In 1934 under Pius XI, a Pontificio Collegio Pio Brasiliano was detached from the Collegio Latinoamericano, as had been previously separated from it a pontifical Canadian college in 1888 and a pontifical Mexican college in 1967. The Latinoamericano and the Brasiliano were made the responsibility of the Jesuits 'ad perpetuum'.

At the age of 31, the future Pius IX had belonged to the MUZZI mission, the first Pontifical mission in Latin America (Chile 1823–95) and had been profoundly marked by this experience.

2. *Acta et decreta Concilii plenarii Americae latinae in Urbe celebrati anno Domini MDCCCXCIX*, Romae, Typis vaticanis, 1900, CX–X462 p., plus an *Appendix* of 779 pages. Present were 14 archbishops and 40 bishops. Among the eight consultors all resident in Rome were the Spanish capuchin, Vives y Tutó (who was appointed cardinal during the council) and Fr Wernz, the future general of the Jesuits.
3. The second was held at Medellín (Colombia) in 1968, the third at Puebla (Mexico) in 1979. Paul VI attended the first one and John Paul II the second one.
4. The United States, which is a member of the OAS, does not belong to CELAM. Cuba and Puerto Rico, which are members of CELAM, are not members of the OAS, the first because of its exclusion, and the second because of its political status.

   Similarly, there used to be an Episcopal Conference of Central America and of Panama. Since its replacement by national bishops conferences, it continues only as a Secretariat.
5. *DTC*, 'Amérique latine', T.1, col. 1081 (Paris: Letouzey and Ané, 1900) quoted in the encyclopaedia *Catholicisme*, t.1., col. 458 (ibid., 1948).

   The Episcopal Conference of Brazil (CNBB) is the second most numerous in the world after that of Italy. In 1977, there were 637 ecclesiastical jurisdictions in Latin America of which 217 were situated in Brazil. The number of Catholics was estimated at 284 million out of a population of 336 million. These figures have to be treated with great prudence.
6. Mission 'Economia y Humanismo', *Estudio sobre las condiciones del desarrollo en Colombia* (Bogotá: Présidence de la République, 1958) 2 vols, cartes. Louis-Joseph Lebret (1897–1966) subsequently founded IFRED, which is a centre specialising in the problems of development. Since his death, a Centre Lebret has been created (9 rue Guénégaud, 75006 Paris) and is directed by Fr Vincent Cosmão and publishes as a periodical bulletin *Foi et Développement*.
7. Two North American scholars have written theses on the work of Fr Vekemans. One purports to establish his links with the CIA while the other denies them. The answer to this question involves a series of problems which the sociologists must address. These are the links between sources of finance, channels of distribution, research programmes, relationships between power and knowledge and the way each of them is used, or between the disinterestedness of the researcher, the strategy of his intervention, the interests of his work and the publication of his results. More generally is involved the interplay of multiple finalities implied by the series of operations and politico-ideological divergences between researchers. An academic conflict of a normal type is thus complicated in the heat of action by factors which are blind to nuances.
8. This is from Alex Morelli (1919–79)'s posthumous publication, *Hacia*

una Iglesia popular (Mexico, 1980). 'This continent is a volcano' he used often say. Having arrived in Montevideo in 1959, and having been expelled from Uruguay in 1965, he received from Edmond Michelet a diplomatic passport which facilitated his work. He took up residence in the great shantytown of Mexico city, Netzahualcoyotl (more than 2 million inhabitants).

9. Dial, published from 47 quai des Grands Augustins, 75006 Paris.
10. In 1977, France provided 400 *Fidei Donum* priests, of whom 130 were resident in Latin America.
11. The new form of Catholic Action was initially seen by enthusiastic lay people as an alternative to the general Catholic Action on the Italian model which enjoyed the support of the bishops, JEC, JAC, JOC, ACI, ACO, MIJARC . . . These movements became rapidly politicised and this is a constant of the development of Catholic Action simply for over a century now. This was also the time when people read the Jerusalem Bible, translated Chenu, Congar, Lubac, sang the psalms of Gélineau, when the University Centre of Mexico modelled itself on the Centre Richelieu of the Sorbonne. . . . The dominant ideology was that of development, and it was not yet contested by the theory of dependence and the consequences which follow from it.
12. 'La démocratie chrétienne en Amérique latine', *Le Monde diplomatique* (February 1981), pp. 7–12 (various authors). 'Amérique latine: à la recherche d'une nouvelle démocratie', *Panorama démocrate chrétien* (Rome, revue de l'Union mondiale démocrate chrétienne), IX (1978), 1, 99 p. (divers auteurs latino-américains et le Fr Vekemans); Peter Molt, *La Démocratie chrétienne en Amérique latine*, and various Latin Americans, *Amérique latine: pour un projet de société communautaire* (Rome, 1971), (Cahier 7 and 8 of the Institut international démocrate chrétien d'études).
13. The most recent criticism is Roland Gaucher, *Les Finances de l'Église de France* (Paris: Albin Michel, 1981) ch. VI. (The CCFD is compared to Secours Rouge.)
14. The State made a contribution to the erection of the new basilica which was inaugurated when the solidity of the old building gave grounds for worry.
15. With the war of the *Cristeros* (1926–8), studied by Jean Meyer: *La Cristiada*, 3 vols (Mexico: Siglo XXI, 1973–4); *Apocalypse et Revolution au Mexique: La guerre des Cristeros* (Paris: Gallimard-Julliard, 1974) 244 p. (Coll. Archives); *La Cristiade, L'Église, l'État et le Peuple dans la Revolution mexicaine (1926–1929)* (Paris: Payot, 1975) 246 p.
16. When Jean Paul II visited Mexico for the Episcopal Assembly of Puebla (1979), President López Portillo saluted him at the airport. This was the minimum requirement of courtesy. When the President's daughter married in 1981, the newspapers were full of details of the civil ceremony without ever mentioning the religious ceremony which had taken place in the strictest privacy of the presidential residence.
17. The confiscation of the property of the clergy which was subsequently sold to lay purchasers.
18. On this period, Rodolfo Ramon de Roux, *Église et société en*

Colombie (9 April 1948). *Fonctions sociales et fonctionement de l'institution catholique* (Paris, 1981), 334 p. (third year thesis, École des hautes études en sciences sociales).

19. Charles Conlacines, *Chili. L'Église catholique (1958–1976)* (Paris: L'Harmattan, 1977) 274 p.
20. Vicaria de la Solidaridad del Arzobispado de Santiago de Chile (which published the Bulletin *Solidaridad*).
21. Can one then speak of a 'disintegration of the Catholic ideological block' or suppose that this integration was more apparent than profound? It was only in 1931 that the Holy See brought about the creation of a Catholic Action complemented by the Catholic trade unions and subsequently by Christian Democracy. This however was but a development of the traditional core. While the appearance of Christians for Socialism is something new, the detestation of conservative catholics is a simple reappearance in force.
22. Charles Antoine, *Le Sang et l'espoir. Ces chrétiens d'Amérique latine* (Paris: Le Centurion, 1978) 148 pp. A detailed but non-exhaustive chronology is to be found in *América latina Boletin* (October 1978) published by the International Student Christian movement and the Jeunesse étudiante chrétienne internationale (JECI): *'Padeceran persecucion por Mi Causa'. Diez anos de conflicto Iglesia-Estado en America latina*, 320 pp.
23. Leader of the Golconde group which had published in January 1969 a 'Manifesto for Socialism'. This text declared itself in favour of the revolution and the institution of a socialist-type society.
24. 'L'Église paie un lourd tribu en Argentine', published in *Le Figaro* of 20 February 1978, under the signature of Jean Bourdarias: how then could the Argentinian bishops remain silent?
25. The classic text is Gustavo Gutiérrez, *Teología de la Liberación: Perspectivas* (Lima, Peru: CEP, 1971); translated into French: *Théologie de la Libération. Perspectives* (Bruxelles: Edns Lumen Vitae, 1974), 343 p.; Rubén A. Alves, *Christianisme, opium ou liberation?* (Paris: Edns du Cerf, 1972), 195 p.

    While there have been priest guerilleros, such as Camilo Torres, and then Domingo Latin, both of whom were killed in combat, there was also the non-violent way illustrated by Adolfo Perez Esquivel, *Le Christ au poncho* (Paris: Centurion, 1981), 160 p. (The author received the Nobel Prize for Peace 1980.)
26. It is as if from within their political independence, the Latin Americans had become conscious of an economic and social dependence for which marxism provided them of a model of analysis. Similarly, as if within their colonial dependence, the Africans had felt a loss of their cultural identity and thus felt that they never had acceded to their authentic Christian personality. For their part, western theologians under the influence of liberal society, explored a theology of secularisation and then in reaction to this, a theology of revolution. These are the new paths of political theology which has a rich and long past.
27. Charles Antoine, *L'Église et le Pouvoir au Brésil. Naissance du militarisme* (Paris: Desclée de Brouwer, 1971), 270 p.; José Comblin,

Le Pouvoir militaire en Amérique latine. L'idéologie de la Sécurité nationale (Paris: Jean-Pierre Delarge, 1977), 235 p. (bibliography); Marcio Moreira-Alves, *L'Église et la politique au Brésil* (Paris: Edns du Cerf, 1974), 266 p. (bibliography).

28. Charles Antoine, *L'Intégrisme brésilien* (Paris: Centre Lebret, 1973), 121 p.

    Another question is what the ideology of national security, and more generally, Latin America, owe to maurrassisme. See Miguel Rojasmix, 'Charles Maurras en Amérique latine', *Le Monde diplomatique* (November 1980).

29. Pablo Richard, *Origine et développement du mouvement 'Chrétiens pour le Socialisme', Chili, 1970–1973* (Paris: Centre Lebret, 1976) 166 p. See also Pablo Richard, *Mort des chrétientés et naissance de l'Église* (Paris: Centre Lebret, 1978), 25 p.

    More general and theoretical: Giulio Girardi, *Chrétiens pour le socialisme* (Paris: Edns du Cerf, 1976) 206 p. (bibliography, pp. 149–60).

2 The Catholic Church and Politics in Latin America: Basic Trends and Likely Futures

Daniel H. Levine

Religion and politics in Latin America today often seem a mass of conflict and contradiction.* There is debate over the meaning of events and bitter struggle to shape and control them. There is also confusion. Contradictory claims abound, and the evidence to sort them out is scarce and unreliable, at best subject to very divergent interpretations. All this conflict and contradiction stems from almost thirty years of unprecedented change in both religion and politics.

This chapter identifies central tendencies and explores the bases of patterns in the change so visible over recent years. Even the most casual glance at recent Latin American experience with religion and politics turns up lots of change over little time in institutions and areas once generally considered static and stodgy. So much change is hard to grasp and absorb under any circumstances. In any case, Latin America is big and diverse, embracing countries with radically different cultural traditions, social and economic structures, and political histories. Even if we were to argue (for purposes of discussion) that 'religion' has a single sort of influence and impact, it should be no surprise that its expressions vary according to circumstance. Constraints and opportunities, urgent needs and felt imperatives, are bound to differ from revolutionary Nicaragua to stolid Colombia or authoritarian Chile. They also vary within nations by region and social level, and over time as well as societies themselves change. A first step in making sense of all this change and variation is thus to accept that it is real, normal, and inevitable. But acknowledging contradiction as real does not condemn us to accept confusion as inevitable. Some of the confusion arises from lack of clarity about basic concepts. Two noteworthy cases in point are the notion of 'politicisation of religion' and the meaning given to participation.

Critics often describe the current Latin American situation as one of the 'politicisation of religion'. What does it mean to speak in such terms? Describing developments in this way implies that in earlier (presumably happier) times, religion was not politicised. But in Latin America religion and politics have been joined ever since the Conquest. The common complaint is then less about the relation between religion and politics as such, than it is about religiously based challenges to the *existing* order of things. Concern with 'politicisation of religion' works from a false premise: that 'politics' is only (or principally) a matter of challenges to established arrangements.

Clearly, when we speak of religion and politics, Church and politics, or Church and State now, at issue is not the 'politicisation of religion', as if this were some simple index which rises or falls, levels on a hypothetical religio/political thermometer. What has changed is not religion's political involvement or salience, but rather the following three elements. First, there is less unquestioned unity around core institutions led by bishops. Second, the ideological direction of criticism has shifted: there is great dissatisfaction with capitalism and intense struggle over the validity of marxist analysis in religious discourse. Finally, the social location of the process has moved, with popular groups taking a greater role. Such groups bring their own agenda to the encounter with institutions, respecting but not necessarily following to the letter directives received from above.

The issue of participation is similar. Lately, there has been considerable stress on the growth of participation in both religion and politics throughout the region. As part of a general move away from the formal and legalistic categories which dominated earlier research on 'Church and State', scholars and observers working throughout Latin America have turned to more dynamic themes of religion and politics, exploring how elites, institutions, and formal documents link up with other levels of reality in systematic ways. In this vein, much work has been done lately on popular classes, grassroots movements, and their often conflicted ties with high politics and the 'big structures' of Church and State.

But despite this reorientation, much research remains elite-focused, concerned above all with the development of structures and agendas created in the churches and projected outward to popular groups. Studies now commonly ask how institutions view the people and make a legitimate place for them in doctrine, ideology, and structure. But suppose we invert the question, and ask instead *how* people view the institution? How do average men and women see the big structures of religion and politics? How and why do they organise in certain ways? What specific needs and goals do they bring to the encounter with the high politics of power and meaning religion and politics embody and project?

Reformulating concepts in this way makes for a richer portrait of reality. For much of the drama of recent experience arises from the convergence of heightened concern for participation in the churches and in religion generally with the growth of national security states, and thus with political closure, expanded repression, and restricted opportunities for participation of any kind.[1]

This conjuncture gave a decisive push and direction to religious and political ferment in key cases all across the region. But why did repression magnify pressures for participation and enhance their legitimacy, and not lead to apathy and accommodation? First, where they took hold, new religious ideas legitimated activism in theory and through their translation into innovative forms of grassroots organisation. Second, the very experience of participation provided nets of solidarity which encouraged members in continued resistance. Finally, political closure drove new clients into these structures, which often were the only outlets available.[2]

At issue here is no longer a simple opposition of religion to political power: for this, Latin American history provides ample precedent. What is new is the language of opposition and its carriers: liberation theology as worked out by average people in the grassroots groups known widely throughout the region as base Christian communities or CEBs. Much has been written on liberation theology and CEBs, and I will not go over this familiar ground here.[3] But a few key traits may well be noted. Moving beyond condemnation of specific rulers or regimes to challenge whole economic, cultural, and political systems as unjust and sinful, liberation theology has crafted a different discourse about religion, society and politics. In turn, the CEBs have opened the way to new kinds of practice. These are generally small, socially homogeneous groups (mostly poor people) which meet regularly to read and discuss the bible, and to reflect on community life and problems from this perspective. Their normal practice encourages self-expression, sharing and solidarity, and active participation in the collective affairs of daily life.

Both liberation theology and CEBs gain added political salience from the conjunctures in which they emerge. Each enhances participation and activism; each crystallises at a moment when any collective action is viewed with deep suspicion. As a result, each quickly becomes a target for repression by threatened elites. Civil and military rulers fear popular organisation just as they fear *any* uncontrolled action. They fear it even more when it comes legitimated by the moral and organisational force of religion. Church authorities are also afraid. They fear loss of authority, as grassroots groups develop a sense of autonomous collective identity, with new norms of legitimacy and alternative styles and sources of leadership. Loss of authority means specifically decay of *hierarchical* authority and unquestioned obedience.[4] The result of the process has been to make Church–State issues salient once again. Indeed, over the last 10 or 15 years, conflict between Church and State all over Latin America has arguably been more intense and visible than at any point in the previous century. Conflicts arise and find expression in this format once again because churches (ecclesiastical institutions) are drawn into confrontation with states in defence of grassroots groups. A typical sequence begins with apparently innocuous community activities: discussion groups are formed, co-operatives established. Because authorities are so fearful, any collective action draws repression, leading to statements and actions by church leaders in defence of pastoral agents and group members. From such modest beginnings, conflict has repeatedly escalated to higher and broader levels, ending in general challenges to the logic and legitimacy of authoritarian rule.

This process is often termed 'radicalisation', but while radicalisation is clearly present, more is at issue. The particular version of faith and commitments at work in these cases is especially open to radicalisation. The pervasive stress on activism, participation, and themes of equality and justice in recent Latin American Catholic thinking make groups and leaders especially sensitive to undercurrents of power and privilege in any situation.[5] Once the cycle of conflict gets under way, such new religious orientations, reinforced by mutual support in different kinds of group structures (more participatory in theory and practice), become self-sustaining in ways unlikely in the past.

Church–State issues are thus salient once again, but note how much the content of typical disputes has changed. Traditional concerns over education, marriage and divorce, state subsidies and the like are mostly gone. Instead, centre stage is held by issues of human rights, justice, social criticism, and by a broad conflict over the proper role and place of popular classes in the social order. Two brief examples may help clarify the altered quality of this old confrontation. The first is from El Salvador, and concerns the career of Monsignor Romero. The second draws implications from the Brazilian bishops' consistent promotion of popular participation.

Most accounts of the process in El Salvador date the shift in Romero's general stance from his reaction to the murder of Fr Rutilio Grande and the subsequent escalation of violence against pastoral workers, catechists and CEB members. But more is at issue here than simple reaction. As Jon Sobrino has pointed out,[6] Romero's confrontation with the State grew directly from his commitment to the people, a stance later enshrined at Puebla as a 'preferential option for the poor'. For Romero, the poor were not to be seen in abstract terms, as the poor and humble in general. He insisted on seeing them as he found them, among the impoverished and oppressed of everyday life in contemporary El Salvador.

Being poor and with the poor these specific groups of poor people had a few highly concrete implications. First, it meant putting the institutional weight of the church on their side with services, protection, access to media, buildings, and to facilities of all kinds. Second, it meant putting the moral weight of the Church on their side by preaching, denouncing injustice, and announcing the possibility of a new social order. Third, it required identifying with the poor and sharing with them. This meant taking on a simple life style and also promoting, trusting and backing popular leaders. Initiatives like these did not rest on any desire on Archbishop Romero's part to confront the state. Rather, they grew from a vision of the Church which located it firmly in the world, and thus in practice blurred hitherto sharp lines between religion and politics. In a speech at Louvain Romero put it this way:

> The Church's option for the poor explains the political dimensions of the faith in its fundamentals and in its basic outlines. Because the Church has opted for the truly poor, not for the fictitiously poor, because it has opted for those who really are oppressed and repressed, the Church lives in a political world, and it fulfills itself as a church also through politics. It cannot be otherwise if the Church, like Jesus, is to turn itself toward the poor.[7]

The Brazilian example is similar, but gains added weight from the force of episcopal unity. Here we find not a single extraordinary leader (like Romero), but a general institutional reorientation. At the heart of this change, and critical to Church–State conflict throughout the period of military rule (1964–85), has been consistent episcopal stress on popular participation: supporting popular initiatives, trusting leaders, encouraging alliances. This process has been well documented[8] and one example will suffice here.

In preparations for the Extraordinary Synod, called by Pope John Paul II in late 1985 to review and evaluate the previous two decades of change, Brazilian bishops consistently supported CEBs and liberation theology as legitimate and vital religious innovations. At Rome, they thus assumed the same role they have long taken in Latin American organisations like the regional bishops' conference, CELAM. In both forums, Brazilians engaged more conservative Latin American bishops (especially Colombians) in heated dispute over a wide range of issues. In marking out their positions, Brazilian spokesmen did not rely on a narrow vision of the institution and its needs. On the contrary, they argued

> I'm not the local branch manager of the International Spiritual Bank Inc. I learn as much from my people as they learn from me. They confirm my faith as much as I confirm theirs. When I arrive on horseback or in a jeep, I do not preside all the time. When you ask me what I think, I tell you what their views are.[9]

The following sections of this chapter review central tendencies of change since 1958. The process is first considered over time, and then through analysis of variation in contrasting cases. Throughout, special stress is given to how religion and politics influence and shape one another. The chapter concludes with speculation on likely trends for the future.

REALITIES: CHANGE AND VARIATION

The overall period is dated from the papacy of John XXIII to the present. In the Church, this takes us through four Popes (John XXIII, Paul VI, and the two John Pauls). It is deeply marked by the Second Vatican Council and its opening to the world, both in general terms and through the impact of reforms in liturgy and ritual which open up religious participation enormously. In social doctrine, the period sets out from Pope John's two encyclicals (*Mater et Magistra* and *Pacem in Terris*) which open doors to learning from the social sciences, to collaboration with marxism, and generally to an option for the poor. These themes are carried forward in Vatican II, and take general shape in Pope Paul's *Populorum Progressio*, which sets the issues in a general context of concern for 'modernisation and development'. Late in Paul's tenure such social and political themes yield to stress on birth control (*Humanae Vitae*), on preaching the gospel, and to a vague fear of the loss of unity. The period closes under John Paul II with a burst of conservative activity, devoted in organisational terms to reaffirmation of unity, and doctrinally to attacks on liberation theology. The Extraordinary Synod of late 1985 marks a convenient end point.

If these 'events' of the Church are set against a social and political time line for Latin America, the conjunctures are suggestive. In political terms, the period is marked off by revolutions 20 years apart in Cuba and Nicaragua. The Cuban experience has enormous appeal early on, and spurs a new kind of Catholic political reformists, epitomised in Christian Democracy, which reaches its high point with victories by Eduardo Frei in Chile (1964) and Rafael Caldera in Venezuela four years later. But although Christian Democracy offered a new outlet for Catholic political energies in open societies like Chile or Venezuela, in other cases alternative visions of religion and politics begin to bubble up at the same time. Only two years after Frei's election in Chile, Camilo Torres is killed in Colombia. Torres was a former priest who moved to revolution as an outgrowth of his general Christian commitment to justice. While he has found few imitators, the ideals Camilo Torres espoused remain alive, in a call to change *beyond* reform, and to political action beyond electoral vehicles. In any case, Christian Democracy was not the only 'model' to appear on the Latin American scene in 1964. That year also witnessed the military coup in Brazil, which set a standard for the next twenty years of authoritarian rule in the region. The Brazilian example was followed in the 1970s by profoundly reactionary regimes in Uruguay and Chile, and (in fits and starts throughout the period) in Argentina.

The trajectory of Christian Democracy in Chile is central to our story. In its rise to power, the party carried a surge of optimism about reform. It helped create a new place and direction for Catholic political energies, breaking with the alliances of the past. Christian Democracy soon divided and ran out of gas in Chile. Electoral defeat itself was less significant than the fact that both Left and Right

	POLITICAL EVENTS LATIN AMERICA	*SIGNIFICANT RELIGIOUS EVENTS*	*RELIGIOUS EVENTS CATHOLICISM*
1958			Pope John XXIII elected
1959	Revolution in Cuba		
1960			
1961			*Mater et Magistra* publ.
1962			Vatican II opens
1963	Military coup, Brazil		*Pacem in Terris* publ. Pope Paul VI elected
1964	Christian Democratic victory, Chile		
1965			Vatican II closes
1966		Camilo Torres killed in Colombia	
1967			*Populorum Progressio* publ.
1968	Christian Democratic victory, Venezuela	MEDELLÍN CONFERENCE Pope to Colombia	*Humanae Vitae* publ.
1969			
1970	Socialist victory, Chile		
1971		*A Theology of Liberation* publ. López Trujillo elected Sec. Gen. CELAM	*Octogesima Adveniens* publ.
1972	Meeting CpS, Chile		
1973	Military coup, Chile	*Tierra Nueva* founded	
1974			
1975			
1976			
1977	Rutilio Grande killed in El Salvador		*Evangelii Nuntiandi* publ.
1978		Archbishop Romero named El Salvador	Pope John Paul I elected Pope John Paul II elected
1979	Revolution in Nicaragua	PUEBLA CONFERENCE Pope to Mexico	
1980	Coup in El Salvador	Archbishop Romero killed Pope to Brazil	
1981			*Laborem Exercens* publ.
1982		Jaruzelski Coup in Poland	
1983		Pope to Central America	Ratzinger Instruction
1984			
1985	Civilian rule, Brazil, Uruguay, Argentina	Pope to Peru and Venezuela	EXTRAORDINARY SYNOD Leonardo Boff silenced
1986		Pope to Colombia	Ratzinger II

Figure 1 Selected Religious and Political Events, 1958–1986

abandoned the party. The Catholic Left turned to stormy alliances with marxism, forged in the 1970 Allende campaign and confirmed in tumultuous meetings of Christians for Socialism (Cristianos Por el Socialismo, CpS) in Santiago in 1972. The Catholic Right returned to traditional links with conservative parties, and also to extremists in the military and in organisations like TFP (Tradition, Family, and Property). As the initial Christian Democratic impetus decayed, Catholic political energies divided, reformist optimism faded, and a notable backlash against the 'politicisation' of religion and the churches got under way throughout the region.

Once presumably united around a reformist agenda (Christian Democracy, *Populorum Progressio*), Latin American Catholicism splits. At one extreme we find a Camilo Torres, and close to him movements like Chile's CpS, Colombia's SAL (Sacerdotes Para América Latina), or the Movement of Third World Priests in Argentina. On the level of theory, it is around this time that a long period of discussion and reflection crystallises in the publication of Gustavo Gutiérrez's landmark *A Theology of Liberation* which gave a name and focus to many of these concerns.

The meeting of the Latin American Bishops' Conference (CELAM) at Medellín in 1968 seemed to empower and legitimate many of these elements. But in retrospect Medellín looks more like a peak than a marker on the road to growing commitments with change. Soon after, the guard changes at CELAM. Monsignor Alfonso López Trujillo of Colombia was elected secretary general in 1972, and began a systematic reorientation of the organisation: training institutes, publications and staff were all purged. López Trujillo also promoted an ideological counter to liberation theology, joining with Roger Vekemans to found the journal *Tierra Nueva* in Bogotá in 1972. *Tierra Nueva* soon became a central voice in the attack on liberation theology and related 'progressive' issues and movements.[10]

Consider for a moment the contrasting examples of Camilo Torres and Roger Vekemans. Although the two are rarely spoken of in the same breath, a comparative look may be instructive. They take off from a similar starting point of social science analysis and Christian reformism, but soon move in opposite directions: the first to guerrilla activity, the second to extended ideological combat with liberation theology. In his brief career, Camilo Torres moved from sociological research and small-scale reformism of a Christian Democratic sort to general political organisation (the ill-fated Frente Unido) and finally to guerrilla struggle. In his longer trajectory, Vekemans emerges from Belgian Catholicism, long a seedbed for Christian Democratic groups and ideas. He worked in Chile for many years in sociological research and most notably in popular organisations closely linked to the Christian Democratic Party. After Allende's victory, Vekemans and his team moved to Colombia, founding *Tierra Nueva* and operating what amounts to a continental clearing house for the counter-offensive against the Left. Stung by the Chilean experience, Vekemans and his group have now mostly abandoned direct political action.

Out of the original Christian Democratic impetus, Camilo Torres moves radically leftward, a precursor of much that was to come in the twenty years since his death. Vekemans is more complex, because it is less a matter of his move rightward, as a question of how general shifts in the ideological spectrum pushed an originally reformist (not even 'centrist') position identified with Christian Democracy to one end of the range of available alternatives.

The polarisation epitomised in these two cases grew steadily through the 1970s, and surfaced at a particularly critical moment at decade's end. The region's bishops gathered again in 1979 at Puebla to weigh changes since Medellín and chart a course for the future. The story of Puebla has been told well and in detail elsewhere[11] but a few major points should be noted. Puebla marks the inauguration of a vigorous new Pope, his appearance in Latin America (the first of five such trips over seven years). It also coincides with successful revolution in Nicaragua, and with the enormous escalation of violence in El Salvador. Church people played a visible role in both processes, often in close concert with opposition groups. After Puebla, violence continues to grow in El Salvador, claiming Monsignor Romero among its victims less than a year later.

Most of these trends have continued since the Puebla meetings. Over the whole period, violence has grown and unity has declined. Violence appears for the churches in part through the onslaught of national security states, which has claimed pastoral agents, CEB members, bishops, priests and sisters among its many victims. Violence also appears through the issue of class conflict: a major charge against liberation theology has been its supposed endorsement of violent class conflict through a partisan stress on preferential options for the poor. If we take unity to mean obedience to hierarchically constituted authority (as do most bishops), then unity has visibly declined. Norms of unquestioned obedience, and the general expectations of passivity on which they rest have all been put into question.

John Paul II has made Latin America a priority, travelling to the region many times since his inaugural visit to Puebla. He regularly condemns violence.[12] stresses the 'non-political' character of the Church's mission, and underscores the need for unity and discipline in the ranks. Some have seen in all this a 'Polish model', noting the Pope's experience with Polish Church traditions of clerical dominance, episcopal unity, and tight authority relations. But there is an alternative Polish model which provides a suggestive conjuncture with the push for greater popular participation in Latin America. This model rests on the example of Solidarity. From early 1980 until General Jaruzelski's December 1981 coup, Solidarity was clearly a different kind of 'Polish model', and showed the possibilities for an autonomous popular movement to grow, erupt into hierarchical and closed structures, and pull them into new sorts of commitments and challenges. But this is clearly not the model the Pope has in mind.

If we attribute a Polish model to John Paul II, it would have to be one stressing ecclesiastical discipline and unity. In the Polish tradition, reinforced strongly in this century, the very idea of 'Church' hinges almost exclusively on bishops, clergy, and dioceses. These hold the 'sacred deposit' of truth (to use an old phrase) and give it to masses who also belong, but not in the same way. It is a trickle down theory of religious life, well fitted for social or political contexts which are themselves elitist and authoritarian in character. The point has been made sharply by Leonardo Boff in the book which prompted his silencing:[13]

> Throughout its history, the Church has defined itself at times with the ruling classes and at other times with the lower classes. The unequal social structures, revolving around ownership of the means of production, slowly came to predominate within the Church itself. An unbalanced structure in the means of 'religious' production was created; in socioanalytical language (so as not to give a moral connotation) there has also been a gradual expropriation of the means of religious production from the Christian people by the clergy. In the early years, the Christian people as a whole shared in the power of the Church, in decisions, in the choosing of ministers; later, they were simply consulted; finally, in terms of power they were totally marginalized, dispossessed of their power.
>
> Just as there was a social division of labor, an ecclesiastical

> division of religious labor was introduced. A group of functionaries and experts was created, responsible for attending to the religious needs of all through the exclusive production of the symbolic goods to be consumed by the now dispossessed people. . . . It is clear that a Church so structurally unbalanced is in harmony with the social realm that possesses the same biased means of production. The Church has often become the legitimating religious ideology for the imperial social order.

Building a Polish model for Latin America thus means reinforcing norms and values of hierarchy and discipline while amplifying the voice of key Latin American leaders like López Trujillo (named Cardinal by John Paul II). Autonomous grassroots groups must be brought to heel and 'depoliticised'. From this vantage point, 'politics' is identified with conflict and violence, withdrawal and neutrality are urged, activism deemphasised, and spiritual values stressed. The 'preferential option for the poor', seemingly enshrined at Puebla, is qualified as 'not exclusive', and reworked as a 'preferential love for the poor and young' – quite a different sort of commitment.

Over the whole course of events, there are two high points where the weight of thought and action shift direction and new 'packages' are conceived and put together. The first is from Vatican II and the rise of Christian Democracy, peaking in the period around Medellín. There is general openness to change, a new critical discourse about society and politics is invented, and significant ideological and organisational innovations get the stamp of religious legitimacy. The decline of Christian Democracy, followed by the experience of CpS, Allende, and military rule in Chile all mark the end of this period. The publication of *A Theology of Liberation* comes near the close. The second starts to crystallise after deep divisions in the mid-1970s. One end of the spectrum is held down by liberation theology and a 'radical ideal' of base Christian communities which makes them central to the construction of a new order in society, politics, and culture.[14] The confrontation of key episcopal conferences like Brazil or Chile with national security states reinforces this group. The other end of the spectrum takes form with the change of command in CELAM, and the turn of key Catholic institutions to critical stances on marxism and politics. The whole process comes together around the time of Puebla and the Nicaraguan revolution. It continues through the violence in El Salvador, the rise and fall of Solidarity in Poland, and the growing, concerted attack on liberation theology

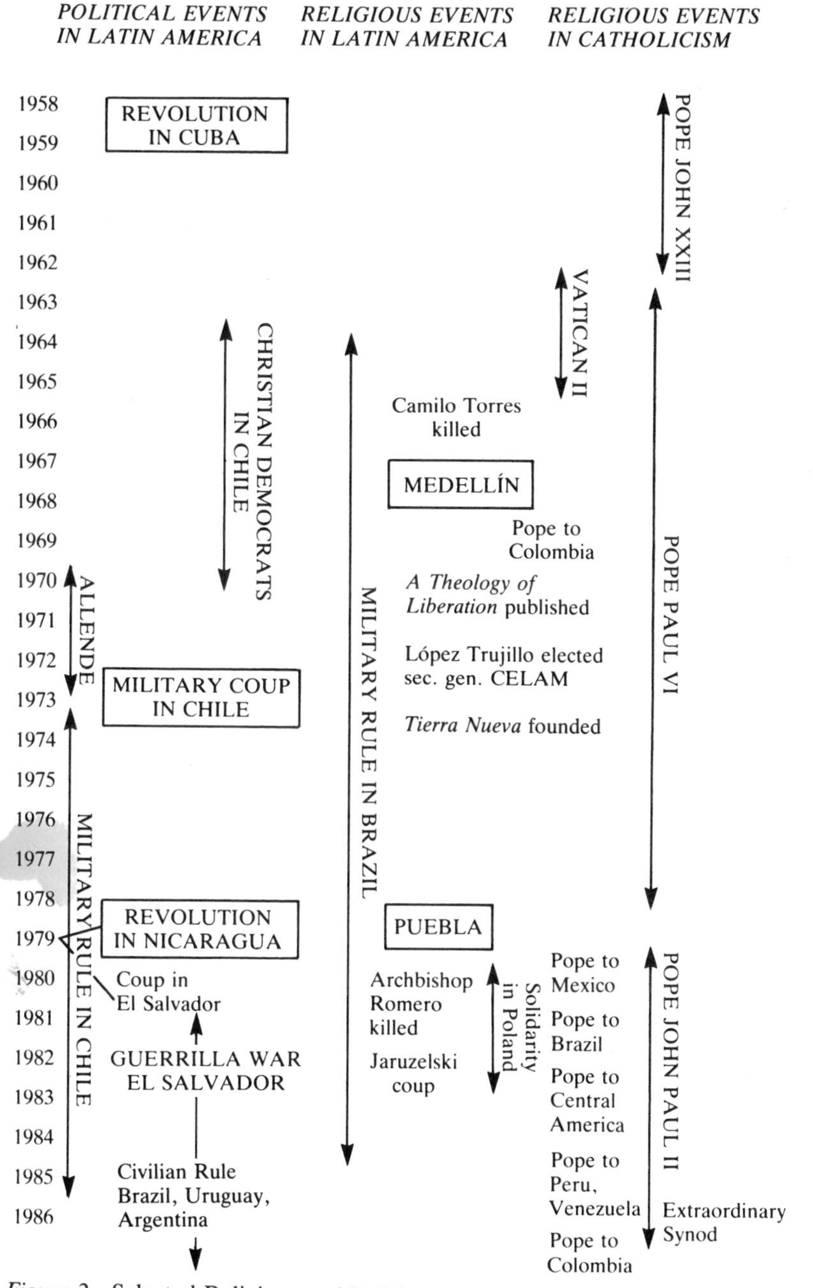

Figure 2 Selected Religious and Political Events, 1958–86

which peaks with the 1984 Ratzinger Instruction and the Extraordinary Synod of late 1985.

If we were to draw a curve through Figure 2, tracing some mythical level of enthusiasm for radical or liberationist ideas and solutions among church officials in Latin America, the line would rise slowly through the 1960s, top off around Medellín, and thereafter drop sharply from the mid-1970s on. This general trajectory holds for key cases like Chile, and has been advanced strongly throughout the region by Colombian Church leaders. The major counter example is Brazil.

This overview highlights the changing nature of political outlets for Catholicism and the altered meaning given to 'politics' in Catholic discourse. In the first period, the churches stood with Christian Democracy. These parties offered an apparently ideal way to free the institution from earlier partisan entanglements. Now the bishops could safely leave 'politics' to reformist Christian elites, acting 'on their own'. The 'Church as such' (the ecclesiastical institution) was not compromised, and specific Catholic political parties (for example, Dom Leme's Catholic Electoral League in Brazil) seemed a thing of the past. But as Christian Democracy soured, the idea that such an alternative could get the Church 'out of politics' proved illusory.

Church leaders did strive to 'get out of politics' by abandoning older alliances, but pressures for political action of new kinds grew. First came cases like Camilo Torres, for whom 'politics' was a Christian imperative, part of a generalised revolutionary (but still non-partisan) challenge to the established order of things. Then, groups like CpS called for partisan political action, but now in alliance with the Left. CpS and similar groups legitimated their 'politics' through ideas soon to crystallise as liberation theology. Later, liberation theology itself, above all as worked out in the daily experience of many CEBs, brought 'politics' to the Churches in two related senses. The first came with Church elites defending base groups against repression and in the process clashing with civil and military authorities. The second came as claims to grassroots autonomy and egalitarian notions of power and authority challenged conventional expectations of power within the churches, bringing politics home to the institution itself.

This succession of political outlets has been accompanied by a shift in the stance the churches have taken with regard to regimes and political systems generally. From unquestioned supporters of the established order, the churches moved through periods of major criticism to a current 'official' stance (much contested to be sure) of neutrality. Looking over the period as a whole, one may well ask: did the Church change, or is it the spectrum which shifted, giving new meaning to what are much the same positions? The question suggests how much the Catholic Church's political projection is marked by circumstance, and by the sort of opposition it encounters. In the first period noted earlier, the major threat was underdevelopment and the core response was to be Christian Democracy and reform. But in very little time the perceived threat changed, from underdevelopment to repression. Threats from the 'right' helped put even moderate Churches on the 'left' end of the range of alternatives.

What drives change on these dimensions? What does it mean? The answer is only in part a matter of how transformations within religion are magnified by political threat or pressure. More generally, we need to look at how people 'see' the Church, and at the implications of this new 'seeing'. The outcomes visible across the region cannot be reduced to a simple function of repression turning the churches in one direction or another. There must be a prior ideological change within the churches, the development of new outlooks and legitimations which undergird decisions on where to stand, with whom, and for what. In fact, repression has been broadly similar in Brazil, Chile, Uruguay, and Argentina, but only the first two found the churches in determined and vocal opposition, promoting and defending popular movements. Conflict and violence have been similar in El Salvador and Guatemala, but in the first case Archbishop Romero and a host of grassroots workers put the Salvadorean Church in the midst of conflict, closely aligned with the popular movement. In contrast, under Cardinal Mario Casariego, the Guatemalans pursued 'neutrality', and with rare exceptions condemned 'politics' in and for the churches.

These examples suggest that while the years since 1958 show tremendous change, change does not occur all at once. Moreover, change is not irreversible, nor is it all there is to the process. There is also resistance to change, and there can be much creative innovation in the name of conservative choices. To illustrate the dimensions of variation more fully, I close this section with a look at Colombia and Brazil, generally considered to hold down the conservative and progressive ends of any ideological spectrum in today's Latin American Catholicism.[15]

There has been so much commentary pointing up differences between these cases that it may be instructive to begin with a few similarities. Each episcopal conference is highly organised, well staffed, and unified around a shared 'project'. Each has a coherent programme, and plays it out consistently at home and on the world scene, working hard to develop international Catholic support (in CELAM or the Vatican) for national and regional initiatives and judgements. Differences arise first from the contrasting models of 'Church' which prevail among the two hierarchies. Colombia's bishops work with an image of 'Church' rooted in hierarchy. Distinctions of rank and office are maintained and affirmed, and authority as hierarchy is made central to the legitimate constitution of any religious activity. In contrast, the operative Brazilian model is more communitarian; as noted, it rests on acknowledgement that 'Church' has constitutive sources and dimensions beyond the hierarchical.

The point of this comparison is not to articulate 'models of the Church' in an abstract way, but rather to see how these are worked into normal practice, and experienced on a day to day basis by real men and women. Models have an impact as they shape practice, and make some kinds of behaviour seem right, proper, and possible. Colombia's bishops vigorously attack democratisation within the churches, reserving special fire for liberation theology, the 'popular Church', and autonomous CEBs. In contrast, the Brazilian position rejects distinctions of popular from institutional Church as a false dichotomy: all levels share in and contribute to the same experience.[16]

Historical differences underlie these contrasts. The Church has long been dominant in Colombia, and since the late nineteenth century has been identified with cultural and national unity. Conservative victories in the previous century's civil wars enshrined this dominance in law, practice, and popular expectations. The general position has eroded only marginally, if at all, in recent years. From this starting point, Colombian bishops have generally striven to preserve, protect, and defend. In Brazil, regalist tradition and a dominant State left the Church weak and dependent. These weaknesses were reinforced by Brazil's notable cultural and religious pluralism, and have led the Church over the years to search for ways to create and extend links with popular classes. Recent political changes have also marked each Church's overall stance very strongly. Until the 1940s, the Colombian Church was firmly allied with the Conservative party. This alliance was shaken by inter-party violence after 1948, which left hundreds of thousands dead over the next fifteen years. The horrors of political violence in Colombia further reinforced a dread of popular mobilisation, which in effect became identified with chaos and slaughter. In the aftermath of the violence, the Church moved from pro-Conservative to partisanship to 'neutrality' in favour of the established order. Now officially indifferent between Liberals and Conservatives, the bishops remain fearful of alternatives: challenging parties and alternative political structures are both ruled out.[17] Even if new visions were to thrive in the Church, where could they find allies? In political terms, electoral democracy has been the rule through most of this century, and politics remains dominated by the traditional political parties. The system is relatively open, and this openness has served as a safety-valve, letting opponents blow off steam. There has been no threat of radical revolution, no sharp turn to repression. Hence, there is no dictatorship to drive opponents together, no major leftist group or coalition, no significant popular movement with which to join forces.[18]

For the Church, the result has been a consistent and thorough programme linking conservative ideas with bureaucratic and organisational growth. The Colombian Church does not just sit and sigh for the good old days. It articulates and projects a conservative message with great vigour, sponsoring the 'right kind' of groups (carefully monitored and linked to clergy and hierarchy). Independent and thus 'unreliable' initiatives are delegitimised, isolated, and where possible, destroyed.[19] The contrast with Brazil is very sharp. There, initial openness to change was magnified many times over by the heavy hand of post-1964 military rule. As the Brazilian Church experimented with new programmes and strategies, repression radicalised its pastoral agents while driving an available clientele into church structures. Clients themselves grew in number and accessibility over the post-war years. In sociological terms, Brazil has seen considerably more mobility and popular organisation than Colombia in this period. One might say that politics was inevitable for Brazil's bishops, thrust upon them by the constriction of alternatives. New ideas about popular organisation and a general religious enhancement of popular experience converged in Brazil with social and political currents promoting a similar project. Did the Brazilian Church *cause* the popular movement? Did the 'people' erupt into the churches?[20] Such questions are often asked, *but they are the wrong questions*. The point is not to sort out sources in this way, but rather to see how initiatives in religion, social life, and politics reflected and reinforced one another. The conjuncture is critical. It makes sense of the appeal of ideas, and helps explain the availability of clientele and the appeal of organisational innovations in recent decades.

Brazil and Colombia contrast sharply on all the dimensions considered here. The comparison shows that although Catholicism may be one Church and one religion, it takes very different forms in specific contexts and circumstances. Why do activist and democratising notions take hold and appeal in one context and not another? Why does liberation theology seem welcome in Brazil, and condemned in Colombia? One anonymous commentator put it this way: 'Liberation Theology is like a tree. If you plant it in the right place, it is good for the place and good for the tree'. By the testimony of Brazilians themselves, planted in Brazil it has enriched the Church. Planted in El Salvador, it found prophetic leadership and committed activists and flourished. The tree withered in Colombia. The ground is hard, and the plant neglected.

FUTURES

What is the future for religion and politics in Latin America? What will happen? In this concluding section, I will identify a few central tendencies of change and project them into the future.

First, there will be no major drop in the salience of 'religion and politics' considered together, as a set of issues. This will continue to confound the expectations of those who associate 'modernisation' with secularisation, and thus reduce religion to epiphenomenal status.[21] Although their joint salience will remain high, the nature of the relation between religion and politics will alter. Major changes will accompany the degree of openness or closure in the political system generally. If the apparent trend to civilian rule and democracy should consolidate and spread, the centrality of religious groups in political organisations and action will fade. More outlets will be available: popular groups will be less driven into the churches, and the churches as institutions will no longer stand alone as vehicles for collective action. It is ironic that the very military regimes which complain so bitterly about 'politicisation of religion' are surely among the major promoters of what they deplore and condemn. All across the region, the expansion of authoritarian rule clearly magnified tendencies to radical thinking and political confrontation in the churches as within religious groups generally.

Despite the fact that greater political openness should reduce pressures for political action, the churches and religion generally will remain important to the formulation of political issues and phenomena. Part of this presence will derive from the continued impact of the kinds of activism initiated over the last 15 years. The new discourse about justice and equality, rooted in biblical and religious themes, has become very widespread and should remain vital in religious life. There will of course be continued struggle to control the specific texts and images used and discussed, but the ideological centre of gravity of discourse has shifted. Further, while CEBs will probably be less salient *per se* in political matters, they will continue to play a subtle, long-term role by eliciting and promoting new sources and styles of leadership – making them normal and legitimate. The groups as such may move out of the centre of action, but the leaders they develop should diffuse throughout society.

Second, there will be no major schism or division within Catholicism. Conflict will continue, with sharp disputes on the dimensions noted here: conservatives *versus* progressives, institutional elites *versus* popular groups, episcopacies *versus* religious orders. But although such groups differ strongly, and fight to advance contrasting programmes and positions, all remain within the fold. Liberationist sympathisers are prone to recognise the religious legitimacy of Catholic radicals while seeing conservatives as inspired purely by instrumental considerations of power or institutional convenience. At the same time, conservatives often charge radicals with using religion solely for political ends. But in fact all work from deep religious conviction, all claim to be 'good Catholics', and all resist being read out of the Church.

Third, there will be a decline in *new* popular initiatives, especially those given to assertions of grassroots autonomy. This will result from sustained pressure by the Vatican and most of the ecclesiastical hierarchies in the region. It is hard for grassroots groups to resist such pressure indefinitely. They value ties to the institution for the religious legitimacy, collective identity, and sense of tradition and moral worth they carry. They also need the mediating networks the institutional Church can provide. After all, with rare exceptions these are groups of very poor people, short on time, resources, and allies. All this makes them vulnerable to pressure. The next ten or fifteen years are likely to see a notable struggle between competing models of CEBs. The fight will go on in neighbourhoods, towns and villages, religious orders, dioceses and nations, as well as in international forums where institutions and episcopacies espousing alternative views will struggle for control.

The prospect of sustained pressure on popular movements raises a fourth possibility, with major implications for the future social composition of Catholicism. There is evidence that the combination of political salience with vocal opposition to injustice, inequality, and repression has alienated much of the Church's middle- and upper-class clientele while drawing rural and urban popular sectors closer. The former complain that the churches are contaminated by marxism: too 'political' and insufficiently spiritual. The latter see old social distances reduced (in everything from liturgy and ritual to details of the dress or dwelling of priests and sisters). Innovations like CEBs have also made access to religion easier for poor people, and popular views of the institution have shifted ground in many cases.

What will happen if the new 'Vatican line' should win out and the grassroots initiatives so highly touted in recent years are radically constricted or eliminated? Will the Church 'lose' these groups, as it is often said to have 'lost' the working class of Europe in the nineteenth century? It is possible and many liberationists believe it likely. But it is not inevitable, for hierarchical opposition to radicalised and autonomous CEBs does not mean opposition to grassroots organisation as such. The real alternative 'on the ground' is not 'CEBs or nothing', but rather a choice between kinds of grassroots organisation. In Latin America today all sorts of groups call themselves 'CEBs'. Without exception, they meet regularly, they study and discuss the bible and use biblical texts as a basis for reflection and action. Most typically engage in some kind of mutual aid and community improvement. With all these similarities, how do they differ? Critical differences arise from the dependent and deferential ties to hierarchy which characterise conservative structures. Such groups work on what we might call a 'Colombian model'. They are closely monitored by 'reliable' clergy or sisters, who provide the texts, set the agenda, and manage all ties and decisions vertically. Independent links to other popular groups are discouraged. If this 'model' of organisation and action should prevail, we may expect a typical group agenda to be more explicitly spiritual and less political. The typical scope of group action will be more personal and localised, less focused on collective action and structural change.[22]

Finally, the clearest tendency is for *more conflict within religion about politics*. Who will the Church stand with, and who will stand with her? What will religion mean to average people in Latin America as they face the hopes and joys, the fears and challenges of political life? Clearly, much will depend on how religious ideas and structures fit with changing experience, and on who makes the match. In this chapter, I have stressed how the special character of recent Latin American experience stems from the convergence of religious change with repression and political closure. This conjuncture gains added force from a series of related social transformations such as notable declines in rural isolation, growing proletarianisation, substantial migration, and the growth of literacy, all of which combine to undercut the authority of traditional elites, while empowering new capacities and dispositions for collective action. Together, these processes make people available for new kinds of organisations, values and commitments, and explain why new ideas, like those of liberation theology or CEBS, 'fit' the needs and practices of emergent groups.[23]

Understanding this process in all its richness and complexity requires attention to fundamentals of thought, structure, conflict, and action. One thing scholars must not do is to organise research reactively, running after the last event or the most recent incident to come to light. In practical terms, this usually means reacting to 'crises', a surefire recipe for instant scholarship of poor quality. In any case, the whole notion is suspect for it ignores the long-term roots of single events, and thus obscures the dynamics of motivation and commitment which make events happen in the first place.

The analysis laid out here rests on a different perspective. It takes off from change in ideas, works outward to social class, structures, and institutions, and then back again, through ideas, to action. Obviously, there are other perspectives on change, and one can readily imagine a worthwhile programme of research grounded in issues of class or organisational dynamics.[24] But it is a peculiar value of studying religion that the subject itself strongly reinforces our sense of the creative power of ideas, and of their ability to move individuals and groups in new ways, along unanticipated tracks. In the final analysis, the way we think about things organises what we see and how we interpret events, as well as what we seek and how we go about getting it. Of course, this is not just a matter of ideas alone, as if they were simply 'in the air' in some vague way. Ideas are closely linked to structures; they are carried by institutions and worked out in the ordinary routines and expectations of all sorts of groups.

The point is not to freeze 'religion and politics' in any one form, the same now as in past or future, identical here as there. Instead, research must address the formation of packages, clusters of elements and legitimations, and then specify who puts them together, under what circumstances, and for what ends. How can we make our concepts and categories fit experience better? The first and most basic step is to listen: to hear what people say and then to consider action and structure using their own logic as an interpretive guide. This means respecting the autonomy and validity of religious and political categories, and searching for how they influence and draw on one another in institutions as in ordinary life. It also means paying special attention to the relation of popular groups with elites and institutions. Respecting the autonomy and validity of each, we can begin to figure out how, in changing, each changes the other, and in the process together rework the ties that bind them over the long haul.

NOTES

* An earlier, longer version of this chapter was presented as 'From Church and State to Religion and Politics and Back Again', at a Conference on 'Latin American Politics and Society: A Cultural Research Agenda', held at Georgetown University, Washington, DC, 15–17 May 1986. I am grateful to Enrique Baloyra, Margaret Crahan, Eusebio Mujal-Leon, and Renato Poblete for reactions and comments.

1. For more detailed comparative analysis of the implications of this conjuncture, see Daniel H. Levine and Scott Mainwaring, 'Religion and Popular Protest in Latin America', in Susan Eckstein (ed.), *Power and Popular Protest: Latin American Social Movements* (Berkeley: University of California Press, 1989). See also Daniel H. Levine, 'Religion and Politics: Drawing Lines, Understanding Change' *Latin American Research Review* 20:1 (Winter 1985) 185–201 and Daniel H. Levine (ed.), *Religion and Political Conflict in Latin America* (Chapel Hill: University of North Carolina Press, 1986).
2. For further comment on this point, see Levine, 'Religion and Politics', and also Philip Berryman, *Religious Roots of Rebellion: Christians in the Central American Revolutions* (Maryknoll: Orbis, 1984).
3. Cf. Daniel H. Levine, 'Religion, Society, and Politics: States of the Art', *Latin American Research Review* 16:3 (Fall 1981) 185–209, Levine, 'Religion and Politics', and the studies reviewed there.
4. Leonardo Boff stresses parallels and mutual influence between religion and politics in these terms:

   We must recognize that in the past few years, especially after Vatican II, extremely important steps have been taken. Just as the Church previously took on Roman and feudal structures, it is now taking on structures found in today's civil societies that are more compatible with our growing sense of human rights. This is the often argued 'democratization of the church' . . . p. 44.

> There is no real conflict between the ecclesial institution and the ecclesial communities [CEBs] . . . The real tension exists between a Church that has opted for the people, for the poor and their liberation and other groups in the same Church that have not made this option, and who have not made it concrete or who persist in keeping to the strictly sacramental and devotional character of faith. (p. 126)

Leonardo Boff, *Church: Charism and Power, or – Liberation Theology and the Institutional Church* (New York: Crossroad, 1986).

5. Cf. my review of Ana Carrigan's biography of Jean Donovan, *Salvador Witness*: Daniel H. Levine, '"Whose Heart Could be so Staunch?"' *Christianity and Crisis, 22 July 1985.*
6. Jon Sobrino, 'A Theologian's View of Oscar Romero', in *Archbishop Oscar Romero, Voice of the Voiceless* (Maryknoll N.Y.: Orbis, 1985) pp. 22–51.
7. Oscar Romero, 'The Political Dimension of the Faith From the Perspective of the Option for the Poor', in *Voice of the Voiceless*, pp. 182–3.
8. For example, in Thomas Bruneau, *The Political Transformation of the Brazilian Catholic Church* (Cambridge: Cambridge University Press, 1974), Thomas Bruneau, *The Church in Brazil: The Politics of Religion* (Austin: University of Texas Press, 1982), and Scott Mainwaring, *The Catholic Church and Politics in Brazil, 1916–1985* (Stanford: Stanford University Press, 1986).
9. Cited in Peter Hebblethwaite, *Synod Extraordinary* (London: Darton, Longman & Todd, 1986) p. 37.
10. I review the origins and trajectory of *Tierra Nueva* and other Latin American Catholic journals in 'Religion and Politics'.
11. For example, in Philip Berryman, 'What Happened at Puebla', in Daniel H. Levine (ed.), *Churches and Politics in Latin America* (Beverley Hills: Sage Publications, 1980) pp. 55–86.
12. But see Juan Luis Segundo's comment on the Pope's highly selective criticisms of violence in Segundo, *Theology and the Church: A Response to Cardinal Ratzinger and a Warning to the Whole Church* (Minneapolis: Winston Press, 1985) pp. 107–36, 151–2.
13. Leonardo Boff, *Church, Charism and Power*, pp. 112–13.
14. This point is developed more fully in Daniel H. Levine, 'Religion, the Poor, and Politics in Latin America Today', in Levine, *Religion and Political Conflict*, pp. 3–23.
15. This comparison is developed in considerable detail in Levine and Mainwaring, 'Religion and Popular Protest'.
16. One suspects Brazilians might agree with Hebblethwaite's comment on the notion that the young see the Church more as an institution because there is too much talk of institutions, and not enough of God. He notes, 'this is just plain wrong. People regard the Church as an institution because that is how they experience it. The remedy is not to talk more about Jesus, but to make the local communities more

welcoming, more human, more an expression of *koinonia*'. *Synod Extraordinary*, p. 139.

17. On the violence, see Daniel H. Levine and Alexander Wilde, 'The Catholic Church, "Politics", and Violence: The Colombian Case', *Review of Politics* 39:2 (April 1977) 220–49.
18. For more detailed analysis of Colombia, see Daniel H. Levine, 'Colombia: The Institutional Church and the Popular', in Levine, *Religion and Political Conflict*, pp. 187–217, and also Daniel H. Levine, 'Continuities in Colombia', *Journal of Latin American Studies* 17:2 (November 1985) 295–317.
19. One unintended consequence of the hierarchy's success is the characteristic extremism of alternative visions in Colombia. It is hard to get them started, and harder still to make them survive. When they *do* get off the ground, pervasive repression in the churches drives them to extremes: a middle ground is hard to find. In this light, the short and sharp trajectory of Camilo Torres makes sense.
20. Thomas Bruneau offers a careful evaluation of such issues in his 'Church and Politics in Brazil: The Genesis Of Change', *Journal of Latin American Studies* 17:2 (November 1985) 271–93.
21. I discuss the status of such assumptions in current research in my 'Religion and Politics in Comparative and Historical Perspective', *Comparative Politics* (October 1986).
22. See Levine, 'Colombia: The Institutional Church and the Popular', in *Religion and Political Conflict*, and Levine and Mainwaring, 'Religion and Popular Protest' for more detailed analysis and commentary.
23. See Levine, 'Religion and Politics in Comparative and Historical Perspective' for a fuller analysis.
24. Cf. Bruneau, *The Political Transformation of the Brazilian Catholic Church*, or Brian H. Smith, *The Church and Politics in Chile: Challenges to Modern Catholicism* (Princeton: Princeton University Press, 1982).

3 The Vatican's Latin American Policy

Peter Hebblethwaite

To determine the Vatican's 'policy' towards any particular region, we usually have to proceed indirectly. For the Church has no forum in which such policies might be discussed and debated. So what the Vatican's policy towards Latin America is will have to be deduced from the appointment of bishops, the appointment of nuncios (and their instructions, when known), documents from the Roman Curia and papal speeches.

But in the pontificate of Pope John Paul II, the student has a valuable new aid in the study of the Vatican's Latin America policy: papal journeys to Latin America. If Vatican interest in Latin America could be measured by distances travelled and words uttered then that part of the world was high in the priorities of Pope John Paul II. He remarked in the plane on his way to Mexico in January 1979 that 'Humanly speaking, the future of the Catholic Church is being played out in Latin America'.

One of the most unnoticed and most important of the papal journeys was to the island of Santo Domingo in October 1984. Santo Domingo is the Caribbean island where Columbus made his first landfall in 1492. The Pope recited the prayer Columbus's sailors recited on landing:

> Blessed be the light
> And the true Holy Cross
> And the Lord of truth
> And the Holy Trinity.
> Blessed be the dawn
> And the Lord who sends it to us;
> Blessed be the day
> And the Lord who sends it to us.[1]

John Paul recalled Columbus's prayer to make the point that the discovery of America was, deep down, a religious act. So he called upon the Latin American Church to prepare for 1992, the five hundredth anniversary, with a 'novena' of years.

Of course the discovery of America was not just 'a religious act' in a chemically pure state. Only the previous year, 1491, the Moors (Moslems) had been finally driven out of Granada after eight centuries of bitter struggle. Among other things, Columbus's voyage was an attempt to get round and attack Islam in the rear. The Portuguese had already 'got behind' Islam down the west coast of Africa; Columbus's venture was to attack them from the other side. In other words, both Spanish and Portuguese monarchs and explorers saw their maritime adventures as a continuation of the medieval crusades. And motives were always mixed: besides the gospel there were always thoughts of glory and gold.[2]

So celebrating 500 years of evangelisation in Latin America was neither simple nor straightforward. The Pope recognised this when he said that this encounter between the Iberian peninsula and the peoples of Latin America was 'the beginning of universal history in its process of interaction, with all its benefits and contradictions, its lights and shadows'.[3] But that was not enough to exorcise the ghosts of the past. Though aware of ambivalence, John Paul's reading of Latin American history remains on the whole positive. Indeed he moves over to the attack:

> A certain 'black legend' marked not a few historiographical studies which for some time concentrated primarily on aspects of violence and exploitation which occurred in civil society during the period which followed discovery.[4]

It seems difficult to pin all the blame on anti-clerical prejudice and shift the responsibility to the State ('civil society'). Whole peoples were wiped out by syphilis and other western diseases. Massacres, sexual abuses, slavery, offences against human dignity as ghastly as any in recorded history took place. What is more, some of this was done in the name of Christ and thus theoretically justified. Thus in 1519 Oviedo, following Aristotle, claimed that since some races were naturally inferior, they were therefore destined by the natural law to be slaves. The Indians are lazy, vicious, cowardly, lying beasts, sodomites, idolators; it follows that if they are decimated by disease, this is but the just punishment of God.[5] It strains credulity to sweep all this under the carpet and to say, as the Pope does, that 'political, ideological and even religious prejudices have also presented negatively the history of the Church on this continent'.[6] Pope John Paul nearly always uses history *apologetically*, to clear the name of the

Church. This is understandable for a Pole, brought up in a country where the official intellectual establishment uses history to prove its favourite theses about ecclesiastical obscurantism.[7]

However, John Paul adds that we should approach the fifth centenary celebrations 'with the humility of truth, without triumphalism or false modesty'. If we take this approach, then we will 'give thanks to God for her successes and learn from her mistakes, so as to project a renewed Church towards the future'. It is in that spirit that I will address the question: what is the Vatican's Latin American policy today?

Let us go back, for the last time, to the point of Columbus's discovery. His voyage was financed by the Spanish Crown. Had the Spanish Crown, therefore, right of conquest over the Indies as they were known? Yes, said the papal bull, *Inter Coetera* of 3 May 1493. Alexander VI, the notorious Borgia Pope, 'informed that the peoples living in these islands and continents believe in a sole Creator God, and are sufficiently well disposed to embrace the Catholic faith and practice sound morality', named Ferdinand and Isabella 'lords of the lands and continents discovered and to be discovered, with full, free, simple and absolute authority and jurisdiction'.[8] From which the King and Queen of Spain concluded that they were now the owners of the 'new world'. The 'Reformation' had not yet happened, but thoughtful minds wondered whether the Pope had any business making such fateful decisions. The first 'Vatican policy' towards Latin America consisted in leaving it all to the Spanish (and later Portuguese) Crown.

One of the most thoughtful of contemporaries was Bartolomé de las Casas. He was a priest, a colonist and a slaughterer of Indians in Hispaniola from 1502 and Cuba from 1512. He was 'converted', that is granted the grace to see how the gospel fitted his situation, while preparing a sermon in 1514. This was within a decade of the conversions of St Ignatius Loyola and Martin Luther and, for Latin America, it was of comparable importance. Las Casas freed his Indian slaves, gave up his lands, and in his memoir of 1516 became the advocate of the Indians at the Spanish court. The authority of the King of Spain over the Indians, he argued, is unlawful because according to the natural law all men are free and responsible since they are created in the image and likeness of God. And such rights are inalienable. Consequently what the Pope was really saying in

1493 was not that the Spanish Crown was free to enslave or massacre these people, but that the King was entrusted with the stewardship or administration of these territories. Las Casas hoped indeed that the Indians would be converted, but pointed out that the only way to achieve that goal was to treat them as brothers, put oneself at their service, and thus convert them by gentleness.[9]

Las Casas establishes a link between the early colonial period and the Church of today. For Las Casas was talking about the defence of human rights long before the Enlightenment and the French Revolution popularised the notion (as 'the rights of man'). That is why Latin American theologians regard liberation theology not as some foreign import coming in crates marked 'Made in Cuba' or 'Made in Moscow'. They see it rather as a part, the best part, of their own tradition.[10]

This rediscovered 'tradition' is of great pastoral relevance right up to the present. For Jon Sobrino SJ, Archbishop Oscar Romero, the murdered Archbishop of San Salvador, was not so much a 'new' type of bishop as a traditional 'model':

> In analysing his episcopate, it is essential to realize that he made the defence of the poor his principal ministry. He thus restored something of great importance for the understanding of episcopacy: it began at the time of colonisation, but was afterwards lost. At the time of colonisation the bishop was, *ex officio*, the 'protector' of the Indians. On the assumption, all too correct, that the Indians were going to be marginalized, exploited and annihilated, the bishop had the task of protecting them from exploitation by either the military or the colonists. This deeply Christian and ecclesial insight into the role of a bishop goes back four centuries, and was revived in our day by Archbishop Romero. The poor, the oppressed, anyone in need, knew this, and turned to him for help. . . . What he succeeded in doing was 'institutionalizing' the preferential option for the poor. To 'institutionalize' here does not mean to bureaucratise or trivialise. On the contrary, it means that not only should Christians make this option for the poor as individuals, but also that the Church, as such, should opt for them and should also place its institutional resources at their service.[11]

Now you can begin to see why I devoted so much space to history: it raises live and controversial issues in Latin America.

The *modern* history of the Church in Latin America begins not with the Second Vatican Council (1962–5), whose agenda was too 'European', but with the second meeting of the Latin American Bishops' Conference (CELAM) which took place in Medellín, Colombia, in August 1968. Medellín 'applied' Vatican II to Latin America. It took its stand on *Gaudium et Spes*: 'To carry out such a task, the Church has always had the duty of scrutinizing the signs of the times and of interpreting them in the light of the Gospel'.[12] Medellín was the 'new Pentecost' for Latin America.

Its main achievement was to re-express the Christian concept of 'salvation' in terms of liberation, *liberación*, not only from individual sins but from the sinful structures of society. This was legitimate and pastorally timely. Salvation had always carried with it hidden metaphors such as 'bringing health'. But now the dominant image was that of redemption or liberation from captivity. It had a lot to commend it in Latin America where the much-trumpeted 'decade of development' was proving a disappointment. In 1969 SODEPAX – the short-lived joint commission between the Vatican and the World Council of Churches – produced a mimeographed report hopefully entitled: *In Search of a Theology of Development* (SODEPAX, 1969). A young Peruvian Indian theologian, Gustavo Gutiérrez, explained how, after Medellín, the notion of 'development' was unviable and that it had been replaced by 'liberation'. His 1971 book, *Teología de la liberación, Perspectivas* (Lima: CEP, 1971) developed these ideas further.

But it would be quite wrong to imagine that the bishops somehow 'invented' liberation theology at Medellín. They rather gathered up available theological insights and stimulated new ones. They put into words what was 'in the air'. The theology that emerged after Medellín was uneven in quality, sometimes frenetic in tone, but it was an expression of a new-found vitality and hope. The clumsy old slumbering giant that was Latin America was waking up with a pride in the continent that was no longer seen as dependent on Europe. 'We have faith in God, in man, and in the values and future of our continent', they declared. Fateful words.

What emerged in the early 1970s was a new way of doing theology. It was rooted, local and committed. It was not *about* liberation but *for* liberation. It was not an abstract reflection on revealed truth so much as an analysis of local situations of injustice in which God 'took the side of the poor'. The image of God changed: no longer a remote 'Providence', maintaining law and order, keeping everything as it was ('the rich man in his castle, the poor man at the gate'), the God of liberation theology was the God of Exodus, with his people in their oppression, leading them out of it towards the promised land. This 'analysis' led to 'praxis'. If that was marxist language, so be it, though there was little evidence at this time of much close familiarity with Marx, still less of direct contact with the communist parties of Latin America who claimed to be his heirs.

In 1971 liberation theology registered some notable successes, which seemed to confirm that it was moving out of its Latin American *habitat* to influence the universal Church. The first success came in *Octogesima Adveniens* (15 May, 1971), a papal letter addressed to Cardinal Maurice Roy, then President of the International Justice and Peace Commission. It had the sweep and the scope of the encyclical it just failed to be. Pope Paul VI declared himself 'incompetent' (in the technical sense) to offer a universally valid message on social justice: 'In view of the varied situations in the world, it is difficult to give one teaching to cover them all or to offer a solution that has universal value. This is not our intention *or even our mission*'.[13] The task abandoned by the Pope was now assigned to 'Christian communities' dotted round the world. On them fell the onus of diagnosing their own situations in the light of the gospel. The Latin Americans felt that Paul VI was vindicating the policy they had pursued since Medellín. *Octogesima Adveniens* also contained a subtle passage on the four elements in 'socialism' ('marxism' was not named): continual struggle against domination and exploitation; the exercise of power in a single-party state; an ideology based on historical materialism and the outright denial of transcendence; and finally 'a scientific approach to social and political realities'.[14]

The problem was to know whether these four elements could be unscrambled. Paul VI maintained, though a little nervously, that they could not: if you bought the 'struggle' or the 'analysis' you would end up with 'dialectical materialism' in your shopping basket before you could say 'Karl Marx'. But many Latin Americans said that they were actually making the distinctions denied by Paul VI. They wanted neither marxist atheism nor dialectical materialism – evidently incompatible with Christian faith; nor did they regard the Soviet Union with its one-party state as the model of a liberated society. Moreover, in speaking of 'the scientific approach', Paul VI could be taken to mean that marxism, in so far as it was 'scientific', held no more terrors for Christians than did biology.

If there was a certain ambiguity about *Octogesima Adveniens*, the Synod of 1971 was quite clear that the preaching of justice was 'a constitutive dimension' of the preaching of the gospel.[15] It was not a pious afterthought or an optional extra. Religious orders built structures on this insight. The 32nd General Congregation of the Society of Jesus in 1974 stated that 'the mission of the Society of Jesus today is the service of faith, of which the promotion of justice is an absolute requirement'.[16] Others, especially sisters owing allegiance to Jesuit spirituality, followed this example. No longer merely the passive object of mission, the Latin American Church was now the active agent of its own transformation, and the universal Church was beginning to learn from its original experience.

But with these successes, a reaction set in. In 1972 Eduardo Pironio was elected president of CELAM after being its secretary general for five years. This had the paradoxical result of leaving the decision-making in the hands of the conservative bishop, Alfonso López Trujillo of Medellín, Colombia. López Trujillo, who became secretary general of CELAM at the youthful age of 37, immediately proceeded to transfer its main departments to Bogotá, Colombia, and to employ Roger Vekemans, a Belgian Jesuit, and a professional critic of liberation theologians. Rumoured to be financed by the CIA, Vekemans also conducted a campaign of vilification against the Allende regime in Chile (where he had previously worked). In Rome, López Trujillo could count on the support of Cardinal Sebastiano Baggio.[17] As prefect of the Congregation of Bishops, Baggio controlled episcopal appointments; as president of CAL (the Pontifical Commission for Latin America), he had at his disposition CELAM's information service in Rome (they shared the same building) and was responsible for all aspects of Latin American policy formation. Sympathetic to Opus Dei, Baggio was hostile to liberation theology, inclined to give military dictators the benefit of whatever doubt was going, suspicious of Jesuit independence and social commitment, and an implacable foe of the marxism that he believed was infiltrating the Latin American Church. Thus from 1973 the battle-lines were already drawn up for a conflict that continued for the next decade and beyond. The combatants were already in position. The central issue – the true nature of evangelisation – was already identified.

Conveniently, the 1974 Synod on the theme of 'Evangelisation' provided a forum in which these matters could be debated. It had been selected by those who felt that the 1971 Synod had been hijacked into saying that justice was 'a constitutive dimension' of preaching the gospel. This was made quite clear in the draft text (known as *Lineamenta*) which provided an outline for the discussions. Under the heading 'Apparent contradictions in evangelisation that have to be harmonised', it homed in on liberation theology and recent Latin American debates:

> There are those who describe evangelisation as though it were something only on the spiritual and religious level, meant only to free men from the bonds of sin. Others, however, describe Christ as the new Moses and consider the Gospel is ordered to human development, at least at the present moment of history. Some ask whether one should speak of two finalities (albeit closely related ones) or whether both these aspects blend into one.

At this point a new actor entered the scene whose importance was not grasped at the time: Cardinal Karol Wojtyla, Archbishop of Kraków, Poland. He was *relator* of the theological section of the Synod discussions. His task was to present a position-paper at the start of the debate, to draw the conclusions from it, and to work on the final report.[18]

Cardinal Wojtyla's theological report disappointed the Latin Americans. It made no reference to the accounts of experiences given in the first two weeks of the Synod, not surprisingly since it had been written in advance during Cardinal Wojtyla's summer vacation in the Masurian Lakes. Accordingly, its method was one of deduction from first principles rather than inductive from pastoral experience. For Wojtyla evangelisation begins with Christ's mandate to the Apostles and is continued through the mission of bishops and pastors. It consists in 'conversion and liberation' by the power of the sacraments, but the liberation in view is from sin and Satan. Salvation consists in conversion from the 'world' and its false values. The 'world' is seen simply as the recipient of the Church's message, the object of its pastoral concern. True, proclaiming the gospel does have political implications, but these are essentially *indirect*:

> All these things (social, economic and political structures), even though they do not directly concern the mission of the Church, have nevertheless an immediate and very close relation to the Church's task of diffusing and defending justice and peace in the world. In this sense work in favour of social and economic liberation belongs to the exercise of evangelisation, as many documents of the papal *magisterium* show, especially from the end of the 19th century.[19]

The last phrase refers to *Rerum Novarum*, Leo XIII's 1891 encyclical. It implied that Karol Wojtyla believed that 'Catholic social doctrine' still had a role to play – even though only in 1971 *Octogesima Adveniens* had cast doubt on it. Prompted by Vatican II and impelled (they believed) by Paul VI, liberation theologians had worked out an alternative approach to the Church and politics which depended on the discernment of 'the signs of the times'. This is the fundamental divide in the *perception* of the Latin American problem. There is a straight line from this 1974 paper to the address at Puebla in 1979 and the two Instructions on Liberation Theology of 1984 and 1986. The only difference is that in 1974 it did not much matter if a Polish cardinal misunderstood Latin America. It is infinitely more serious once he becomes Pope.

The Puebla meeting of CELAM in February 1979 was eagerly awaited. It would be the first opportunity for Pope John Paul II to state his views on liberation theology (for the story I have just told had passed largely unnoticed). On the eve of the meeting an embarrassing cassette was discovered which threw light on how López Trujillo was preparing for the event. It was a draft letter, never intended for publication, to Archbishop Luciano Cabral Duarte, a notoriously conservative Brazilian. It urged him to 'prepare your bomber planes. You must start training the way boxers do before going into a world championship. May your blows be evangelical and sure'.[20] López Trujillo rejoiced in the election of the new Pope because he had already 'spoken very clearly against the deviations of the Latin American Church'. New episcopal appointments confirmed that this was indeed the papal policy. Leonardo Boff, the Brazilian Franciscan, would soon be 'called to order'. Finally, López Trujillo deplored the presence at Puebla of Fr Pedro Arrupe, who was there against López Trujillo's better judgement and 'thanks to the pressure of others'. In most organisations, such revelations would have put an end to a man's career. But López Trujillo, far from faltering, went from strength to strength and became a Cardinal on 2 February, 1983.[21]

These revelations also throw light on the purpose of Puebla 1979 compared with that of Medellín in 1968. As seen by its principal orchestrator, Puebla was designed to permit the Latin American Church to recover from the mistakes of Medellín which had launched a runaway movement that subsequently became uncontrollable. Pope John Paul's Puebla speech was a clear expression of what would be the theological basis of his Latin American policy. He made his purpose plain from the outset. They had to build on the foundations of Medellín, but 'without ignoring the incorrect interpretations of it that have sometimes been made'. He singled out four 'incorrect interpretations' as of fundamental importance.

The Pope stressed that bishops or pastors were '*teachers* of truth, not a human or rational truth, but the truth that comes from God'. This truism was a reminder that bishops should not justify their positions by claiming to speak 'in the name of the people'. They were teachers, not tribunes, of the people. This judgement was also a reaction against the tendency of liberation theologians to make their 'situation' the starting-point, and so place *orthopraxy* (living the gospel by identifying with the oppressed) on the same level as *orthodoxy* (having the 'right ideas'). Pope John Paul gave the primacy to orthodoxy: 'Over and above unity in love, *unity in truth* is always urgent for us'.

Second, John Paul attacked the notion that a distinction could or should be made between the institutional or official Church, which is judged harshly, and 'a new Church, springing from the people and taking concrete form in the poor'. This is inadmissible because preaching the gospel (evangelisation) is 'not subject to the discretionary power of individualistic criteria, but to communion with the Church and her pastors'. John Paul had an explanation for such deviations: they were the product of 'familiar forms of ideological conditioning' which in his *thesaurus* means 'marxism'. This was very abstract Polish-philosophy-professor-talk; and it was impossible to know who the Pope had in mind; certainly not the Sandinistas, who were then on their last lap to Managua, the capital of Nicaragua.

Third, John Paul disputed the liberation theologians' contention that the gospel should be 'read from the point of view of the oppressed'. This practice led to interpretations that were 'theoretical speculations rather than an authentic meditation on the Word of God'. However, his conclusion that such presentations of a political Jesus 'did not tally with the Church's catechesis' was relatively mild in tone at least.

Lastly, in the final section of his Puebla address, John Paul sketched out his own alternative version of liberation theology. It could not be based on 'atheistic humanism' (marxism once again), because man needs the more-than-human to protect him against tyranny. It should on the contrary be based on 'Catholic social doctrine' which insists on the dignity of every human person: 'This *complete* truth about the human condition constitutes the foundation of the Church's social teaching, and is also the basis of *true* liberation'. The Church's social teaching, he added, 'was still valid and necessary, even though some people seek to sow doubts and lack of confidence in it'.

As he spoke, John Paul was seated between Baggio and Cardinal Aloísio Lorscheider of Brazil. There can be no doubt which of the two found the address more gratifying. It was a thorough-going onslaught on the main tenets of liberation theology, which were caricatured in the process. Thus that bishops sought to speak 'in the name of their people' was a sign of their pastoral responsibility, not necessarily an abdication of their teaching role. Nor had people gone around disparaging Catholic social doctrine: it was simply that it had ceased to apply to the sub-continent where, despite a brave effort by Eduardo Frei in Chile in the 1960s, it had not proved capable of providing a model for a more just and fraternal society. However, Pope John Paul's address could claim not only the authority of the papal office, but the intrinsic authority that came from being Polish and therefore having a first-hand experience of what living in a 'socialist state' was like. But being Polish was double-edged: it meant that he might miss the originality of what was happening in Latin America.

Thus from the point of view of the Vatican's Latin American policy, the principal lesson to be derived from the Puebla address was that the main problem of the continent was the threat of a marxist-inspired unorthodoxy which would imperil the Church's unity. Latin America was 'perceived' not as an exciting place where new and fascinating theological developments were springing up (that was how the Latin Americans saw themselves), but rather as somewhere where theological deviations had prospered and proliferated and would have to be checked.

The rest of the story is little more than a working out of the logic of that 'perception' of Latin America. Papal visits to Latin America have repeated the same themes with very little variation. Theologians are seen as those through whom dangerous opinions enter the Church.

However, the moves against them have not proved very successful. Attempts to condemn Jon Sobrino SJ failed because of the resolution of the new General, Fr Peter-Hans Kolvenbach, and the ineptitude of Sobrino's accusers (who were reduced to quoting the dust-jacket as evidence of a 'deviation'). In October 1984 the entire Peruvian hierarchy was brought to Rome (at its own expense) in order to secure a condemnation of Gustavo Gutiérrez; but, although the bishops were evenly divided, none was forthcoming.

The case of Leonardo Boff is an even more paradoxical instance of the impotence of power in the Church. When both his religious superiors and his episcopal conference had refused to condemn him, Cardinal Joseph Ratzinger summoned him to Rome for a 'conversation' on 7 September 1984. Boff was accompanied by Cardinals Arns and Lorscheider – thus refuting the fantasy that he had invented some 'popular Church' at odds with the hierarchy. Even when Boff was silenced in April 1985, it was not for his alleged marxism but for 'neo-Protestant' trends. The letter conveying the ban explained: 'The Congregation (for the Doctrine of Faith) feels obliged to declare that Leonardo Boff's options, here analysed, are such as to endanger the sound doctrine of the faith, which is the task of the same Congregation'.[22] This was the first instance of someone being condemned for his 'options' (*opzioni* was the Italian term). Boff claims his 'option' is for the poorest. One might be tempted to think that Boff's silencing was a greater danger to faith than anything he might have said. In any case the ban was lifted, on Holy Saturday 1986, without either explanation or apology. All one can conclude is that the *will* to deal with liberation theologians like Boff is certainly there, but the actual method of ousting them has not yet been discovered.

Now it would be quite wrong to present these examples of Vatican ineffectualness as simply the result of disobedience. They are, partly, at least, the result of doubts about whether the Vatican is the appropriate body for formulating the policy of a local Church. For in Vatican II theology, the local Church is not just a fragment of the Church universal: it has its own subsistence, reality, duties and responsibilities. Archbishop Denis Hurley, of Durban, South Africa, drew the lessons at the Extraordinary Synod late in 1985:

> Concerning relations between the Holy See and local Churches and the collegial and consultative bodies formed by local Churches, our conference calls for the clearer recognition of *the principle of subsidiarity*. In the social teaching of the Church, we find this recommended to the world. We do not always find it easy to practise it ourselves. Local Churches are entrusted with the vast burden of evangelisation in all its dimensions, but when it comes to even minor matters of Church law and doctrine, the same trust is not always in evidence. *Had the principle been respected in the matter of Father Leonardo Boff O.F.M ., a good deal. of adverse*

publicity would have been avoided. We need greater faith in the presence and power of Jesus and the Holy Spirit in all parts of the Church.[23]

Though the wily Hurley mentioned Boff, it seems more likely that he had in mind the Irish Dominican, Fr Albert Nolan, who made history in September 1983 by refusing the post of Master General of the Dominicans, preferring to work with the oppressed blacks of South Africa.

Though every effort was made to prove the contrary, the Extraordinary Synod marked a turning-point in the Vatican treatment of liberation theology. The reason was, I believe, quite simply that its opponents 'went over the top'. There was first of all an obsequious statement read out by Cardinal Ernesto Corripio Ahumada, Primate of Mexico, expressing 'gratitude in a special manner to the Congregation for the Doctrine of Faith, for reproving the errors of a certain theology of liberation which, with the so-called *iglesia popular*, has caused so much harm to the faithful people'.[24] This was laid on not merely with a trowel, but with a spade.

That was at the meeting of cardinals which preceded the Synod. At the Synod itself, there was an ominous silence about liberation theology, as though, like *Solidarnosc* in Poland, it had simply ceased to have official existence. The remark of Hurley quoted above did not find its way into the official bulletin, and a Vatican spokesman indeed denied that it had ever been made. But on 30 November 1985, Darío Castrillón Hoyos, another Colombian and present secretary general of CELAM, let fly against the so-called popular Church which pretended to be with the poor, but was not, feigned to be with the peasants (the *campesinos*) but was compromised with trades unions and political parties, and had turned the Mass into a political meeting. Some said he was talking about Nicaragua, but he did not say so. His final charge was that liberation theologians had as their aim 'to grab the *magisterium* of the Church from the hands of the Pope and the Bishops'. The Synod, packed though it was, could recognise that this was, to say the least, a somewhat incomplete account of liberation theology.

The other side of the coin was conveyed in *written* interventions by Bishop José Ivo Lorscheiter, president of the Brazilian Bishops' Conference, and Cardinal Aloisio Lorscheider. Lorscheiter carefully explained that liberation theology, far from being the work of a handful of way-out and audacious theologians, was rather the fruit of the pastoral work of the Latin American Church as a whole. It was not, he said, 'a theology of violence, and does not legitimate violence. It is not a theology which takes up or appeals to marxist ideology. It does not apply to Latin America concepts borrowed from European "political theology" '. But if it was none of those things, then Ratzinger's shafts had missed the target. Lorscheider took up the theme of the Church of the poor. The people of Latin America, he said, are for the most part rich in Christian faith but poor in almost everything else. So there are two reasons for listening to the people: 'They are a faithful people and a poor people, and as such they are loved by God with special predilection'.[25] I do not claim that these interventions reversed the course of the Synod. They did not. But they prepared Pope John Paul to understand that what López Trujillo and Castrillón Hoyos were telling him was not the whole truth, and omitted the most important factor of all: life itself.

Whether this analysis is correct or not, there was certainly a changed atmosphere when representatives of the Brazilian Church met from 13 to 15 March 1986 with members of the Roman Curia in the presence of the Pope. There was frankness on both sides. Pope John Paul spoke of a new style of *ad limina* visit and a new way in which he could exercise his *ministerium Petri*. From the point of view of the Vatican's Latin American policy, the novelty was that for the first time an episcopal conference was invited to 'a new form of collegiality, thanks to which the Pope and his collaborators now know better the realities of the Brazilian Church'. It had taken a long time to reach this point; in the past, Latin American policy had dropped down from on high.

The main effect of the new approach could be seen in the papal letter, dated 9 April 1986, which was carried to Brazil by Cardinal Bernadin Gantin, Baggio's successor. He read it out on 12 April, 1986. The Brazilians welcomed it with tears and *alleluias*. No wonder, for it represented a complete reversal of what they had been accustomed to hear and what John Paul himself had told them at Fortaleza on 10 July 1980. They heard the Pope say: 'You have performed an inestimable service to Brazil, and beyond that to other Churches and the universal Church'. From scapegoats, they had become exemplars: 'As pastors you have been extraordinarily close to your people, sharing in their joys and sorrows, as ready to educate them in the faith, to open to them the path of Christian life, as to succour their needs, have compassion on their afflictions and trials, and bring them hope'. There were no quibbles about the option for the poor, no emphasis on the 'dangers' of base Christian communities. Moreover, the Paschal Letter (it came as an Easter present) declared that liberation theology was 'not only opportune but useful and necessary' and that it represents 'a new stage' in the on-going development of theology.

The difference between this and the negative 1980 judgement is not so much that the Pope has changed his mind as that he has listened to different advisers. The 1980 judgement was from the outside, and it was based on hostile denunciations coming from a minority of Brazilians who fed the Pope's own pre-judgements. The 1986 assessment is based on what the Brazilians are trying to realise in a very difficult situation, and it accepts broadly their own evaluation of the situation. Essentially designed to secure peace with the Brazilian bishops, it has no wider implications, and certainly does not imply any change of heart.

NOTES

1. *L'Osservatore Romano* (English edition), 19 November 1984, p. 5.
2. Roland Mousnier, *Histoire Générale des Civilizations*, IV, *Les XVIe et XVIIe Siècles* (Paris: Presses Universitaires de France, 1967), p. 374.
3. *L'Osservatore Romano* (English edition) 19 November, p. 5.
4. Ibid.
5. Mousnier, *Les XVIe et XVIIe Siècles*, p. 434.
6. *L'Osservatore Romano* (English edition), 19 November 1984, p. 5.
7. See Maciej Pomian-Srzednicki, *Religious Change in Contemporary Poland: Secularization and Politics* (London: Routledge & Kegan Paul, 1982). 'Successful defence', remarks the author, 'became to the Church just as important and positive an action as successful attack', p. 56.
8. Mousnier, *Les XVIe et XVIIe Siècles*, p. 434.
9. Ibid., p. 435.
10. Argentinian Enrique Dussel, who now teaches church history in Mexico, is the President of the Commission for the Study of the Latin American Church (CEHILA). He has done more than anyone to bring out the 'originality' of the Latin American tradition.
11. Jon Sobrino, *Romero, Martyr for Liberation* (London: Catholic Institute for International Relations, 1982) pp. 48–9.
12. *Gaudium et Spes*, sections 4 and 44.
13. In my forthcoming biography of Pope Paul VI, I will examine this question more profoundly. It seems that Paul VI was knocked sideways by those (including Cardinal Suenens) who said he should

not have produced *Humanae Vitae* without collegial consultation. So, the Pope concluded: no more encyclicals.

14. *Octogesima Adveniens*, 33.
15. J. Neuner and J. Dupuis, SJ, *The Christian Faith* (London: Collins, 1983) No. 2159.
16. *32nd General Congregation of the Society of Jesus* (1974) Decree 4, 2.
17. Baggio was born 16 May 1913, in the diocese of Vicenza, Italy. Between 1938 and 1946 he did his stint as a junior Vatican diplomat in El Salvador, Bolivia and Venezuela. Between 1953 and 1969 he was nuncio to Chile and after an interval in Canada became nuncio to Brazil. A cardinal in 1969, he became Prefect of the Congregation of Bishops in 1973 until he went into semi-retirement in 1984. As can be seen, he had first-hand, though somewhat out-of-date, experience of six Latin American countries.
18. His interventions can be studied in Giovanni Caprile, S.J., *Karol Wojtyla e il sinodo dei vescovi* (Rome: Vatican Press, 1980), Other data on the 1974 Synod comes from my own records.
19. Ibid., p. 214.
20. John Whale (ed.), *The Man who leads the Church* (London: Collins, 1980) p. 88.
21. There were some indications, early in 1986, that López Trujillo was no longer the dominating force he had been. Pope John Paul's letter to the Brazilian Bishops (12 April 1986) showed an understanding and appreciation of their position never manifested before or since.
22. *L'Osservatore Romano* (English edition), 9 April 1985.
23. *Convergence*, 2 (1986) p. 23.
24. P. Hebblethwaite, *Synod Extraordinary* (London: Darton, Longman & Todd, 1986) p. 105.
25. Ibid., p. 126.

4 CELAM: The Forgetting of Origins

François Houtart

Any study of the Latin American Bishops' Conference (CELAM) is an initiation into the history of Latin American Catholicism over the past thirty years. Since 1956, CELAM has been closely involved with all the events of the religious and social life of the continent, and its development has been deeply influenced by all the great social movements. These movements, and the logic inherent in any institution which has to survive and continue in a particular society, are an integral part of CELAM. Thus, both its discourse and its action reflect the phases of the economic and political organisation of the continent, and the successive concepts of the Church over this period.

It is possible to distinguish three main periods in the political and economic organisation of the continent. These showed significant national variations. Firstly, there is a populist period linked to a certain recognition of the people as the object of social policies. The second period is one of military or right-wing dictatorships challenged by revolutionary movements. The third period is marked by a certain movement towards democracy as a new form of bourgeois hegemony. In the economic field, these different political periods coincide with an initial national industrialisation producing substitute products. This is followed by the large-scale introduction of multinationals or by the emergence of agrarian capitalism. The nature of the developments depends, of course, on the nature of the country or region. During the 1980s, the general economic crisis saw the countries of the region become debtor nations.

At the time this analysis begins, some thirty years ago, the life of the Latin American Church was characterised by an awakening to new practices of evangelisation. These contrasted with the traditional forms of relationship between the Church, the landed oligarchies and the conservative parties. There was then the era of ecclesiastical reforms, promoted by the Second Vatican Council, and applied in Latin America in 1968 after the Medellín Conference. Finally, a period of restoration commences in the early 1970s. It is on the basis of this periodisation that I am going to analyse the development of CELAM.

I. FROM THE CREATION OF CELAM TO THE SECOND VATICAN COUNCIL

1. Preparation

The creation of the episcopal conference in 1956 followed earlier meetings of Latin American bishops. During the colonial period three provincial councils met at Lima. In 1899, Leo XIII summoned a plenary council in Rome on the occasion of the fourth centenary of the 'discovery' of America.[1] In the history of the Church, this was the first Council of the bishops of the Latin American continent. It brought together thirteen archbishops and forty bishops. The assembly examined several questions. The main one of these was the unification of ecclesiastical discipline, because there existed at that period an extraordinary diversity and complexity of laws and of disciplinary norms, not only in Latin America, but in the whole of the Church.[2]

In 1955, on the occasion of the international eucharistic congress at Rio de Janeiro, the Latin American episcopate again met together in 'conference'.[3] This was the last such meeting. Cardinal Piazza, who presided over this conference, did not hesitate to say that it had 'neither precedent nor counterpart in contemporary ecclesiastical history'. It was summoned by the Holy See, presided over by a cardinal of the Curia in the name of the Pope, and its conclusions were revised by Rome before being published.

More people participated in this conference than in the Council of 1899. There were 7 cardinals, 90 bishops or ordinaries, and in addition, the presiding cardinal and his deputy, 5 foreign prelates and 6 apostolic nuncios. While the Council of 1899 had been preoccupied with legislation, the Conference had as its object, the elaboration of a pastoral programme.

Pius XII inaugurated the meeting and had a document[4] read in which he identified the religious problems of the continent. According to the Pope, there were certain deficiencies in the Catholic way of life and a shortage of both diocesan and regular priests. He also stressed the necessity of having a positive attitude:

> If circumstances demand it, new apostolic methods must be adopted, and new paths followed which, while remaining in conformity to the tradition of the Church, will be better adapted to the demands of the present time and will benefit from the conquest of civilisation.

The Pope also encouraged the episcopate to remain united and to co-ordinate its action. He urged the bishops to encourage vocations to the priesthood and the lay apostolate. He concluded by stressing the importance of social action by Christians which was all the more necessary 'as it is a problem closely related to religious life'.

In the final declaration of the Conference which was inspired by numerous preparatory documents submitted by the bishops, four principle questions were raised: the shortage of priests, religious education, social problems, and questions relating to the Amerindian populations. It was decided to create a Latin American Episcopal Conference (CELAM), composed of the representatives of the national episcopal conferences. Its functions were to be the following:[5]

- to study the problems facing the Church in Latin America,
- the co-ordination of different activities,
- the promotion and support of Catholic charitable agencies, and finally,
- the preparation of further Conferences of the Latin American Episcopate whenever summoned by the Holy See.

The location of the general secretariat of the conference was put to a vote: 32 votes were cast in favour of Rome, 30 in favour of Bogotá, 16 in favour of Rio de Janeiro, 6 in favour of Lima and 2 in favour of Santiago in Chile. On the face of it, it is surprising that so many bishops voted in favour of Rome. This can be explained by the tradition which saw Rome as the centre of Latin American ecclesiastical activities. This was notably the case during the preceding plenary council. It is also to be explained that interventions by Rome at this period were much more numerous in the internal affairs of Latin American dioceses than in European or North American dioceses.

It must be emphasised, however, that the majority of the episcopate voted in favour of a Latin American location: 54 votes were cast in favour of cities situated on the continent. Bogotá got the largest number of votes. That choice is explained by its central geographical location. After further consultation with the Latin American episcopate, Pius XII decided to locate the Secretariat there, stating that its very functions required residence on the continent. Thus, the initiative came from Rome, and not from Latin America.

2. Structure and Functions

CELAM, composed of delegates and substitute delegates elected for two years from the national episcopal conferences, was also given a president and two vice-presidents. The general secretariat comprised 5 under-secretariats which respectively dealt with the following matters:

- the preservation and propagation of the faith,
- the clergy, religious institutes and vocations,
- education and youth, and finally,
- the lay apostolate and social action.

From the beginning, the Holy See had considerable power over CELAM. While it reserved to itself the right of summoning the conferences of the episcopate the annual meetings of CELAM were mandatory. Only in the case of extraordinary meetings of CELAM is their time and date fixed by the Holy See. The agenda of ordinary meetings, however, has to be approved by the Holy See. The Holy See can also add certain items to the agenda and modify it. It has similar powers with regard to the conclusions; they have to be approved by Rome and the Vatican can add to these conclusions.

It is also the Holy See that appoints the secretary general of CELAM. It directs his work, requiring a report every three months. It remains the prerogative of the Holy See to create eventually new sections within the under-secretariats. Finally, it also reserved to itself the right of publishing certain items in the CELAM bulletin.

The Latin American episcopate as a whole was not convinced of the necessity for a Latin American organisation. Some bishops considered the initiative as something which risked diminishing local episcopal authority. Many considered it an additional administrative and financial burden. However, the early working of CELAM was characterised by a phenomenon which might appear surprising at first sight. In the face of the lack of interest of an episcopate which was largely conservative, the elected delegates to the conference were those who already had wider contacts and who reflected a tendency which was clearly more progressive than that of the episcopal body as a whole. CELAM was remarkably dynamic as a result. Not only did it co-ordinate existing pastoral strategies, but it also set about promoting a series of new initiatives.

Thus, CELAM helped to organise episcopal conferences where they were not already functioning. In 1960, CELAM encouraged the creation of a Conference of Major Religious Superiors (CLAR), with headquarters also in Bogotá. Various under-secretariats called meetings, each in its particular area of responsibility. A bulletin was published from January 1957 onwards, and circulated to the whole of the Latin American episcopate.

3. The First Annual Meetings and their Themes

The first annual meetings of CELAM set out the main parameters of its future development. In Bogotá in 1956 problems of organisation dominated the agenda. A second meeting was held in 1957 at Fomeque, in Colombia, where six themes were treated. The first concerned the collaboration of religious with CELAM. As a matter of fact, in certain Latin American countries religious were more numerous than the diocesan priests; consequently, they played a very important role in the life of the Church in those countries. Thus, the meeting of CELAM sought the particular co-operation of religious in the following fields: preaching, catechetics, the celebration of Masses in parish churches, confessions, the lay apostolate, social action and specialised apostolates.

The second theme concerned the establishment of national episcopal secretariats, and particularly their relationships at the level of the parish, of the diocese and at the national levels. The co-ordination of the lay apostolate was the third theme. The fourth theme concerned the apostolate in Catholic universities and the moral and religious assistance to students studying abroad. The fifth theme was the major UNESCO project of the extension of primary education in Latin America. And finally, the sixth theme was that of the Catholic press, and notably the press agency, Noticias Católicas, published in Washington by the services of the NCWC (the North American Episcopal Conference).

The third meeting of CELAM was held in Rome in 1958. This location was chosen because many Latin American bishops had decided to go to Lourdes on the occasion of the centenary of the apparitions. They had decided also to visit Rome to attend the celebration of the centenary of the Pio Latino College, the seminary of Spanish-speaking Latin Americans.

John XXIII addressed the bishops present. First of all, he said:

> Learn to distinguish the essential from the accessory. This is indispensable for your action today. Then take a wide view of

> things. Don't forget that we are at a moment of construction and conquest, and that your vision should be orientated towards the future.

Finally, he asked the episcopate to discover the common heritage of the Latin American countries. This search, he said, is not only a duty, but also one of the most efficient means of advancing spiritual interests in each of the dioceses. This was a response to certain reticences of the episcopate.

The meeting of CELAM in Rome examined five themes. The first concerned the defence of the faith and some directives were given. These stressed the need to organise intensive courses for the pastoral formation of priests, the foundation of biblical institutes, the teaching of the catechism in rural areas and the promotion of the liturgical movement.

The second particular pre-occupation of the meeting was catechetics and the recruitment of lay people for catechetical work. Caritas[6] was the third theme. The episcopate examined the way to organise this institution in the most efficient way possible in each country. The fourth theme concerned bilingual rituals, Latin-Hispanic or Latin-Lusitanian. The fifth and last theme examined the rules of the general secretariat.

Communism in Latin America was the principal subject of the fourth meeting of CELAM which met at Fomeque in Colombia in 1959. This theme was obviously linked to the social situation on the continent and to the then recent Cuban Revolution. The final declaration affirmed the necessity to transform social structures in order to promote justice. It explained how communism sought to gain the masses in Latin America, and why the Church had to adopt a firm position in the face of that danger.

In 1960, CELAM, meeting at Buenos Aires, dealt with pastoral problems. Four papers on basic problems opened the discussion. Monsignor Larrain, the bishop of Talca in Chile, analysed the pastoral problem by examining its fundamental bases – theology, and the human sciences. Theology was necessary, he argued, for the orientation of pastoral action. Without it, one risked being restricted to a series of formulae not in direct relationship with essential work. In addition, he said, sociology and psychology were indispensable. Without them one had a purely theoretical pastoral approach which did not take sufficient account of reality. Monsignor Larrain then studied the functions of the diocese and of the parish from this perspective. He concluded with a series of proposals. These were:

- the foundation of a theological commission in Latin America for the study of the basis of pastoral theology;
- the organisation of a Centre of Latin American Socio-religious Research;
- and the organisation of a Latin American Institute of Pastoral Formation.

Monsignor Marqués, the bishop of Puebla, Mexico, then spoke on the problem of pastoral action at the level of the diocese. He stressed particularly the means required for the accomplishment of such a plan. Priests, religious and nuns should be redeployed. It was necessary to co-ordinate the institutions of the parish, of education, of Catholic Action, of assistance and charity and of social action. This implied, he said, serious preparation. It necessitated a systematic study of diocesan reality and of its needs and also an inventory of the Catholic resources available with a view to their practical application.

The problem of pastoral action in rural areas was the theme of the third main paper; presented by Monsignor Alfredo Rubio Díaz, the bishop of Girardot in Colombia. After giving a striking description of the pastoral reality of rural Latin America on the basis of the data contained in the study carried out by FERES (Fédération internationale des institutions catholiques de recherches sociales et socio-religieuses),[7] Monsignor Rubio arrived at the following conclusions:

- The great majority of Catholics in rural zones had not been evangelised.
- The fundamental problem was decentralisation of pastoral action – urgently necessary for the promotion of catechetics, for a life of prayer and for the apostolate.
- It also obviously supposed a totally new vision of lay collaboration. Without such a decentralisation, purely formal pastoral structures did not touch the actual life of groups of people.

Monsignor Rubio also stressed the necessity of being present, and of actively collaborating with all plans for agrarian reform, on condition however, that they be inspired by the principles of the Church. This would bring about a just solution to the terrible problems of the social and human situation of the peasant masses. In conclusion, Monsignor Rubio called for the constitution of an efficient Christian rural movement in each country, a Latin-American pastoral plan, the creation of an Institute of Pastoral Formation for the clergy, and the continued pursuit of socio-religious research.

The urban parish, the object of the fourth and final paper was given by Cardinal Antonio Caggiano, Archbishop of Buenos Aires. He outlined first the phenomenon of the concentration of population in large cities. He then noted that the parish should be the base of the whole urban apostolate. He insisted on the importance of traditional organs such as the Confraternity of Christian Doctrine, the Confraternity of the Holy Sacrament, Catholic Action and organised charity.

In its final declaration, CELAM stressed the necessity of co-ordinating different apostolic works by means of a realistic, efficient and methodical plan of action. The conference also stressed the need in Latin America for a more organic and community-based concept of the parish, as well as a new vision of the role of lay people in the pastoral action of the Church.

The declaration also stressed the problems of the standard of living in rural milieux, and launched a solemn appeal to Christian rulers and to the faithful to take this problem in hand in an efficient manner so as to permit the peasants to acquire land in accordance with the requirements of social justice.

4. The Lessons for the Future

I have dealt at length with the origins of CELAM because they contained important lessons for the future. The numerous contacts, established by the many meetings and journeys, constituted a dynamic factor in a Church which had lived more on the heritage of the past than in response to the challenges of the future.

From the point of the sociology of the ecclesiastical institution, one can note the fact that the initiative for the creation of CELAM came from the top. While it resulted from a desire to instil a new spirit in local Catholicism, it also took its place in the context of an adaptation of central power to the new possibilities of communication, rather than to a true decentralisation. Such a process however, is not linear – it is dialectic. A new situation had been created. Thanks to funds made available at that time, particularly from Germany, initiatives taken by certain secretariats or by the delegates of CELAM were able to receive the material support which they needed. Before long, that process created tensions and even conflict. The Holy See set up the Pontifical Commission for Latin America (CAL) in Rome in 1958 in order to co-ordinate and monitor more efficiently regional initiatives and international co-operation in Latin America. In 1960, during the preparation for the Buenos Aires meeting, tension between the commission and the general secretariat of Bogotá nearly paralysed the entire activity of CELAM.

Such pastoral orientations, especially those which arose from the Buenos Aires meeting, already pointed to future developments. The decentralisation of pastoral institutions and the introduction of lay people into pastoral roles, were the prelude to what were going to become the base Christian communities. The call to renew theology was going eventually to give rise to the theology of liberation. This reflection on the social problems of the continent laid the markers for new positions which would bring a certain number of Catholics, both lay and clerical, to revolutionary commitment.

During the 1950s, the Catholic interpretation of society and Christian social doctrine were heavily inspired by the current of thought developed in France by Jacques Maritain, whose very name inspired passionate responses in certain Latin-American countries. The work done on the ground by the Juventud Obrera Católica (Young Catholic Workers, JOC) had had an influence beyond worker milieux, and also offered a more concrete perspective for approaching social problems. It was in this framework, strongly orientated by an inter-class concept of the common good, that during this first period both the theoretical orientations of a social doctrine and the practices of development of the Latin-American Church evolved. They were appropriate in the context of populist regimes in Brazil, Argentina, Colombia and Mexico, as well as in that of the Alliance for Progress founded by President Kennedy. In Latin America this current is called *El Desarrollismo*, or the ideology of development.

II. CELAM AND THE SECOND VATICAN COUNCIL

The experience that the active bishops had acquired in the framework of CELAM was to become central to their action in the Second Vatican Council. The delegates were used to meeting regularly and they had learned what was meant by the functioning of an assembly. Moreover, they had already discussed the main questions concerning the problems of the contemporary Church. This was particularly so in the case of the two vice-presidents, Monsignor Rafael Larrain and Dom Helder Câmara. Thus, the former was among the bishops who, right from the outset of the council intervened to bring about a complete revision of procedure. As for Dom Helder Câmara, he organised informal meetings regularly between the bishops and the experts, and this had a real influence on the elaboration of the conciliar texts.

CELAM as such had not been authorised to be present at Rome at the beginning of the Council. It was the initiative of the African bishops, who installed their secretariat in Rome, which encouraged the people responsible to transfer the general secretariat of CELAM to the Italian capital and to open an office there. It had been thought that the Latin American bishops would follow the lead given by the episcopates of Spain and Portugal which were notably conservative on the question of Church renewal. The opposite was the case. The majority of the Latin American episcopate followed the orientations of the bishops who had been more active in CELAM. These last mentioned, who had close contact with the more open milieux of the American and European episcopates, clearly identified themselves with the partisans of reform.

So as to explain to the council fathers of other continents the fundamental reasons for the attitude of CELAM, the Presidency arranged for distribution, to each of those bishops, of a work translated into different languages giving a synthesis of the principal data contained in the FERES socio-religious enquiry.

If the influence of the Latin American bishops manifested itself in all the conciliar documents, their intervention can be seen particularly in the Pastoral Constitution on the Church in the Modern World (*Gaudium et Spes*). Thus, one can argue that the very existence of CELAM was a key factor in the direction taken by the Second Vatican Council. It must not be forgotten that one-third of the council fathers came from that continent.

III. FROM VATICAN II TO THE MEDELLÍN CONFERENCE

A conference of Latin American bishops, summoned by the Holy See and organised by CELAM, was held in Medellín, Colombia, in 1968. The agenda dealt with the application of conciliar thinking to the Latin American Church. Between the end of the Vatican Council in 1964, and the Medellín meeting, CELAM had organised a great number of meetings dealing with the different areas dealt with by the secretariats and on which Vatican II had made pronouncements.

The most important of these meetings was probably that held at

Mar del Plata, Argentina, in 1966. It was devoted to the problems of justice and development, and inspired the policies subsequently decided upon at Medellín. The final declaration was entitled 'The Presence of the Church in the Development and the Integration of Latin America'. It is interesting to note that a copy of this was given by a delegation of Latin American bishops to the secretary general of the United Nations, U Thant.

Medellín was a most important event in the history of the Latin American church. It brought together 130 participants with voting rights, the majority of whom were bishops delegated by the different episcopal conferences, as well as 13 representatives of the Conference of Religious (CLAR). The preparation for the conference had not been easy. There was tension between the pontifical commission for Latin America and CELAM. The Holy See wished to maintain a tight control not only over the content of documents, but also over the organisation of the conference. Thus, the Vatican's approval was necessary for the nomination of the subjects to be treated by all rapporteurs, the length of each of the interventions and the discussions, the choice of experts and other organisational details as well. Four experts invited by CELAM were rejected at the last minute by the Holy See.

However, the dynamics of the conference made it possible to define a series of new tendencies, thus reaping the harvest of the experience gained from twelve years of running CELAM. There were two notable developments at Medellín which were going to have a great influence over the Latin American Church in the following years. One was the support given at the pastoral level to the development of base Christian communities. The other was the legitimacy brought to the development of liberation theology. It has to be pointed out that military dictatorships were beginning to appear in the 1960s, notably in Brazil, and that Central America as a whole was ruled by extreme right-wing regimes, that under the influence of American military advisers the doctrine of national security had been adopted in several states and that guerrilla warfare had broken out in several countries with various degrees of success. Camilo Torres had been killed in a guerrilla action in 1966.

IV. FROM MEDELLÍN TO PUEBLA

It is not surprising that the more conservative elements of the Latin

American episcopate as well as those of the Roman Curia, did not view favourably the new directions taken by the conferences of the Latin American episcopate supported by CELAM. As a result, a dual corrective mechanism was applied: a firmer control of the co-ordinating bodies of Catholicism in Latin America, and a policy of episcopal nominations which was designed to counteract the new developments.

The statutes of CELAM were modified at the meeting at San José, Costa Rica in 1970. It was decided to have the presidents of the episcopal conferences sit alongside the elected delegates at the meetings. This reinforced the control of the national episcopal conferences and concomitantly the weight of the conservative elements. This was seen in the meeting at Sucre, in Bolivia, two years later. It was in 1972 during this meeting that the auxiliary bishop of Bogotá, Monsignor López Trujillo, who was known for his conservative views, was elected secretary general of CELAM. Thus began a process of concentration and rationalisation of the different bodies. The different sections of CELAM were progressively relocated in Bogotá. The Pastoral Institute of Quito, the Liturgical Institute of Medellín, the Catechetical Institute of Manizales were merged into a single body based in Bogotá.

From 1972, criticism of liberation theology became more and more frequent. By this time, Monsignor (now Cardinal) Trujillo declared that there were two theologies of liberation, one founded on a spiritual tradition (of Latin American origin) and another of European origin which stressed political action. According to him, only the first one was valid and not flawed by external intervention. In 1973 it was decided not to celebrate the fifth anniversary of the Medellín Conference 'so as not to engage in triumphalism'. Extremely severe condemnations of the movement Christians for Socialism were published at this time.

The positions taken by CELAM were characterised by a concentration of power in the hands of the secretary general, close links with the Holy See and an orientation which increasingly resembled a counter-reformation. In 1974, at the annual meeting, which took place this time in Rome, the statutes were again modified and the same persons were confirmed in office for four years. In 1978 a new conference of the episcopate was to be organised to celebrate the tenth anniversary of Medellín. Because of the death of Paul VI and then of John Paul I, however, the conference was postponed for a year. It finally took place in Puebla in Mexico in 1979.

Conference preparations were laid with the object of correcting the pastoral and theological directions of Medellín. The secretary general of CELAM, Monsignor Trujillo and Cardinal Baggio in Rome, worked in close collaboration. This manifested itself in several ways, both by who was invited and who was excluded and in the manner in which the conference was organised. The opening address of the conference was delivered by Pope John Paul II who clearly warned the bishops against certain tendencies in the theological and pastoral fields. There were 367 participants of whom 187 had voting rights. Only five representatives of CLAR, the Conference of Religious, were allowed to vote in comparison with thirteen at Medellín. None of the liberation theologians were chosen as experts. But their discussions outside the conference sessions, together with the more progressive bishops, prevented the conference from ending in disavowal of the conclusions of Medellín. There was no explicit condemnation of the theology of liberation or of the base Christian communities. The conference could not turn back the tide. The final text voted by the bishops was modified in several places by the Holy See before publication. While these modifications were generally minor, they were also significant in some areas.

Admittedly, what was happening in Latin America reflected a profound revolution in the Church. Even if the Holy See, through the voice of John XXIII and of Vatican II, had given a certain reforming impetus, the apparatus of central power had remained in place and was generally directed by the same people. The tension between a redefinition of objectives and the permanency of an ecclesiastical organisation was bound to give rise to conflict. This facilitated a relatively easy recovery of control by the most conservative elements.

V. THE INSTITUTIONALISATION OF THE RESTORATION

Several months after Puebla, Monsignor López P. Trujillo was appointed president of CELAM. Shortly afterwards he became a cardinal. On the occasion of his receiving the red hat, Pope John Paul II expressed appreciation of the role he had played in rectifying the theological currents in Latin America. During the eighteenth assembly of CELAM in 1981 the new cardinal made the following statement about the liberation theologians:

> the problem is not that they speak out strongly on behalf of the

poor, but that they make ideological use of a Marxist instrument of analysis in contradiction with the magisterium of the Church.

CELAM became the main base of the opposition to the theology of liberation. A series of meetings were organised. One held at Rio de Janeiro in 1982 was devoted to christology. Cardinal Ratzinger was invited to attend. The well-known sequel of this invitation was the publication of two documents by the Congregation for the Doctrine of the Faith which were particularly critical of the theology of liberation, the silencing of the Brazilian theologian, Leonardo Boff and the pressures exercised on the Peruvian episcopate in relation to Fr Gustavo Gutiérrez.

CELAM also began an active campaign against the direction being taken by the base Christian communities. A meeting on ecclesiology was organised and Monsignor Jérôme Hamer participated in it. He is currently the Cardinal Prefect of the Congregation of Religious but at that time he was Secretary of the Congregation for the Doctrine of the Faith. When Cardinal Dom Paulo Evaristo Arns of São Paulo presided over a meeting of the base Christian communities of Latin America in 1980, CELAM brought considerable pressure to bear to minimise its effects.

Reference must also be made to the action of CELAM in Nicaragua. No sooner had the Sandinista revolution succeeded than CELAM, thanks notably to the financial support of private American foundations, organised a series of campaigns in conjunction with the local episcopate for the education of priests, nuns and lay people. Some of the most conservative elements of Latin American Catholicism took part. The official purpose of the meetings was to prepare cadres of the Church to counter the ideological action of a regime which was considered marxist and therefore anti-religious. In 1983 during the annual meeting held at Port-au-Prince, Monsignor Quarracino, who had been secretary of CELAM during the presidency of Cardinal López Trujillo, was elected to the presidency. The conservative approach was thus confirmed both at the institutional and personal levels, and notably by the choice of the new secretary general, a Colombian bishop who was close to Cardinal López Trujillo. In 1985, just before the Extraordinary Synod took place at Rome, CELAM published a work which it had distributed to the bishops who were to attend. This document was a veritable active accusation against the new popular forms of church organisation, particularly in Nicaragua, but also in Mexico, in Chile, in Peru and so on.[8]

Thus one can note that CELAM has become an organ of restoration within the framework of Latin American Catholicism. This follows the Cardinal Ratzinger line. The present position stands in marked contrast to CELAM at its foundation. Then it was directed by a section of the Latin American episcopate which was more open to change largely because the conservatives had not taken any interest in the new structures. There was a change of attitude, however, when the importance and efficiency of these new structures became evident. Little by little, the conservatives took control of the council and of its different organs. They marginalised the other currents of thought and of action and co-ordinated all these activities with the people who were favourable to a restoration in the universal Church. It must also be remembered that CELAM played an important role in the organisation of Papal visits to the continent and particularly to Central America.

The history of CELAM's thirty years of existence illustrates quite clearly the sociological mechanisms of an institution in a process of change. We have seen how a dynamic minority succeeded in transforming an institution which was little inclined to change from the inside. At the same time, institutional logic reproducing existing structures linked on the one hand to an authoritarian concept of the Church and on the other to a hegemonic vision of the social space necessary for its action, completely reorientated what was being done in practice.

The case of CELAM thus poses the theoretical problem of the relationship between the manner in which an institution defines itself and its institutional presence in civil society. It is clear that the development in Latin America of base Christian communities as a new ecclesial form constructed from the bottom up, and favouring the emergence of new religious roles both masculine and feminine, was in conflict with the exclusively hierarchical concept of the religious institution where only that which is an initiative of authority or that which is in a relationship of submission to such authority appears as legitimate.

It is also clear that both the content and the manner of development of the theology of liberation are fundamentally opposed to the explicit or implied theological vision of this authoritarian concept of the Church. This is because liberation theology is founded on the perception of a social reality as one which is conflictual in its structures. For liberation theology is constructed on the basis of this situation of conflict which it makes its 'space' of theological reflection and one of the criteria of its concrete truths, that is to say, of its fidelity to Jesus as a historical person.

The fact that CELAM has been an important channel for the defusion of these two influences, one in the domain of ecclesiastical organisation, and the other in that of the production of theological meaning, has obviously made it suspect in the eyes of those partisans of the concept of the Church described above. Indeed, the episcopal conference of Medellín had shown on the one hand a willingness to organise the popular masses as a dynamic form of social transformation, and on the other render legitimate the beginnings of a new theological reflection.

Reaction soon manifested itself and confirmed its presence by recovering control of the institution through a gradual reorganisation of its sections, and through a gradual replacement of the people in charge. This, of course, is only one of the aspects of the 'restoration' of which Cardinal Ratzinger has spoken. Other policies with the same finality will be pursued, for example, that of episcopal nominations intended to modify, when this is necessary, the orientations of local episcopal conferences, a policy of support given to certain religious organisations (notably Opus Dei) or to certain movements (like the charismatic movement) which promote the same concept, or a policy of pressures exercised on the financial aid agencies and on the ecumenical bodies which have supported the new initiatives in Latin America.

Sociologically, the institution possesses efficient means of medium-term action, and this permits it to make certain concessions in order to avoid ruptures which would be too brutal. CELAM now risks considering the process as a linear one, without perceiving that it is in fact a dialectic one, and that the basis of future contradictions exist already. This is because its ecclesial concept, and its orientations, both religious and social, are in conflict with the daily experience of a great number of its members.

NOTES

1. Leo XIII's apostolic letter, *Cum diuturnum*, published on 25 December 1898. See Mgr Pablo Correa Leon, *El Concilio Plenario Latinoamericano de 1899 y la Conferencia Episcopal Latinoamericano de 1955* [Communicacion a la reunion del CELAM in Bogotá, 1956.]

2. It is interesting to note that this work played an important role in the preparation of the code of canon law that was published in 1918. The points which were treated at the Council related to ecclesiastic personnel, the Mass, the sacraments and Church property.
3. Although bearing a *prima facie* resemblance to the Council of 1899, this Conference was of a very different character. While a council is a legislative body which makes canonical regulations and laws, a conference is a consultative meeting in the course of which the bishops study a certain number of themes of common interest, exchange experiences and enter into agreements.
4. On 29 June 1955, Pius XII published the apostolic letters *Ad Ecclesiam Christi*, addressed to Cardinal Piazza who was going to preside over the conference (A.A.A. XXXXVII–1955) pp. 539–44.
5. Article 97, chapter 6 of the conclusions of the Conference of Rio de Janeiro.
6. The Catholic Aid Organisation.
7. Between 1958 and 1962, a socio-religious research project was organised by the Fédération internationale des institutions catholiques de recherches sociales et socio-religieuses. Its results were published in 40 volumes.
8. *CELAM otra Iglesia en la base* (Bogotá, 1985).

5 Latin America and the Special Rome Synod

Jon Sobrino

The Extraordinary Synod of Bishops was celebrated in Rome from 24 November to 8 December 1985. It was called by John Paul II to celebrate the twentieth anniversary of the Second Vatican Council and to evaluate what has happened since the Council. Present were 165 Synodal Fathers, of whom sixty per cent came from the Third World and about a fifth from Latin America. In this commentary we want to present, in the first part, the most important events that occurred during the Synod. In the second part, we will offer an initial evaluation of its significance, leaving till later more detailed theological analysis. Both in the presentation and the evaluation we will take into special account the reality of Latin America and its Churches.

The Synod began with a report from Cardinal Daneels in which he synthesised the replies of the episcopates to the questionnaires which had previously been sent out to them. This report had the beneficial effect of dissipating some doubts and fears created by the publication of the book by the Prefect of the Congregation for the Doctrine of the Faith, Cardinal Ratzinger, *The Ratzinger Report*. As is widely known, this book, translated into various languages, expressed great pessimism with regard to what had happened in the Church since the Council. Though it did not blame the Council in itself, the book created a climate of mistrust in relation to the Council and even went so far as to ask for a restoration in the Church. Various bishops and theologians expressed themselves as being against the theses of the book (in Europe, a hard-hitting article by Hans Küng stood out; in Latin America, twelve liberation theologians commented on it and criticised it in a short book published in Brazil, *Vatican II and the Latin American Church*) and, a few weeks before the Synod, Cardinal Koenig brought out his own book, *Church, Where Are You Going?*, which was considered as a reply and a counter-balance to Ratzinger.

In this climate of mistrust and fear, Cardinal Daneels' report had the virtue of calming people and of creating an atmosphere of freedom in which the Synodal Fathers could express themselves. As the Cardinal said at a press conference: 'One does not hold a Synod about a book'. The Synod was not going to centre on the Ratzinger book, which does not mean, as we shall see, that it did not have great influence on the direction of the Synod.

The second stage began when the Synodal Fathers made their prepared interventions, which could not go beyond eight minutes. More than a hundred of them spoke, and they did so freely. Since these interventions were not so much a debate as a presentation of a vision of the Church in the various countries, the interventions taken together offered a mosaic of the situation of the Church, its diversity as well as the serious tensions within it. Various positions gradually appeared on the issues of the relation of the Church to the world, on centralism or collegiality, on Churches that are vital or languishing.

We can cite some significant examples of what happened. Various bishops (Malone, President of the Episcopal Conference of the United States, the Norwegian Gran, and the Italian Cardinal Poletti) treated of the theme of collegiality, asking for it to be extended to the episcopal conferences. More radical was the Ukrainian Archbishop Maxim Hermanuik, who asked for the constitution of a permanent Synod of Bishops which would assume the legislative power which at present the Pope shares only with the Curia. The latter would be left with a merely executive role. As an innovative proposal of the first world Church we might consider also the request of the Archbishop of Salzburg, Karl Berg, to reflect more deeply on birth control and the denial of the sacraments to Catholics who are divorced and remarried.

From the third world, the Archbishop of Bombay, Simon Ignacio Pimenta, who spoke in the name of all the Asian episcopates, requested a deepening of Vatican II's teaching with regard to Christianity's relationship with other religions in a new context. He characterised this context as follows: the continent of Asia is today victim, on the one hand, of a western culture which exercises an influence which is increasingly pernicious and destructive of the values of local cultures; and on the other hand, victim of the great oriental religions which exercise an ever greater influence, especially on the young.

With regard to Latin America, various bishops spoke and, as was expected, gave differing views. Some adopted a thoughtful position in the face of the positive fruits of the Council and of the present dangers. Others accented the negative point of view sharing a special fear of the so-called Popular Church (Cardinal Obando, Darío Castrillón, secretary general of CELAM, Raúl Primatesta, the Argentinian, who went so far as to request the Synod to affirm the obligation of the State as such to recognise God and the right of the Church to promote its cult according to the natural law). Another group expressed itself along the lines of Medellín, which they recognised as the great fruit of the Council as far as Latin America was concerned (among this group were Julio Terrazas, President of the Bolivian Episcopal Conference, and the Brazilians, Cardinal Aloísio Lorscheider and Ivo Lorscheiter, President of the Brazilian Episcopal Conference). These insisted that the Council ought to be a light, not a limit, for episcopal collegiality, and to lead to an increase of powers for the episcopal conferences. Similarly they emphasised especially the prophetic mission of the Church, the option for the poor, attentiveness to the Word of God, the articulation of faith and justice, the specificity of the theology of liberation, the integral liberation of man, human rights and so on.

After these interventions, Cardinal Daneels presented a second report which constituted the third great moment of the Synod and which represented a qualitative change. In his report, the Cardinal tried to review what had been said in the interventions and proposed a certain orientation for the future work of the Synod and for its final documents. In the presence of so many and varied view-points, preoccupations and problems, Daneels concentrated on three points which gave the impetus for the selection and treatment of the principal problems. It is necessary to deepen our understanding of the Council in three directions: (a) the 'sacred' as a counterweight to secularism; (b) the concept of the Church as 'Communion', so as to overcome a purely sociological approach, to which it is vulnerable; (c) the 'theology of the Cross', so as to moderate the excessive enthusiasm with which the post-conciliar Church looked on the world and to put a brake on *aggiornamento*.

This report decided the future of the Synod. As can be seen, the concerns treated are more those of the first world than of the third. Vatican II is implicitly praised, but two of its essential points have fallen into the background: the missionary character of the Church and its reality as the people of God. These first world concerns were those insisted on by the influential group of German speaking bishops, and particularly by Cardinal Ratzinger, whose version of these problems appears in his book and in his intervention, 'The Church as Mystery'.

After this report, the Synod worked in language groups with a view to elaborating a message and a document. In these groups important points were treated and debated. The Canadian Bernard Hubert, President of the Canadian Episcopal Conference, for example, drew attention to the danger of the Church limiting its concerns to its internal life and so forgetting about the world. 'The struggle for justice and participation in the transformation of the world appear fully as a constitutive dimension of the preaching of the gospel.' According to him, the Synod ought to affirm in its message the desire of Christians to participate constructively in the more serious problems of our time, among which he mentioned the debt of the third world and the threat of a nuclear conflict. Though this proposal was debated in one of the smaller groups, it was not accepted.

As far as the more specifically Latin American problems were concerned, two very different postures were present in the group discussions and were reflected publicly in the press conferences. Dom Aloísio Lorscheider constantly insisted on the decisive importance of the Church as the people of God, a people who are poor yet rich in faith, on the necessity of listening to this people, and of the Church being converted to them and so on. Dom Ivo Lorscheiter made a clear defence of the theology of liberation, which he characterised as a fruit of Vatican II, born of the Church, useful and necessary for its pastoral action. Other Latin American bishops, among them Darío Castrillón, expressed themselves along opposing lines. In brief, there appeared the known division among the Latin American bishops. On the one hand there was a defence of the Church of the poor, of the theology of liberation, of the principle of subsidiarity, that is, of greater autonomy for the local Churches. On the other hand, there were attacks against the so-called popular Church, against a certain liberation theology haunted by the phantasm of marxism attributed to it, and an unbreakable adhesion to Roman centralism. These arguments did not appear in the plenary session nor are they reflected in the final document; they do however reflect the reality of the Latin American Church.

After the work in groups, and not without upsets, the Synod decided to produce a *Message of the Synod to the People of God*, and to publish, with papal approval, a document with the title *The Church, subject to the Word of God, Celebrates the Mysteries of Christ for the Salvation of the World*.

In the *Message*, the current situation of the world is presented in sombre tones, although its ultimate positive destiny is exalted. There is emphasis on the meaning of the 'mystery' of the Church, on the call to holiness and on the necessity of avoiding false sociological or political interpretations of the nature of the Church. Although in the beginning it was thought of directing this message, as did Vatican II, to 'all men', in the end it is directed only to the 'People of God'.

The *Document* consists of an introduction and four chapters. In the introduction, Vatican II is praised; the bright side and the dark side of the post-conciliar period are analysed and encouragement is given for a more profound reception of it. The first chapter treats of the Church as mystery, of the necessity to return to the sacred, to sanctity, to the sacraments, to the renewal of the religious life. In the second chapter, the living sources from which the Church draws her life are analysed: the Word of God and the liturgy. There is insistence on the task of evangelisation and a warning against the confusion which some theologies have caused, to overcome which dialogue between bishops and theologians is called for. Liturgical renewal is praised, but the document insists on correcting abuses and on explaining the theological basis for the sacramental discipline and for the liturgy. As a new proposal 'it is desirable that a catechism or compendium of the whole of Catholic doctrine, both on faith and morals, be written which would serve as a point of reference for the catechisms or compendia to be written in the various regions'. In fact, it is well known that such a catechism is already being written. In the third chapter, the Church as communion is analysed. There is insistence that the analysis of the Church from the purely organisational perspective and from the perspective of power be superseded; and that communion does not deny diversity. On the contrary, it is within unity in pluriformity that collegiality, the episcopal conferences and the oriental Churches are approached. It insists on participation and co-responsibility in the Church. In the fourth and last chapter, the mission of the Church in the world is analysed, recalling *Gaudium et Spes* and proposing the criterion of the 'theology of the Cross' as a means of realising this mission. The concrete problems which it treats are: *aggiornamento*, inculturation, dialogue with non-Christian religions and with non-believers, the preferential option for the poor and human development. Among the suggestions mentioned was an examination of the social doctrine of the Church with respect to the promotion of justice in changing circumstances.

This is a short synthesis of what happened in the Synod, which may be supplemented by the reader consulting the documents themselves. What we propose to do now is make an initial general evaluation of the Synod, recognising the Synod as an event of the Universal Church and seeking its significance for Latin America.

In itself, the Synod was an important ecclesial event, as its participants have recognised. However, the most important element, because the most lasting, has been the elaboration – fragmentary and not always explicit – of an ecclesiology. The fundamental thing is that it has sketched an image of the Church which it presented as agreeing with that of Vatican II and as an adequate concretisation for our world. We will look at some important aspects of this.

The Synod event itself is presented as 'communion', that is, a realisation of the proposed ecclesiology. The Fathers noted the atmosphere of prayer, fraternity, dialogue and study. It is certain that the Synod did project that image, unlike, for example, Puebla, where the tensions were much more evident. It does not seem possible to doubt the communion and the subjective liberty among the Synodal Fathers, all of which is to be praised.

However, we must examine events a bit further. Without knowing exactly how the Synod was prepared in the different dioceses and countries, we can say that in some there was participation by the grassroots, by the totality of the people of God, as for example, in Brazil; in others there was not this type of preparation. It does not seem extravagant to think that the people of God were not actively present in its preparation. In this sense, the Synod showed communion on the level of the bishops, which is important to underline, but not necessarily at the radical level of the people of God. Indeed, had it been such, the themes and the approach would have been different or at least more ample.

Also we have to look at the freedom of the Synodal Fathers. Undoubtedly they expressed themselves freely. We cannot ignore, however, the atmosphere that was generated before the Synod. Ratzinger's book, to which we have referred, provoked many contrary reactions and his pessimism was not reflected by the Synod. It was, however, we believe, very important, and even decisive for the limiting of the subject matter treated by the Synod, something supported by the German-speaking bishops. In this book it is clearly said that what is most urgent is the treatment of ecclesiology and general lines for this are proposed. 'My impression is that the authentically Catholic meaning of the reality "Church" is tacitly disappearing . . . . Behind the *human* exterior stands the mystery of a *more than human* reality, in which reformers, sociologists, organizers have no authority whatsoever' (*The Ratzinger Report*, Leominster

1985, p. 45–6). This approach and this solution are already present in the second important report of Daneels and in the final document.

John Paul II assisted in silence at the interventions, which undoubtedly facilitated the subjective freedom to speak. However, it is beyond doubt that in the final documents there is present not only his magisterium – which would be obvious in the Catholic Church – but also what we might call his theological style, which is more transcendentalist than historical, and his ecclesiology which is defined absolutely in terms of unity. In one further, concrete point he introduced his own theology: the theology of the Cross. Already during the Council he proposed it during the debate on *Gaudium et Spes* but on that occasion without success. The document of the Synod included it in a relevant manner, while insisting that the theology of the Cross 'does not exclude the theology of creation and of the incarnation, rather it obviously presupposes them'.

With these reflections there is no desire to deny the right to formulate various theologies nor the fact that one or other may be the determining one. However, it is remarkable that this theology, and only this one, was imposed and that the ecclesiologies of the people of God, those of Medellín and Puebla, are practically absent. All this produces the impression that in this important point of ecclesiology, the fundamental issue had been already decided.

Although almost two-thirds of the Synodal Fathers came from the third world, the problems treated in the final document tended to be those of the first world: secularisation with its negative consequences of secularism, indifference, atheism, consumerism, dehumanisation, the loss of the meaning of life and so on. The problem is real and of radical importance for the Church, and the Synod did well to take it into consideration.

I must come back, however, to draw attention to the almost exclusive concentration on this point (secularism) and on the form it takes in the first world and on the response which is given to it. In a universal Synod, it should have been necessary to justify concentrating on this problem, since, as presented, it is not the problem of the third world. It would seem that there are traces here of a certain priority given to the first world over the others, or of a way of thinking which assumes that what happens in Europe is of definitive and significant importance and programmatic for all.

Notable also is the attention given to 'mystery', without however any profound analysis of what is being talked about. Positively, 'transcendent and divine realities' are referred to: negatively, it is opposed to secularism. It is a pity that the Synod has not analysed this point in depth, for what is at stake is none other than the theological dimension of Christian and human existence. 'The sacred', 'mystery' is none other than God, and seen thus, the problem is truly universal. What happens is that the problem of God is seen in different forms in different parts of the world. In Europe, faced with secularisation and atheism, one will speak of 'the return to the sacred'; in the third world, one will speak of the struggle against idolatry, a problem just as real, but more radical than the former for the Church and its theological dimension.

One also notices the lack of a Christian analysis of 'the sacred' starting from Revelation, since one cannot presuppose that it is already known what is secular and what is sacred prior to the manifestation of God in Jesus Christ. Even though – one will object – a Synod has not time to treat everything, it seems to us that if, in fact, the problem of the sacred and mystery was treated, the Synod ought to have paid at least minimal attention to what it is and to how one approaches it since Jesus. Would that the document had observed the dialectic between 'sacred' and 'profane', between 'transcendence' and 'incarnation', between 'faith' and 'the practice of Justice' and so on. Had this been done the Synod would have been able to achieve a greater universality, since the problem of the mystery of God is present in Europe, in Latin America and its theology of liberation, and in Asia and Africa with their variety of religions. It would be good if in future synods and councils the Church tackled the themes of theo-logy and Christo-logy without reducing all to ecclesiology, since the latter's life depends on the former.

Finally the facility with which the presentation of a Church as mystery is proposed as a solution for the problem of secularism is striking. All that the document says, one supposes, is correct. However, the basic hypothesis is not so obviously correct: because the Church has appeared more as a sociological reality than as a mysterious one it has promoted secularism, therefore the return to the Church as mystery will help promote the opposite. No-one denies that an insistence on the mystery of the Church can help create an atmosphere favourable to 'the return to the sacred'; in fact, other phenomena, such as the proliferation of oriental religious cults, suggest this. It is clear, however, that this is not the way the Church should proceed, firstly, because its sacredness comes to it given by Jesus Christ and not simply through the meaning of or the desire for transcendence and the non-worldly; secondly, because that part which the Church played in shaping the high point of secularism came not from the loss of mystery but from her historical practice. Would that the Church, following the Synod, would present itself truly as mystery to the world. To do this would demand being truly worldly as Jesus was and in the way that Jesus was – in poverty, denouncing in truth, willing to risk persecution and death – and so make present the mystery of God in this world. This would demand the abandoning of what is worldly in the sense of wealth, and power, and the wisdom of this world, of all of which the history of the Church is full.

The Synod recognised the validity of Vatican II and was grateful for the inspiration which it found present in it. On the juridical level, one supposes that it could not be otherwise. It is nonetheless important that the Synod said so and that it recognized that in Vatican II there is present not only true doctrine but also inspirational principles for today. In the message it says: 'encouraged by this joyful hope for the Church and for the world, we invite you to know better and completely the Second Vatican Council, to make a study of the Council more open and available. We call on you to unite yourselves to our effort. We also commit ourselves to employ all the methods at our disposal to help respond to all the demands which the Council directs to the Church'.

It is not possible to speak more clearly of the importance of the Council. None the less we cannot ignore that the Synod approaches the Council from a certain point of view and with certain emphases. In one form or another all the important points of Vatican II, or almost all, are in the document. However it is necessary to analyse what is the importance that is attributed to each and to see which are given prominence and which are not. The impression which the document gives is that the point of view has changed on two issues that are essential to the Council: the relation of the Church to the world and the treatment of the Church in itself as the People of God.

As far as the first issue is concerned, it will certainly be said that 'the Church by its very nature is missionary', that is, it exists not for itself but for the world. However, throughout the text the dialectic between identity and mission is not sufficiently elaborated, and does not arrive at the radical statement of *Evangelii Nuntiandi* that the identity of the Church consists in its mission. In this way, the Church in itself is favoured above its mission, and in the determination of the latter the world to which it is directed does not have the role which Vatican II gave it. In Vatican II, the 'signs of the times' are important for knowing what the Church ought to do (GS 4); more than that, they are where the presence of God and his will are to be found (GS 11). The Synod admits the first, but does not consider the second. On this issue there has been a going back from Medellín and Puebla. There is no truly theological reflection on the world and the incarnational aspect of mission is not emphasised so much.

As far as the second issue is concerned, there is in the Synodal documents a striking silence: there is no mention of the people of God. The message is directed to them, as distinct from non-believers, but afterwards the term is merely mentioned, not analysed nor given the relevance it was accorded by Vatican II. Why this incomprehensible silence? The reason would seem to be already expressed in the Ratzinger book. 'Behind the concept of the Church as the People of God, which has so exclusively been thrust into the foreground today, hide influences of ecclesiologies which de facto revert to the Old Testament; and perhaps also political, partisan and collectivist influences' (*The Ratzinger Report*, p. 47). In other words, it is a 'dangerous' image of the Church. It is certain that in Vatican II it is not the only image of the Church, and for that reason the Synod did well to recall the others also. However to simply suppress it when it acquired decisive relevance in the Council is surprising. To do so on the ground that it is dangerous is not very convincing; from the point of view of its being dangerous any image of the Church can be such since it is limited and capable of being manipulated. Exactly the same thing could happen with the image 'communion' which has the inherent danger of making the Church concentrate on itself. One has to go on and analyse whether the danger of the image comes from the wrong use which can be made of it or if it comes also from the questions it poses us, in which case the danger would be healthy and productive. There is no doubt that the concept, 'the People of God', highlights the historicity of the Church, the necessity of incarnation in history, her pathway between fidelity and infidelity, her hope. It also brings to the fore the fundamental equality of all in the Church. What should have been done was to take the concept, 'the People of God', analyse it properly and make the appropriate distinctions about the dangers within it. In any case, it is once again surprising that a Synod convoked to celebrate Vatican II should ignore one of its most central statements.

What significance for Latin America have all these issues that were so central to the Synod? We have already said that the Synod dealt mainly with a Central European set of problems. This means that, properly speaking, there was not, except in excessively vague terms, any treatment, illumination, critique or encouragement of the current Latin American agenda: base Christian communities and their ministries, theology of liberation, and, more fundamentally, the theological approach of the Church starting from the signs of the times, her decidedly prophetic and anti-idolatrous mission, her incarnation among and solidarity with the poor, her immersion in historical liberation, her relationship with other liberationist groups and so on.

In spite of this, we still have to ask ourselves what the Synod says to Latin America, in view of the fact that it was a Synod of the universal Church. We will look at it under three important headings.

The insistence of the Synod on the sacred can help a deeper study of, and the giving of greater value to, popular religion. This is important for the communities as well as for the people in general, for their self-awareness, their organisation, their struggle and their faith. It may lead us to treat seriously the religious manifestations of the indians and the negros. It may encourage us to continue developing the so-called spirituality of liberation, which is nothing other than a treatment of the theological problem of man. It may lead us to dialogue honourably with unbelievers, especially with those in the liberation and revolutionary movements.

As far as the Church as communion is concerned, progress on this front in Latin America is greatly to be desired, since there are divisions; and many facts show the lack of, and inability for, dialogue on the part of those who adopt positions more or less consequent with Medellín and the theology of liberation. In any case, communion would have to be given an historical form along the lines of Puebla's formulation: communion 'and' participation. This latter element is mentioned by the Synod, but one gets the feeling that it is understood only as collaboration. For example, one rejoices that 'many lay people offer themselves for the service of the Church'. However, participation is more than collaboration with the hierarchy, it is the realisation *in actu* of communion. To participate is to take part, giving and receiving, in the faith, in the hope, in the love of the Church; it is also to share in its organisation, liturgy and doctrine, as has been shown in Latin America by the Church of Brazil and that of Monsignor Romero.

As far as the theology of the Cross is concerned, it is not really necessary to mention it in Latin America, since life and faith and theology are made of it. However, it does have to be adequately situated historically. It is not a case in Latin America of emphasising the Cross as a historical and Christian existential fact: that can be taken as said. It is a question of emphasising the cross of crucified peoples, at whose service intervenes invariably the subjective cross. The theology of the Cross becomes therefore the theology of the incarnation and of discipleship, of the defence of the poor, of the attack against the oppressor, of persecution and of martyrdom. Also, paradoxically, it becomes the theology of hope and of the resurrection, because in the poor is the Lord: they are the light of the nations, they maintain hope, they save.

It remains to be seen what will be the fruits of the Synod and its impact in Latin America. If in fact it sends the Church in Latin America back to Vatican II, to Medellín and Puebla, its fruits will be noteworthy and the Synod will have achieved what it set out to do. To do this, however, doctrine is not enough, no matter how important it may be. One must start from reality. This involves looking at not only the realities treated by the Council but also how it came to treat of those realities. In a remarkable text, even if only said in passing, the Synod says: 'the Greek for witness is *martyrium*. In this regard, the more ancient Churches of Europe can learn much from the young Churches, from their dynamism, their life and witness, leading to martyrdom of blood in the strict sense'.

If these are not simply words, then we are being shown here a very important pathway for the future of the Church. It is said that there is ecclesial vitality – in the young Churches, says the document, but also in many renewed communities of the first world – and to a large extent this comes from the Council. It is a pity that the Synod focused itself, in fact, more on the negative in the hope of finding a solution. The fact of having chosen the problems of 'the most ancient Churches of Europe' led it to choose this approach and to pay this price. If one adopts, however, the opposite point of view and analyses what is positive in the post-conciliar period, a more adequate pathway is offered for the future, including the future of the languishing churches. One ought to continue speaking of mystery, of the mystery of God, the Father of our Lord Jesus Christ, the God of the poor and the God of life; of ecclesial communion, the true body of Christ, which bears in its flesh the marks of his passion and the hope of his resurrection, of a communion as a true fraternal community, the true people, with whom God has made a convenant, and with them all without exception; of the theology of the Cross, as the mystery of evil in the crucified peoples and as the mystery of salvation, the expression of generous love which maintains hope and sets in motion the reign of God.

It is good that the Synod has focused on the post-conciliar problematic, but more important still is to build on the life that already exists. However, that is not found at the centre, but at the edge, not in Jerusalem but, as the scriptures say, in Bethlehem the unknown. There it is. That is the place that truly nourishes the hope and the orientation of the Church. It is this that the Latin American Church offers as a help so that the beautiful and utopian words of the message of the Synod may become a reality:

> We were not created for death but for life. We are not condemned to division and war, rather we are called to brotherhood and peace. Man was not created by God for hatred and mistrust, rather he was created so as to love God. He was made for God. Man responds to that vocation through the renewal of his heart. There is one pathway for humanity – and we already see signs of it – which leads to a civilization of participation, of solidarity and of love, to a civilization which is the only one worthy of man. With all of you we propose to work so that this civilization of love may win through, as is God's plan for the whole of humanity as it waits on the coming of the Lord.

This chapter was translated by Leonard Martin and Raphael Gallagher.

Part Two
Theological Perspectives on the Latin American Reality

6 Central America: The Political Challenge of the Faith

Jon Sobrino

The Central American Church, virtually unknown until about ten years ago, is now known throughout the world, and, whether admired or feared, continues to be news. Seen from the outside, two things have powerfully attracted attention on account of their newness: the involvement of the Church in struggles for liberation and even revolution (in Nicaragua, El Salvador and Guatemala) and the cruel and massive persecution of Christians which has produced abundant martyrs (in El Salvador and Guatemala above all, but also in Honduras, Nicaragua and Panama). Behind these spectacular new developments, however, something more fundamental has happened: a new evangelisation of Central America and a central-americanisation of the Gospel. In Central America there has appeared a Church of the poor or popular Church, and this is ecclesially the most radical new development. The words of Gustavo Gutiérrez, 'the history of the Church in Latin America divides into before and after Mgr. Romero', are a tribute to the martyred archbishop, but they also underline the type of Church that he symbolised in Central America. Let us consider in what follows the historical and evangelical principles that make this Church a new development, in order subsequently to analyse its present problems and its future. Needless to say not all the Church in Central America is as we shall shortly describe it; but that Church exists, it is the newest, and the one that must be taken into account when judging the present vicissitudes of the Church.

I. THE NEWNESS OF THE CENTRAL AMERICAN CHURCH

The most important new development is that the Central American Church has found its place, its identity and its mission in the reality of Central America, a process that began quite rapidly after Medellín.

This fundamental historical reality is the extreme poverty and the hope of liberation. Both the poverty and the hope are historical realities, and for this reason the Church, by attending to them, has been able to make itself Central American; they are also realities to which the Gospel is directed, and for this reason the Church, by taking them up and responding to them adequately, has been able to make itself more evangelical and Christian.

The Central American Reality

In Central America the extremely grave reality described by Medellín and Puebla is a truth that cries out. In the first place, there is 'the destitution that marginalises large human groups' (Medellín, Justicia I), the situation of inhuman poverty that is 'the most destructive and humiliating scourge' (Puebla, 29); in the second place: destitution as a product of 'unjust structures' (Medellín, Justicia 2), and thus a real sin; in the third place: the unjust destitution which is in itself 'institutionalised violence' (Medellín, Paz 16) that 'conspires against peace' (Paz 1), and thus a sin that brings close, and entails, destruction and death. On the other hand, it is also true that there exists 'a longing for total emancipation, for liberation from all servitude, for personal growth and collective integration' (Medellín, Introduction 4). An oppressive poverty which leads to death or a desire for liberation are then the fundamental features of the historical reality of Central America with which the Church has to come to terms.

Recognising that this is the situation and that here we have the most important fact about Central America is above all an act of profound honesty about reality, an act that is in itself conversion, for previously things were not seen in this way; it is also the presupposition and foundation for a recovery and growth of the Church's identity and mission, for neither of these can be fulfilled apart from that honesty, and with it they can both grow in a Christian way.

This vision of the Central American reality is correct not only historically but also theologically. Poverty 'cries out to heaven', and thus says something important about God; hope is 'a longing of the Spirit', and thus says something important about the Spirit of God.

What poverty says in theological terms is that God's creation is threatened, vitiated or annihilated, since poverty in Central America – unlike the meaning it may have in the first world – signifies real closeness to death, a closeness that is slow but real. For that reason, as has been said, 'the poor are those who die before their time' (G. Gutiérrez). This means that eschatology, the final fulfilment, is not the only issue facing the Church, something for which it must work and hope, but that protology, life, that which is in the beginning, also continues to be a fundamental issue which the Church must tackle.

Moreover, in Central America poverty is not simply a slow death, but a death that is also violent and rapid when the poor desire and struggle, even nobly, to escape from their unjust poverty. Then they are arrested, imprisoned, tortured, murdered; and they disappear. The Central American reality then becomes peoples crucified like the servant of Yahweh (I. Ellacuría) who shoulders, and succumbs beneath, the weight of the world's sin, whose face is disfigured and made repugnant (look at those who have been tortured), who goes like a silent sheep to the slaughterhouse (look at the thousands of unnamed people murdered), who is held to be wicked and Godless (look at how they are judged to be criminals and subversives), and buried like an evildoer (look at the secret graves). That poverty, as a slow or violent death, is what cries out to heaven from the earth and what reveals heaven's judgement on and against this earth. But the longings for liberation – which have little or nothing to do with the bourgeois ideals of progress, of consumerism or of dehumanising materialism – also reach heaven, and from heaven that hope is blessed and encouraged.

The Response of the Church

To define things in such terms means that, in response to the question of its ecclesial identity and mission, the Church (in advance, as is logical, and even though Christian faith may already be obviously active) has understood and recognised itself to be a creature in this world and before God, and in such a way that nothing it may subsequently say about itself can cancel out that status as creature and the primary responsibility that derives from it. The Church in Central America has recovered that fundamental status as creature and as a result has defined its ecclesial nature at a level that is strictly theological. This implies, very concretely, a demand to choose, like anyone of good will or any group, between life and death; in theological terms, the demand to choose between the God of life, who gives life and who wants his creatures to live, and the false divinities – false but existing – who attribute to themselves the characteristics of the divine: ultimateness, untouchableness, exacting submission and making limitless demands, the idols of death, who deal out death and demand victims in order to subsist like the god Moloch.

Thus it is that in Central America the fundamental problem of faith passes necessarily through this theological moment, formulated as a choice between alternatives that are mutually exclusive and in conflict: mutually exclusive because the one divinity excludes the other, and in conflict because the one divinity acts against the other. Thus it is also that the alternative to Christian faith is not, in the first place, simply atheism, but idolatry: not the absence of faith but the active (and perverted) faith in idols, which may be designated first and foremost as active, absolutist capitalism and the doctrine of national security. In the words of Monsignor Romero: 'In this no neutrality is possible. Either we serve the lives of the Salvadorean people or we are accomplices in their deaths' (Speech in Louvain, 2 February 1980). And these Salvadorean and Central American peoples are the immense majority who are poor.

This type of theological faith is the presupposition and foundation of what is new in the Church. Undoubtedly there are many other things that the Church has done and should do: when mentioning the lives of the poor, for instance, we have not said everything about the will of God for them nor have we mentioned the demands He also makes on them. But without that option one cannot speak of faith nor can one speak of God.

That faith is necessary and immediately translates itself into primary attitudes and activities that correspond to the will of a God of life. Against the covering up of reality – which, like every sin, tries to conceal itself from itself – faith entails discovering and proclaiming the truth of reality, of unjust death and of the desire for life. Against misery and cruel suffering, faith calls forth mercy – like that of the high priest, Jesus – to succour and relieve it. Against injustice, faith supports the struggle for justice with its ingredients: the prophetic denunciation of the structures of death, the demand for necessary structural changes and for the most suitable and efficient means to attain them. Against the resignation and fatalism that the idols of death wish to instil, faith becomes the encouragement of hope. In other words, against idolatry faith becomes faith in the God of life.

This faith that is demanded of the Church is an ultimate, for one cannot go further than what has been described, though it will need to be made concrete and explicit in Christian terms. It is demanded urgently, since the clamour of the poor is 'clear, growing and, on occasions, threatening' (Puebla 89), and mediates to us the Pauline cry 'the love of Christ drives us on'. With that faith the Church enters into Central America historically and theologically. That faith does not make it abdicate or relativise its condition as creature; instead it draws it into solidarity with the Central American poor and with all those who are honestly concerned for their hope and liberation.

In the reality of Central America this is the first logical step taken by the Church, apparently simple in its theoretical formulation, but costly and also fruitful. It is important to underline it above all so that it may be understood in other places in which the fundamental problem is not one of life or death. But that is what it continues to be in Central America. In the admirable words of Monsignor Romero to Leonardo Boff: 'It is necessary to defend the minimum which is God's greatest gift: life'.

The positioning of the Church in this way within the reality of Central America and before God is the root of its change and of its newness. Obviously what we have just described is Christian; but it seems to us extremely important to stress that what is Christian also refers back to – and deepens without separation – the 'being-human' of the Christian. From this there has emerged a new identity and mission of the Church in conformity with Vatican II and Medellín which we shall describe as briefly as possible and systematise according to the procedure of Jesus himself and of the Spirit of Jesus. We shall interpret ecclesial identity and mission as a following of Jesus starting with what his Spirit is unveiling today.

Incarnation

The Central American Church sees in the *incarnation* of Jesus the first demand to which it must respond. The Pauline statement, repeated and made central in Medellín, that Christ 'being rich made himself poor', acquires the value of a paradigm and implies a historical change of epochal dimensions. The incarnation is not one demand among many, nor merely an evangelical counsel or an ascetic practice. It simply means determining the place in which it is natural for the Church to be and from where it can carry out its mission. To put it in the most general terms, the Church has to become incarnate in the world of the poor.

That incarnation is in the first place a profound conversion. It is not just better knowledge of the world of the poor in order to develop in better ways the pastoral activity of a Church already constituted logically in advance of its incarnation. It is not just adaptation to the surrounding world, as requested by Vatican II, in order thereby to overcome the ecclesial triumphalism of centuries. It is not just dialogue with the world out of mutual respect and with confidence in mutual enrichment. It is in the first place conversion, and radical conversion, because the world of the poor means for the Church a radical 'other' that demands a radical change. Historically, the poor are an 'other' for the Church, precisely because they have been rediscovered in their truth and are no longer as they were once thought to be. Theologically they are an 'other' because previously they had not been taken into account as privileged recipients of the Church's mission, and much less in the formulation of the contents and modes of evangelisation and in the construction of a Church of the poor. This new development is what makes incarnation a conversion in so far as it involves a demand for radical change and also repentance for not having seen things in this way before nor having acted in accordance with a correct vision.

That incarnation is described since Medellín as solidarity of the Church with the poor. This solidarity has shown itself in Central America as a going, even physically, to the world of the poor. The movements towards insertion into that world by various priests and by a much larger number of nuns, the redistribution of human and physical resources in favour of, and in real contact with, the poor, the reorientation of the Church's traditional platforms and mechanisms (schools and universities, the media, pastoral work of a social and humanitarian kind, reorganisation of curias, priests' councils, clergy meetings and so on), all these take seriously into account the popular masses of the poor as primary recipients of their activity and, increasingly, as their inspirers and motive-force. In this descriptive sense the Central American Church is very different today from what it was fifteen years ago. There is much greater closeness to the poor and, above all, that closeness has become a major criterion for judging it.

That incarnation, in theological terms, involves resolving in a Christian sense the first fundamental problem of the Church: its place in history. In becoming incarnate among the poor the Church is simply recovering its origins. It is not mere rhetoric to affirm that the Church sprang up at the feet of One crucified. Nor is it rhetoric to say that in the beginning of the first Christian communities most of the members were poor, the little and the despised ones of the world, as Paul says. The christological root of the Church is here: in the concrete reality of Jesus. But its pneumatological root also culminates in that incarnation, for an important part of the Spirit's activity was to recall that the One who had risen from the dead was none other than the One who had been crucified; and an important part of the Spirit's present activity has been to return the Church to its true place.

The recovery of its true place is extremely important for the Church because from there it can grow, and away from there it is threatened with ossification and falsification of its own being. That incarnation in the world of the poor resolves, concretely, two important problems for the Church. The first is the tension between belonging and not belonging to the world, the proper relation between history and transcendence. An incarnation of the Church that is not in the world of the poor leads it historically to become worldly in the sinful sense of the word, to adopt consciously or unconsciously the values and attitudes of the world, above all the mastery and use of power in the manner of the powerful of this world. This type of incarnation does not make history into a place for transcendence; instead transcendence has to be maintained parallel to history, without converging with it, and often running against it, negating in history what is affirmed in transcendence. In the world of the poor the Church becomes 'worldly' in the positive sense of the word: taking flesh, and weak flesh, like the Son, and this permits it to encounter transcendence in history without parallelism and in principle without reductionism. Poverty – as understood in the profound intuition of St Ignatius – tends to generate 'insults and injuries', from which springs humility and from humility spring all the virtues. Poverty is the place from which history grows, gives more of itself, and thus can be placed in relation to the transcendence of God. The other world, that of wealth, does not make history grow towards salvation, but towards sin; and thus it is not the place in which to encounter transcendence.

The second problem is the tension between past and present in revelation and faith. The Church possesses the deposit of revelation; but to avoid this degenerating into possession of a simple deposit, and to make it productive instead, is not something to be merely wished for, but something which has to *happen*. The poor are, on the one hand, privileged recipients of the love of God, and in this they say and go on saying something important about the God of love. And, moreover, as Puebla says so well, the poor possess an 'evangelising power' (n. 1147); by what they are and suffer, they teach *sub specie contrarii* the will of God and move others to conversion; by their positive actions and by the values that are specifically theirs as the poor (solidarity, humility, hope) they evangelise positively. In this context the words spoken by Monsignor Romero in Louvain are striking and unnerving: since becoming incarnate among the poor the Church has been learning and making concrete the realities of sin and grace, damnation and salvation, God and Christ.

Evangelisation

Incarnated among the poor, the Central American Church has put into practice the call to follow Jesus interpreted, first and foremost, as *service of God's Kingdom*. It has rediscovered that service as evangelisation, but in a sense which is very clearly defined, as in Isaiah and Luke, precisely through being in the world of the poor. To evangelise is to announce and initiate the good news of God's Kingdom directly among the poor. In formal terms this means recovering for the Church's mission the communication of, in the first place, good news, something which may become doctrine but which in itself is more than doctrine: it is a joyful truth, which must be preached and received with joy because it points to a joyful reality. The recovery of the Gospel as good news, and the transcending of a more doctrinaire understanding of it, is a fundamental change that will shape the direction of the entire mission of the Church.

In practice evangelisation is carried out, as Vatican II says, through words and deeds. In so far as it is a matter of verbal proclamation, evangelisation has concentrated on proclaiming and sustaining the hope of the poor, a task in no way routine and one made possible basically by the credibility of a Church incarnate in this way and faithful despite persecution, as we shall see. And alongside proclamation there is denunciation, a task more often forgotten in the understanding of evangelisation, even in *Evangelii Nuntiandi* whose other chapters are so important for their treatment of evangelisation. That denunciation is one form of evangelisation – apart from being the fulfilment of an unavoidable ethical demand – makes sense because its direct purpose is to defend the poor and to offer the oppressors good news also *sub specie contrarii*.

As for evangelising deeds, these are all those actions intended to convert the good news into a good reality. Miracles and exorcisms, which are two sides of the same coin, are the practical applications of mercy at the immediate level of actual suffering and at the structural level of a renewal of reality. Evangelisation then becomes liberation from all slaveries and with the intention of bringing about the fullness of the Kingdom of God. However, as this evangelisation takes place among the poor, liberation in history is an essential moment, the criterion for verifying the honesty with which the other kinds of liberation are aspired to and – if it is carried out in a Christian way – it provides the foundation and the demand for the other kinds.

Abundant signs of all this have been given by the Church in Central America. Proclaiming the good news has entailed countless meetings and reorganisations of pastoral activity, doctrinal documents, the creation of institutions of social care, the direction of refugee camps, reorganisation of the means of social communication, and much else. Denunciation, accompanied by polemics and the unmasking of what pretends to be God's will, has been carried out in pastoral letters and homilies, and in the creation of institutions to defend human rights. Both proclamation and denunciation have been practised on various occasions by the hierarchy but also by the ecclesial communities themselves and by their pastoral agents. The new historical element in liberation has been introduced into the Church's mission, both by judging reality from the viewpoint of the poor and by proposing urgent structural changes that would be in their interest. On important occasions the need to struggle for them, and to organise on a popular basis, has been made plain, and, in truly extreme cases, so has even the legitimacy of popular insurrection against a cruel and permanent dictatorship, as in the case of Nicaragua.

What is important in all this is the understanding of the Church as a true sacrament of salvation and the introduction into salvation of those elements that the poor demand because of their very reality as salvation; the understanding of the Church's mission as true evangelisation and not just as the transmission of a teaching which may be followed by good works

Persecution

A Church made incarnate and evangelising in this way has been massively and cruelly persecuted in Central America. In this respect it reproduces in its life the following of Jesus interpreted as *fidelity to him in person even to the Cross*. The facts are known. More than thirty priests, religious and nuns, including an archbishop, Monsignor Romero, have been murdered; many others have been libelled, attacked, captured, tortured and expelled. A whole diocese in Guatemala had to be abandoned and Monsignor Gerardi, president of the Episcopal Conference, was expelled from the country. If this has happened in the green wood (Luke 23:31), one will understand what has happened to catechists, lay leaders and ministers of the Word, who are in the main peasants, workers and so on. Here the victims number thousands. This persecution has deep historical roots and, in that sense, is no more than the expression of a thorough-going incarnation, as has been said also of the Cross of Jesus. The Church is persecuted because it gets in the way and annoys. Very shortly after Medellín, the Rockefeller report warned against that type of Church, and affirmed that if it became a reality it would endanger the interests of the United States. The CIA also has encouraged that persecution as is testified by explicit documentation, for instance in the well-known case of Bolivia. President Reagan's advisers have renewed the attack on it in the Santa Fe document.

If opposition to the Church has been prepared from outside Central America, oligarchies, armed forces and local governments have done the same more overtly. The persecution of the Church is the response of the idols to a people that first and foremost wishes to be free. The persecution is just one expression of the more generalised repression, though qualitatively it is important and even decisive. The Church annoys because it deprives the *status quo* of authority and religious justification and because it sustains the hope of the poor, a fact which seems simple but which is explosive because the poor, once filled with hope and capable even of continuing cheerful, are not a defeated people. That is why there is persecution: to slow down and wipe out the processes of liberation. That is also why, in addition to clear and brutal persecution, the Church is attacked indirectly through the encouragement and financing of alienating sects and through the creation of new institutions, like the Institute for Religion and Democracy in Washington, designed to bring about a return to a liberal Christianity.

When the persecution is considered in Christian terms, one must affirm first of all that it expresses the full consequence of following Jesus. The Church is experiencing what happened to Jesus and for the same reasons: because it opts for and defends the poor, and does so against the powerful. Like Jesus it has been accused of religious blasphemy and political subversion, and the same conclusion has been reached in its case as in his: it is deserving of death. But that persecution proves the truth of this Church, which completes in its flesh what is lacking in the passion of Christ, and which is thereby becoming truly the body of Christ in history; a Church which is carrying out the act of greatest love, that of laying down its life for its friends, and which is in this way becoming holy.

Persecution restores the Church to its place before God. It must, first of all, assimilate its surprise that its persecutor is the Western, Christian world, and in the name of supposedly Christian values, all of which involves a very serious re-questioning of how God is understood. But at a deeper level persecution makes it participate in the loneliness of Jesus on the Cross, in his dying prayer, in his fidelity to God even when all that is heard is his silence. Here there is a profound experience of God, one that is scandalous in itself, but purifying. The Church, in the midst of the sighing and weeping of the high priest of Hebrews, is becoming faithful to God.

Resurrection

That crucified Church is also living the *resurrection* of Jesus. To live in this world like resurrected beings is simply to live in the circumstances of history with the Spirit of the Risen Jesus. This Jesus has appeared to it anew, bearing the wounds of the crucified One certainly, but also with the Spirit who gives life, recreates and makes all things new.

Within the Church that Spirit is revealing itself in an unprecedented creativity at the pastoral, liturgical, doctrinal and theological levels. That Spirit has united the Church and all the ranks within it, bishops and peasants, priests and intellectuals, nuns and workers. That Spirit has opened the Church to other confessions so that there exists a true ecumenism in action. The Spirit has given freedom, not primarily in its liberal sense of freedom-for-oneself, but freedom to interpret the gospel as spirit rather than as a letter that can be turned into doctrine, and from here stems the new, but profoundly faithful, understanding of the gospel. Freedom above all to love, to give and to give oneself out of love. It is the freedom of Paul who enslaves himself in order to serve all people and the freedom of Jesus whose life is taken by no one but laid down freely by himself.

The Spirit has given joy. In the midst of incarnation and persecution there has recurred the gospel paradox of joy and happiness. Good news can be greeted only with joy, and it is this important tautology that has been recovered. The gospel has become the precious pearl or the hidden treasure which, once found, can demand everything – the sale of everything – but which gives the deepest meaning to life and death. For this reason, as many observers have noted, the Christians of Central America are not sad people, but men and women of dignity, hope and joy; they are oppressed but not overwhelmed. If it is true that on their crosses they depict the One who was crucified, it is also true that present in them is the spirit of the One who rose from the dead. This resurrected Church relates to God in all fullness. It does not restrict itself to believing in and responding to the God of life, even though it begins by concentrating on this and henceforth maintains it as something central. It truly believes in God as a Father in whom one can trust and as an Utopia that draws one to itself and towards which one must journey. To believe in God the Father means resting in him and seeing in his fatherhood the ultimate model of Christian life: 'Be perfect as your heavenly father is perfect' (Mt 5, 48). To believe in God as Utopia means feeling called and moved to realise in history those Utopian realities that in history are so difficult to realise and reconcile: justice and freedom, struggle and peace, truth and reconciliation. In other words this Church believes in the fullness of God without on that account making relative something that goes on being fundamental to God's will, the life of the poor. With and towards God it journeys on through history. The root of that profound faith lies ultimately in the fact that the Church has passed through the trial of persecution and its faith is rooted literally in the blood of martyrs.

This is what is new, historically and theologically, in the Central American Church. If we had to sum it up in one word we would say that the gospel has been made Central American. Believers no longer need to borrow their identity as believers from something that is not Central American. The Gospel speaks to them directly. They accept and bless any mediation of the Gospel, even though it may come from outside; but what is deep no longer comes from outside, from Europe or North America, and it corresponds with what is most intimate within them. This new development is epochal in kind, and that is why the historical and the evangelical co-ordinate so well, why they refer to and empower each other instead of separating or becoming diminished. Because of it one can speak of a resurrection of the Church, of its re-invention from below (L. Boff), from Central America.

II. THE PROBLEMATIC AND FUTURE REALITY OF THE CENTRAL AMERICAN CHURCH

We have spoken so far of what is new in the Central American Church. This newness is a reality which makes the Church very different from what it was fifteen years ago, a Church whose existence cannot be denied. Even in places where it is not present, it is conspicuous by its absence, with the result that it has become a criterion at least for judging and classifying the various modes of being the Church. At the present moment there is a reaction against Medellín and the type of Church that we have described, and also a maturing of that Church. The question therefore arises: how real, in historical terms, is that Church, and what are other modes of being the Church? In order to classify them we shall choose two criteria that accord with the rise of the Church since Medellín: an historical criterion, their relationship to the historical reality of Central America, and a theological criterion, their constitution as a Church based among the poor.

The Historical Criterion

The historical criterion can only be justice for the popular masses. But since this affirmation is accepted by practically everybody it is of no great help. More helpful is the precise criterion of the struggle for justice in the particular movements of liberation and in the revolutions actually occurring in the area. This helps the task of classification because in the face of these realities people are, in practice, divided.

As has been well said by Ignacio Ellacuría, whose analysis we are following, there are, in the midst of injustice and repression and in the midst of revolutions, three stances: (i) 'anything rather than communism'; (ii) 'neither this nor that'; (iii) 'all risks necessary must be taken to end the situation of injustice and violence'.

(i) The first stance is not expressed very explicitly, even though in practice there is a tendency towards it in the odd bishop who turns up to bless counter-insurgency wars and in a few anti-Sandinista bishops in Nicaragua. The central thing is that communism is seen as intrinsically evil because materialist, atheistic and irreconcilably antagonistic to the Church. It is the theology of Reagan according to which it is better that a child should die of hunger than be deprived of its faith; a theology repeated by a Nicaraguan bishop. This stance entails the real death of the Church described earlier. It does not begin with, nor does it maintain as central, the cries of destitution and of hope; instead it begins with, and is guided by, an ideological prejudgement (or prejudice) by which it judges reality and relativises what since Medellín cannot be made relative.

(ii) The second stance is more usual and extends between wide limits. It does not want the present reality nor the revolutionary radicalism that might supervene. It does good and important things, defends human rights, and pastoral work of a social and humanitarian kind, denounces – ethically rather than prophetically – oppression and repression, permits the Church to take some risks and encourages or tolerates the base Christian communities so long as they do not involve an excessive politicisation or a great hazard for the Church. On the other hand it tends to be on good terms with governments and even armed forces in order to avoid greater evils, it supports the processes of formal democratisation in the hope that they may become a reality and not have to face the possibility of revolution being the only solution; and it supports reforms. It criticises revolutionary movements for what they do wrong, naturally enough; but also with a certain *a priori* inclination against them, though it recognises that in the cause for which they struggle there is a fair amount of justice. In practice, and notwithstanding the good things mentioned, it is rather inclined to refrain from questioning the democratic Western world and to be suspicious of revolutions.

(iii) The third stance is less common. It was coherently defended by Monsignor Romero, and is supported by many base Christian communities and those who work with them. The bishops of Nicaragua also defended it when legitimising the insurrection against Somoza, though one should not forget that his regime did not find in the Church a serious obstacle until the end. This Church does not please CELAM, nor the Vatican, nor the nunciatures. Its attitude towards revolutionary movements is not ingenuous; it does not approve of much of their ideology nor of all their activities, certainly not the terrorist ones. But it sees in them something more just than their adversary, and it also sees a need for many things they fight for to be introduced into society if this is to be just and viable for the poor. In El Salvador at the present time a negotiated settlement to the conflict is being sought, one that – at least in theory – would involve introducing a fair amount of what is radical in the revolution into the solution for the nation. This Church, again without ingenuousness, does not lay down as an absolute what might happen to the Church if the revolutions succeeded, even though this might result in a loss of privileges for it, or some limits to its mission. Its criterion for judging political and revolutionary processes is not its own self, the advantages or disadvantages it might find, but the good of the popular masses. And if it should have to pay a price, that would be all to the good and, in any case, a penitential contribution on the part of the Church, which so needs to pay this price for its past history.

Alongside its stance towards communism, there is the Church's view of violence on which it also usually divides. Of course, none of the types of Church desires and encourages violence on principle to the extremes of a war which in itself and directly spells destruction, death and dehumanisation. But violence and its causes are present and therefore cannot be ignored. In the face of this situation the most common stance is that 'violence is evil wherever it comes from'. None the less, the first type of Church seems to accept violence when it comes from governments and armies fighting against revolutions. This is so at the moment in the case of certain bishops in Nicaragua and of several other bishops in the region in the face of United States activities (militarisation of Honduras, support for armies in El Salvador and for the *contras* in Nicaragua) which are not condemned with an intensity that corresponds to the massive and destructive scale of the intervention.

The third type of Church is more considered and precise in its condemnation of violence. It does not merely repeat that violence is evil wherever it comes from, because in principle violence could become legitimate and above all because that routine repetition is of little use in pastoral orientation and can come to mask the truth. The first thing it does is, like Monsignor Romero, to classify, make a hierarchy of and hence judge the various types of violence. The first, the fundamental and the worst form of violence is structural injustice, truly 'institutionalised violence' in the words of Medellín. The second form is that which serves the first by violent acts: it is the repressive violence of armies, security corps and paramilitary groups. The third is the violence of response, on the part of liberation and revolutionary groups, when these commit acts of disproportionate violence and certainly when they practise terrorism. Alongside these forms of violence worthy of condemnation, and in the same order, it admits in principle the possibility of legitimate violence, in the form, for instance, of a popular uprising, based on the traditional teaching of the Church and with its conditions set out in *Populorum Progressio* and Medellín. This is what in practice was done in their day by the Nicaraguan bishops, and this was the teaching set forth by Monsignor Romero.

To choose as criteria for classification the various stances adopted towards revolutions and violence may cause surprise, but it is important because these realities do exist and divide people. It is also the historical, though tragic, way of showing whether the Church is incarnate in reality or distancing itself from reality subtly or crudely. In fact only a small part of the Church is facing those problems with courage and clarity.

It should be added that this part of the Church is trying to face those problems in a Christian way. It does not *a priori* bless revolutions nor (as more often happens) condemn them; instead it analyses them and tries to imbue any type of struggle with a Christian spirit, in the manner exemplified by Monsignor Romero. As far as revolution was concerned, Monsignor Romero emphasised positively the need for a radical and authentic change whose main agent would be the people. Hence his defence and encouragement (along with Monsignor Rivera) of the *organización popular* but always from a Christian point of view. His positive purpose in doing this was to ensure that the *organización popular* might be really at the service, and in the interests, of the popular masses, an expression of true love; his negative purpose was to help it overcome the temptations typical of those movements, such as disunity, self-projection, substitution of the people by their leaders, dogmatism, the reduction of everything to the organisation and the manipulation of the religious dimension.

As for the violence, he insisted that any change involves a real struggle which in theory could become even an armed struggle. But he always insisted on the use of peaceful means of struggle, he always proposed dialogue as the best way of resolving conflict and he condemned what he called the mysticism of violence. Above all he struggled and called on others to do everything possible and impossible to avoid having to reach the point of a legitimate insurrection.

In any case he insisted that Christians should imbue any political process with the Spirit: mercy in the presence of real suffering, not considering it merely as the price the people have to pay; strength in suffering and repression; a clear eye to see what the processes themselves are becoming, without deceiving oneself or others; respect for the peoples' consciousness, above all their religious consciousness; hope that draws sustenance not only from particular victories but from faith in God; a striving for reconciliation, for openness to forgiveness, as a way of avoiding closure of all future to one's adversary, without which no people can survive. This means making the processes human through the Christian spirit and also – to use a lamentable but unavoidable expression – humanising conflicts.

It is not central to the Church's calling to be an expert on revolutions or, even less, on violence. But to take a position, and an honest one, on these realities, which are inevitable, historically, in Central America and which really exist, gives credibility to what is central to the Church in its relations with the world: its own message of Christian liberation, its positive activities in favour of justice (defence of human rights, proposals for radical change, humanitarian work and so on) and in favour of peace (dialogue and reconciliation, the use of peaceful means), its criticism of what is limited and sinful in revolutions and of the mysticism of violence. A Church that remains firm with integrity in the face of these realities indicates truly that it is not concerned with itself but with a world that must be transformed in the direction of God's Kingdom; that it does not abdicate its nature as creature as if unaffected by what affects any human being; that it is not triumphalist either, as if it had precise answers for everything and did not have to become incarnate in all that is ambiguous in history.

The Theological Criterion

The theological criterion for classifying the Church is its stance towards what may be called the Church of the poor or popular Church. What this Church is, in positive and ideal terms, has already been set out in the first part above. However, that mode of being the Church is divisive. One cannot deny the newness of that Church, nor its cost. That Church is demanding, it knows persecution and martyrdom, it turns upside down the traditional good relations desired with governments and so on. Here is the basic problem, though there have been attempts to reinterpret it by making the popular Church a Church inspired by marxism and hostility to hierarchy. Without denying possible exaggerations, both accusations may be said to be fundamentally erroneous; they are excuses, rather than reasons, for outlawing it. The basic problem – apart from the demands it makes – is that this Church, because of its newness, produces an initial uncertainty and insecurity in the Church's internal organisation and pastoral work. To put it in graphic terms, it is not easy to 'know how' to be a bishop, priest, theologian and so on initially in a Church in which the poor are speaking for themselves.

Following the earlier classification we may say that the first group condemns the popular Church, as in the case of several bishops in Nicaragua, without even entering into dialogue with it, though admittedly it is true that in some Christians there is an excessive identification of Christian faith with the Sandinista movement. The second group supports the base Christian communities, as an important expression of the popular Church, so long as they keep a low political profile, or it tolerates them with greater or lesser tension. This is what happens practically throughout the region.

The third group retains the original intuition of Medellín concerning the popular Church, an intuition qualified but not denied at Puebla: 'a Church that seeks to become incarnate at the popular levels of the continent and that, in this respect, springs from the response of faith made to the Lord by those groups' (n. 263). Despite many problems associated with that Church and its limitations and sins, the communities are considered to be a gift of God to the Church, energisers of its pastoral work, its liturgy and its theology, places of apprenticeship in important Christian values, examples of commitment and generosity.

These two criteria adopted here to classify the various modes of being the Church are connected. Both the historical criterion and the theological one presuppose either a real incarnation in society or a subtle evasion of it. What must be stressed is that the Church of the poor is in principle the correct response to the real world of Central America, the one that preserves what is just in revolutions, and the one that tends to heal what is limited and sinful in them. It is not surprising therefore that in general the same Christian groups are to be found in both classifications, whether the criterion be historical or theological.

The Future

The Church of the poor, which we began by presenting in ideal terms and which is represented historically by the third group, is the most novel by comparison with past history, and large enough to be spoken of not as a mere passing incident but as an ecclesial and social reality. Nevertheless, it is small by comparison with other modes of being the Church. But this smallness must be understood properly. It is not a closed 'sect' nor a 'diaspora' (as Rahner prophesised the Church would be in a European world gripped by galloping secularisation), but a 'leaven', that is, it is small but incarnate in the totality of the Church and fermenting all of it. Viewed historically it is the place in which the Church is not simply alive or surviving but growing; it is in other words the future of a Church that would wish to go on being Central American and to respond to the reality of Central America.

One foresees that this ecclesial future will be influenced by two powerful and conflicting movements. On the one hand a conservative reaction and on the other the maturing of the Church of the poor.

The Central American Church is involved in the conservative reaction of the Church in Latin America and throughout the world. Considered as a whole it is not living through the shining moments of Vatican II and Medellín, but is tending instead towards restoration. Clear signs of this reaction are (i) the search for administrative safety starting with episcopal conferences that give the impression of being united even though this may involve concealing strong differences among their members, and of being more authoritarian than before, without the previous dialogue with the grass-roots of the Church; (ii) the selection of bishops from the first and second groups, a clear example being the recent award of a cardinal's hat to Monsignor Obando; (iii) doctrinal safety in the training of seminarians, even though this may mean extremely impoverished academic and pastoral formation, as in the case of seminarians in El Salvador and Nicaragua; (iv) attacks on, or ignorance about, liberation theology among almost all members of the hierarchy, even though Monsignor Rivera has defended publicly the liberation theology being elaborated in El Salvador; (v) the tendency in episcopal statements towards pure orthodoxy or towards a purely ethical analysis, without the earlier prophetic voice of Monsignor Romero and, to a greater or lesser degree, without a praxis that corresponds to the magnitude and urgency of the evils being denounced; (vi) an exaggerated ecclesial triumphalism when judging the problems and dangers in the region, condemning on principle every evil and every evil person, without the Church recognising its own involvement in what is wrong through what it has done or failed to do; (vii) an excessive influence of ideology on judgements about historical reality so that in the last resort the Western world might not be endangered; (viii) finally, and by way of generalisation, an impoverished pastoral leadership and an impoverished development of pastoral strategy, in favour of more traditional and less controversial forms of pastoral action.

In the face of this reaction, the Church of the poor, the base Christian communities and those who work with them insist that the revolution of Medellín, or at least that of Puebla, must be maintained, even though they have become more realistic and realise that situations change, and even though they have reflected also on themselves and see the need for maturation. Important signs of the continuing life and maturing of the Church of the poor are: (i) the preferential option for the poor, at least on the level of formal statement, an irreversible gain not to be scorned; (ii) self-criticism by the Church of the poor, which is striving (successfully) to ferment the personal and transcendent values of faith, and to connect them with liberation; (iii) greater autonomy of the communities in relation to popular movements, not in order to dissociate themselves from them, but in order to empower them with what is specific to the faith; (iv) the development of an authentic spirituality, evangelical, historical and popular, in which there is emphasis on following Jesus, and on the spirit in which this should be done, on working for God's Kingdom and on faith and confidence in the Father of Jesus, on prophesying within the Church and on loyalty to it; (v) the maturing also of liberation theology which has, in Central America, been a force behind liberation processes, but which is now drawing increasingly for its theology on the real faith of the communities and accompanying the process in all its vicissitudes; (vi) the renewed importance given to large-scale popular piety, respecting its rhythms and refraining from imposing anything on it prematurely; (vii) lastly, the very fact that this Church is continuing forward despite all its difficulties both external (attacks from within and outside the Church) and internal (its own limitations and sins), which indicates that its faith, its hope and its charity are profound.

What the future holds for the Central American Church, held in tension between reaction and fidelity to Medellín, has yet to be seen. But for the moment it must be affirmed that the Church of the poor has a consistency of its own which enables one to speak of its future, all the more so since it has endured the most difficult trial, namely itself: the overcoming of its own limitation as the creature that it is. Unlike in the times of Vatican II, the direction of the Church is not being imposed or simply given from above (hierarchy and theology), but is now also rising up from below; it is rising up as an objective reality, not as leadership that has been sought after or – even less – that is individualistic. The movement of reaction is being opposed, in other words, objectively by a new force that is fundamentally nothing other than the Gospel rooted among the poor.

The Church of the poor therefore has a future in Central America. We should wish to add that such a Church is not only possible but necessary. It is necessary, in the first place, for the reality of Central America. Before the Church had made an option for the poor, they had already opted for the Church. The Church is able, and in some cases it alone is able, to give hope and direction to their journey towards liberation. When one considers the future of Central America, the interminable years of war in El Salvador, the destitution and extermination of indigenous peoples in Guatemala, the attempt to suffocate Nicaragua (that is, three million human beings), the militarisation of Honduras, its loss of sovereignty and its perennial poverty, then the Church must act as the sacrament of salvation and this it can do only as the Church of the poor.

But that type of Church is a necessity too for the future of the Church itself. From a Christian point of view, that Church is the structural context in which the gospel can go on being read with the eyes of the poor, that is, read simply, and not be ransomed again by the powerful or watered down in the Church of a Christendom in which the gospel is preserved in terms of culture and ambience but no longer has much connection with the good news of Jesus, his denunciations and his demands. It is necessary to avoid what is happening abundantly and regrettably in various places in the first world: the perception only of God's silence or of the anger with which he reveals himself against those who imprison truth in injustice. With all its limitations it is the Church of the poor that maintains the presence in history of the gospel and of God.

But in addition a Church of the poor is the Church that will preserve sufficient credibility to go on being active and influential in society in the future. As Monsignor Romero used to say, changes will occur with the Church or without it. But when they do occur, it will be asked what the Church did to favour them. In this matter the Church must be clear and not confuse short term triumphs and advantages with the battle of future centuries. The alienation from the Church, the indifference towards it – more harmful even than attacks on it – the decline of the faith in so many parts of the first world should put the Central American Church on its guard. The latter must ask itself if the best way to avoid something similar happening here (the loss of intellectuals, of the working class, of social movements and even of part of the middle class in Europe) is to aim at a Christian order and ethos that has the necessary support of, or at least normal relations with, the powers of this world, or to continue along the evangelical path proposed by Medellín. A Church of the poor that would accompany them in their sufferings and hopes, in their liberation movements, with all the reservations necessary but also with encouragement and Christian criticism, that would commit itself to them and lay down its life for them, is what, in human terms, guarantees the Church's future for a long time, and perhaps even its freedom and its survival, but in any case it is what guarantees that the Church will be the Church of Jesus.

7 Liberation and New Creation: A Theological Conversation

Enda McDonagh

I. THE INNOVATIVE IMPACT OF LATIN-AMERICAN LIBERATION THEOLOGY

In theology as in other disciplines important changes in method and subject-matter occur from time to time. Sometimes these changes prove to be no more than transient fashions: 'Death-of-God' theology in the late 1960s appears now to belong to that category. Its exact contemporary, just developing in Latin America at that time and subsequently known as liberation theology, has proved to have much greater staying power and much greater impact on Christian theology beyond the geographical and cultural confines of its origins. Indeed it has become the major theological influence throughout the Christian world over the last two decades. And that influence is undoubtedly due to the theological profundity as well as the social relevance of the original intuition which discovered in this traditional Christian word and metaphor the key to so much that Christianity might offer to the fearful, struggling people of our time. This chapter seeks to review sympathetically yet critically some of the major achievements of that paradigm shift in Christian theology, to link it with another potentially transforming Christian metaphor, that of 'New Creation', and to relate both to the first world, European and Irish location of the author.

While liberation theology is now used to describe theological activity far beyond the boundaries of Latin America and its poor, the original, classical (if it is not premature to invoke the term) and still normative form of liberation theology is considered to be that of Latin American theologians. Gustavo Gutiérrez, Juan Luis Segundo, Jon Sobrino, Rubén Alves *et al.* provide the standard reference points for developments from Africa and Asia as well as important resources for theologies of black liberation in the USA and women's liberation in the western and wider world. The plurality of Latin American theologians instanced (and the list could and should be much extended) suggests a plurality of theologies. There is a rich diversity in Latin American theology of liberation so that one might even speak of liberation theologies, but they belong to a single recognisable family. This family coherence permits the reviewer to survey some of the major creative influences of liberation theologies without the necessity of detailing some interesting and indeed significant differences between Gutiérrez, Segundo and Boff, for example.

II. A NEW ROOT METAPHOR

Paradigm shifts in science such as the one from classical physics to quantum theory are finally expressed in symbolic language, the symbolic language of master equations and, for physicists, the very secondary but still inevitable symbolic language of particles and waves. In theology the use of symbols appears more obvious and, from the physicist's perspective, less controllable. However, the 'hard' sciences are at present experiencing a certain modesty-shock about the nature and precision of their own symbolic language. Paradigm shifts tend eventually to relativise the new as well as the old. Theologians whose symbolic language focuses on the interactions between God and humanity or between God and cosmos, rather than simply cosmic interactions, have had a variety of symbols available to them from the Jewish and Christian traditions. Like other scientists, theologians have not always adverted to the symbolic and metaphorical character of their basic language. Again it is only with the change of paradigm or root metaphor (to invoke another metaphorical description) that the symbolic nature of all theological language is exposed anew with its limitations and its possibilities. To describe the language of theology as symbolic is of course to advert to its limitations, inevitable in any attempt to describe the ultimately mysterious, but it is also to underline its possibilities as the ultimately mysterious seeks human modes of expression. It is perhaps natural to dwell on the limitations of the earlier metaphors, symbols and paradigms and on the possibilities of the new. It is however foolish, even with the more cumulative nature of the hard sciences, to ignore the truth-achievements of former symbols and paradigms or the necessary limitations of their successors. Theology, in both its 'wisdom' and 'way' forms, like philosophy and politics and unlike the physical sciences, cannot claim such a clearly cumulative history. Can one argue that Karl Barth and Karl Rahner superseded Augustine and Aquinas as one might argue that Einstein has superseded Newton? Beyond that, Christian theology focuses on particular foundational people, events and experiences, in Israel and Jesus, to which it must continually return. These people, events and experiences provide the basic account of the interaction of God with humanity and cosmos and the basic words and symbols to describe it. Paradigm shifts in theology are undoubtedly influenced by the contemporary context but they draw on the normative accounts and originating metaphors of Israel and Jesus.

In the period prior to and including Vatican II, Catholic theologians, frequently influenced by their Protestant colleagues (for example, Oscar Cullmann and various predecessors) acquired a new consciousness of the historical dimension of God's interaction with the world. And this interaction was seen in predominantly healing or salvific terms. Salvation, salvation-history or history of salvation became the dominant image or root metaphor in theological discussion, replacing the earlier dominant language of redemption. Both of course were drawn from the biblical accounts of Israel and Jesus and had been extensively used separately and together at various times in the history of Church and theology. The emphasis on the historical and on the 'healing' of salvation as against the 'buying-back' of redemption fitted the academic and social contexts of the Church and theology at least in Europe and the first world in the 1960s. And the richness of language and symbol yielded very significant results in so many of the documents of Vatican II, including those on the Church, on revelation, on religious liberty, on ecumenism and on the Church in the modern world. The historical healing which the salvation-history paradigm emphasised enabled the Catholic Church to reach out in joy and hope (*Gaudium et Spes*) to all people of good will, to other churches and religions, to the aspirations and needs of contemporary humanity. God's interaction with humanity and cosmos was interpreted in a positive and hopeful manner as leading to the progressive healing and transformation of humanity. This also was the time of Kennedy's New Frontier, of the Alliance for Progress with Latin America, of the exploration of space leading to the first human being on the moon and of so many other positive achievements and aspirations. History and salvation seemed to be marching firmly in step.

The promoters of Vatican II in Latin America encountered a rather different reality. The Alliance for Progress had made little impact on the poverty and oppression of the masses expected to respond to the hopeful and joyful message of the Council documents. Healing or salvation seemed a very inadequate symbol to meet the needs of the millions oppressed and enslaved both economically and politically. Harking back to God's intervention in bringing his people out of the slavery of Egypt (Exodus), to Jesus' own programme as announced in the synagogue at Nazareth (Luke 4; Is 61) and to Paul's interpretation of the Jesus event as a setting free (Galatians and elsewhere), Latin American theologists settled on the great biblical metaphor of liberation as the basis for their reflection and activity.

It was of course, as in Exodus, Luke and Paul, to be a liberation in history and not only beyond history. The historical emphasis so recently and effectively recovered would join the liberation metaphor in seeking to explore the meaning of God's activity among the poor and oppressed of Latin America.

III. MATTER AND METHOD OF LIBERATION THEOLOGY

The new root metaphor of liberation arose out of the particular challenge posed by the actual conditions of Latin America to the message and resources of the gospel, of the histories of Israel and Jesus. The fuller configuration of the metaphor and its developed theological usage require more detailed analysis. Unlike physics where a single equation or series of equations in the powerfully symbolic language of mathematics focuses the new paradigm, theology and its paradigms are continuously on the move between foundational Jewish and Christian experience (with events and people) and the contemporary experience of the theologians, seeking to question, interpret and illuminate the one by the other. This movement and the more precise description of its poles help identify more exactly the basic features of liberation theology without of course ever reaching for the concentration and precision of $E = mc^2$. Divine-human interaction is not translatable into such symbolic language.

Theology as a study of divine-human interaction focuses, in liberation theology, on the socially human, the human being in society as distinct from the human being as individual.

Even the historically conscious salvation theology of Vatican II was still strongly individualist in character. It was no longer simply the salvation of souls but of persons in their historical as well as their eschatological existence but it remained heavily individualist in line with the personalist and liberal presuppositions of the Council. With liberation theology and its European contemporary, political theology, the salvation of society as against that of the individual person was emphasised. The history of salvation yielded to the salvation of history. In biblical terms this involved fresh attention to the great social image of the Kingdom. Parallel to the developments in physics it emphasised the necessity of field-theory as opposed to particle-theory. The interrelation between Jewish-Christian foundations and the contemporary Latin American situation moved Christians to recognise liberation in society in history as the immediate expression of God's action in the world. Exodus became a biblical and theological paradigm once again.

The theological turn from person to society, from salvation to liberation could not and did not ignore the continuing significance of the person, although it may have obscured it for some people. Critics of liberation theology have stressed this obscuring, although defenders might fairly respond that the obscuring of the social in earlier theologies was much more serious and that the necessary historical balance could be achieved only by strongly emphasising humanity's social existence.

Salvation of the person by grace, by God's spontaneous activity, had always required attention to the complex composition of the person, to some psychological analysis. Paul provides many early examples of this psychological theologising. Augustine proved original and masterful as he extended his own self-analysis, which reached its climax in *The Confessions*, through a thicket of theological problems dealing with grace and human salvation to his reflexions on the inner life of Godself in *De Trinitate*. Aquinas and Bonaventure, in their objective and subjective ways, employed all the resources of psychology available to them. In the twentieth century psychological developments particularly from the psycho-analytic tradition have influenced the theologies of sin and conversion, sexuality and marriage, power and weakness, dying and grieving. And from Paul to the theologians indebted to Freud and Jung, conflict within the person has been a particular concern as manifesting the focus of God's saving activity, the struggle between good and evil, between grace and sin and the role of God-given yet utterly human freedom in that struggle.

Liberation and other social theologies have followed, consciously or unconsciously, this pattern of analysis and reflexion. For them the analysis has naturally been analysis of society, social analysis. They have sought with the aid of various developments in social analysis, including marxist analysis, to understand the conflict within society between grace and sin, between good and evil, between powerful and powerless, between oppressor and oppressed. They have observed how far the God-given freedom of all has been operating and how far that freedom has been restricted or eliminated for some by the political and economic power of others. In social terms the graceful action of God has been seen to be directed to the restoration of freedom to those restricted and deprived. God's social concern is the liberation of the oppressed. God's call to humanity in Jesus Christ is a call to liberating activity, in particular to Christians to enter freely into the liberating process whereby all are set free from contemporary enslavements, whether political, economic, racial, sexual or other. The social concerns of theology demand new methods, social analysis and engagement with the liberation of the oppressed.

Critical reaction to the use of social analysis has ignored the strong tradition of personal analysis in theology and implicit analysis of society. Paul in his letter to the Romans, Augustine more explicitly and self-consciously in *The City of God*, and Vatican II in *The Church in the Modern World*, offer striking examples of attempts to understand the social context of the gospel. More detailed criticism focuses on the use of marxist tools of analysis and on the emphasis given to conflict in society. The diversity of liberation theologians prevents any complete consideration of such criticism here. The more influential authors, Gutiérrez, Segundo and Boff, adapt the marxist tradition of analysis in ways that escape any suggestion of materialist determinism. Their exposure of the conflict on economic and other grounds is simply a revealing of reality, of sinful reality in need of God's liberating and transforming grace. While the economic basis of the conflict is stressed it is not used in a simply reductionist and exclusivist way. However, sympathetic readers of liberation theology might sometimes wish for greater attention to sources of oppression other than economic, despite the latter's immediate and urgent significance in Latin America and indeed other countries in the third and first worlds.

The engagement in the struggle for liberation, against the sins of oppression which are structured into society, is in this context the answer to a divine call to follow Jesus in caring for the poor, the excluded and the oppressed. This is the response of faith, the loving, practical faith, perhaps better described as the trinity faith-hope-love.

Theology as faith(-hope-love) seeking understanding, in the hallowed definition of Anselm, derives from this faith-hope-love of practical engagement in the struggle. The primacy of such engagement, of praxis, is in reality the primacy of a living and loving and hoping faith, the authentic Christian response to the call to discipleship in the context of oppression. In such faith, recognition and engagement go hand in hand. Theory and praxis in their basic sense belong together. Orthopraxis and orthodoxy are two sides of the same coin of tribute to God. Opposition between praxis and theory, or between orthopraxis and orthodoxy, or the primacy of one over the other, which are sometimes asserted by advocates and critics of liberation theology, cannot be maintained in principle. In actual situations, primary attention to one or the other may be required. In the contemporary Church and world the restoration of balance would suggest far more attention to orthopraxis.

IV. LOCATING THEOLOGIANS AND PARTICULAR THEOLOGIES

The new modesty of the hard scientists such as physicists, in so far as it exists, derives from their involvement with the process they wish to observe. They can no longer see themselves as detached observers, examining from the outside some physical event. The very activity of observation, their activity, is part of the event. They belong within as participants and not just outside as observers. Theologians, as the physicists' one-time predecessors in the claim to serve the queen of the sciences (and in the associated risks of arrogance), have also much to be modest about including their involvement with that which they would observe and analyse. The social location of theologians, in first, second or third worlds, with the privileged or the deprived, makes them much more clearly participants in the historical and social events of which they would give an account. Their claim to detached observer status and to its kind of objectivity, is even less valid for theologians than for physicists, as it indeed is for the practitioners of all the human as distinct from the physical sciences. Participation-free theology, like value-free social analysis, is a myth which liberation theologians have fully exposed.

Awareness of social location does not of course invalidate the theological enterprise, although it does relativise it. Such awareness also strengthens theology, enabling it to attend to the larger truth of the theologians' participation in the process under analysis, with their cultural presuppositions and economic and political pre-engagements. It permits theologians to decide consciously on their engagement, rather than operate unconsciously out of it. It allows theologians to recognise the side of the social divide to which they belong, and to change sides if necessary. It allows and requires purification of faith in the following of Jesus.

Such locating of theologians in social structure but also in time and place and culture reveals the contextual and thus particular character of all theology. Theology was always particular to time and place. The universal character of the Christian Church demanded a certain universality of theology also, evidently based on the universal claims and significance of the Christ-event. But that universality was not intended to be uniformity, as the particular theologies of Mark and Paul and John clearly attest. Communication and communion between the early and particular Churches as well as the call to communicate with the wider non-Christian world was the way to a universality which respected particularity. Where that universality lapsed into imperialism the particularity was ignored or suppressed. Recent European theologies have sometimes yielded to the temptations to imperialism. Within the Roman Catholic tradition Latin American liberation theology has proved a powerful challenge and check to that. It would be sadly ironic if its restoration of the particular should lead to imperialist claims to be the only way of doing theology in the wider world. At present that is not a real danger. The many fresh insights of Latin American theology may stimulate new theological visions around the world without indulging in (self-contradictory) imperialist claims.

V. FROM LIBERATION TO NEW CREATION

No particular symbol as paradigm, however well-rooted in biblical and Christian tradition, can comprehend the range and depth of the divine activity in the world. Liberation, with its indisputable biblical credentials, has proved more fruitful than many other symbol-paradigms. Its translation from its Latin American economic origins to other third-world countries and its adaptation to first-world oppressions based on race and gender offers further testimony of its rich potential. African and Asian theologies together with black and feminist theologies in North America and Europe belong to the same liberation family and have been greatly influenced by developments in Latin America. Of course, North America and Europe have their own internal economic oppressions, heavily qualified by race and gender – the 'poor black woman' may symbolise the furthest reach of oppression the world over. Within the first world then, theology must take account of economic privation as well as race and gender.

In Ireland, for example, this applies urgently to the growing numbers of unemployed and of emigrants. This is in addition to theology's responsibility to confront the first world with its exploitation of the third world. More sophisticated analysis of first world-third world relations and Christian engagement on the side of the oppressed are the preconditions for first-world theologians as they set about reflecting on their faith-hope-love.

What is envisaged here is a planet-wide movement for the transformation of human relationships from privilege and exploitation by the few into a community of freedom, justice and solidarity. These basic Kingdom values of Israel and Jesus, given such powerful secular expression in many democratic and social developments of our time, are still far from realisation in first, second or third worlds. In the struggle for the realisation of these values many people and movements, secular and religious converge. Christians and their theologians have the responsibility to engage in this struggle as some partial realisation of that inbreaking Kingdom or reign of God, while continually lifting their eyes and those of their colleagues in the struggle, to the further horizons of history and eschatology. The faith-hope-love which keeps awareness of and commitment to the inbreaking, graceful and liberating God is essential to human fulfilment and at times to authentic human survival. All this applies to western theologians no less than to southern and Latin American.

The politico-economic thrust of liberation and liberation theologies is clear and essential to the present condition of humanity. It expresses well the justice and freedom, the human-rights aspirations of so many people, where these rights are not understood in some narrow, individualist fashion but taken to include social and economic rights. Solidarity (in earlier language, fraternity) and peace, with the implied reconciliation of divided and hostile peoples, are no less essential to the transformation of human relationships sought in history and beyond. Peace movements throughout the first and second worlds, for example, emphasise an aspect of human fulfilment and Christian promise which may seem remote, distracting or deliberately intended to maintain the oppressive status quo in Latin

America and other third-world situations. To say that justice and freedom must come first is not necessarily to opt for violent opposition to present oppression with its inherent violence. It may be to refuse to opt for a cheap reconciliation that permits the destruction and oppression to continue. Genuine reconciliation must be based on equality, on justice. It will involve, as Gandhi, that great promoter of it, realised, mutual emancipation, the emancipation of the oppressor as well as of the oppressed. However, such emancipation depends first of all on the resistance of the oppressed. For Gandhi this should be non-violent, but it should be persisting and developing resistance to the point where it effectively displaces the oppressors and creates new relationships of mutual respect and equality. For very many oppressed groups, religious minorities in Eastern Europe or in many Islamic countries today, racial minorities and women, such Gandhian resistance is the only practical way. In other instances where the oppressed are a majority it would seem the more appropriate Christian way. However, the choice can be authentically made only by those within the oppressive situation and committed to changing it.

Where all this is leading in conflict situations as small and as intense as Northern Ireland or as large as South Africa or as diffuse as economic relations between first-world and third-world countries, is towards a transformation of people and structures, towards what Paul, picking up on Genesis, called New Creation. As a comprehensive symbol in confronting the chaos of human society with divine and human creativity, it offers an important complement to the symbol/paradigm of liberation with its sharper political connotations.

The large sweep of Christian and human concern for the planet earth as well as for its peoples, which has surfaced in the environmental/ecological/green movements, may no longer be regarded as the preserve of some wealthy and eccentric elite. Chernobyl alone convinced many people of the close connexion between human survival and care for the earth. Economic exploitation of people and rape of the earth's resources are very closely connected, as the destruction of the rain forests in Brazil underlines. Care for one another, for all living things, animal and plant, for the physical resources of the earth, its air and water, its energy, all belong together in our creative or co-creative responsibility. In face of historical destructiveness towards one another and the planet, the new responsibility can in Christian terms be undertaken in hope based on divine promise and achievement of new creation in Jesus

Christ. While the slow, often powerful, struggles for personal and social liberation continue they may be fitted into that broader vision of a new heaven and a new earth which the ever-new creativity of our God offers to us and seeks to achieve with us. From liberation to new creation is the way which the followers of Jesus must take not simply for themselves but, after Jesus' own example, for all.

Part Three
Politics and the Gospel in Central America

8 God and Man in Nicaragua

Conor Cruise O'Brien

God is central to the current public debate in Nicaragua, and both sides constantly invoke His name. On all the main roads, near the larger centres of population, there are huge printed posters reading simply:

PARA NOSOTROS NO HAY
MÁS QUE UN SOLO DIOS
1 Corinthians, 8, 6.

'For us there is no more than one single God'. But someone has been going round adding to each poster, in large manuscript, after 'DIOS', the words:

. . . EL DIOS DE LOS POBRES!!

The 'one single God', without further qualification, is the God of the Nicaraguan Catholic hierarchy, led by Cardinal Miguel Obando y Bravo, Archbishop of Managua. And this is also the God of Nicaragua's middle-class opposition, all of which – including Protestant oppositionists – looks to the Cardinal as its political leader. The posters are assumed to be funded by the Cardinal's North American friends.

'The God of the Poor' is the God of the governing Frente Sandinista de Liberación Nacional, of the three (formerly four) Catholic priests who are members of the government – in defiance of the hierarchy and of the Pope – and of the many Catholic (and some Protestant) clergy and lay men and women, Nicaraguan and non-Nicaraguan, who have worked among the Nicaraguan poor, and who see the Sandinista Government as generally promoting the interests of the poor.

Both sides are deeply in earnest, with passions that approximate to those of civil war. Indeed they are very closely related to the civil war now being waged, with outside support, in many parts of Nicaragua.

The Cardinal's public position on the war has been identical, in essentials, to that of President Reagan. Like the President, the Cardinal calls for immediate negotiations between the Sandinista government and the American-backed *contras*. In adopting this position, the Cardinal sees himself as doing his duty as a Christian leader, seeking peace, *la paz*. The Sandinistas, on the other hand, believe that they are the ones who are seeking peace, through negotiations between the two sovereign governments concerned, the United States and Nicaragua. The Sandinistas see *la paz* as withheld by the United States' refusal of direct negotiations, and by its humiliating insistence that, instead, the Nicaraguan government must negotiate with the *contras*, the paid paramilitary agents of the United States.

It follows that the Sandinistas regard the Cardinal as promoting war, not peace, and helping the cause of Nicaragua's enemies.

The Cardinal genuinely does not see the issue in this light, but the light he does see it in does not tend to make relations with the government look any better. The Cardinal has consistently refused to condemn *contra* atrocities. Asked why, he adopts an agnostic position. He has read allegations about such things, in the government press, he says, but, as he knows a lot of things the government press says are not true, he cannot comment. (*Newsweek* interview with Joseph Contrera: 18 November 1985.) This hardly holds water. The Catholic clergy, anywhere in a Catholic country, are in a position to provide their bishops with a very good national news service; they do not have to be dependent on a government-controlled press. And the *contra* campaign of terror against peasants in northern Nicaragua is notorious; so much so indeed that President Reagan, at one point, was driven to claim that the Sandinistas were in the habit of dressing up as *contras*, in order to commit atrocities, to discredit the *contras*.

The Cardinal's claim not to know did not go down well with some, even, of his senior clergy, in the exposed areas. 'Tell him to come to my parish' said one of these, 'and help me bury the dead'.

It is not, however, just a question of not wishing to know what the *contras* may have done. It is a question of signalling support for the *contras*. After receiving his Cardinal's hat from the Pope in May 1985, and before returning to Nicaragua, the new Cardinal said Mass in Miami: a Mass attended by the *contra* leadership and by the photographers. *Contra* leaders Adolfo Portocarrero and Edén Pastora were prominent in the audience at the Mass. 'I do not object to being identified with the people who have taken up arms', he commented after the ceremony.

In Miami, with a confidence enhanced by the new and signal mark of the Pope's approval, the new Cardinal went a step further than he had ever gone, while he was no more than an Archbishop. But it was a step in the direction in which he – and following him the Nicaraguan hierarchy – had been moving for more than five years; initially hesitantly, but openly and with conviction from 1983 on. The Pope's visit to Nicaragua came on 4 March of that year. I shall come back to that event, momentous in the history, not merely of Nicaragua and Central America, but of Latin America as a whole and of the Catholic Church. It is enough for the present to say that, in its immediate impact, the visit was a disaster for the Sandinistas, and that it fortified the position of Archbishop Obando and his supporters, at least for a time.

Later in that year, the Sandinista government, under growing pressure from the Reagan Administration's efforts to destabilise it, introduced compulsory military service: Servicio Militar Patriótico (SMP). The response of the Nicaraguan Episcopal Conference, in a document called 'General Considerations on Military Service', was to call in question the legitimacy of the Nicaraguan State itself, in its existing form, and to legitimise rejection of its authority, specifically in the form of refusal of military service. (Implicit legitimation of an opposing form of military service was left to later, in Miami.)

La Prensa, on 1 September 1983, published the bishops' explosive challenge under the appropriate title 'Nobody can be obliged to take up arms for a party'. The bishops said, among other things:

> The absolute dictatorship of a political party, which is constituted by force as the only arbiter and owner of the state, its institutions and every type of social activity, poses the problem of its legitimacy as well as the legitimacy of its institutions, including the army. . . . It is not correct to mix, confuse or identify the concepts of fatherland, state, revolution, and *Sandinismo* . . . . The attitude towards this Bill, for all those who do not share the Sandinista Party ideology, has to be that of 'conscientious objection' and no-one should be punished, persecuted, or discriminated against for adopting this position.

The document ends with the words 'May the Virgin Mary, Queen of Peace, help us to live according to charity so that this Holy Year of Reconciliation may produce in each of us and our society sincere fruits of justice, love and peace'.

The document embodying the general considerations on military service of the Nicaraguan Episcopal Conference is something of a curiosity in the history of the post-Reformation Church. Medieval Popes, and Counter-Reformation Popes, de-legitimised princes, and then sought to depose them, with considerable abandon. But in more recent times – and especially in the twentieth century – the instruction to 'Render unto Caesar the things that are Caesar's' has not generally been interpreted as including an obligation to verify the credentials of each particular Caesar. In Latin America, in particular, the Church has generally felt no need to challenge 'absolute dictatorships' of the right, or to insist on that blood-fraught revolutionary (or counter-revolutionary) distinction between 'the regime' and 'the State'. But in little Nicaragua, as out of one of its volcanoes, the old Hildebrandine fires erupted, with the assertion of the right and duty of the Church to pronounce on the legitimacy of princes, and to prepare their deposition. As in the other parts of the world, in the closing years of the twentieth century, the notion of Holy War is showing that it has not yet lost all its power to intoxicate and to inflame.

It is fair to note at this point that, in the last five years of the Somoza dictatorship (1974–79), Archbishop Obando and the rest of the Nicaraguan hierarchy were increasingly critical of the regime, and strongly so in the dictator's last year. After the fall of the dictator, the Frente Sandinista – in words which it was later to regret – acknowledged the significant role which the bishops, 'especially Monsignor Obando y Bravo', had played in the revolution, in that they had 'valiantly denounced the crimes and abuses of the dictatorship'. But until 1978–79 – when Somoza was visibly collapsing and bereft of American support – the Archbishop never seems to have attacked him in the fundamental way in which he has attacked the Sandinista regime, or with the same accents of Holy War. To denounce abuses of power is not as radical as to deny the legitimacy of power.

But it is not *really* Holy War, most of the Cardinal's opponents claim. The 'General Considerations' are only formally a doctrinal document; they are in reality a political document, dictated by the social conservatism of the Cardinal and some of his colleagues, and by their desire to help to bring about the restoration of the old order (minus Somoza) under the benign hegemony of the United States. There is certainly some truth in that view of the matter, but it can be exaggerated, and sometimes is. Thus the Sandinista newspaper, *Barricada*, likes to depict the Cardinal as a puppet, manipulated by Ronald Reagan. This is not credible. It is impossible to watch the

Cardinal, or listen to him for an hour or so, without being aware that, whatever else may be said about the man, he does not belong to the order of puppets.

On the first Sunday of our stay in Nicaragua, my wife and I went to the little Church of San Domingo de las Sierritas, near Managua, to hear the Cardinal say Mass, and preach. San Domingo is a pretty little church, high and cool. It lies in a relatively affluent area, and the congregation was a middle-class one. There were also several television crews: the Cardinal is always news. We followed the crews into the sacristy, where the Cardinal was christening a baby, and being filmed. I thought an elderly nun, beside the Cardinal, looked a bit tight-lipped about the publicity – distracting from the sacrament – but the Cardinal had clearly given permission. International publicity, after all, is part of his armoury in his struggle against the Sandinistas and their allies.

After the christening, we all went back into the church. By mistake, my wife and I took the places intended for the parents of the christened baby, beside the grandparents. Nobody even murmured. Nicaraguans are an usually gentle people, in most contexts. The Cardinal is something of an exception. Even when saying Mass, he seemed that morning to be spoiling for a fight. As he put on his vestments, I thought he looked like a boxer getting ready for the ring. He is a small, powerfully built man, now running to fat; markedly Indian features – more so than most of his congregation; bullet head, thick neck, heavy jaw. His most marked expressive characteristic – perhaps especially marked that day – is that the corners of his lips turn sharply down. As he sat at the altar, while lessons were being read, the tips of his short fingers, joined in prayer, crossed the line of his mouth. My notes carry the hieroglyph:

That the Cardinal was cross was obvious; that he was cross with the Sandinistas and their allies was also obvious. I think now that he had other, stronger reasons for being cross, though I did not guess at them at the time.

The Cardinal read out, in a firm, strong, clear voice a letter of the Nicaraguan episcopate on 'The Eucharist, Source of Unity of Inspiration', dated 6 April 1986. It was a well-written statement, in a high Castilian style, with classical overtones: 'They blame the Church for silence, while they silence it . . . .' It contained a long passage – which the Cardinal read out with especial resonance – attacking what the Cardinal and his followers call 'the popular Church' (*iglesia popular*) meaning those who regard themselves as followers of *el Dios de los*

Pobres (who retort with the phrase '*iglesia institucional*', applied to people like the Cardinal and his supporters). The attack on the *iglesia popular* began with the words:

> A belligerent group of priests, religious, nuns and lay people, insisting that they belong to the Catholic Church, in reality, by their acts, works actively in undermining the unity of the same Church, collaborating in the destruction of the foundations on which rests unity in the Faith and in the Body of Christ.

These words – and much more to the same tune – were spoken with passionate conviction. But there was another passage, read with no special emphasis, which may be of more significance, as regards the evolution in 1986 of the struggle between Church and State in Nicaragua (and the related struggles within the Latin American church). This passage was part of a section headed: 'The Church, Waging Peace'. The key sentence in the passage read:

> We judge that any form of aid, whatever its source, which may lead to destruction, pain and death for our families or to hatred and division between our peoples is to be condemned.

At the time I thought that passage was pretty anodyne. I thought that because I was not then aware of how far the Cardinal – especially in 1985 in Miami – had committed himself on the *contra* side. Against that background, the sentence looks a lot more interesting. And it has aroused interest, especially among that 'belligerent group' which the belligerent Cardinal so detests. Government press censorship did not allow that episcopal letter (or several others before it) to appear in the newspapers. But it was readily available from diocesan press offices in Nicaragua, and became the subject of delighted comment in the April issue of *Envío*. *Envío*, a monthly review published by the Instituto Histórico Centroamericano, in Managua, reflects the views of an influential group of Catholic intellectuals (priests and lay people) who are, as they say, in Managua, 'with the process'. The process in question is the revolutionary process, especially in its social aspects; being 'with the process' implies broad support for the Sandinistas, without necessarily being committed to support all their policies and actions. At the end of an article entitled *La Iglesia de los Pobres en Nicaragua*, *Envío* singles out that passage from the Nicaraguan hierarchy's statement, underlining parts of it, calling it an historic step, *paso histórico*, and claiming that it means 'the condemnation of the military aid of Ronald Reagan's administration to the counter-revolution'.

Certainly, it comes a lot nearer to meaning just that than anything the Nicaraguan bishops had ever said before; and it even seems an implicit condemnation of the Cardinal's own position at Miami, less than a year before.

It does not seem an unreasonable inference that a section – perhaps a majority – of the Nicaraguan hierarchy is becoming refractory against the Cardinal's leadership, in relation to the civil war. As regards the *iglesia popular*, he still calls the tune, but no longer on the *contras*, it would seem. Some of the bishops, especially from the northern and eastern dioceses, where they know most about *contras* at first hand, are believed to have had misgivings about the Cardinal's lead on this matter for some time, on moral and humanitarian grounds. Others, more politically minded, may well feel that the Cardinal's line simply does not make sense today, in terms of the Church's interests. The *contras* have never looked as if they could overthrow the Sandinistas, and they look even less like it now than they did in 1983–84 (which was their peak). To call, as the Cardinal has regularly done, on the Sandinistas to negotiate with the *contras* is to call for what is not going to happen. Nobody who knows anything about the Sandinistas believes that they would negotiate with the *contras* even if Managua were about to fall, which it is not, or not to the *contras*. If it does fall, it will be to the invading armed forces of the United States.

To support the weaker side in a civil war, in the hope that it may be about to be rescued by foreign invasion, is an extraordinary high-risk policy, which prudent churchmen – whatever their personal political inclinations – would always wish to avoid. It rather looks as if prudent churchmen may currently be a rising force in the Nicaraguan episcopate, and that they may be beginning to rein in their impetuous Primate, the 'Cardinal of Central America'.

If all that is so – as I believe – it is not surprising if the Cardinal looked a bit grim at Mass that April morning in San Domingo de la Sierritas.

The Cardinal is still a force – a force of nature indeed – but he and what he represents may no longer be quite the force they were, in what looks in retrospect like their heyday: the period that began with the Pope's visit to Nicaragua in March 1983, and ended in May 1985 with the Cardinal's visit to Miami, in all the *hubris* of the new red hat.

The Pope's visit to Nicaragua is perhaps the most important, and certainly the most dramatic, episode in the great struggle between the institutional *un solo Dios* and *el Dios de los Pobres* in Latin America in the late twentieth century. Both sides in Nicaragua had looked to the Pope for a blessing, legitimising their particular interpretation of the Church's teaching. The Archbishop, of course, knew the Pope. The champions of *el Dios de los Pobres*, for their part, seem to have been counting on John Paul II's social teaching, which seems strongly on the side of the third world, and hostile to capitalist values and the consumer society. And the Pope had presided, very early in his Pontificate, over the second Conference of Latin American Bishops at Puebla de los Ángeles, in Mexico, which had committed the Church to 'the preferential option for the poor' seen by some as the furthest the institutional Church has gone – since its adoption by the Emperor Constantine – in recognising *el Dios de los Pobres*.

In Managua in May 1986, I asked a young Jesuit, an ardent and active liberation theologian – and so very much 'with the process' in Nicaragua – where he thought the Pope stood on liberation theology. 'The Pope', said the Jesuit, '*is himself* a liberation theologian!' His eyes flashed as he said that, and then he laughed painfully, as at some unbearable paradox.

My own guess is that the Pope sees himself as not merely *a* liberation theologian but as *the* liberation theologian. It is for *him* to say how far liberation theology can legitimately go, and where it is to stop. It is for him to determine in what sense God is in very truth *el Dios de los Pobres*; and also for him to repudiate false, and potentially heretical or schismatic, interpretations of those words.

Many other Catholics, in arguing about this or that formula of the Second Vatican Council, tend to ignore the *First* Vatican Council which in 1870 declared 'the Roman Pontiff' – subject to certain conditions – to be 'endowed with that infallibility which, according to the will of the Redeemer, is vouchsafed to the Church when she desires to fix a doctrine of faith or morality'. Liberal and progressive Catholics tend to assume that the resolutions of Vatican I have somehow been superseded, implicitly rescinded, or qualified out of existence, by Vatican II (1962–65). Pope John Paul II makes no such assumptions. In the Encyclical *Redemptor Hominis*, at the very beginning of his pontificate, he took care to quote Vatican I, as well as Vatican II, when he touched, rather enigmatically, on the subject of 'infallibility'. Since then, John Paul II has conducted what is in essence a Vatican I pontificate, while making copious and adroit use of the style and formulae of Vatican II. Thus John Paul II, like Vatican II, is all in favour of 'ecumenism'; but he also makes it clear that the Church unity which he favours is to be 'around the Successor of Peter': a Successor of Peter who is also the successor of Pius IX, never repudiating Vatican I. 'Consensus', too, the present Pope favours, and 'dialogue', just like Vatican II; except that now, when bishops meet, it is the Pope who registers the true meaning of their dialogue, and issues the document which embodies what he says is their consensus. It is all rather Orwellian, and it seems fitting that the pontificate of John Paul II should have included the year 1984. But the Orwellisms are dictated by the necessities of the situation, which require the re-edification of one kind of Church, behind the facade of another. The central meaning of this pontificate is to restore papal authority seen as badly damaged by the effects of the Second Vatican Council. That restoration is no easy task; especially as it must perforce be conducted in terms of the very principles which did the damage.

The Pope's concept of his own authority is simply not compatible with the versions of liberation theology, and of *el Dios de los Pobres*, which are fervently embraced by those Catholics who, in Nicaragua, are 'with the process' of the revolution. On the other hand, it was natural for a pope, bent on restoring authority within the Church to come to the support of an Archbishop whose own more limited authority was being challenged and subverted in Nicaragua. What was being challenged and subverted was not just the authority of Miguel Obando y Bravo, but the very concept of hierarchy, the whole structure, of which the Pope himself is the apex.

And the challenge was – and is – not a petty, parochial or peripheral one. It is true that Nicaragua is a small and poor country. But the very fact that it is small and poor is a source of strength for it in the great debate within the Catholic Church. Tiny Nicaragua, standing up to the greatest power on earth, David against Goliath, evokes the admiration of millions of people throughout Latin America; and Latin America is where nearly half the world's Catholics live now, and where more than half of the world's Catholics will be living by the end of the century. (And end of the millennium; not irrelevant, for the present Pope is very conscious of the approach of the Church's second millennial year, over which he personally hopes to preside.)

And as for poverty, many Latin Americans wonder why a Church committed to a preferential option for the poor should be severe on the government of Nicaragua, simply because it contains priests who are committed to *el Dios de los Pobres*, while almost all other Latin America countries are blatantly committed to *el Dios de los Ricos*?

So – contrary to mundane appearances – this formidable Pope, in taking on Sandinista Nicaragua, was taking on an adversary no less formidable than himself: an adversary representing forces which may possibly defeat the entire purpose of his pontificate and leave papal authority in ruins throughout Latin America – and thus weakened throughout the rest of the world – before the end of the millennium, whether Karol Wojtila lives to see that ecclesial climacteric or not.

The mere existence of that tremendous latent challenge goes a long way to explain why the Pope found himself engaged in a confrontation, when he visited Nicaragua in March 1983. But it is also necessary to take account of certain preceding chronology:

October 1978	Karol Wojtila becomes Pope John Paul II.
January 1979	Second Conference of Latin American Bishops at Puebla de los Ángeles in Mexico.
July 1979	Managua falls to the Nicaraguan Revolutionary forces. Inauguration of the Sandinista regime.

Puebla was the first major challenge in the new pontificate. The previous Conference of Latin American Bishops at Medellín, in Colombia, had seen some notable victories for *el Dios de los Pobres*. Some of its formulations have the marks of Latin American liberation theology. Medellín endorsed 'the clear perception that in man everything is mediated politically'. 'In our evaluation of popular religion', declared the Medellín bishops, 'we may not take as our frame of reference the westernized cultural interpretation of the middle and upper classes; instead, we must judge its meaning in the context of the subcultures of the rural and marginal urban groups'.

For liberation theologians, Medellín marked a notable advance; some hailed it as 'the new Pentecost'. It followed that, for conservatives, Medellín was a disaster. As Paul Johnson writes, in his admiring *Pope John Paul II and the Catholic Restoration*: 'The turning point, at which the ultra-radicals captured a section of the episcopate and first acquired a major voice in policy was . . . the Conference of Latin American Bishops held in Medellín in that fatal year 1968, the high tide of 1960s illusions'.

Pope Paul VI had been present at Medellín, without appearing to make much impact there. John Paul II went to Puebla, where he showed a mixture of firmness and ambiguity, which has proved to be characteristic of his pontificate. His main aim was to reassert the *Magisterium*: the authority and discipline of the Universal Church, under the Successor of Peter. Medellín had seemed at times perilously close to launching a separate Latin American Church. But in reasserting papal authority, the new Pope had to take account of Medellín, as an accomplished fact, which the Latin American bishops were not about to reverse. So he handled Medellín, at Puebla, much as he has handled Vatican II; he took over the style, while seeking to infuse into it a different spirit, tending towards more conservative interpretations. It is a subtle strategy, and works well in Rome; whether it can be made to work in Latin America is another matter. The partisans of *el Dios de los Pobres* were not displeased with Puebla, which gave them that famous 'preferential option for the poor'. 'Medellín and Puebla' are commonly cited together, by radicals, with shared implied approval. The radicals also took favourable note of some of the Pope's Medellín-style language during his Mexican visit: his calls for 'bold transformations' and 'daring innovations to overcome the grave injustices of the past'.

On the whole, the Pope's Mexican visit of 1978 probably gave a lot more aid and comfort than he intended to radical Catholics in Latin America. His biographer, Mary Craig, ends her chapter on that visit with the words: 'The Church in Latin America had received a shot in the arm and renewed hope was in the air'.

It certainly was. A little more than six months after Puebla, on 19 July 1979, Managua fell to the Sandinistas. 'Bold transformations' and 'daring innovations' were indeed under way. The Pope must later have wondered whether his own language in Mexico – his 'shot in the arm' – had helped 'the process' in Nicaragua.

Certainly, the radical currents in the Church, set in motion by Vatican II, and swelled at Medellín, contributed to the Nicaraguan process. And the result of the process was something unique in history: a revolutionary government including four Catholic priests, having widespread Catholic support, and regarded by a significant section of the Catholic Church as an earthly manifestation of the will of the God of the Poor. For these believers, the process is to culminate in *el Reino de Dios*: the Kingdom of God. For them, nothing less than that is what is at stake in Nicaragua.

In Sandinista Nicaragua – that is, among Sandinistas in Nicaragua – those words, 'the Kingdom of God', crop up, in speech and in print with a frequency disquieting to the secular visitor, and to some religious visitors as well. What is most striking is the *casual* way in which the words are used. People refer to the coming Kingdom of God as if they were waiting for a bus.

I think it was that casualness that first brought home to me how serious these people are. You can actually feel around you, in Nicaragua, something going on that you know cannot be switched off, either from Washington or from Rome: that most intractable thing, a new kind of Faith. And the Faith in question is not confined to those Sandinistas who are specifically identified as religious. The powerful *comandante* and Minister of the Interior, Tomás Borge – widely regarded as the most formidable marxist in the Sandinista directorate and in the government – speaks of the Earthly Paradise and of Hell and Antichrist and of 'the integration of liberating Christianity with the Revolution'. Daniel Ortega, now President of Nicaragua, announcing to a large crowd in Managua his nomination of the Jesuit, Fernando Cardenal, as Minister for Education, gave that integrationist concept a simpler form in the slogan: *Pueblo de Sandino! Pueblo de Cristo!*

And the cult of the revolutionary dead, which is such a conspicuous part of *Sandinismo* is powerfully expressive of the same linkage. These dead are invariably referred to in countless official statements and inscriptions as *héroes y mártires*: not merely national heroes but also martyrs, witnesses, through their death, to their Faith in the God of the Poor.

This 'synthesis of Christian vocation and revolutionary conscience' – as the FSLN has called it – has become a subject of deep concern to the Holy See. It seems to be widely supposed that what worries the Holy See about Nicaragua is the infiltration of marxism into the Catholic Church. But I think that is Washington's worry rather than Rome's. The present Pope has had ample reason to take the measure of marxism, and there can be little in his experience that could lead him to see marxism in itself – as distinct from Soviet material power – as a particularly dangerous adversary. As it happened, the Pope was in Poland, for his triumphal visit, in that summer of 1979, in June, just as the Sandinistas in Nicaragua were sweeping towards their final victory.

The huge and loving crowds that came out for the Pope in Poland welcomed him in the name of Faith and Fatherland. That potent combination had been able to set at defiance all the efforts of successive Polish governments, backed by Soviet power, to make marxists out of the Polish people, or even any significant part of the Polish youth, growing up under marxist rule.

In Poland, Faith and Fatherland have been aligned for centuries, and still are. In Latin America, they have not been, up to now, but in

Sandinismo they are. That is the profound originality of *Sandinismo*, and the source of much of its power. (There is certainly also a marxist component in *Sandinismo*, but it is in my opinion subordinate to the nationalist component, and to a great extent a vehicle for the expression of that. I shall come back to this.)

No-one knows better than John Paul II the power that lies in the conjuncture of Faith and Fatherland. All the more reason therefore to view with alarm the form that the conjuncture has taken in Managua. For the Sandinistas, unlike the Poles, have not been content to take their Faith on trust from Rome, but have been issuing their own definitions and interpretations, through their own trusted theologians, much as happened in the Reformation lands in the sixteenth century. And as Martin Luther found his princes, so the liberation theologians of Latin America have found *their* princes, in the nine *comandantes* of the Frente Sandinista de Liberación Nacional; with, no doubt, other princes to come, in other parts of Latin America. Putting it another way, and invoking the memory of another reformer, Managua is a potential Geneva for Latin America.

But the comparisons are only valid in so far as we remember that the original reformers were not setting out to form new churches, but to reform the universal church. Similarly, the liberation theologians and Christian Sandinistas are not at present setting out to found a new church or churches in Latin America but to make over the universal church in the image of the God of the Poor.

Whether the project is to lead to a breakaway church or churches, or alternatively to a reform of the universal church, according to the prescriptions of Latin American liberation theologians, it must look equally abhorrent, from the point of view of a Pope bent on restoring and consolidating papal authority.

Nor can the Pope's forebodings have been in any way allayed by the stream of liberation theology that began to flow from the presses of Managua in the immediate aftermath of the Sandinista revolution. I have one such publication before me as I write. It is called *Cristianos Revolucionarios*. It is one of a series of 'popular pamphlets', *Folletos Populares*, published by the Instituto Histórico Centroamericano of Managua, who are also the publishers of the monthly review *Envío*, which I mentioned earlier.

Cristianos Revolucionarios embodies the results of a seminar on 'Christian Faith and Sandinista Revolution' held at the Universidad Centroamericana de Managua in September 1979, when the Sandinista regime was just two months old. The cover shows a young man with a beret, wearing a crucifix around his neck, and carrying an automatic rifle in his left hand and Molotov cocktail in his right. But the cover seems likely to have been less disturbing, to Vatican circles, than some of the contents of the pamphlet (contents which incidentally are much more academic and subtle than the garish cover of the *Folleto Popular* seems to promise). One section of the pamphlet is boldly entitled: 'Jesus Christ is not enough for us [*No nos basta Jesucristo*]'. The section argues that, as well as the gospel, revolutionary practice is needed and also 'a theory' – which, while not explicitly named, is clearly some form of marxism. The pamphlet goes on with some brilliance to explain the double position of the revolutionary Christians, within the revolution, and within the Church. They do not want to divide *either* the revolution *or* the Church, but to be an integral part of both. Far from seeking to create 'a parallel Church' (*una Iglesia paralela*) as their enemies claim, all the revolutionary Christians demand is 'a space' (*un espacio*). What do they want the space for? They want the space in order to 'confess [in it] explicitly how we belong [*nuestra pertinencia*] to the only Church of Christ [*la única Iglesia de Cristo*]'. It is to be 'a space in which the popular classes would be able to appropriate [*apropiarse de*] the religious symbols, [and] in which this historical subject which was the people [*que era el pueblo*] will be able, as a people, to read the Bible and, reflecting on reality, to make theology [*hacer teología*]'.

It is against a background of a spate of publications of that kind that the reactions of the Nicaraguan hierarchy, and of the Vatican, to the initial friendly overtures of the Sandinista Government have to be understood. In October 1980, the National Directorate of the FSLN issued its communiqué on religion. This was certainly intended to be a conciliatory document; as I mentioned earlier, it praised Obando personally. The Sandinistas sincerely pride themselves on their magnanimous and positive approach to religion, and on having altogether abandoned that doctrinaire hostility to all religion, which had hitherto been common to all revolutions claiming any degree of marxist inspiration. The key paragraph of the Sandinista communiqué ran:

> We do not encourage nor [sic] provoke activities to divide the churches. Religion is the exclusive business of Christians and it does not concern political organizations. If there is division, the churches ought to look for the causes within themselves and not

> attribute responsibility to supposedly evil outside influences. Yes, we are frank in saying that we would look favourably upon a Church that, without prejudice, with maturity and responsibility, worked in the common effort to develop more and more avenues for dialogue and participation that our revolutionary process has opened.

What the Sandinistas had failed to realise was that their friendly overtures would be far more frightening to many bishops – including those of Managua and of Rome – than the normal degree of doctrinaire hostility to be expected from a purely marxist government. With proper marxists, churchmen knew where they stood: marxists in one sphere, the Church in quite a different one: a tidy and tenable state of affairs. This new stuff was quite different. Not that liberation theology in itself was all that new; by 1979, liberation theology had been around for a little over a decade, since its beginnings in Germany in 1967. What was new in Nicaragua – and most alarmingly new – was that for the first time liberation theology had the *backing of a State*: a most undesirable precedent, for Latin America in particular.

The Vatican was, as usual, slow to react. But Archbishop Obando was prompt. His opposition to the Sandinista regime began as soon as those *Folletos Populares* started to promote liberation theology with official approval. That FSLN communiqué altogether failed to mollify him. As he must have seen it, those 'avenues of dialogue' which the FSLN was calling for could only lead into that ominous *espacio* demanded by the liberation theologians. As he saw the matter, not merely was the temporal sphere encroaching upon the spiritual, but a revolutionary State was making use of a fifth column within the Church in order to subvert the hierarchy, and promote schism and heresy.

From these sources, and not from any nostalgia for the old social order, or need to do Washington's bidding, sprang the Archbishop's implacable hostility to 'the process'. But of course that hostility made the Archbishop a natural ally both of those who *were* nostalgic for the old social order, and of President Reagan, with whose inauguration the opening of the Archbishop's attacks on the Sandinista regime approximately coincided. And the Archbishop's complaints helped the President with the demonisation of Sandinista Nicaragua. Thus the President, in claiming that the Church was persecuted in Nicaragua, could clinch that claim by quoting the Archbishop. To the general public, 'religious persecution' conjures up visions of churches being closed down by force, and of systematic physical ill-treatment of priests and nuns. Nothing of the kind has been going on in Nicaragua. Obando, indeed, genuinely believes that the Church is being persecuted there. What he has in mind, when he talks about persecution, is, primarily, state encouragement to liberation theologians, secondarily, denial of access to the media, for himself and his colleagues, through government censorship, and thirdly, a certain amount of rough barracking at times in the past by left-wing parishioners: the so-called *turbas divinas*. Those are the realities on which the charge is based. But the picture which the word 'persecution' brings to mind is different, and more frightening.

The battle between the Archbishop and the Sandinista government was well and truly locked when Pope John Paul II came to Nicaragua on 4 March 1983, to be welcomed by both sides.

In Managua, in April 1986, my wife and I watched the Pope's visit, on video, just as it had been broadcast at the time, for many hours, live on Nicaraguan television. We watched the video in the house of a woman whom I shall call Victoria. Victoria is a believing and practising Catholic and she is also 'with the process'. The Pope's visit had been a painful and distressing experience for her – and for many others like her – and she cannot have enjoyed the replay. On the other hand, she wanted us to see how it had been. Also, our presence there that evening was a distraction for her, at a time of suffering and anxiety. Her seventeen-year-old son, who had volunteered for his Servicio Militar Patriótico, had left the previous day for one of the 'war zones', penetrated by the *contras*. She told us how his ten-year-old brother had dressed up that day in his clown outfit, in an effort to cheer them all up. As it happened, within a few days of our visit, Victoria had to call on another mother whose son, a class-mate of Victoria's son, had just been killed by *contras*. The boy's parents were *not* 'with the process', and the boy had not volunteered; he had been conscripted. In the circumstances, Victoria had wondered whether her condolences would be accepted. But they were.

Victoria is a member – in reality, a kind of leader – of one of the base Christian communities in one of the poor *barrios* of Managua. The *comunidades* were set up under the impetus of Vatican II and Medellín, in an effort to remedy the shortage of parish clergy, chronic in Latin America. Most, though not all, of the *comunidades* appear by now to have become vehicles for liberation theology, and the *comunidades* generally are regarded with suspicion by conservatives in the Church. The *comunidades* were anxious to play their full part in the great event of the Pope's visit. And Victoria's *comunidad* had spent weeks preparing a big banner which they carried out to Sandino Airport, Managua, on the big day, 4 March 1983.

In any case there we were, in Victoria's living-room, watching the Pope's visit, a little more than three years after the event.

There is the Pope's plane on the tarmac, and a long wait. My note reads: 'Plane pregnant with Pope'. The Pope gets out and then, in accordance with established custom, kisses the ground of Nicaragua, which is hot. Rather neatly, the commentator says that the Pope is kissing the ground *'de Nicaragua libre'*. But that is the commentator, not the Pope. The nine *comandantes de la revolución*, who make up the national directorate of the Frente Sandinista are all there. Victoria's *comunidad*'s banner is there. It is a good big banner and it reads: *BIENVENIDO JUAN PABLO EN LA TIERRA DE SANDINO*.

There were other Sandinista slogans: 'Welcome to free Nicaragua, thanks to God and the Revolution'; 'Between Christianity and revolution, there is no contradiction'. And then there were what *Envío* was later to call 'more generic' slogans used by 'those Christians opposed to the process': 'I am happy the Pope is coming'. 'John Paul II, Nicaragua is waiting for you'.

The first to greet the Pope are the papal nuncio and a foreign office official. First sign that all is not well. Normally, the greeters should be the Archbishop of Managua (as head of the Nicaraguan hierarchy), and the Foreign Minister, Miguel d'Escoto. Presumably the Frente objected to the Archbishop, because of his political role (as they see it). And the Pope must have objected to the Foreign Minister, since Miguel d'Escoto is a priest (of the Maryknoll Order), who has stayed on in the government of Nicaragua, contrary to Church discipline. But both Obando and d'Escoto are around there, somewhere.

Now Daniel is welcoming the Pope on behalf of the three senior *comandantes* – Daniel Ortega, Co-ordinator of the National Directorate (and later elected President of Nicaragua). The press – except *La Prensa* – always calls him just Daniel, and so does everyone in Nicaragua who is 'with the process'. Daniel, with his spectacles and his mane of brown hair waving in the breeze, seems like a young, progressive headmaster anxious to make an impression on an extremely distinguished visitor. Too anxious, as it turns out.

I quote from my rough notes, made as I watched the Pope listen to Daniel:

> 'You are being received by a heroic people ... 50,000 dead – social and moral changes'
>
> Pope looks as if he had toothache; holding jaw with left hand.
>
> 'American threat ... worthy riposte to *intervención Norte-americana*.' *Barricada*-type speech goes on.
>
> Pope's head bowed more and more on hand.
>
> Daniel quotes from early (1912) letter of Nicaraguan Bishop to Yanks.
>
> Pope folds arms on chest.
>
> Long, long old letter. Daniel very boomy.
>
> 'The soldiers killed ...'

The reference here is to seventeen young soldiers killed by *contras* four days before the Pope's visit. The memory of these soldiers – all secondary school-boys – powerfully affected the ceremonies surrounding the Pope's visit. And that memory, and thoughts related to it, were also strongly present in Victoria's living-room, while video made those scenes come alive again.

Daniel went on with his speech, getting a bit hoarse and wavery as if knowing that what he was saying was not going down too well. He spoke of the inalienable right to religious liberty, and then of Christians 'basing themselves on faith corresponding to the revolution'.

Pope back to holding jaw.

The Pope's response to Daniel's ill-judged discourse – even *Envío* says that it 'took longer than the time allotted' – seemed quite gracious, probably because most of it had been written out before hand. My notes read:

> 'Thanks God in land of lakes and volcanoes .... Noble people, rich in Christian traditions ... sincere thanks to junta, and [*sic*] for its deference in coming to greet me ...'

This reference is significant, in that it seems to show that the Pope was indeed hoping – as the then Vatican Secretary of State, Cardinal Casaroli, is known to have hoped – that relations with the Sandinista regime might improve. The Pope, in thanking the junta – meaning the national directorate, of the nine *comandantes* – rather than the *government* seems to have been making an important point. The government included the four priests, who were *not* however members of the directorate (or junta). The overture to the junta, ignoring the government, seemed to imply that if the Sandinistas would drop the four priests – thus symbolising a propensity to draw back from involvement in Church affairs – relations with the Vatican could be normalised. So the Pope seems to have been trying to mend some fences. But it did not work out that way, not by any means.

In any case, even if he did mean to mend fences with the Sandinistas, he was not going to do so by publicly letting down the embattled Archbishop of Managua. He saluted his brother bishops, *hermanos obispos*, 'especially our beloved Miguel Obando'. Then a light, quick slap over the knuckles for Daniel, when, after sympathising with 'those who suffer from the results of violence from whatever quarter it comes', the Pope condemned not only 'hatred' but also 'sterile accusations'.

Then the government had to be greeted. This was the first really tricky bit, since the government included those four priests. Still, governments are governments whatever they may contain, and the Pope has always greeted governments on his tours. Victoria told us that a way had been found round the difficulty, or so it was thought. The Pope was to pass along the line of government members, acknowledging the government's collective existence by some kind of comprehensive salutation, without having to greet each individual member. It was a sensible idea, but this was one of those days where everything that could go wrong, did. One member of the government, apparently not having grasped the nature of the problem, stepped forward to greet the Pope. And then the fat was in the fire.

The next thing on that screen is the spectacle of the Minister for Culture, Father Ernesto Cardenal – a frail person with long white hair and a white beard – taking off his black beret and kneeling before the Pope, for a blessing. And the Pope, instead of blessing, wags a finger of admonition, saying sternly 'You must regularise [*arreglar*] your situation with the Vatican'.

'Ernesto cried', said Victoria, 'and everybody came over to comfort him.'

Ernesto Cardenal is something more important, in the eyes of many Nicaraguans, than either a Minister or even a priest. He is a poet – one of the two most distinguished living Nicaraguan poets – in a land where poets are esteemed and appreciated, to an extent, I think, unknown in any other part of the modern world. It happens that the other leading Nicaraguan poet – Pablo Antonio Cuadra, director general of *La Prensa* – is one of the bitterest enemies of the Sandinista regime. He and Ernesto – who are cousins – were once also close friends, now separated by politics. 'He was like a son to me', Cuadra told me. Clearly affection – though not the possibility of civil conversation – had managed to survive even the intense heat of antagonistic Nicaraguan politics.

When the Pope snubbed Ernesto, many Nicaraguans – all those who were 'with the process' and probably quite a few others as well – felt themselves snubbed, in the person of this admired and beloved Nicaraguan. Ernesto himself, though hurt, did not take the snub so heavily, or lose his sense of humour. He tells of how stricken his mother had been by the Pope's attitude. 'I thought he would treat you like a father', she said, 'But he *did* treat me like a father', said Ernesto. 'He just didn't treat me like a *mother*.'

Ernesto might feel no rancour, but others did, on his behalf. From the moment of the Pope's wagging finger, over Ernesto's uplifted face, the visit went sour, for many of those who – like Victoria – had worked hard to prepare a welcome for the Pope.

Victoria, like others we met, was puzzled, as well as distressed, by that rebuke. It seemed disproportionate, gratuitous, petty; a needless piece of humiliation, for the enforcement of some trifling and archaic ecclesiastical regulation. That is pretty much how I saw it myself, while I was watching that painful scene on video. But later, after I had looked more closely at what is at stake in Nicaragua for the Church – as the Pope conceives the Church – I felt rather differently about it. The Sandinista fusion of religion and politics – not only religion and marxism, but also *religion and nationalism*, which is much more dangerous – puts at risk, throughout the whole vast spiritual battleground of Latin America, the Pope's mission to restore the *Magisterium*, the teaching authority of the papacy. Ernesto is a committed and enthusiastic agent of the Sandinista fusion. So when Ernesto knelt before the Pope, the Pope had to see, not just an estimable if misguided human being, but an insidious, incarnate threat to the universal church, and to the Pope's own mission. And not just a threat, but a trap as well. If the Pope gave Ernesto the blessing Ernesto was asking – guilelessly as it seemed, but perhaps with some guile in the background somewhere – would the Pope not be seen as blessing the Sandinista fusion itself? And if so, would he not – the Pope – be conniving at the sabotage of his own great mission, and of the Church entrusted to him?

Considering all that accumulated thunder in the air, I am

surprised, in retrospect, at how lightly Ernesto got off. But that was certainly not the general impression at the time.

Thinking over that scene now, in terms of the forces represented by the protagonists, it is not Ernesto I am sorry for. It is the Pope. But I shall come back to that.

After that unpromising start, the Pope went on to León, a former capital of Nicaragua, for a purely religious ceremony, the Celebration of the Word. There was a large crowd. 'Nobody did anything that day', said Victoria glumly, looking at the scene. She also alluded to the cost of the visit. As soon as they realised that the visit was going to do them more harm than good, the Sandinistas, quite naturally, began to regret their investment in preparing to receive the Pope. Quite a large investment for impoverished Nicaragua: 'Approximately $3 million and two months supply of gasoline . . . used in bringing the people to Managua', according to *Envío*.

Then the Pope went to Managua and to the disastrous and chaotic last phase of his eleven-hour visit to Nicaragua. This was the Mass celebrated in Managua's main square, the Nineteenth of July Plaza. The crowd, which filled the plaza to overflowing, is said to have been the largest ever assembled in the history of Nicaragua: between 600 000 and 700 000 persons, or about one-fourth of Nicaragua's total population. But not all of these, by this time, were well-disposed to the Pope. The incident with Ernesto in the morning had set up a ferment.

The day had been terribly hot, even for tropical Nicaragua: 40°C (104°F). Tempers were frayed and distinct factions – Sandinistas and Obandists – made themselves heard: 'The Catholic chorus' according to *Envío* 'wanted only traditional religious songs to go out through the loudspeakers. But those controlling the audio, from the Sandinista system, were playing songs from the Nicaraguan *Campesino* Mass'.

This was already a bit rough, from the Pope's point of view. His very ears, during his own Pontifical Mass, were being assailed by the – to him – revolting strains of Sandinista fusionism and the dubious hymnal of liberation theology.

Then the Pope delivered his homily, and the whole thing came apart.

According to Victoria the text of the Pope's homily had been cleared with the Sandinista National Directorate. 'They thought it was all right when they read it', she said, 'but when *he* read it aloud, it sounded quite different.'

I suppose that, on paper, the concepts of the homily – Church unity, the *Magisterium* and so on – may have looked abstract and abstruse, unlikely to arouse passion, or much interest. But when the Pope actually delivered this part of his homily, with barbed and fiery eloquence, it became apparent that he personally was very angry indeed, and that his anger was directed against the Sandinista process, in its relation to the Church:

> Church unity is put into question when the powerful factors which build and maintain it – the one faith, the revealed Word, the sacraments, obedience to the bishops and the Pope, the sense of vocation and joint responsibility in Christ's work in the world – are brought up against earthly considerations, unacceptable ideological commitments, temporal options, or concepts of the Church which are contrary to the true one.

'The word "true"' notes the *Envío* writer ruefully – 'was said in a tone of surprising firmness and with a sharp intonation'. (The *Envío* writer also noted sardonically that the Pope, in the course of this homily mentioned 'bishops' fourteen times and 'peace' only once.)

The Pope's tone – probably much more than what he said – sent up the temperature of the crowd. But it rose further – 'emotions boiled over' according to *Envío* – when the Pope called the *iglesia popular* 'an absurd and dangerous project'. There were shouts of 'We want peace' (*Queremos la paz!*), 'People's power!' (*Poder popular!*), 'They shall not pass!' (*No pasarán!*). '*Silencio!*' shouted the Pope. '*He*'s not a Pope of the poor!' proclaimed a voice from the crowd. 'Look at his dress!' '*Silencio*', again. Then the Mothers took the stage, spreading further waves of emotion, which spilled over into the living-room where we were watching the scene, three years later. The Mothers are the members of Nicaragua's Association of Mothers of Heroes and Martyrs: that is, of sons who fell in the revolution, at the hands of Somoza's National Guard, or in the current fighting at the hands of the *contras*. There are about fifty of these Mothers – including some of the Mothers of the recently killed seventeen – and these last were there, very near the altar and the Pope. 'The blood of our boys is crying out!' called one mother. 'We want a prayer for our Martyrs!' called another. The Pope, who was saying Mass, was unresponsive. Later another Mother called out 'We can offer you now only the sorrow . . . the Reagan government . . .' (her voice faded away). This particular interruption came at the actual moment of the Pope's Consecration of the Host, and was to give rise later to Vatican complaints about 'profanation of the Eucharist', during the Pope's visit to Nicaragua.

Victoria still, after three years, felt outraged by the Pope's refusal, as she saw it, to have the common decency to say a prayer for those dead boys, at the request of their recently bereaved Mothers. I could understand and respect her feelings, but I also thought I could understand how the thing must have looked to the Pope. He must have felt, as in the case of Ernesto, that he was being set up. That association, heroes *and martyrs*, represented the very thing that was anathema to him in Nicaragua. The mere fact that he was asked for a prayer 'for our martyrs', made it impossible for him to say such a prayer, without tending to legitimise a cult which he regards as 'absurd and dangerous'. So he remained deaf to the entreaties of the Mothers, and there must be many, besides Victoria, who will never forgive him.

In any case, it was obviously a very angry – though controlled – Pope who took off from Sandino Airport that hot March evening. Whatever thoughts he may have entertained about mending some fences with the Sandinistas were banished, and would stay banished for years to come. Obando's harsh picture of what *Sandinismo* was like seemed abundantly vindicated. The Pope left to Obando the vestments he had worn during his Nicaraguan trip. And two years later the Pope made Obando a Cardinal. All those feverish preparations the Sandinistas had made for the Pope's visit, and the money they had invested in it, had only helped (so it seemed) in the strengthening and promotion of their most implacable enemy.

That fourth of March, the day of the Pope's visit is remembered in Nicaragua as *El bochorno de Managua. Bochorno* is a beautifully appropriate word. The dictionary gives the English for it as: 'sultry weather . . . embarrassment'. The effects of the sultry embarrassment took a long time to wear off: more than two years in fact. In this period, Miguel Obando was riding high, and well into the political domain: legitimising resistance to military service, delegitimising the regime, and then – as a new Cardinal – fraternising with its enemies (as related earlier). He seemed to be daring the government to do something about him. The problem was that it did not seem possible to do anything about him, without appearing to persecute the Church, and making the Pope into an open enemy. The minister responsible for public order – Tomás Borge, senior *comandante* and Minister for the Interior – publicly confessed that, though he could handle the other enemies of the revolution, he did not know what to do about Obando's counter-revolutionary activities: a most unusual confession for this powerful and resourceful *comandante*, and exemplary Sandinista.

But there was one minister who thought he *did* know what to do about Obando, and who acted on his thought. This was Miguel d'Escoto, Minister for Foreign Affairs and Chancellor; and one of the three priests now in the Government (the others being the brothers Ernesto and Fernando Cardenal). Miguel d'Escoto was born in Hollywood, California, in 1933 and educated in the United States, where he joined the Maryknoll Order. As Foreign Minister, he has travelled enormously – seeming at times to be in orbit – and much of the weight off Nicaragua's unique problems in foreign affairs seems to be carried by the Vice President, the cool and politic Sergio Ramírez (who is close to Daniel Ortega, and often consulted by him). It would be easy, but wrong, to infer from that that Miguel d'Escoto is a bit of a lightweight. Like each of his priestly colleagues, Miguel carries considerable moral and intellectual, and even spiritual, authority within the Sandinista structures. *Comandantes* come and ask him questions about God, unlikely as I know that will appear in Washington. Like Ernesto, Miguel has the gift of inspiring affection as well as respect. When I asked a young Irishwoman, in Managua, who knows Miguel well, what he was really like, she replied simply: 'Miguel is a *dote* [a darling]'! But as well as being a dote, Miguel is something of a prophet. Also he has a sense of theatre. He was not born in Hollywood for nothing.

Through this combination of gifts, Miguel was able to find the way to lift Sandinista spirits out of the uneasy leaden aftermath of *el bochorno*, and also the way to wage spiritual war against Miguel Obando. The way was through a form of sacred drama, which Miguel d'Escoto called *la insurrección evangélica*. The 'evangelical insurrection' was carried out in two parts: the *ayuno*, or fast, and the *Viacrucis*, the Way of the Cross.

The *insurrección evangélica* began with the Foreign Minister's perception that – in his own words – 'the government as a government cannot find an answer to a theological war'. It was the task of the Christian Sandinistas, specifically, to man that trench: 'We Christians have our own special arms which we must use: prayer, fasting, processions with hymns, vigils . . . .'

The first phase of the *insurrección* was the fast for peace, *el ayuno por la paz*. Here, of course, Miguel d'Escoto was consciously following in the footsteps of Gandhi and Martin Luther King. But he was following in his own way, and also breaking some new ground. His fast was unique in that it was carried out *by a member of a government*, with the support of his colleagues. The government knew of his undertaking in advance, and it had their approval, informally. Daniel Ortega used to drop in to see him, during his fast. The idea of a government, through one of its ministers, using a fast as a religious-cum-political weapon is, I believe, wholly unprecedented.

The fast was also different from the Gandhi and King fasts, in that it was not a pacifist fast, although Miguel d'Escoto uses a lot of apparently pacifist language. His commitment to non-violence is personal and teleological, and does not exclude enthusiastic backing, in the present, for the Sandinista Army, the Ejército Sandinista. In this respect, d'Escoto is less like Martin Luther King than he is like one of Cromwell's preachers; and indeed there seems to be something more Cromwellian than Catholic about *Sandinismo* generally (as I think John Paul II would agree). Teófilo Cabestrero, who has written a history of the d'Escoto fast (*Un Grito a Dios y al Mundo*, A Cry to God and the World) tells of a message from the fasting priest to the army, on the twelfth day of the fast. The message was conveyed to the army by Father César Jerez, SJ, head of the University at Managua, and d'Escoto's strongest supporter in the *insurrección evangélica*:

> At a solemn *acto de ascensos* – [passing-out parade] – of the *Ejército Sandinista*, Father César Jerez read out to the soldiers a message from Father d'Escoto in which he praised their heroism and spoke to them of Christ and of [His] wish for [*voluntad de*] non-violent, prophetic methods, in order to bring about the coming of the Kingdom of God; he tells them that he is opening a new trench for peace with these means, fasting and prayer.

The idea of an encomium on non-violence being officially read out in the course of a military ceremony may seem odd to us, but it apparently does not seem odd to any of them: priests, soldiers or politicians. It is all part of *Sandinismo*. The *insurrección* itself did sometimes seem odd, even to Sandinistas, but it turned out to be oddly effective.

The *ayuno* began in the first week of July and d'Escoto kept it up for thirty days; others joined in for part of that time. D'Escoto was fasting, and keeping open house, and talking away, in a parish house in one of Managua's *barrios*. As Cabestrero describes it:

> Here come, on visits of solidarity to Father Miguel, young students, disabled people, villagers from Niguinohomo [Sandino's birthplace], peasants from Río San Juan, Nicaraguan poets who give a night-time recital, combatants from nine Battalions of Irregular Warfare [*Batallones de Lucha Irregular*] who embrace Father d'Escoto, play the *Misa Campesina* and are applauded by the assembly.

And so on. It was an on-going show as well as a fast. And there were side-shows as well: a nocturnal panel on 'Prophetism' in Managua; a singing rosary at dawn in Estelí; processions and vigils all over Nicaragua, all part of the *insurrección evangélica*.

And d'Escoto himself continued to prophesy; the frontispiece to Cabestrero's book shows the fasting priest-minister clutching a microphone in his right hand. This was early in the fast – and d'Escoto had been quite fat before he started – but his bearded face has already a set, hollow look and his sunken eyes are gleaming behind his horn-rimmed spectacles. He seems to be holding on to that mike as if it were some kind of lifeline; if he cannot eat, at least he can talk. He talks well, spontaneously, urgently, pungently; and – during the fast – a little feverishly. He talked to Cabestrero about the spiritual significance of Ronald Reagan's mendacity.

He had been listening to a speech of Reagan's, as he fasted, and it had hit him hard. The President has lied, he said, 'with such a mastery, with such a great capacity for lying, for saying what is not so, and for saying it with such serenity and such conviction, that I, without becoming angry, felt an enormous sadness. And there came about a change in my vision of the problem that confronts us.... I thought, there is more in this than just a pathological obsession.... And one day, alone in my room, I thought that this incredible capacity for lying reveals something like [*como una*] a case of diabolical possession'.

But the primary target of the *insurrección* was not Reagan: it was Obando. Obando was generally not named, in this first phase of the *insurrección – the ayuno* – but the hierarchy was frequently either named or otherwise evoked. Right at the beginning, at the concelebrated Mass of twenty priests, which was the solemn opening of the *ayuno por la paz*, on 7 July 1985, one of the concelebrants, Monsignor Arias Caldera, said: 'May they depart from our sky, the crows who fly with the eagle of the North'. No-one had to be told who the crows were, or the eagle. Later, d'Escoto, thinking aloud, was more specific:

> Then I saw the Church all bloody, guilty by omission and even more guilty than Reagan, because of the responsibility of its mission . . . . These are terribly sad things, like the conspiracy of the synagogue with the Empire and the forces of evil in order to condemn Jesus, things on which I have meditated much in retreat [*en retiro*].

Obando must have thought it was a funny kind of retreat.

The *ayuno* ended at the beginning of August 1985, after thirty days. D'Escoto had said he would keep it up until he was convinced that his spark – *chispa* – had got a fire going. By August, he thought – with reason – that there was a fire. The *ayuno* had caught the imagination of many Christians in many parts of the world, and especially in Latin America. Messages of 'prophetic solidarity' poured in from almost every country in Latin America and from many other countries. Thirty-five bishops (not all of them Catholic bishops) signified their support for the *ayuno*.

In Lent 1986, Miguel d'Escoto, having recuperated his strength after the fast, started out on the second phase of the evangelical insurrection: *el Viacrucis por la paz*, the Way of the Cross. The *Viacrucis*, with its stations of the cross, is a traditional expression of Nicaraguan popular piety. D'Escoto intended his *Viacrucis* to be just that, but also to be an expression of support for the Sandinista position on peace, and so of insurrection against the position of the Nicaraguan hierarchy.

From a conservative point of view, of course, the d'Escoto *Viacrucis* represented an attempt to hijack a traditional devotion for political purposes. *La Prensa* – which of course is on the Cardinal's side – subjected d'Escoto's *Viacrucis*, throughout its progress, to a running fire of ridicule. I have sometimes wondered why the censors let that stuff through. *La Prensa* is subject to strict governmental pre-censorship. If people on *La Prensa* were able to mock that *Viacrucis*, it is because the censors decided to let them do so. This might be attributed to divided counsels within the Government, but I doubt whether that is the explanation. The Ministry of the Interior is responsible for censorship. The responsible Minister is *comandante* Tomás Borge. Borge is a subtle person, and if he let that mockery get by, it must be that he thought it would do the cause of the mockers more harm than good. And indeed mockery is not a particularly appropriate way to discredit a modern simulation of the *Viacrucis*, in the eyes of Christians. For Christians have to recall that mockery entered largely into the intentions of those who organised the *real Viacrucis*.

The traditional Nicaraguan *Viacrucis* is a local affair. D'Escoto's was larger and longer – '*un gran Viacrucis*' – setting out from Jalapa on the Honduran border, on the first Friday in Lent, 14 February 1986, and reaching Managua, 300 kilometres away on 28 February: two weeks of hot, dusty walking. Few of the pilgrims went all the way – perhaps no more than forty, including d'Escoto. Many more – from 5 000 to 12 000, as reported – went along for a single stage of around 20 kilometres. Pilgrims stayed in peasant houses; peasants came out with plants and flowers as well as holy images. Not all that many peasants, but some peasants, for every stage. The pilgrims were accompanied by a car with a public address system which transmitted hymns and political speeches, alternately. Mothers, young men and children appeared, carrying crosses.

The parish clergy is sparse in rural Nicaragua, and it was divided on the *Viacrucis*. In several centres, the church doors were shut against the pilgrims, and in one, the church door carried a placard reading 'Don't make politics out of the *Viacrucis*!' But in other places, the parish priest welcomed the pilgrims, blessed them and walked with them.

The high point of the journey was in Estelí where, on 22 February 1986, the bishop, Monsignor Rubén López Ardón personally ordered the Cathedral – which had previously been kept closed – to be opened to the pilgrims, embraced and blessed d'Escoto before about 20 000 people, himself asked for d'Escoto's blessing and said a prayer for peace. He recognised (according to the *Viacrucis Boletín*, No. 15) 'that the motives of this pilgrimage are of authentic Christian faith in the pursuit of peace and life'. The bishop's statement was highly significant because it showed that the Nicaraguan hierarchy is no longer united behind the Cardinal, whose detestation for everything d'Escoto stands for is notorious. In fact the advent of d'Escoto's *Viacrucis* had obliged the Bishop of Estelí – whose northern diocese has suffered more than most from the depredations of the *contras* – to stand up and be counted. And he had – apparently after initial hesitation – chosen to be counted on the side of the pilgrims and not that of the Cardinal. It was the most notable victory to date of the *insurrección evangélica*.

Monsignor López Ardón also expressed the hope, at Estelí, that 'the procession towards Managua' should be 'oriented with maturity', meaning that he was asking d'Escoto to lay off the Cardinal. But there was no chance that the leader of the *Viacrucis* would do that. The whole enterprise was directed against the Cardinal's betrayal – as d'Escoto saw it – of both Faith and Fatherland. D'Escoto was now referring to Obando by name. 'It is intolerable', said d'Escoto at Condega,

> that the medals of honour which the Government of the United States has offered to Cardinal Obando in order to make a political tool out of him [*para instrumentalizarlo politicamente*] should be accepted. If the attitudes of certain Bishops don't change, we Christians will one day find ourselves in the painful position of asking ourselves: 'Can we celebrate the Eucharist in communion with those who use their religious influence against our people?'

These words – with their strong hint of impending schism – were stuff to make even liberation theologians hold their breath. D'Escoto is their prophet, and they love him, but he frightens them. But then they also feel that that is what a prophet is *for*.

At Managua, in the Cardinal's own Archdiocese, on the last day of the *Viacrucis*, d'Escoto changed his tone, though not really his tune. Addressing a large crowd in front of the gaunt shell of Managua's Cathedral (ruined in the 1972 earthquake) Father d'Escoto held out his arms and entreated 'Brother Michael', *Hermano Miguel*, to come and join the *Viacrucis*. To no-one's surprise, *Hermano Miguel* did not respond.

It is hard to gauge the impact of such a strange event as the *insurrección evangélica*. D'Escoto himself refuses to do so; he leaves all that to God, he says. Within Nicaragua, the *insurrección* never amounted to a mass movement. The maximum turn-out was that 20 000 at Estelí – a drop in the ocean compared with the 700 000 or so who came out to see the Pope in Managua. Yet the size of the turn-out – the 'gate' – is not necessarily what counts most. The intensity of the commitment behind the presence may count more. And d'Escoto's movement was one of high intensity. The psychic force of the storm it produced was enough to crack, at Estelí, the hitherto monolithic facade of the Nicaraguan hierarchy. And note had to be taken of that by all, both in Latin America and in Rome, who were concerned over the balance between the forces represented by the slogan, *un solo Dios*, and those represented by the slogan *el Dios de los Pobres*. *El bochorno* had been the round of *un solo Dios*. The *insurrección* round went to *el Dios de los Pobres*.

Whether by coincidence or not, the succeeding months have witnessed a certain relaxation of the ecclesiastical pressures against the Sandinistas, both from the Nicaraguan hierarchy and from Rome. As mentioned earlier, the Nicaraguan hierarchy, in its April 'Letter on the Eucharist' appeared to distance itself from the *contras*, whom Obando had previously appeared to back. A very senior Sandinista with whom I discussed this shift had a down-to-earth explanation of it, unconnected with the impact of the *insurrección*. (This particular Sandinista is of a cool, pragmatic temperament, and so not a natural d'Escoto fan.) 'The bishops' he said, 'were up for the *contras*, as long as they thought the *contras* might be going to win. But now that the *contras* don't look as if they could ever win, the bishops draw aside a bit.'

I suspect that the two explanations – *insurrección* and *contra* failure – may not be incompatible or unconnected. The Sandinistas look a tougher nut to crack now than they did a few years back. And *one* of the things that makes them hard to destroy is the spiritual fire-power concentrated against the theological enemies of *Sandinismo*, by Miguel d'Escoto and his *compañeros*, out of 'the new trench for peace'.

During 1986, too, Rome greatly relaxed its pressure on 'liberation theology' – the culture from which *Sandinismo* derives so much of its vital force. The 'Instruction on Christian Freedom and Liberation' issued by the Vatican in April 1986 was welcomed by perhaps the most eminent liberation theologian, Gustavo Gutiérrez of Peru, as 'the end of an era'. And it does indeed signal the end of the open season on liberation theology which the Vatican had been conducting, especially since the Pope's visit to Nicaragua: the attempt to stamp out 'deviations and risks of deviation' conducted on the Pope's behalf by Cardinal Joseph Ratzinger, prefect of the Congregation for the Doctrine of the Faith. Through Ratzinger, John Paul II was addressing a magisterial '*Silencio*!' to the worshippers of *el Dios de los Pobres* in Latin America. But it simply did not work. Those concerned just carried on as before – or worse, from the Pope's point of view, as in the case of Nicaragua's *insurrección*. What the April Instruction does – without of course acknowledging the fact – is to register the failure of an effort to exercise papal authority. Although John Paul II is generally regarded as a particularly strong Pope, that Instruction is one of the weakest documents ever to reach the world under the authority of a Roman Pontiff. Decoded, the message that went out *urbi et orbi* in April was: 'as you won't listen to what I've been trying to tell you, now I'm going to tell you something different, which I hope you'll like a bit better'.

What both the Pope and the Nicaraguan hierarchy have been finding out and acknowledging in their way is that *el Dios de los Pobres* is what Edmund Burke found 'the nature of things' to be: 'a sturdy adversary'. I mean *el Dios de los Pobres*, not as He might be defined, contained and sanitised in Rome, but as He exists in the minds and hearts of those who call upon His name, throughout Latin America. His power was felt in Estelí in February, and in Managua and in Rome in April.

I said earlier that when I looked back on that scene in which the Pope admonishes Ernesto, the one I feel sorry for is the Pope. The reason for this is that Ernesto and his friends are engaged among living realities – the cause of the poor, the defence of Nicaragua – whereas the Pope has dedicated his life to the resuscitation of an extinct abstraction: the *Magisterium*, the teaching authority of the Church, of which the supreme exponent is the Pope. Some people think that the Pope is succeeding in bringing back this authority; that is the meaning of the phrase 'the Catholic restoration' used by Paul Johnson and others. It is true that this Pope is far more popular than any Pope has been before. But popularity is not to be confused with authority. Catholics love this Pope, but when he solemnly tells them that they must behave in some way that they do not find convenient, they just do not take a blind bit of notice of him.

The critical test, by which the *Magisterium* has been seen to fail, in our time, is that of contraception. If there is one matter in which the Church's teaching, in the second half of the twentieth century, has been clear and firm, that is the matter of contraception.

Pope Paul VI laid down the law on that, for Catholics, in the Encyclical *Humanae Vitae*: Pope John Paul II in *Familiaris Consortio*, has corroborated and fortified the law laid down in *Humanae Vitae*. The message of the *Magisterium* is crystal clear: Catholics are *not* to use contraceptives. And Catholics have gone right on using contraceptives: not only in North America, but in Catholic countries like Ireland and Poland, where Catholic education is strong, and Church attendance very high. If the very poor, in the poorest regions, still do not use contraceptives, this is not because they are mindful of the teaching of *Humanae Vitae* and *Familiaris Consortio*, but because they *are* very poor, and therefore ignorant, and therefore do not yet understand about contraception.

Then John Paul II brought the weight of the *Magisterium* to bear against the liberation theologians, but again the thing did not work. The spring seems to be broken.

John Paul II is getting to look more and more like the popular misconception of an international Canute, magisterially perambulating all the strands of the world, before huge and admiring audiences, without the slightest effect on the tides.

The contemporary failure of the *Magisterium* seems to have far reaching implications for Latin America. The revolutionary Christians fought for their *espacio*; the traditionalist counter-attack has failed, and the revolutionaries now seem to be secure in control of that *espacio*, where they have 'appropriated' the symbols of the Catholic Church – such as the *Viacrucis* – with the emotional loyalties that go with these. Along with the revolutionary process, a new Reformation is in progress. Only the revolutionary reformers of *our* time do not need to break with Rome. They can keep the Roman symbols – and the Roman sacraments which is more important – without Rome's retaining any vestige of real authority over them. Rome may discipline theologians for what they publish – though Rome seems by now to have realised that that too can be counter-productive. But what Rome cannot possibly do is to supervise how Christianity is taught by thousands of ordinary priests, nuns, other religious, Delegates of the Word, and other lay people among the poor of Latin America. Many, probably most of those – those that are in regular contact with the poor, that is – have been radicalised by their experiences among the poor. Specifically, they have been radicalised by their experiences of what the rich, in most parts of Latin America, have been prepared to do to the poor and to those who try to help the poor. The Church of *el Dios de los Pobres* has its twentieth-century martyrs in Latin America, of whom the most venerated is the murdered Archbishop Romero of San Salvador. The teachers of the poor are teaching Christianity as a revolutionary doctrine, and there is nothing 'the Church' can any longer do about that. More than that, the Vatican, in calling off its crusade against 'deviations and risk of deviations' has itself 'deviated' into giving a kind of blessing to *los Cristianos Revolucionarios*. The most remarkable words in the April Instruction of 1986 are those which proclaim it 'perfectly legitimate that those who suffer oppression on the part of the wealthy or politically powerful should take action'. (A later passage makes clear that 'armed struggle' may be included under 'action'.)

Cardinal Obando may well wish to try to turn the words 'or

politically powerful' into a kind of charter for the *contras*, but that is not how these words are likely to be read by most people in Latin America who know about them. Most people – whether of left or right – will read these words, in the context of the Instruction that embodies them, as meaning that the Vatican can no longer be relied on as an ally for conservative forces in Latin America. If that interpretation is right, as I believe it to be, Miguel Obando y Bravo's life-line to Rome is endangered, within less than a year of his receiving that red hat for services to conservatism. Put not your trust in pontiffs.

Now all this has an important bearing on the prospects for *Sandinismo*, and also on the prospects for efforts to contain or extirpate *Sandinismo*. But before I try to explain the bearing and the prospects, as I see them, I had better try to explain what *Sandinismo* actually is: also, of course, as I see it.

Sandinismo is apparently regarded in Washington as an essentially alien ideology, cunningly decked out in some kind of Latin American fancy-dress. I don't know whether they really believe these things in Washington, or whether they only pretend to believe them, but if they do believe this one, they are in fundamental error, and headed for more unnecessary trouble. *Sandinismo* is a thoroughly Latin American ideology, with deep roots in Latin American history, and specifically in the history of Nicaragua. Far from being an alien phenomenon in Nicaragua, *Sandinismo* is a native response to alien domination: the alien domination in question being that of the United States. Perhaps that is the basic reason why *Sandinismo*, viewed from Washington, looks so alien.

Augusto César Sandino (1895–1934), the eponymous hero of this ideology, became a national hero to the Nicaraguans for the same basic reasons as those for which Joan of Arc became a national heroine to the French: he fought the foreigners who had invaded his country, and he was murdered by the servants of those same foreigners. (English historians – in the case of Joan – and American ones – in the case of Sandino – may define the issues differently, but I am talking about how the issues appear to *nationalists*, of France and Nicaragua, which is what matters in considering *Sandinismo*.)

The particular foreigners whom Sandino fought, at the head of a small but resolute band of guerrillas, were the US Marines, who were in Nicaragua, at the invitation of Nicaragua's Conservative faction, from 1909 to 1933. Sandino fought the Marines, with varying fortunes, from 1927 to 1932. He was successful to the extent that the

Americans were unable either to subdue him or buy him off – the latter being extremely unusual at the time in Central American politics, civil or military.

The last of the Marines left Nicaragua on 2 January 1933. They did not leave because they had been defeated by Sandino – as the simpler sorts of Sandinista rhetoric suggest – but because US policy had changed in favour of something subtler. But Sandino had probably quite a lot to do with the change in policy. The indomitable guerrilla leader had been news throughout the world and had caught the imagination of nationalists, not only in Latin America, but as far away as China. The publicity was judged to be bad for the United States. And it was possible to protect US interests by other means. The means consisted of the Nicaraguan National Guard, selected and trained – and originally commanded – by US Marines. The new commander of the National Guard, selected by the US Ambassador, was Anastasio Somoza Debayle, the founder of the dynasty which was to rule Nicaragua until the Revolution of 1979. On 21 February 1934, Sandino and two of his generals, after dining in Managua with the then President of Nicaragua, Juan Bautista Sacasa, were abducted by members of the National Guard, driven out to Managua airfield and shot by firing squad. Two years later Somoza – who had been at a poetry-reading while Sandino and his comrades were being shot – ousted Sandino's host, Sacasa, and made himself President.

A marked feature of *Sandinismo*, as mentioned, is its cult of heroes and martyrs. Sandino himself is the supreme hero and proto-martyr. '*Bienvenido a la Patria de Sandino*!' says a large sign at Sandino Airport, Managua, recalling the scene of the original martyrdom. There are portraits of him everywhere: a skinny, morose little man, invariably wearing a ten-gallon hat, and looking like a figure out of a 1920s cowboy movie. You see sketches of him in chalk on rocks along the Nicaraguan country roads; just lines, like a match-stick man, identifiable only by the hat. And in at least one place, an economical artist paid homage to Sandino by the simple hieroglyph:

Sandino's status as a martyr may appear a bit anomalous, since Sandino was not a Christian, although he did believe in God. Like many mavericks in the 1920s, he was a theosophist and a spiritualist. But Christian Sandinistas of today insist that whatever Sandino *thought* he was, he was indeed a true Christian martyr: one who fought and died for the God of the Poor. He refused to call himself a Christian, because the most eminent Nicaraguan 'Christians' of his day – like that Bishop of Granada who blessed the US Marines – were in the service of the enemy. These, however, were not really Christian at all, but worshippers of Mammon. Had Sandino lived to see the advent of liberation theology, he would have proclaimed himself a Christian revolutionary. And on that last point, at least, I think the Christian Sandinistas are probably right.

To the US media of his day, of course, Sandino was no kind of hero or martyr, Christian or other, but a bandit and a red. A bandit he certainly was not. The question of whether he was a red is more complex. In several ways, he *was* a red. In his Mexican years – 1922–26 – he associated with communists and other revolutionary ideologues and picked up some of their outlook and vocabulary. He was not a marxist – no-one who was into theosophy and spiritualism could reasonably be described as a marxist – and although he did often use the language of class war, I think it clear that, with him, the class struggle was secondary to the national struggle. This appears in the fact that Sandino stopped fighting once the Marines had been withdrawn. The *social* structure in Nicaragua was not changed by the departure of the Marines. The fact that Sandino spent his last evening on earth with the very 'moderate' President Sacasa seems to indicate that social conditions did not arouse in Sandino the same elemental passions that drove him on, over five years, to fight the foreign foe on Nicaraguan soil.

The primacy of nationalism also appears in the incident that led – according to his own account – to Sandino's departure from Mexico and return to Nicaragua. A Mexican revolutionary acquaintance of his, dismissing the possibility of revolution in Nicaragua ever, said that every Nicaraguan was a *vendepatria*. The mere thought of being taken for a *vendepatria* – a man prepared to sell his country – was so unbearable to Sandino that he determined to return to Nicaragua and raise an army to fight the US Marines. And the expression *vendepatria* is even now the most deadly insult in the Sandinista lexicon. It is the word with which they brand people like Archbishop Obando.

In general, all Sandino's most passionate utterances, all those that are treasured by contemporary Sandinistas, are expressions of exalted nationalism. I could cite a number of examples, but there is just one that sums them all up. This consists of the four words of Sandino's that are the national motto of Sandinista Nicaragua: *Patria Libre o Morir*! Give me liberty or give me death.

The second hero and martyr in the Sandinista pantheon is the poet Rigoberto López Pérez who in 1956 killed Anastasio Somoza Debayle, at a party in León, and was then shot down by Somoza's bodyguards. President Eisenhower called López 'the murderer of a friend of the United States', but of course to Sandinistas he is not a murderer but the executioner of Sandino's murderer. López's deed and fate were an inspiration to *Sandinismo*'s third hero and martyr, who was also its leader and principal ideologue, Carlos Fonseca Amador, co-founder along with Silvio Mayorga and Tomás Borge, of the Frente Sandinista de Liberación Nacional in 1961. (Both Fonseca and Mayorga were later killed by the National Guard.)

In long 'Notes' which he wrote on López, Fonseca quotes Machiavelli's epithet on tyrannicides: *rarisimos*. Fonseca also quotes some of López's own poetry, including the lines:

> Nicaragua is getting back to being
> (or may be for the first time)
> a free country
> without affronts and without stains:
> *una patria libre*
> *sin afrentas y sin manchas*

According to Fonseca the words 'or may be for the first time' have 'an extraordinary revolutionary transcendence' in their context. It is, I believe, this sense of national humiliation – Fonseca himself writes of *la patria humillada* – which supplies the basic drive of *Sandinismo*. Up to July 1979 the Sandinistas fought to wipe out what they regarded as the humiliation of their country. And since July 1979 – and especially since Ronald Reagan became President – they have been fighting to avert the re-imposition of national humiliation on their country. And to Sandinistas, national humiliation is precisely what Reagan insists on, when he refuses to negotiate with them, and tells them to negotiate with the *contras*. It is not in the nature of Sandinistas to negotiate with *contras*. *Not* negotiating with *contras* is what their tradition, their whole intellectual, moral and emotional formation is all about. *Patria Libre o Morir*.

As well as being inspired by Sandino, López and the Nicaraguan experience, Fonseca and his *compañeros* were immediately inspired by the Cuban revolution, which had triumphed in Havana just before they established the Frente (in Honduras). Unlike Sandino, Fonseca and his *compañeros* were intellectuals, and committed marxist-leninists; and through them marxism-leninism became an element in *Sandinismo*. According to the thinking of President Reagan and his fellow-believers this automatically makes Sandinistas into accomplices in the international communist design, masterminded by Moscow. This kind of thinking is apparently impervious to the massive historical evidence which refutes it. In the 1950s, people like Reagan, by exactly this same reasoning, believed that the Chinese communists, being marxists, were *ipso facto* tools of Moscow. Those who, knowing China, argued that this was not the case, and that Chinese nationalism was still a major force in Chinese communism, were dismissed as naive – and in many cases also dismissed from their jobs. But the equation 'marxist equals tool of Moscow', far from being called into question after it broke down in China, is still being applied, with exactly the same overbearing confidence, in Central America.

In fact, those Sandinistas who were, and are, marxist-leninists are no more apt to toe the Kremlin line than the Catholic Sandinistas are to toe the Vatican line. Carlos Fonseca despised the Moscow-line marxist Nicaraguan Socialist Party, for being more faithful to the Moscow line than to Nicaragua. He called these Moscow-liners 'false marxists'. Fonseca and his friends were 'the true marxists'. That is a pretty solid refutation of the Reagan equation.

A good clue to the real nature of *Sandinismo* is contained in the Sandinista oath, as quoted by Fonseca, (who probably drafted it) which runs as follows:

> Before the image of Augusto César Sandino and Ernesto Che Guevara, before the memory of the heroes and martyrs of Latin America and all humanity, before history. I put my hand on the black and red banner which signifies '*Patria Libre o Morir*', and I swear to defend with arms in hand *el decoro nacional* [national decorum/decency/respect] and to fight for the redemption of the oppressed and exploited of Nicaragua and of the world. If I fulfil this oath, the liberation of Nicaragua and of all peoples will be a reward; if I betray this oath, a shameful death and ignominy will be my punishment.

You could take that oath, in good conscience, without being a marxist. But you could not sincerely take it, or repeat the Sandinista slogans, without being a nationalist. Within the Sandinista complex, nationalism and commitment to the cause of the exploited, are as it were 'required' subjects. Marxism and revolutionary Christianity are optional, at least as far as the rank and file are concerned. And even if all the nine *comandantes* are marxists, as has been widely believed, their marxism is still their own home-made version, not made in Moscow.

I believe that marxism – even of the home-made variety – is now recessive within *Sandinismo*, and that the revolutionary Christian element is becoming dominant. Education has been entrusted to Sandinista Jesuits. Fernando Cardenal is Minister for Education, and César Jerez – Miguel d'Escoto's friend – is head of the Universidad Centroamericano. Perhaps even more significant is what looks quite like a 'conversion' on the part of Tomás Borge. Borge – as the only survivor out of the three founders of the Frente Sandinista – is virtually the custodian of the Sandinista faith. And Borge – as noted earlier – has been increasingly using the language of *Christian* Messianism – 'the Kingdom of God' – rather than the marxist variety. Granted Borge's immense authority, this can only make the Christian element less 'optional', and more central, within *Sandinismo*.

I think that, in the early days of the revolution, revolutionaries like Borge were a bit wary about their Christian partners. Might not these *compañeros* defect, or at least wobble, when the theological heat was on? But that matter was put to the test, and the *compañeros* in question (with few exceptions) came out of it with flying colours. Paradoxically, it was the Pope's visit, *el bochorno de Managua*, that did most to increase the influence of the very people whose influence he (the Pope) wanted to diminish: the Christian Sandinistas. For there was the Successor of Peter in person, wagging a finger of reproach at these *compañeros*, and they had neither defected nor wobbled. On the contrary they had launched their counter-offensive, the *insurrección evangélica*. And finally, in the Vatican Instruction of April 1986, it was the Pope, not the Christian Sandinistas and liberation theologians, who was seen to give ground. The prestige of the revolutionary Christians had never been higher than it was in 1986.

I think it would now be more accurate to speak of *Sandinismo* as a *faith* rather than an ideology. It is the most formidable kind of faith, the kind that is emotionally fused with national pride. And this kind of faith is now alight in every corner of Latin America. It is true that it is not the *only* kind of faith around. Latin America is now a melting pot, where faith is concerned. The traditional Catholic Church is collapsing, not just on one side but on two. On one side are the Christian revolutionaries, enlarging that *espacio* of theirs, appropriating the symbols, and so on. On the other, lots of Catholics have been defecting to the Protestant fundamentalist sects. The Latin American bishops, in their reply to the Pope's Instruction, sought to ascribe the inroads of the fundamentalists to the activities of the CIA. I think the bishops over-estimate the CIA. It looks as if there are a lot of people who are attracted neither to the old kind of Catholicism nor the new one, and who are looking for a different kind of faith; more individual, more quietist. But it is the new Catholicism that has the *political* dynamic, the capacity for revolutionary social transformation, and the capacity to fuse with national pride – as in earlier times millennialist Puritanism did, first in England and then in North America.

Is it necessary for the United States to take on the new faith, by storming the new Geneva: Managua?

In what remains of this chapter, I shall briefly consider three arguments by which it is alleged to be necessary to proceed in this way.

The first is that the new faith is not really a faith at all, but a disguise under which Soviet power advances; the second, that even if the new faith *is* native to Latin America, it is basically hostile to the USA; and the third that the new Faith is intrinsically oppressive and totalitarian.

As regards the first part, I have already discussed the native roots of *Sandinismo*, and shown – I hope – that one of its essential characteristics is the restoration of national pride. People who are as fiercely and proudly nationalist as the Sandinistas are, are not going to hand their country over to a new master, once they have got rid of the old one. Or rather, they are not going to to that *voluntarily*. They could be pushed into it. They could be pushed into it if they felt it was the only alternative to surrendering to the power of the United States. The Cuban precedent is there. The more 'successful' Reagan's pressure on Nicaragua is, the more Nicaragua is likely to be forced in that direction. If Soviet power does indeed come to extend into Central America, it will be courtesy of Ronald Reagan.

There is more substance in the second point. Latin America nationalism, including *Sandinismo*, *is* anti-American; or anti-*North*-American as they say, since Nicaraguans are Americans themselves. Sandino himself was fiercely and loudly anti-North American: as well he might be, seeing that the people he was fighting were the US Marines, in his own country.

Latin American nationalism has always had to define itself *against* US power. For Latin American nationlists, the national humiliations which they so deeply resented were consequences of the direct or indirect applications of US power. The 'affronts' and 'stains' which Rigoberto López Pérez felt he had to wipe out at the cost of his own life, came from in the USA. For all these people, the eagle is, and long has been, a bird of ill omen.

At Sandinista rallies, the participants have a custom of breaking into ritual chants, at certain prescribed moments. Among these chants, there is one little number which runs:

Aquí, allá
el Yanqui morirá!
(Here, there
the Yankee will die!)

Being against *el Yanqui* is central to the Sandinista culture. But it is also important to see just what *el Yanqui* means in this context. *El Yanqui* is not just any old Yankee. Thousands of real, live Yankees come to Nicaragua every month, without needing a visa, and are welcomed warmly – as several of them told us – by Nicaraguans of all descriptions, both Sandinistas and others. *El Yanqui*, as in that ditty, is the North American who seeks to impose his will on Latin America. *That* is what must die.

Culturally, Nicaraguans (including Sandinistas) are closer to the United States, in some ways, than most any other Latin American people. One morning at breakfast in the Hotel Intercontinental, Managua, I was reading *Barricada* – the official organ of the *Frente Sandinista* – when my eye was caught by a headline:

Yanquis Vencidos (Yankees beaten)

Who, I wondered, had managed to inflict a defeat on the Colossus of the North – and if they had, why was *Barricada* running the story on page 14? Then I read the story and found that the people who had beaten the Yankees were the Cleveland Indians.

El beisbol is the national game in Nicaragua, and a national passion, for Sandinistas as well as others. You can see people playing it in every village, and kids practising on small patches of waste land, in any poor *barrio*. The only riots that took place during our stay in Nicaragua were between two lots of baseball fans. And all the papers – even *Barricada* – give lots of space, not only to Nicaraguan baseball, but also to *US* baseball.

It is curious that the two Spanish-speaking countries where baseball is the national game – Cuba and Nicaragua – are also the two which have managed to shake off US political hegemony. Baseball must be character-building.

The United States, it seems to me, would possess a tremendous *natural* attractive power over Latin America – a natural gravitational field – if successive US administrations were not forever counteracting that pull by pushing the countries concerned around, in misguided and counter-productive efforts to make them more 'pro-American'. These are precisely the efforts that have in fact made them *anti*-American to the extent that they are.

There is, I think, very little personal hatred in Nicaraguan anti-Americanism. Not even personal hatred for Ronald Reagan; Miguel d'Escoto did indeed fancy that the President might be a victim of diabolical possession, but even that was more in sorrow than in anger. There has been nothing in Nicaragua, about Reagan, that at all corresponds to, for example, the torrent of frantic and obscene iconography which Buenos Aires directed at Margaret Thatcher, at the time of the Falklands War. Sandinistas, indeed, understand Ronald Reagan rather better than most foreigners do. They understand and up to a point respect, his talk about 'standing tall', because 'standing tall' is what *Sandinismo*, too, is all about. They recognise in Reagan, *to that extent*, a partly kindred spirit. 'Ronald Reagan', one Sandinista told me 'is the Che Guevara of imperialism'.

What Sandinistas cannot accept – and will resist, literally to their last breath – is the insistence that, for Americans to be seen to stand tall, Nicaraguans must cringe.

Neither the 'communist' point nor the 'anti-American' point, as justifying intervention in Nicaragua, has any validity, in my view. There remains the third point: 'totalitarian oppressive . . .'.

I am concerned in this chapter primarily with *faiths*: with the element of faith in *Sandinismo*, and with *Sandinismo as* faith. But it is necessary at this point to consider, more succinctly, the nature of the Sandinista polity.

The dominant characteristic of the Sandinista polity is government by a revolutionary elite: the Frente Sandinista itself, headed by the nine *comandantes de la revolución*, the National Directorate. This governing principle was already established in the formation of the Frente itself, twenty-five years ago, and maintained throughout the revolution. The revolution is not held to have been completed by the fall of Somoza but to be still continuing; the present phase being the defence of the revolution against the counter-revolutionary forces in the pay of the United States.

In this phase, as in the earlier ones, the Frente sees itself as the Vanguard of the People, *la Vanguardia del Pueblo*. Those who make up the vanguard are, in Fonseca's words 'joined to the people and guiding it', *juntos al pueblo y guiándolo*. This concept may be Fonseca's – and so *Sandinismo*'s – principal debt to Lenin, but it is a lot older than Lenin and is probably inherent in every revolutionary 'process'; the Cromwellian Saints and Robespierre's Jacobins saw matters in essentially the same light, subject to wide rhetorical variations.

The principle of rule by a revolutionary elite was overlaid, not superseded, by the general elections held in November 1984. Not that the elections seem to have been rigged. There were many international observers around, including western parliamentary delegations, and most of these agreed that, on the whole, the elections were fairly conducted – and a lot more fairly than most in Latin America. But of course the mere fact of being the incumbents gave the Sandinistas an enormous advantage, in conditions where voters had no previous experience of free elections. More fundamentally, it is extremely doubtful whether the opposition even if it had won an electoral majority, would thereby have attained real power. Throughout the whole thing, the Army remained the *Ejército Sandinista*, the police the *Policía Sandinista*. Elsewhere in Latin America, even the fairest elections generally lead to no change in the real structure of power, because the elected civilians never attain more than nominal control over the armed forces. And I do not believe that the Frente would have allowed even a victorious opposition to de-Sandinise the armed forces.

Indeed it seems clear that the Frente could not, *consistently with the Sandinista faith to which it is committed*, have accepted anything of the kind. At least as long as the revolution is threatened by the counter-revolution – and God knows how long that may be – no proper Sandinista can possibly consent to letting the *vendepatrias* take over again, either by elections or by force.

The idea of democratic process has no special sanctity in Sandinista eyes – or in many other Latin American eyes either. Elections may be tactically useful, in certain conditions, but no Sandinista could permit them to prevail against the truly sacred things: *La Revolución, la Patria, el Reino de Dios*. It is a question of faith, and articles of faith are not changed by counting heads. The same sacred things are also felt to be more important than freedom of expression. If censorship is useful for the defence of the revolution, then let there be censorship is the Sandinista position.

The Sandinista elite is unquestionably 'joined to the people', in that – unlike other Latin American juntas – it has worked to improve the conditions of the poor and to provide humane government. I would define the nature of this state as elitist and authoritarian, but not totalitarian, and not physically oppressive; although it can be held – and is held by the opposition – that rule by an elite and press censorship in themselves constitute oppression. That may be so, but, if so, it is a milder form of oppression than the word generally conjures up or than prevails in most of Latin America. The security forces are more restrained, and less apt to throw their weight around, than in other Latin American countries. The penal system is mild; this is no *gulag* State. And people – although not free to publish attacks on the regime in the media – feel absolutely free to attack it in private conversation, or from the pulpit. All that may, of course, change, under the pressures of the war, and other pressures. I am speaking of how things were in 1986. The picture projected by the Reagan administration of present-day Nicaragua as a sort of totalitarian inferno is very far from the truth – as even American Embassy officials occasionally admit. In its early years, the regime made remarkable progress in the eradication of illiteracy and disease, and the replacement of sub-standard housing. But these achievements are now at risk – and there have been set-backs in all these fields – because of the economic pressures on Nicaragua and because of the disruption of production in the countryside – and flight of population – caused by *contra* attacks on villages and co-operatives. There are now shortages of virtually everything, even water. Even the privileged guests of the Hotel Intercontinental in Managua have to do without a water-supply on Tuesdays and Fridays every week. In some of the *barrios* people count themselves lucky if they *get* water on two days a week. People are experiencing great hardship. One young mother – not an enemy of the regime – said to me with passion: 'Day after day, things are getting worse and worse'.

So in terms of making life miserable for most Nicaraguans, the Reagan pressures have been quite successful. But the success would only make some kind of sense – even of a nasty kind – if the misery were putting the skids under the Sandinistas. It is true that if elections were held now it is *possible* though not in my opinion likely – that the public hardship might result in a majority against the Frente. But, as argued above – and as Washington must know – the Sandinistas have no intention of letting themselves be put out of power in this way. Nor are unarmed masses of people about to rise up and expel the Sandinistas. The pressures could only have effect if they tended to split the Sandinistas themselves, including the Ejército Sandinista. But they do not work that way; quite the contrary. All this pressure, coming from Washington, tends to unite Sandinistas because it threatens the most cherished deity in their pantheon: *el decoro nacional*. Nicaraguans feeling a sense of national pride – almost always defined with negative reference to the United States – tend to rally behind the Frente in answer to so blatant a challenge from the North. Some Nicaraguan nationalists did initially rally to the *contra* cause – around the theme of 'the revolution betrayed' – but several of these have now given up, the most prominent being Eden Pastora. After these defections, the *contra* cause has been looking more and more like what the Sandinistas always said it was: a *vendepatria* enterprise.

It is true that there are sizeable numbers of Nicaraguans who care very little about *la patria* or *el decoro nacional*. For those in the Atlantic provinces for whom Spanish is not the first language, and whose religion is not Catholic – English-speakers of Jamaican origin and some Indians – neither the notion of *la patria* nor – consequently – *Sandinismo* can have much appeal. I was reliably informed in Bluefields that about four-fifths of local young males subject to call up have left the country rather than undergo their Servicio Militar Patriótico. And it is also because a lack of 'Nicaraguan' feeling in these provinces – and consequent resentment of Sandinista efforts to mobilise support – that the *contras* were initially able to make headway in this region; though they subsequently lost much support, because of the indiscriminately brutal behaviour of many of their number. Today the prevailing attitude in these provinces seems to be one of 'wait and see', with little enthusiasm either for the Sandinistas or for the *contras*.

But it is on the Spanish and Catholic Pacific side, where most of the population is, that *la patria* is, and has its devotees, the Sandinistas. The Sandinistas cannot, in my opinion, be driven from Managua except by the direct use of US force. And if they are driven out of Managua they will still go on fighting, as guerrillas, and others will join them, and US forces will have to stay there, in order to prevent a Sandinista come-back. And in that way, bogged down in Nicaragua, the United States will be taking on the forces of nationalism, not only in Nicaragua, but throughout Latin America. That did not work out well in Indo-China, and I do not think it would work well in Latin America either.

It is true that in the past the US has been able to intervene in Latin

America repeatedly and with impunity. But things are a bit different now; there is a new spirit around. In particular, the new alignment of *el Dios de los Pobres* and *la patria* – Faith and Fatherland – is shifting the balance. Pope John Paul II took on that formidable alliance, without quite knowing what he was taking on, and then found that he had to back away. I hope that Ronald Reagan and George Bush too may back away, before it is too late.

9 The Rise and Fall of Social Catholicism in Costa Rica

Rodolfo Cardenal

The so-called thesis of the two spheres, of Church and State, which characterised the first decades of the 1900s, led to the consideration of national reality independently of faith. The Costa Rican people were very religious with regard to helping with the construction of churches, attendance at worship and observance of formal morality; but in electoral matters they followed their own judgement, ignoring the directions of the clergy and the episcopate. The latter wanted Catholic governments who would recognise the Church as a power and treat it as such. In addition, they sought to avoid the election of communist candidates. The Church's mission was understood in anti-communist terms. This was clearly demonstrated during the banana strikes in the early decades of the twentieth century, when the episcopate understood the workers' demands as communism. The Church understood its mission to be halting the advance of communism.

Apart from opposition to communism and the illusory social reforms in which the Church made common cause with reduced groups of liberal coffee planters, the thesis of the two spheres was upheld, that is, the clergy abstained from intervention in social matters. This tendency was accentuated during the 1930s but accordingly the people experienced disorientation. The disorientation and the helplessness of the believing people were the constant concern of this Church, except for a brief period of major social reforms which resulted in the Costa Rican welfare State.

THE UNLIKELY ALLIANCE

The most creative moment of the Costa Rican church was during the 1940s when Monsignor Víctor Sanabria, archbishop of the capital, with great vision assisted in the building up of the welfare State which has characterised the social and political order of Costa Rica. Before arriving in San José, Monsignor Sanabria, still bishop of Alajuela in 1938, had already shown his concern for the impoverished masses.

The initiation of the so-called social reforms was due to President Rafael A. Calderón, who had studied in Cardinal Mercier's school, was familiar with the social encyclicals and cited them frequently as he did the Decrees of Malines. The first social reform was the creation of social security in October 1941. This institution of social services was planned in the greatest secrecy in order to avoid the opposition of the coffee oligarchy. Calderón's government sought popular support only after it had legally established social security. However, Archbishop Sanabria had already defined his position in a pastoral letter, 'On Just Wages' (*Sobre el justo salario*) dated 29 June 1941. In it he denounced poverty, insufficient clothing and malnutrition. He defended the social function of wealth and the obligation of the State to intervene in the economy to benefit the poor. Likewise, he also defended the right of the Church to intervene and announced his support for social legislation, social security and benefit taxes (*impuestos de beneficencia*) for hospitals. The archbishop was not followed by his clergy; only a minority supported him in this venture.

The so-called 'social guarantees' followed; that is, minimum pay, maximum working hours, equality of pay for both sexes, the right to belong to a trade union and the right to strike. The State committed itself to promoting co-operatives, procuring housing, demanding minimum conditions of hygiene and security from landlords and improving the technical training of workers. Monsignor Sanabria approved and promised to support this plan which was approved by the Assembly on 2 July 1943. The archbishop obtained a declaration of support from the episcopal conference.

Naturally, faced with opposition from those sectors most privileged (through exportation of coffee and bananas), the government desperately needed popular support to advance reforms and to keep itself in power. The necessary social support came from a 'strange' alliance between the government, the Church represented by the archbishop and a certain number of priests and the communist party. The understanding was possible because all of these social forces concurred in their interest in improving the situation of the workers. The archbishop went as far as to march beside the leader of the communist party in the streets of the capital during a workers' demonstration. The communist party accepted a change in name to broaden its social base, including Catholics.

The Right did not delay in reacting against the archbishop, using everything from the most 'clever' editorials to the most vulgar caricatures. Monsignor Sanabria defended his position, even in front of his own clergy who still did not support him. For Monsignor Sanabria, the agreement was a decisive step towards the unity of all sectors interested in social justice. Those who protested most were the liberals, who claimed the archbishop had never wanted to have dialogue with the Church and had used their opposition to communism to defend their selfish interests.

Monsignor Sanabria recalled that the bishops' warning against communism had not had the desired effect because the people, with that class instinct they had shown they possessed, knew somehow that the Church favoured their enemies, that is, those who had reduced them to poverty by economic exploitation and social domination. However, they had not ceased to be profoundly religious on account of that. Likewise he pointed out that the people did not understand how the Church had attacked communism and had not done likewise with liberal positivism, equally characterised by its materialism and atheism. The people were convinced, Monsignor Sanabria added, of the alliance between the Church and capitalism on account of its silences and its partial denunciations. Then the archbishop moved to the attack. The coffee planters and liberals had become disillusioned with the social doctrine of the Church because they thought 'that the only mission of the Church in these matters was to preach resignation to poverty, or else merely to recommend the fulfilling of the duties of charity.' ('Words to the Reverend Clergy' – *Palabras al Venerable Clero*).

It was now time, therefore, to place oneself on the side of justice and charity 'and since justice is more often on the side of the poor, we shall not refuse to be equally often on the side of the same poor. That is our mission . . .' (*Ibid.*)

At that time the communist party was the only one which seemed to offer to improve the situation of the workers. Monsignor Sanabria was familiar with the brief history of the communist party. Many of its members were anxious Costa Ricans who had unsuccessfully belonged to a reformist party very much tied to the Church. What interested them more than materialist philosophical theses was social justice.

Monsignor Sanabria probably took the unusual step of allying himself with the communists at that time to avoid civil war which he saw as imminent. In fact, when it broke out in 1948, he tried in vain to negotiate between the two sides. His mediation failed because of the intransigence of the government, fearful that if they surrendered, the rebels would put an end to the reforms, and because of the intransigence of the rebels who considered the government communist.

The archbishop's support for Calderón's government was rewarded with the suppression, in July 1942, of the liberal laws of 1884. The suppression of the anti-clerical laws signified the end of the nineteenth-century liberal hegemony and the establishment of a new relationship between Church and State.

The agreement between the archbishop and the communist party, renamed Vanguardia Popular, led to the acceleration of the creation of the Catholic trade union movement by the archbishop, in order to offer an alternative to the existing trade union movement and channel support for the programme of social reforms. The day the code of labour laws was promulgated, 15 September 1943, the archbishop established the Rerum Novarum Trade Union which experienced rapid growth. At the end of 1945 it had 102 trade union branches, but, because of lack of leadership, only eighty-five functioned. The Vanguardia Popular trade union had a similar experience.

This lack of leadership and dependence on a single person brought an end to the trade union. The lack of leadership led to the situation where the union revolved around the personality of the adviser and promoter, Fr Benjamín Núñez. In 1945 Núñez took advantage of the autonomy recognised by the archbishop to move away from his direction and enter into competition with the trade union of Vanguardia Popular, thus violating a previous agreement. Between 1945 and 1948 rivalry between these two was becoming more intense. At the same time, Núñez affiliated his union to the social democratic movement which later became the National Liberation Party (Partido Liberación Nacional).

In the civil war of 1948, the trade unions were aligned with the traditional oligarchy and reformism against the government, social Christian tendencies and the communists of Vanguardia Popular. For the trade unions and the oligarchy, the object was to bring down a supposedly communist government which had annulled elections it had lost.

When it triumphed, the National Liberation Party suppressed Vanguardia Popular and its trade union on 17 July 1948, proscribing communism in public life. When he was appointed Minister of

Labour, Núñez brought with him the best leaders of Catholic trade unionism. Abandoned, the Catholic trade union survived in decline until the early 1960s. As regards the National Liberation Party, it upheld social reforms and consolidated the welfare State.

RETURN TO THE TRADITIONAL

When Monsignor Sanabria died, in 1952, the Church reverted to a triumphalist, Neo-Christian pastoral approach (consecration of the country to the Sacred Heart, parades and processions, the Eucharistic congress), led by the new archbishop Monsignor Rubén Odio (1952–9) and later assisted by Carlos Humberto Rodríguez until the mid 1970s. To render this return to triumphalism possible, Archbishop Odio changed the organisation of the archdiocese. He removed the priests who were most sympathetic to Calderónist social projects and re-emphasised movements pertaining to Catholic Action.

Catholic Action had been founded as early as December 1935 by the archbishop of that time but turned out to be completely inoperable because of lack of co-operation on the part of the clergy. In 1942–3 Monsignor Sanabria re-structured the movement, directing it towards workers and peasants. The previous archbishop had found himself with only five centres and 146 members in the whole country. Monsignor Sanabria's results were no better. In spite of intensive propaganda, the JOC (Juventud Obrera Católica, Young Catholic Workers) did not interest workers. In 1943, only 500 delegates gathered at a demonstration intended to be massive. Faced with this failure, the nuncio and archbishop exerted pressure on the clergy and the rest of the episcopate, and succeeded in establishing the JOC in some parishes. But by 1948 the JOC was completely defunct through lack of training of trade union leaders and complete dependence on the church adviser. It did not take part in the social struggles of the 1940s.

The themes of interest were again Protestantism, communism and Catholic education. The Church placed itself once more comfortably close to the bourgeois interests without intervening directly in social questions. Declarations on social problems were few and when they were made they were extremely vague. Official declarations were characterised by the enunciation of themes of universal application, divorced from national reality. Hence some anti-communist tendencies arose. The most salient feature of the pastoral approach was the systematic campaign of disparagement of Cuba, a campaign which acquired a really violent character. This stance easily enabled Archbishop Rodríguez to identify publicly the interests of the Church with those of the State, which was at that time under President Orlich, 'both powers – that of the Church and that of the State – working in perfect harmony, we, Costa Ricans, shall be able to ... overcome the communist peril and succeed in conquering the social order'. The most positive aspect of this anti-communist campaign was the propaganda of the social doctrine of the Church, presented as the only and the true solution to socialism, to marxism and to communism. In order to promote this doctrine the hierarchy set up the classic but equally ineffective bodies – a secretariat of social action, a Catholic press and a social school in 1963. This last institution was financed by private enterprise, which also imposed its line of worker-boss solidarity, as it considered the social doctrine of the church 'excessively progressive'. This gave substance to Monsignor Sanabria's position.

ON THE PERIPHERY OF ECCLESIASTICAL RENEWAL

The Costa Rican Church remained apart from the ecclesial renewal introduced by Vatican II and Medellín, except in a few isolated cases. In Costa Rica it is generally said that the council was reduced to turning the altar around and saying Mass in Spanish. The explanation for this marginalisation lies partly in the personality of Archbishop Rodríguez, who deliberately kept the clergy isolated from the general outlines of Vatican II and Medellín, and from the international centres encharged with their diffusion. Monsignor Rodríguez had great power in Rome. Complaints about his authoritarian and personalised manner of managing the archdiocese and the whole Costa Rican Church went unheard and even the nuncios who opposed him were replaced. The other bishops finally yielded in the face of the archbishop's unquestioned authority.

The other part of the explanation lies in the secular clergy. Their training and spirituality were inadequate. These clergy, mostly Costa Rican, and numerically great for the population, have been characterised by their lack of intellectual vitality. A decline is evident even in the field of Catholic journalism, something very closely associated with the Central American clergy. The weekly *Eco Católico* (Catholic Echo) lost its force and the *Mensajero del Clero* (Messenger of the Clergy) disappeared in 1970. The German Paulinas, who for a long time ran the major seminary, radically suppressed the intellectual anxieties of the clergy. Their norm was to educate the seminarians to serve a simple people. Therefore, studies after the time of Monsignor Sanabria were rudimentary.

Secondly, the clergy have been the victims of a profound process of becoming bourgeois, assisted by the inclusion of religious instruction in official education programmes. The 'religion classes' at second level became the principal source of income for priests, who in turn became state functionaries. The secular clergy applied themselves mainly to teaching religion, leaving the training of lay people in their parishes in second place.

Other priests became good mediators between the needs of their parishes and the welfare State. Their human qualities and religious character facilitated their playing this role. Rather than train lay people and communities, the priests became astute negotiators of finance for community development projects. Co-operatives, craft markets, technical and cattle-breeding colleges easily found state finance. In this way the benefit of the welfare State was extended to the people.

At other levels this led to close collaboration between Church and State. To erect a monument to the peasant, an assistant minister sought help from the bishops. The bishops sought and obtained the continuation of the legal ordinance by which church marriage had civil effect. They praised the collaboration between the Christian Family Movement and the Ministry of Education. They sought amnesty for 600 prisoners and easily obtained legal representation from the episcopal conference. Each time the peace talks of a strike were interrupted, the bishops were approached. The main political parties have always claimed to be inspired by Christian social philosophy. In ordinary and extraordinary budgets, economic assistance is found for the metropolitan chapter, the curia, church construction, the seminary, Catholic colleges, tax exemptions of every kind.

The religious, who increased numerically from 1950 on, did not change this situation as they concentrated almost exclusively on the Catholic education of urban youth who could pay them. For this they established their own educational centres. The proliferation of Catholic colleges which followed broke with the traditional Costa Rican practice of a single public system of education and has served to provide the moneyed class with an elite educational atmosphere, free from popular 'contamination'. It is noteworthy that the religious did not think of entering the national education system, which was legally, economically and socially possible. Instead of that, they preferred to found their own colleges.

THE FAILURE OF RENEWAL ATTEMPTS

All later attempts at renewal failed. The Costa Rican Church became integrated and linked in the most natural way to the State programme of development and reform. In this way also relations between the two institutions were strengthened. This comfortable arrangement has not allowed the development of work of assistance as advanced by the other Central American churches. As there was no work of assistance, an alternative of conscientisation was closed to the clergy and religious associations. The majority of the priests and religious have accepted the myth which affirms the non-existence of social problems in Costa Rica. This ahistoric conscience has been reinforced by the hierarchy. The few priests and movements concerned about social issues were effectively isolated and neutralised. The most outstanding found themselves obliged to leave the ministry.

The list of experiments which failed is long and depressing. Christians felt helpless and lacking in leadership and direction again. After Medellín a sociological study of parishes was suggested in order to formulate pastoral plans, but Archbishop Rodríguez would not permit it. Presently a reform of catechetics was attempted. This did not flourish either, faced with the strength of the tradition of teaching religion in state educational centres.

In 1967 Fr Javier Solís took on the management of *Eco Católico*. From that base he began to question the prevailing authoritarianism in the archdiocese, while he advocated liturgical and pastoral renewal, and real commitment to the popular sections. Numerous priests and religious reacted aggressively against the 'communist' orientation of the weekly. In 1970 Solís forwarded his resignation, aborting the plans of the archbishop to hand the weekly over to Opus Dei. The final crisis was provoked by an editorial in which disagreement was expressed with an arrangement of the Supreme Tribunal of Elections which left the Block Party of Costa Rican Workers, Peasants and Intellectuals (Partido Bloque de Obreros, Campesinos e Intelectuales Costarricenses) out of the electoral contest.

During the 1970s there sprang up two reformist currents which divided the opposition of the bishops and of the clergy in general.

The first emphasised militant commitment to the popular movements. The second favoured rather teaching and theological formation. Neither of the two succeeded in changing the ecclesiastical disposition of the country which continued to be fundamentally sacramentalist and divorced from the problems of the popular masses.

Some more concerned and aware Catholics and Protestants understood that their faith was common to them and that only 'the lucubrations of the theologians' separated them. This sudden awareness explains the various joint activities such as the Ecumenical Encounter of Young People of Tacarés de Grecia, in July 1970 and the Symposium on Liberation Theology of early 1971. The need for a centre of pluralist convergence led to the foundation of the ecumenical group Exodus (*Exodo*) in 1971. Exodus brought together ministers and lay people interested in renewal. They were Christians who sought greater coherence and integration of their Christian commitment. In this group dialogue with marxists was favoured and promoted, facilitating Christians' membership in popular political organisations and assisting marxists to overcome anti-religious prejudices. In 1972 Exodus founded the ecumenical weekly, *Pueblo* (People) which became the mouthpiece of reforming sectors. It was a means of training through information and journalistic commentary.

To this movement were added JOC and JUC (Juventud Universitaria Católica, Young Catholic University Students) which advocated direct and explicit participation of Catholics and of the Church in the solution of social problems. This participation meant, moreover, identifying oneself with the struggles of the popular sectors. JOC was directed by Fr Walter Aguilar and JUC by the ex-priest Arnoldo Mora. They were very small but active groups. The bishops responded by strengthening the movement of lay people submissive to the hierarchy, like the so-called 'Brotherhoods of Labour'.

These renewalist lines, suffocated by intra-church conflicts, did not flourish. From 1973 onwards these renewalist groups diminished and continued to weaken to the point of disappearance. Many of their members moved on to join leftwing political organisations; others, for example two parish priests, were deprived of their platforms for social advancement by Archbishop Rodríguez. He ordered the transfer of the two parish priests without heeding the protests of their parishioners.

In 1975, in a new attempt, a study group interested in diagnosing national reality and proposing new ways of political organisation was set up. In this group two sectors had fundamental influence: the Christians who had remained close to *Pueblo*, former members of *Pueblo* Student Front (Frente Estudiantil Pueblo) who, having retained radical stances, approached the newspaper, and the Trade Union of Costa Rican Educators (*Sindicato de Educadores Costarricenses*). From this came the base of the People's Democratic Party (Partido Democrático del Pueblo) which sought to present an alternative revolutionary form of politics, different from that of the communist party, but the plan failed.

Concerns persisted. There was probably a much-felt need to analyse national reality and transform it through political action. This need was expressed through the Víctor Sanabria Services Centre (*Centro de Servicios Víctor Sanabria*), founded in 1976, to advise trade unions, parties and popular movements. The Centre worked from the platform of *Pueblo*. However, the lack of a competent team and of adequate selection of staff – the result of insufficient clarification of objectives – likewise, suspicion and the opposition of the traditional Christian sectors contributed to the disappearance of *Pueblo*, of its successor, the magazine *Respuesta* (Response) and of the centre itself in 1980.

In close contact with Exodus and *Pueblo* there sprang up a second tendency to renewal advanced by a small group of religious interested in the training of pastoral workers. The Theological Institute of Central America (Instituto Teológico de América Central – ITAC), founded in 1972, represented the first serious attempt at institutional renewal. However, ITAC was barely tolerated by the secular clergy and the bishops. In 1978 the episcopal conference withdrew from the institute. The seminarians were supported by the religious, who went on strike and demonstrated in front of the cathedral of the capital, but finally they had to submit to the will of the bishops or leave the seminary.

ITAC proved unacceptable because of the authoritarian mentality of the bishops. The latter would not tolerate the running of the institute being in the hands of a collegiate body in which they did not have the final word. Likewise, ITAC proved unacceptable because the bishops wanted a 'manageable product' and not one involving conflict. In 1979 the seminarians returned to their traditional seminary and ITAC was publicly deprived of authority by the bishops.

Similarly, the teaching of theology independently of the bishops' control proved to be unacceptable. In 1974 they opposed the Ecumenical School of Religion, established by the National Autonomous

University. The object of this school was the investigation of religious phenomena and the teaching of theology. The bishops considered it a threat to orthodoxy on account of its ecumenical character. Opposition was greater when the training of teachers of religion for second level was being established in 1976. The bishops were opposed because they feared that the laity with training and university qualifications would supplant priests of the secular clergy. When the curriculum was approved, the episcopate prepared to fight at the level of the commission entrusted with the appointment of religion teachers, which was under episcopal control.

Throughout the 1970s there was no ecclesial, pastoral or doctrinal plan, as a generalised sacramentalist pastoral approach prevailed. To this fervent parishioners responded individually. At the end of the decade there was only a minority who understood their faith as a commitment of solidarity with the poorest. This minority group worked on the banana estates among the casual and seasonal labourers (*precaristas*) and outside parish structures. One growing sector had begun to distance itself, however, from sacramental practice and the Church. Another increasingly large sector of people had been going first to Protestant denominations and in later years to fundamentalist and Pentecostal sects. Not even in this area has the Church been able to be effective and, on account of that, its social influence has diminished considerably.

The State monopoly of public assistance has not left much opportunity for Christian church work. The Church has unloaded all responsibility on the State, trusting that the solution to social problems will come from the continuation and extension of social reforms. This trust has led the Church to view socially and culturally achieved successes with excessive satisfaction. However, that same fact has meant reducing its work to the teaching of religion in state centres and to sacramentalisation. Teaching and celebration of the sacraments have been the main concerns of the Costa Rican church. This is probably why neither Vatican II nor Medellín has had an impact on a self-satisfied church conscience. Those who have tried to awaken this conscience and disturb its complacency have failed.

This chapter was translated by Mary Harris.

10 The Catholic Church and the Politics of Accommodation in Honduras

Rodolfo Cardenal

DISORGANISATION AND ABANDONMENT

Honduras, with a little more than 112 000 square kilometres, was a single diocese up to 1916. But even when other dioceses were created, many of the sees were left vacant. When bishops were appointed, those chosen were often not the most suitable. This is explained by State interferences, the intervention of nuncios and the lack of good candidates.

There were difficulties in 1921 when it was necessary to find a successor to Monsignor José María Martínez y Cabañas who had been Bishop of Tegucigalpa and Comayagua since 1902. A Honduran canon, Monsignor Ernesto Fiallos, who had acted as vicar capitular of the diocese between 1921 and 1923, was the most popular candidate. When Agustín Hombach was appointed, the much respected Fiallos went into virtual retirement. Ten years later, the diocese again became vacant, and the dictator, Tiburcio Carías, wished to impose his former teacher and friend, now the elderly Fiallos, as his bishop. The church chapter, however, chose Benjamín Osorio, an inexperienced parish priest, as ecclesiastical administrator. In 1935 the nuncio dismissed Osorio and appointed Emilio Morales as vicar. The latter was able to win the respect of the clergy and showed talents for management but fell into disgrace with the nuncio. Meanwhile, Carías would not give way on his candidate. Morales was vicar for ten years. Finally, in 1943 the Holy See was able to appoint as archbishop of the capital the Salesian José de la Cruz Turcios, who had to wait until the dictator died to take office in 1946. The new archbishop did not show much interest in episcopal leadership or in ecclesiastical administration. He devoted himself exclusively to visiting rural parishes in which he promoted the building of churches, hermitages, roads and other community development works.

To resolve the *de facto* vacancy the Holy See appointed an auxiliary bishop in 1957: Evelio Domínguez, who retired to a rural parish four years later. In 1962 again the nuncio, with the support of President Villeda Morales, obliged Archbishop Turcios to resign and retire to Costa Rica. In his place they appointed Héctor E. Santos.

In these decades, in the absence of strong episcopal leadership, the nuncios managed the Honduran church as they pleased. Catholic Action was another case of flagrant intervention. The nuncio founded Catholic Action twice, in 1946 and 1952, and imposed the Italian statutes. In both cases it failed. Another nuncio founded a movement of Catholic intellectuals which did not have any great social influence either. It existed while the nuncio was in Tegucigalpa. The same can be said of what he called the Catholic Workers' Circle (Círculo de Obreros Católicos), founded by the same nuncio in 1949 to check communist infiltration. It was not long before it failed.

The diocese of Santa Rosa de Copán experienced similar difficulties. Between 1924 and 1929 the diocese was vacant. When Bishop Navarro died in 1952 there were problems in finding a successor until the nuncio imposed his candidate, contrary to the wishes of the clergy and archbishop. Six years later he had to be dismissed because he was not suitable.

The prolonged liberal reform under the dictatorship of Carías opened a practically unbreachable gap between the existing number of priests and those necessary to serve an expanding population. In 1927 there were only twenty-two per cent of the necessary priests and in 1950 only seventeen per cent. In this decade almost half of the country's parishes were vacant. In 1973 Honduras was the Latin American country with the smallest number of priests: 211, of whom only forty-one were Honduran. The diocese of Olancho, with a territory similar to that of El Salvador, had ten priests.

Apart from the marked anti-clericalism of the upper and most educated classes, the lack of clergy has other explanations. Since 1930 the number of laicisations in an already reduced clergy increased. Among the priests who left the ministry were some trained abroad. Of eight of these only two remained. The deterioration in the training of national clergy was notable. Between 1945 and 1962 the seminary was little more than a secondary school. Its best period was from 1910 to 1945 when it was run by Canadian missionaries. The few existing clergy worked without co-ordination during the long leadership crises in the diocese.

From 1950 onwards this deficiency was made good to a certain extent by foreign clergy. The North American Franciscans established themselves in Olancho and Comayagua. The North American Jesuits settled in the department of Yoro; the Spanish Passionists in Santa Bárbara and the French Canadian missionaries in the south of the country in Choluteca. In twenty years the number of priests doubled. The foreigners did not recruit more helpers in their native countries, but they brought with them sources of finance.

These scanty and disorganised resources were directed towards tackling two great problems for faith at that time. Since 1940 the Honduran Church had suffered great anxiety because of the growing presence of Protestants who had established religious centres and centres of assistance in poor and abandoned towns and villages. For this they had North American economic support. Next, the communist threat appeared, replacing the anxieties caused by the Protestants. The first show of strength by the communist party occurred during the banana strike of 1954. The Church remained aloof from the labour conflict, but faced with the obvious presence of the communist party, the nuncio obliged the bishops to write a pastoral letter in which for the first time they spoke of social problems. However, the emphasis was on the communist threat. Confronted with this danger, the bishops asked the workers not to allow themselves to be deceived by demagoguery and the false solutions being offered by the communists.

Once the conflict was resolved, the bishops did not speak of the subject again until the Cuban Revolution. In a pastoral letter of 1960 they expressed solidarity with the persecuted Cuban clergy. Against this background the holy mission which traversed Latin America arrived in the country. Spanish missionaries arrived in Honduras in 1959 to struggle against 'the onslaught of materialism and corruption'. There were Catholic demonstrations seeking the breaking off of relations with Cuba. In March 1960 the diocesan weekly *Fides* asked the government if it had yet organised the office for commercial control.

Catholic appeals to the government of Villeda Morales (1961–2) were due to the growing sympathy which the Cuban Revolution found among university students. For bishops and some more concerned sectors of the clergy the passivity of the government was official support for the advance of communism. In May 1961 they established a Committee of Democratic Organisations of Honduras (Comité de Organizaciones Demócratas de Honduras) comprising professionals and intellectuals of the most important cities. There were two years of intense anti-communist propaganda activity supported by the Catholic radio. The student section of the committee succeeded in gaining control of the university movement.

The uneasiness of the bishops, encouraged by the nuncio, with the government of Villeda Morales increased with the participation of supposed communists in public administration. The bishops even came to question the president publicly in the National Theatre during an anti-communist evening. The agitation ended with the fall of the government in a *coup d'état* organised by the National Party (Partido Nacional). The *coup* was justified by the 'obvious and intolerable' communism and was followed by persecution of the left wing.

IN THE SERVICE OF INTEGRAL DEVELOPMENT

For nine months in 1959 the twenty-five missionaries who made up the holy mission team travelled throughout the country, preaching powerful and emotional week-long sermons on traditional themes and moral obligations. The mission sought personal conversion, manifest in confession and reception of the sacraments. In the south, the mission had an enormous impact on the revitalisation of old religious organisations and the transformation of their activities into a religious movement of revitalisation. The peasants of the south experienced conversion and reached a new level of participation in local religious organisation.

The religious revival found expression in 1965 in the well-known movement of delegates of the Word in the department of Choluteca. Later this scheme was extended throughout the country and even spread to the north of Nicaragua and to El Salvador. From the start, church ministry was centred on the bible, introduced and explained by the laity. Five thousand representatives gathered at the annual congress of delegates in 1971. However, few parish priests accepted with ease the peasant in the liturgical sphere and at the centre of parochial decisions. In some parishes serious conflicts arose.

After short training each delegate was expected to assume the pastoral responsibilities of his local community. The object was to build a small community around the Word of God. This direct contact between the local communities with the bible led them to discover the relationship between faith and national reality. Each celebration of the Word began with a general discussion on a community theme or the application of a religious theme to daily life. A delegate, usually recognised as a person of great wisdom in his own community, led and directed the discussion. The delegates began to exercise unique social and religious leadership. The training given to the delegates and the manuals supplied to them emphasised that one of the best expressions of the new Christianity was commitment to the so-called Popular Advancement Movement and struggle for the liberation of the peasants.

In those years, specifically in 1959, in addition to the delegates' movement, a Catholic radio station with the object of developing a programme for radio schools was set up. The radio was the most effective means the bishops found of directly influencing people in order to give them religious instruction and liberate them from the communist peril. Naturally, the anti-Protestant element was not missing either. The model for radio schools was taken from Radio Sutatenza of Colombia. The nuncio and the auxiliary bishop Evelio Domínguez were the promoters of the programme.

The radio schools began on a small experimental basis in 1960. In the outskirts of the capital seventeen schools were established with 300 pupils. Teaching material from the Colombian station was used with some adaptations. In each community a monitor was selected who was trained to recruit students, take classes and supervise learning. Both the monitor and the students received all material free.

The results were quick and surprising. The system spread throughout the country, going from 343 schools with 7250 students in 1962 to 754 schools with 14 624 students in 1964. Success was due to a large extent to the fact that the programme of the radio schools was introduced in traditional religious movements with the parish as the centre. The most active monitors come from parish prayer-leaders (*rezadoras*), those chosen to look after a specific saint (*padrinos de santos*) and so on, that is, from families who specialised in local cults. To these were added the new delegates of the Word. Two thirds of the schools were in Choluteca, with Comayagua and Yoro next in order of importance.

Lay religious leaders were motivated to act as monitors in order to combat ignorance (which was understood as the lack of intellectual and moral training). The communities also participated actively showing their conversion and making a Christian commitment. The lay supervisors became the co-ordinators of the schools and the parish priest was an indispensable focus of legitimisation and power that could be delegated.

The monthly meetings of the leaders of the religious organisations, now monitors of the radio schools, were supervised by the parish priest and served as a means of administrative control. Material and information circulated at these meetings. The parish priest's visit to peasant communities no longer had as its sole objective the administration of sacraments but also the supervision of schools and the direction of power.

This movement experienced great and rapid development whenever it moved away from the focus of local power. There was a greater response on the plateau, where the religious traditions were a community force, and less interest on the coast, where there was considerable migratory movement.

The programme of the radio schools and the delegates of the Word extended towards rural development, committing the Church to confronting with rural communities their situation of underdevelopment and social and economic abandonment. The commitment was local and national.

The need for greater technical and financial resources launched the Church on a public and formal commitment venture. To obtain the necessary resources Popular Cultural Action of Honduras (Acción Cultural Popular Hondureña) was established. The direction of this was left in the hands of businessmen and professionals in 1960. A campaign was organised in newspapers and among civic groups, presenting adult education as the most important means of rural development under the patronage of the Church, but always of public benefit. The State contributed 30 000 *lempiras*.

In the countryside local movements, which at times comprised a whole community, sprang up. These were the 'conscious', a cohesive, religiously motivated and intensely active body. The peasants experienced a new form of Christianity and social relations. In particular they experienced the power of the group, which made it possible to carry out community development projects.

After a while the Colombian programmes were abandoned because of their excessively individualist emphasis and there was a movement towards the more developmental schemes of DESAL and the Brazilian model of radio schools. Following the scheme proposed by

DESAL, Popular Advancement applied itself to the construction of a network of basic organisations which would facilitate the organisation and participation of peasants in the national political process. This involved moving away from being marginalised to enter and actively form part of society. Now emphasis was placed on integral development. The radio schools were directed towards promoting the organisation of rural bases, but could not be considered an end in themselves. Between 1962 and 1964 more than 300 monitors received three weeks of techniques of leadership, community development, co-operativism and agriculture.

The message was that they were not only monitors, but also, and above all, that their mission was integral advancement. Therefore, in their communities they should try to improve living conditions, by integrating community development committees. Thus there was a move towards establishing co-operatives for saving and even consumption and production. The co-operatives were founded in municipalities where there were radio schools, making good use of monitors, parish priests and their monthly meetings and visits. The co-operatives were controlled by small producers in contrast with previous cases of co-operativism in which the middle and large landholders dominated. From 1962 onwards the construction of the local infrastructure and the formation of co-operatives occupied increasingly more of the monitors' attention, while religious and literacy activities moved to second place. Again the point of departure was the south, where the programmes of popular advancement sprang up linked to some five parishes.

Between 1964 and 1968 more than ninety co-operatives were organised in the Federation of Lending and Saving Co-operatives of Honduras, supported by the Movement for Popular Advancement and supervised by the Christian Social Movement.

Owing to pressure from the Catholic Office of Relief Services of New York, in 1967, the episcopate reorganised Caritas, promoting a developmental line. The new personnel were recruited among the *cursillistas* (those who had attended *cursillos*) and Christian Social Movement. Caritas aid was channelled through organised peasant groups and geared towards improving the community infrastructure. The so-called Women's Club, founded in Choluteca, was adopted by Caritas. The Club promoted peasant women, giving them a place in community development. Although it was a fundamentally educational programme for women (childcare, health, nutrition, needlework, cookery), many groups committed themselves to community projects related to women. In 1971, the Women's Housewives' Club had 700 centres throughout the country.

Between 1964 and 1965 short social training courses were given to peasants. The movement originated in the university setting of the capital, thanks to the work of the Jesuit J. Fisher. He introduced the courses with the object of spreading the social doctrine of the Church. The social training courses were initiated in Venezuela by another Jesuit, Fr Aguirre. In the university the movement appealed to the Christian Social Student Revolutionary Front, but received a poor response from the professional sectors. Because of that the university leaders took to the country, giving the first courses to the monitors in the south. Through this activity university students and young professionals came into contact with the Movement for Popular Advancement. The impact of the courses culminated in the peasant congress of 1964, from which the peasant leagues grouped under the National Union of Peasants (Unión Nacional de Campesinos – UNC) originated.

The peasant leagues originated and extended through the Movement for Popular Advancement. They received initial training from the Latin American Confederation of Christian Trade Unions which emphasised economic exploitation on the part of the landholders and the economic and political imperialism of the United States. This vision complemented the social doctrine of the Church. The alternative was democracy. In Honduras there was an attempt to establish peasant groups which would bring pressure for agrarian reform and agricultural services.

The UNC was received and accepted within the general scheme of integral advancement and as another programme, but as yet no-one knew the hidden potential of this organisation. Peasant mobilisation energised centres of advancement, which, beginning with the Choluteca experience, had spread throughout the country. The Choluteca centre, founded in 1967, was used to train peasants in group dynamics. Two years later the training courses were directed by the peasants themselves. Around the La Colmena centre there were agricultural services centres to promote the co-operatives in the south.

In 1969, there were similar centres, directed by the clergy but managed by members of the Christian Social Movement, in the departments of Olancho, Yoro, Santa Bárbara, Comayagua, Santa Rosa de Copán and Ocotepeque. The training given in these centres followed the schemes of Choluteca: group dynamics, ideology of marginality, radio schools and committees for community development.

The fundamental characteristic of this new phase was community activism, which signified an important difference from the ordinary practice of local and departmental politics. The new leaders were characterised by their honesty and disinterested dedication, while local politicians had been characterised by their dishonesty and electoral interest.

The parish priests, for their part, considered it legitimate to participate directly in these programmes of development. They were within the well-assimilated theology of development. Among the laity directing Popular Cultural Action of Honduras and the Movement for Popular Advancement there was full developmental awareness and mysticism. Their mission was to create new attitudes and institutions, improving or developing the material infrastructure which was so necessary. The communities organised to resolve their problems, involving their members in the process of decision-making, were the basis of their activity.

The development of these programmes necessitated finance and found it in the international development agencies, especially in AID, which began to give money in 1963. First it financed small local projects, and later, in 1964, it financed the National Federation of Credit Co-operatives. In 1965, CARE, a private North American agency dedicated to helping in cases of emergency and development entered the scene with a finance programme for the construction of schools. The agents of the Movement for Popular Advancement, the parish priests and co-ordinators of the radio schools acted as intermediaries between the North American agencies and the local committees. In this way they avoided the national and municipal bureaucracy, and with it local politicians; they gained experience in how to acquire quick money through the international agencies and all of this permitted the rise of an independent peasant leadership which began to compete with the traditional local politicians.

These sources of finance were exhausted relatively quickly. AID demanded separation from the ecclesiastical hierarchy. The agency hoped that its promoters would become its agents. AID proposed that Popular Cultural Action of Honduras take charge of administering the finance, which meant that the administration of funds would be completely secular and that the archbishop could not intervene in the decisions or veto the policies adopted as he could previously. Initially the hierarchy rejected the proposal, but had to accept it when, in a general assembly of the clergy committed to the programmes, it was clear that work could only continue by accepting the conditions of AID.

Then, in 1968, probably against the wishes of AID, financial control was left in the hands of the Christian Social Movement since the appointed board of directors was joined by professionals from the capital with very little interest in the matter. AID's next step was to interfere in Popular Cultural Action of Honduras, but the latter would not accept the financial attitude of AID, or its tendency to establish credit co-operatives controlled by bureaucratised urban agents more reliable than the peasants themselves. Difficulties increased on competing with the Inter-American Regional Organisation of Workers, controlled by the United States and the National Party (Partido Nacional). AID, therefore, gradually began to withdraw its economic support.

Meanwhile, in 1964, Fr Vincent Prestera introduced *cursillos de cristiandad* in urban areas with the aim of extending social influence beyond the small and active Christian Social Student Revolutionary Front. The *cursillos* were at their most important between 1964 and 1969, when a great number of businessmen and professionals, many of them public servants, joined the movement. The *cursillos de cristiandad* mobilised a sector of the urban middle classes. However, the most concerned went over to the Christian Social Movement and joined the Movement for Popular Advancement, radicalising both. This movement was joined by young teachers of populist inclinations and by lawyers from the departments which had not been co-opted by the traditional oligarchy or by the small circle of the left wing which controlled the university. It was a middle-class movement with strong socio-political interests.

The Association for Human Advancement (Asociación de Promoción Humana), founded in 1965–6 at the request of the DESAL agent to study social problems, plan activities and administer the funds of Misereor, turned to the *cursillos de cristiandad*, to the professionals of Tegucigalpa and San Pedro Sula, offering them a diagnosis of marginality and trying to promote the solidarity of urban centres with the peasants. The life of this institution was brief, and its influence nil as in 1968 it was already dead. Misereor was so interested in it that it sent a Cuban to promote it.

THE RADICALISATION OF REFORMISM

In 1970, the Christian Social Movement controlled four agencies: Popular Cultural Action of Honduras, Caritas, Federation of Lending and Saving Co-operatives of Honduras and the Honduran Development Foundation. All of these had their central offices in Tegucigalpa and teams of promoters in six regional centres for training and assisting the peasants. In 1971 these agencies, the thirty-four radio stations run by the Church and the seven diocesan training centres were organised in a central co-ordinating office, called Council for Co-ordination of Development (Consejo de Coordinación del Desarrollo). Some Canadian, European and North American foundations expressed willingness to finance the programmes of this new co-ordinating body, which they considered the ideal model for promoting development in Latin America. The finance allowed the creation of a decentralised decision-making system at regional and district level. At regional level there were the training centre, the regional supervisors of the five agencies, the co-operatives, the credit committee, the agricultural supervisors and representatives of radio stations where these existed. At district or parochial level there were the co-ordinator of the radio schools, the agricultural instructor, the promoter of housewives' clubs, the co-operative credit committee and the promoter of co-operatives. Almost all of these were peasants with paraprofessional training.

At the end of the decade the movement had grown a lot and had become very complex. Neither the hierarchy nor the parish priests formed part of the decision-making process; this was partly because the clergy were still few and the existing clergy lacked the necessary administrative capacity or did not have sufficient interest to maintain close links with the expanding development agencies in the 1960s. Faced with these difficulties the movement of lay people committed to a socio-economic project of Christian inspiration stood out. The directors of the agencies considered themselves part of an ecclesial movement committed to the transformation of national reality. In fact, some of the agencies were directly linked to the ecclesiastic institutions and the parochial platform continued to be used for many of these activities, with or without the participation of the parish priests themselves. However, an important break had been made.

At this moment a conflict of loyalties arose for the peasants between the institutional church represented by the parish priests and the promoters of the Movement for Popular Advancement. The peasants gave their loyalty to the latter, leaving the parish priest in second place, and the scope for the sacred and institutional was reduced. This was another important break.

That was not all, however, for from 1969 onwards the Movement for Popular Advancement, the Christian Social Movement and to a certain extent a section of the clergy adopted a more aggressive strategy. The leaders of the first two movements abandoned the Christian Democratic theses of Venezuela and Chile. One year previously, in 1968, the Christian Democrat Party (*Partido Demócrata Cristiano*), had been founded, moving away from the thesis of marginality, of co-operative development and of confidence in courses to change the peasants. Links with hierarchy were weakened even further, as some of the leaders of the new party adopted a political line more radical than that of the Church. The conflict was seen in concrete terms in the politicisation of the developmental movement.

An example of the change appeared in the new pedagogic and administrative team which assumed the direction of the radio schools between 1968 and 1970. These new personnel introduced the methodology of Paulo Freire, emphasising the necessity for political education. They began to awaken in peasants a consciousness of secular exploitation and the need to transform that situation of oppression and socio-economic dependence.

Radicalisation was facilitated by the land conflict which began to appear in the south. After the second world war land became scarce in Honduras because of the expansion of commercial agriculture, the accelerated saturation of rural communities with the descendants of the original inhabitants and the presence of up to 300 000 Salvadoreans. In the southern region, in Choluteca, this scarcity was due primarily to the expansion of cotton and livestock, by means of the illegal growth of the big estates. These usurped the rights of the peasants to national and common lands, moving their boundaries over the lands of the peasants. The shortage was felt everywhere and that, more than the unemployment generated in the banana plantations of the northern coast, produced a wave of land seizures.

The situation presented the peasant leagues with a political challenge as from 1964, especially when their rival, the National Association of Honduran Peasants (Asociación Nacional de Campesinos

Hondurenos – ANACH) took the initiative in the south. Until then the leagues, which were reformist in character, had had very limited influence. Alarm spread in the leagues when the Trade Union Federation of Northern Workers (Federación Sindical de Trabajadores del Norte), affiliated to ANACH, appeared in the south in 1968 and began to organise the unemployed and landless peasantry.

The response of the leagues was rapid and effective. In August 1969, the first 600 peasants of the leagues occupied the lands of Namsigüe for the first time. In the following months more leagues were formed and the land seizures became generalised. The formation of regional centres, agricultural credit, technical assistance and texts and contents of radio schools centred around the peasants' organisation to regain national lands. The developmental infrastructure was put at the service of the organised peasants to ensure the occupation of the lands.

Six regional teams in fourteen of the eighteen departments covered 100 000 families, or approximately twenty-five per cent of the rural population. The radio schools had 20 000 students. They provided primary education up to fourth grade, which was officially recognised by the Minister of Education. They included, furthermore, a department of agricultural education.

The popular reformist movement converted its technical and economic capacity into a force for political pressure at the service of the organised peasantry. The movement was identified increasingly with the peasant leagues of the UNC, which already had autonomous local and national structures. It was the leagues which pressurised the social Christians to side with them in the land occupations. The movement which they themselves had brought about was now demanding a radical change of direction of them. The Christian Social Movement publicly attacked the financial and agro-industrial interests of the traditional landowners and the modernising bourgeoisie and the traditional forms of public coercion. These attacks and the new political situation left no doubt about the positions and options of the Christian Social movement.

The landowners of the south were alarmed when they saw the strength of the peasant organisation. The alarm was greater when they observed the favourable government policy towards the peasants, expressed through the National Agrarian Institute. Then, in addition to attacking the government to the point of achieving the dismissal of the director of the National Agrarian Institute, they also attacked the clergy, accusing them of instigating the land occupations. In particular, they accused the radio schools and the Movement for Popular Advancement of being the direct causes of the incursions of 1969 and 1970. ANACH made common cause with the landowners, ridiculing the clergy and the promoters of their puppet agencies. The clergy, for their part, were reserved regarding the legality of the occupations, but did not doubt about supporting the leagues in the face of ANACH attacks.

The commitment of the church of Choluteca to the peasant struggles went as far as the public defence of the peasants' right to occupy lands and to agrarian reform. The *cursillistas* demanded that the bishop of the diocese condemn the seizures, but contrary to what they expected the bishop came out in defence of the peasants' right to occupy national or common lands. He did not allow the occasion to pass without exhorting the landowners to collaborate with agrarian reform, in addition to accusing them of being more concerned about their cattle than about the peasants. The landowners responded with a press and radio campaign against the clergy, which lasted throughout the year 1970. In October they introduced a petition in Congress for the deportation of all Canadian missionaries. The proposal was unsuccessful, thanks to the archbishop's mediation with President López Arellano.

Faced with the strength of these attacks, the Canadian missionaries were doubtful about continuing to support the peasants. During the climax of the campaign the National Party warned the superior of the missionaries that if they gave any support to the Christian Democrat Party deportations would follow. At this moment the hierarchy and most of the clergy withdrew from the popular movement that they themselves had promoted for a decade.

This break with the popular movement is explained by the polarisation of the religious structure to the point where the leaders of the land seizures were the religious leaders themselves. It was not clear for parish priests where the parish ended and the peasant organisation began. For the peasants there was no problem. The peasant leaders defended their positions easily and ingeniously through the bible, which made it more difficult to delimit their jurisdictions and loyalties as well as to delegitimise them.

As was natural, the peasant organisation became increasingly more jealous of its autonomy and that created constant conflicts with the parish priests, who tried to interfere to make their authority and prestige prevail. In the south, for example, there was serious conflict between the missionaries and the peasant organisation. The missionaries wanted to introduce a commercial radio, but the local landowners only agreed to advertise on condition that the leagues were requested to moderate their position. This produced a violent reaction on the part of the leadership of the UNC against the bishop and the clergy.

In Olancho the situation was similar, except that the National Federation of Farmers and Cattle-breeders of Honduras (Federación Nacional de Agricultores y Ganaderos de Honduras) adopted a much more aggressive stance. The 'incidents' of Olancho happened a little later than those of Choluteca. Therefore the stock farmers were more conscious of the need for a radical suppression of the claims of the peasant movement. The bishop, Monsignor Nicholás D'Antonio, was repeatedly accused of being a communist by stock farmers and landholders. He was shamefully interrupted and threatened during a Mass in his cathedral. The stock farmers parked their tractors in front of his residence for two weeks and threatened not to cultivate until the land seizures ceased.

In February 1972 the army had gone into action assassinating eight peasants while trying to obstruct a land seizure at Los Horcones. The facts became known because a Colombian priest, with the consent of the bishop, denounced them. The report had a national impact and raised a wave of protests. On 25 June 1975 the principal landholders and the army assassinated foreign priests Iván Betancur and Miguel Jerónimo Cypher and various peasants: twenty people in all. The army occupied the churches of Olancho and obliged all church workers to leave the diocese. The day of the attack on the centre for peasant advancement in Olancho, the government banned a peasant march which was heading for Tegucigalpa, took control of the El Progreso training centre, closed down two Catholic radios, forbade several religious to practise their ministry and searched priests' houses. Initially those implicated in the Los Horcones crime and the military government tried to hide the massive assassination. Popular pressure and testimonies filtering through the region obliged the government to acknowledge the truth.

The confrontations continued to get worse with the capture of more than a hundred leaders of the UNC. Some landholders from Olancho put a price on the head of the bishop.

THE BREAK WITH THE POPULAR MOVEMENT

The bishops tried to distance themselves publicly from the peasant movement when the latter openly showed its force in 1972. Faced with the events of Choluteca and Olancho, the episcopal conference showed its reservations towards peasant struggles. It rejected violence as a solution and specifically denied its support for the land seizures. With the ambiguity characteristic of this type of declaration it demanded agrarian reform and defended the right of the peasants to organise. It also recognised the right to private property, but added that it was the duty of the State to intervene to safeguard the primary rights of man and not to maintain order purely because it considered it as an expression of divine will. The declaration of the episcopal conference represented a clear retrograde step in the face of the concrete and effective support of the bishops of Choluteca and Olancho for the peasants and the land seizures. Similarly, the bishops expressed their reservations about the attacks on North American imperialism and finally, in effect, abandoned their demands for agrarian reform, for fear of reprisals.

Added to the confusion and fear of the more advanced sectors of the Church was the pressure of the more conservative sectors who saw in the multiple assassination of Los Horcones the logical consequence of a 'semi-communist commitment' on the part of pastoral workers.

The hierarchy and a sector of the people abandoned the peasant struggle and concentrated on the urban middle class and the political elites again, presenting a new populist image while they tried to detach themselves from the popular movement. The nuncio was a determining factor in this change of direction. The middle class enthusiastically welcomed the Church which returned repentant and frightened from its socio-political adventure. The hierarchy and the clergy then concentrated on promoting the charismatic movement which grew rapidly in the cities and from them gradually moved to rural parishes. It is interesting to note that previously the charismatic movement was poorly viewed by the hierarchy because of its lay and independent character. Thus the Church, faced with social conflict, found a comfortable refuge in an apolitical and neutral stance. The ecclesiastical hierarchy bitterly recognised that their alliance with the peasantry had not produced either the desired centralisation or the social power which they had sought. Very much to the contrary, they had been victims of prejudice and persecution.

The episcopate ordered the clergy not to support either the programmes or the agencies of the Council for Co-ordination of Development openly, especially if they were promoting the Christian

Democrat Party. In April 1974 the bishops removed Caritas from the jurisdiction of the above-mentioned council and did the same with the radio schools and advancement centres. In spite of these efforts, the bishops did not succeed in convincing all the landholders of their separation from the peasant movement. In reality, some members of the clergy continued working for the UNC. Furthermore, the Olancho incidents of June 1975 show that there was no unanimity regarding the separation, even at the level of the episcopal conference. Faced with the assassinations and the persecution of the bishop of Olancho, the episcopal conference had to protest and condemn the acts. It assured the peasants of its solidarity, but this was a matter of verbal solidarity, distant and not committed. Thus it abandoned some of the programmes of Caritas, considering them too prone to politicisation.

The bishop of Olancho was dismissed in 1976 and replaced without consulting the clergy of the diocese. The clergy organised and mobilised to the extent of achieving the retirement of the recently appointed bishop amid suspensions and threats. Afterwards, almost all the clergy had to leave the department on account of the harassment of the landowners. Only four priests and three nuns remained.

The Honduran church was both progressive and reformist. It was well within the reformist and developmental scheme to which it gave of its best. It understood the commitment to development as a means of evangelisation and the best means available to bring the kingdom of God close to people. This was probably the best method and there is no reason to doubt the goodwill which existed in this commitment, particularly on account of the consciousness which it created in the peasantry and the experience of organisation and struggle which it afforded the people.

The developmental plan, however, was seen to be insufficient in itself to solve the problems of structural injustice and was, therefore, forced to take a braver step in organising the peasants. The difficulty of the developmental model was shown when there were clear signs of exhaustion. The Church did not wish to go further, accompanying and directing an organised peasant movement which was fighting for lands to which it had a right. With the help of the Church, the developmental movement grew and was consolidated until all its possibilities as a reformist process were exhausted. When it became necessary to devise a new model – more hazardous and exposed to persecution because it challenged the secular power of the landholders – the Church became afraid and retreated, abandoning the peasants to their fate.

This chapter was translated by Mary Harris.

11 Radical Conservatism and the Challenge of the Gospel in Guatemala

Rodolfo Cardenal

INTRODUCTION

The separation of the Guatemalan Church and State was the most violent in Central America and, as Richard Adams affirms, in all Latin America. Nearly all the foreign clergy were expelled from the country with only 119 priests remaining until the end of the so-called liberal revolution. The State confiscated all Church property and suppressed the legal representation of the Church.

For seventy-five years the Church and the clergy were under the strict control of liberal power. That did not, however, entail a loss of popular religiosity; on the contrary. The popular religiosity of former centuries continued as a determining factor of social integration among the largely indigenous population, and, to a lesser extent, among the *ladinos*. The reaction of the indigenous population to the shortage of clergy was to become independent of the sacraments and official rites and to take refuge in 'custom' which combined Catholic practices, vestiges of the Mayan and colonial traditions. 'Custom' was reinforced and became more autonomous in each of the indigenous communities. Therefore, what was weakened was the presence of the clergy and indigenous participation in official worship. In the *ladino* world the effect was the opposite, as the *ladinos* lost interest in any kind of religious organisation.

The few remaining priests dedicated themselves to serving the religious needs and interests of the group of landholders and coffee merchants. Most of the priests remained in the capital. There were a few in the departmental urban areas and scarcely any served the indigenous villages and towns. As the population grew, the Church could not tend to it, having neither the trained personnel nor the economic means. The urban upper and middle classes felt they had no obligation towards the Church. In this way the Church remained poor with few national clergy and without popular support.

During the liberal dictatorship of Jorge Ubico there were small changes. In 1936 it was possible to nominate a nuncio. The archbishop, Monsignor Mariano Rossell, obtained permission for a few priests to enter the country quietly. In 1937, some Jesuits arrived and began to teach in the seminary in the capital. Later the archbishop gave them a parish in the centre of the city. Ubico also permitted the opening of Catholic colleges for the upper classes, directed by the recently arrived religious. In 1943 two priests from Maryknoll arrived and others followed later. Monsignor Rossell also gained the assistance of Marists and Salesians. In these early days the only interest of the Church was to survive and await better times.

The revolution of 1944 and the following decade did not change the opening initiated by Ubico. More religious continued to come. In the years of Jacobo Arbenz, Archbishop Rossell took a great interest in the clandestine political development of the Church. The most important event was the creation of the Movement for National Affirmation of Christianity (Movimiento de Afirmación Nacional de Cristiandad), the organisation from which the Christian Democrat party later came. Meanwhile, the Catholic colleges founded during the Ubico era declared themselves confessional. Later the former students of these colleges led the clandestine political movement against the Arbenz government and were determining factors in the elaboration of the constitution of 1956 and the restoration of the rights and legal privileges of the Church.

CONSERVATIVE AND ANTI-COMMUNIST CENTRALISATION

During the archbishopric of Monsignor Rossell, Church organisation was minimal. He personally controlled all he could. Given that at the beginning of his archbishopric there were very few dioceses, the territory under his jurisdiction was very large. The setting up of new dioceses and the increase in the number of bishops decreased the direct responsibility of the archbishop, who had to leave the organisation of their dioceses to the respective bishops.

The importance of the seminary must not be underestimated. The Church's greatest problem was the shortage of Guatemalan clergy. Up to 1951 the seminary which trained students from secondary level through to ordination was in the hands of the Jesuits and their training was as good as that of the Salvadorean clergy. The majority of the seminarians were from very poorly educated families. As regards the seminary, like the rest of the Church, it did not have sufficient personnel. In 1951 the archbishop closed the major seminary and sent the few seminarians to complete their studies abroad.

In 1960 Monsignor Rossell invited the Sulpicians of Canada to take charge of the recently constructed seminary in the outskirts of the capital. The Club Serra, made up of wealthy lay people, was organised to obtain financial support. The major seminary of Guatemala became the national seminary, while in Quezaltenango and Sololá another two minor seminaries were established. In spite of this increase the traditionally difficult problems remained: a shortage of suitable candidates, a lack of funds for expansion and a shortage of trained personnel.

As the Church remained weak, Monsignor Rossell continued to depend on his close links with a small sector of the upper classes. However, he recognised the responsibility of the Church towards the other popular sectors, especially towards the indigenous population for whom he founded two children's colleges in the capital, the college for boys in 1945 and that for girls in 1949. The archbishop saw the indigenous masses as a potentially revolutionary force and the Church as the institution destined to arrest this radical possibility. The two colleges were a means to this end.

The Church's position changed due to internal and external factors. The Vatican showed concern about the centralism of the archbishop who, furthermore, did not want the establishment of new dioceses. When he was appointed archbishop there were only three. The Vatican, following the advice of the nuncio, appointed three new bishops, all of them foreigners. Consequently, none of them had links with the conservative elites. The reaction of the archbishop and his allies was so violent that the nuncio was withdrawn from Guatemala, but the appointments remained effective. At the time the Vatican also appeared to be concerned about the political identification of the archbishop with Castillo Armas and his National Liberation Movement (Movimiento de Liberación Nacional, MLN).

The other external force which changed the position of the Church in Guatemalan society was the United States which began to support any political or social entity which could mobilise to resist and struggle against the communist threat incarnate in the government of Jacobo Arbenz. The Church had begun its own struggle against communism and did so in the spirit of a crusade. In 1953, Archbishop

Rossell began a pilgrimage throughout the country with the image of Christ of Esquipulas, the most venerated shrine and national image. The object of the pilgrimage was to expel communism. In the words of Rossell himself, 'The presence of the Holy Christ did more against communism than if a hundred missionaries and thousands of books and hundreds of hours of Catholic radio had led the anti-communist campaign'. Likewise he led recitations of the rosary in front of the presidential palace with the same objective.

In the middle of this campaign and another launched by the North American press to convince public opinion that the Arbenz government was communist, a CIA agent asked Spellman, the cardinal of New York, to organise a clandestine contact with the Guatemalan archbishop to co-ordinate the efforts which had previously been independent of each other. Spellman acceded with great enthusiasm and soon the CIA contacted the Guatemalan archbishop. On 9 April 1954 a pastoral letter read in all the churches drew citizens' attention to the presence of communism in the country and demanded that 'the people of Guatemala should rise up as a man against the enemy of God and the fatherland . . . in this national crusade against communism'. The CIA later dropped many thousands of pamphlets containing the archbishop's text from planes in areas far from the capital.

In an attempt to give himself importance, Castillo Armas, 'the liberator' set up by North American diplomats and the CIA, decided to have a Mass of thanksgiving to which much publicity was given, on 21 June 1954 at the shrine of Esquipulas. Thus he hoped to emphasise the merit of the imminent triumph he intended to plan in Guatemala, by identifying himself with the Church. However, his religious mentor, Archbishop Rossell, who was waiting in the capital, did not have full confidence in the Castillo Armas mission. That day he told the United States ambassador that direct intervention by his country could be the only way to protect the 'Christian anti-communists of Guatemala'.

Arduous negotiations took place, some of which were attended by the nuncio, brought along by the United States ambassador. Then, when Castillo Armas was finally proclaimed 'the man of Guatemala's destiny', the archbishop telegraphed the 'liberator' to greet and congratulate him 'in the name of the nation which awaits you with open arms, recognising and admiring your sincere patriotism. May Our Lord guide you and your heroic companions on your campaign of liberation against atheistic communism. You all have my pastoral blessing'.

The support of the archbishop for the liberation movement of Castillo Armas required a new agreement with the State. Castillo Armas encouraged and specifically approved the arrival of foreign clergy and began to treat the Church in a friendly manner. The government of Castillo Armas and succeeding national liberation governments found in the Church an important ally for increasing their control over the growing population and over left-wing groups. In return for this they allowed the Church the legal rights it had before the liberal break. Some rights were recognised by the governments of Castillo Armas and Ydígoras Fuentes, but the full restoration was granted in four articles of the 1966 constitution. Article 67 confirmed and extended the property rights which had been guaranteed in the 1955 constitution. Previously the Church held property, but illegally. The article conceded tax exemption on Church property used for educational purposes and guaranteed the property of titles of those properties the Church had had, even those the government had confiscated.

Article 93 openly declared the teaching of religion in the schools to be of national interest. Consequently, classes in religion were introduced in the curriculum. Article 85 reintroduced the Church as a legal witness for marriage. By this article religious marriages were recognised by the State. The final article, Article 102, guaranteed the autonomy of private universities which specifically permitted freeing the Rafael Landívar University, run by the Jesuits and supported by a fairly rich and conservative group, from the academic control of the national university.

In the years following the revolutionary decade, the Church achieved full legal re-establishment. The growing position of strength and power obtained first in the Constitution of 1955 and later in that of 1966 signified that the State once again was inviting the Church to share in the responsibilities of controlling the country socially. The enthusiasm was not general: some higher sectors linked to the hierarchy considered this an advantage. The indigenous population found the entry of priests beneficial, although there were serious reservations on the part of the most traditional communities. The *ladinos* in the departments were even less interested.

Around the anti-communist movement led by Archbishop Rossell against Arbenz the Movement for National Affirmation of Christianity was formed. The active nucleus consisted of some one hundred people and struggled until the anti-clerical laws were repealed. The leaders of the movement were very close to the archbishop. When the constitution was promulgated, the group dissolved but a few decided to organise in a party which they called Guatemalan Christian Democracy (Democracia Cristiana Guatemalteca). Christian democracy had close relations with the archbishop, that is, he was consulted on important questions. The prevailing feeling was to depend on a progressive party, which would be inspired by the social doctrine of the Church but would also be anti-communist. It involved, among other things, avoiding a repetition of the experience of 1950.

Christian democracy had close links with the Church up to 1956. After that, this relationship became less important as the party grew. After 1966 formal separation became an obsession for the new leadership of the party, more concerned about creating a new model of socio-economic development than about anti-communism. However, the Christian democrat activists persuaded the parish priests to support their party and subsequently they used the organisational network of Catholic Action as a channel for propaganda and recruiting. To be a member of Catholic Action came to imply being a Christian democrat.

THE FOREIGN CLERGY'S CONTRIBUTION: EXPANSION OF THE CHURCH

The foreign clergy grew rapidly and soon outnumbered the national clergy. In general, the majority of these were of pre-Conciliar mentality. While in the capital the Christian democrat party was forming and the Congress was coming under pressure to recover the legal privileges of the Church, its work in the rural parishes gave the Church a new form.

After the fall of the revolutionary government of 1954, the Church expanded visibly and significantly. Undoubtedly, the leadership of Archbishop Rossell and his influence on a nucleus of Catholic laity permitted the expansion to occur easily since legal privileges were guaranteed constitutionally. At the same time the nuncio decentralised the Church and made it more dependent on Rome. The foreign clergy permitted the establishment of contact with other Catholic international centres such as the overseas religious houses of the orders and with the dioceses from which the foreign priests came.

The foreign clergy, secular and religious, were needed to attend to the abandoned indigenous villages. In the indigenous parishes the traditional independence which the confraternities had enjoyed since colonial days were a challenge to the authority of parish priests and pastoral workers. The *ladino* world, which for a long time had been without direct and constant attention on the part of the clergy and had survived successfully without hierarchical ministry apart from the indispensable sacraments, did not respond to the renewed presence of the priests and religious. For the *ladino*, the Church simply did not answer any need.

Thus attention began to be paid to the majority indigenous group and to the developmental problems which they presented. Attention to development and the advancement of the indigenous communities was possible because the religious and the priests received economic support from their respective congregations and from the dioceses from which they came. Otherwise, their work in the poor rural villages would not have been possible. The increase in numbers of clergy led to the creation of new dioceses, which resulted in the decentralisation of the Church, as has been noted above. Although the exact number of clergy is not known, there was a steady increase from the 120 priests of the 1940s.

The priests and religious most active in assisting the social advancement of indigenous communities were the Europeans and the North Americans. In general, the Latin American groups were as remote from the problem as the former Guatemalan clergy. The missionaries, those from Maryknoll, for example, were especially creative.

The foreign clergy brought solutions, but also problems. The easy coexistence found between the foreigners and the *ladinos* was assured in the indigenous parishes by the sympathy of the priests towards the indigenous, and in the *ladino* parishes by the lack of interest in the local population.

The active presence of foreign clergy introduced the inevitable division with the Guatemalan clergy. The division became particularly serious when the nuncio obtained the appointment of three foreign bishops, passing over the objections of the archbishop. This provided the archbishop with an opportunity to show his discontent and even hostility by reverting to nationalism. In his later years he was a great nationalist. Notwithstanding these sentiments, the Guatemalan bishops have always recognised that without the help of the foreign clergy they could not fulfil their ecclesial responsibility. On this occasion it was shown how conservatism and nationalism operated very closely together in the church. Since the 1960s the vast majority of the more progressive priests and religious were foreigners. The Guatemalan clergy became sensitive to the matter, which was also discussed in public on various occasions. Before 1975 several ultra-progressive foreigners were expelled from the country by the government, but none of these incidents upset the good relations between the Church and the State.

These divisions were also evident in prejudices. The Spaniards tended to look down on the Guatemalans, thus continuing the tradition of peninsular superiority over the *mestizo* which goes back to the early years of the colony. The North Americans brought with them racial and class prejudices. Both ethnic groups tended to consider the Guatemalan clergy as bad-mannered and self-centred. Although there were significant exceptions the prejudices persisted and rendered communication among the clergy themselves difficult. Internal communication was not facilitated by the small number of priests and the many demands on them so that, in fact, contacts among them were limited. For the same reason there was no rivalry between the different groups, except for the presence of Opus Dei which operated in a traditionally Jesuit area.

The importance of the foreign clergy was twofold. Firstly, they worked in an area where there were few priests, and, secondly, they were a source of finance. Without this the priest or religious would have to accept a very low standard of living as the rural parishes did not produce enough money to allow him a moderate one. The upper and middle social sectors could be a good source of finance but that involved putting oneself at their service. Foreign support came not only in the form of finance for an individual priest. The German bishops through Miserior and Adveniat provided great sums of money to finance the expansion of the Church. The North Americans channelled money both openly and clandestinely from the government institutions of their country. AID considered priests appropriate elements for promoting development at a local level, especially in the indigenous areas. Likewise the government of Peralta Azurdia, with the same objective, encouraged the Maryknoll missionaries in Huehuetenango to play a determining role in certain matters related to development among immigrants.

Missionaries were also used by the United States government and the CIA obtained a lot of information through them. The majority of them did not realise what they were doing. CIA contacts with the central house of missionaries in New York were routine. Agents obtained information using their apparent friendship with the Maryknoll missionaries and the Jesuits. They asked seemingly disinterested questions without identifying themselves as CIA agents.

ADVANCEMENT AND DEVELOPMENT IN THE RURAL PARISHES

Apart from the traditional responsibilities of parish work, the indigenous parishes in particular actively promoted Catholic Action. In contrast to the situation in other Central American countries this organisation was a very important factor in Guatemala. The organisation of groups of Catholic Action depended on the enthusiasm of the parish priest and the situation in which he found himself. The main activity of Catholic Action was the teaching of catechism and preparation for the reception of the sacraments. Emphasis was placed on the training of leaders and possible leaders of the community, especially the young. Likewise the recruitment of young people was promoted. The catechists already trained were responsible for training others. Once the groups were trained the parish priest gave them other educational, social and moral tasks, such as marriage counselling.

The catechists were the most important factor in regaining the indigenous. Indigenous religious organisation had developed around the so-called confraternities. These were structured by taking age very much into account, so that the highest positions were reached by only a small number of elderly people. This meant that the confraternities were run by elderly people who had successfully passed through the hierarchy of communtiy service offices since their youth. The offices offered social status and therefore the community had special confidence in the office holders. The appearance on the scene of priests of a non-Latin cultural tradition, the Maryknoll missionaries being the first, produced immediate conflicts at a local level. The community matters closely linked to religion quickly attracted the attention of the new priests. In an attempt to eliminate pre-colonial and colonial practices which were considered pagan and incomprehensible, the new priests attacked the indigenous communities' central nucleus of social organisation. In all the parishes and villages to which they went, they encountered these confraternities. In some regions the confraternities were also under other pressures, such as the imposition of intendants instead of local mayors during the dictatorship of Ubico or the presence of political parties during the governments of Arévalo and Arbenz. However, the indigenous organisation was more resistant and the priests were unable to make progress within the authority and power structure of the indigenous parishes.

Where the priests were not expelled, Catholic Action became a convenient instrument for combating the old system. Concentrating on the younger population and training them as catechists eventually caused division in the indigenous communities, separating the young from the old. The parish priests used refusal to say Mass or baptise as a weapon to reinforce the work of the catechists. Belonging to Catholic Action implied a rejection of the indigenous religious leaders (*chamanes*), and confraternities (*cofradías*).

In effect Catholic Action led to new obligations and privileges. Members had their own processions, a separate liturgy and their own internal organisation. When the catechists rushed into opposition to the old religious practices physical violence broke out against them. For this reason proselytising and negative activity was left to the priests. After 1966 Christian democracy tried to present itself as the Christians' political alternative. Then the developmental banner was raised, 'no to communism, no to capitalism, yes to participation'.

The success of Catholic Action varied according to the type of population, failure being clear in the *ladino* parishes. Activity in rural indigenous parishes was not, however, limited to Catholic Action. The North American priests of Huehuetenango and Sololá founded a network of radio schools, based in parish centres. In 1966 there were forty-two schools functioning in Sololá and two in Huehuetenango.

The parish priests and religious worked hard in the foundation of credit co-operatives and unions in their parishes. Some were established on an *ad hoc* basis, that is, without clarity about the principles of co-operativism or a sense of business. Failures soon came but there were also great successes. The most serious deficiency was in appreciation of economic factors. This work of advancement facilitated the acceptance of those involved in communities which were very closed, even for priests, unknown for decades in the countryside.

However this activity, directed with great enthusiasm by the parish priests, caused conflicts. In Quiché a very enthusiastic Spanish priest founded a series of co-operatives including consumer, agricultural, weavers' and credit co-operatives. The organisation included several thousand of the indigenous population. Its success was such that it brought to an end the lending of money by landlords to local usurers and to the credit operations of the *ladino* businessmen. The departmental governor was a military man of little patience with priests and foreigners. The *ladinos* complained bitterly about the progress of the indians. The governor gained the support of the government of Peralta Azurdia and the nuncio ordered the departure of the abovementioned priest from the country. The replacement was more moderate, less progressive and less interested in the development of the indians. At that time it was said that the alliance between the military and the Church against the poor was obvious, but the event illustrates rather the decision of the hierarchy to avoid solutions which would provoke conflict with the State. The national liberation governments maintained good relations with the Church, which would not have been possible if the clergy caused conflict in the public administration. As regards the Church, it showed its political character when it subordinated economic and social development to the State. The priest who was expelled returned to Quiché when the government changed, but the military governor was dismissed due to pressure from co-operativists and in order to avoid more violence.

After Vatican II and Medellín some important pastoral endeavours were relaunched. The most outstanding were the delegates of the Word movement in the dioceses of Huehuetenango, Quizaltenango and Izabal, and the so-called indigenous ministry. The latter attempted to organise the indians and promote exclusively ethnic struggles. The execution of these plans was improved in time though without a clear understanding of the objectives of the so-called indigenous ministry. This ministry, however, increased the number of retreats, courses and religious days which, within a broad pluralism, permitted the politicisation of the indians.

TRADITIONAL URBAN MINISTRY

In the cities the greatest effort was made among the upper classes. The Church was trying to make its presence effective in these exclusive sectors and thus protect what it had gained up to then. There were branches of Catholic Action in the universities, professional associations and for married couples. Retreats were organised for the leaders. In these areas, however, Opus Dei was the most notable institution. In these pastoral activities the idea prevailed that to be a good Catholic one had to be responsible in all areas of life, including professional work. Emphasis varied according to the particular organisation.

The most developed branch of Catholic Action was the university section, made up of a rather small group in the university of San Carlos. The organisation had groups of students in each of the faculties. They met to discuss theological themes and university problems. Like the rural section, this section was concerned about social progress and introducing religious values into daily life. In the mid 1960s the goal of the ecclesiastical adviser was to create teams of university students well prepared to penetrate university associations and exert their influence on them. Quality, not quantity, was the concern. Some students were also members of Opus Dei. In Catholic Action there was considerable emphasis on social justice and its members were of course supposed to be familiar with injustices and be prepared to do something to eradicate them. On graduating, the students naturally were to join the professionals' branch and continue evangelising, act responsibly and work with dedication. However this latter section of Catholic Action had little pastoral impact.

Another organisation which technically formed part of Catholic Action but which functioned autonomously was the Christian Family Movement. This movement was made up of groups of married couples who came together every fortnight to discuss how to live a better family life. In 1966 there were 600 married couples in the capital, Quezaltenango, Huehuetenango, Petén, Zacapa, Verapaz and Esquipula.

The Maryknoll missionaries founded the *cursillos de cristiandad* (short courses in Christianity) movement. The *cursillo* of initiation consisted of a three-day retreat for chosen professional and community leaders. The methodology consisted of strongly moving the participants to bring them to play an active part in Catholicism. The *cursillos* were meticulously planned to achieve the appropriate atmosphere. Each *cursillo* was followed by weekly meetings where problems were discussed. The ideal number of participants was thirty-five; ten from the upper class, another ten from the lower class and some fifteen from the middle class. In this way it was hoped to commit the urban laity of the upper classes to Church work.

The parochial reality from which the *cursillos* arose illustrates the difficulty of urban work in the capital. The archbishop handed over to the Maryknoll missionaries the Villa de Guadelupe, a parish of 30 000 people where there was some of every social class from the most miserable hovels to the residence of the United States ambassador. Even with the economic support of the congregation, the four missionaries appointed considered their task impossible. Confronted with this immense and varied parish, they began the *cursillos* with the aim of identifying individuals who could then help mitigate the shortage of personnel.

Opus Dei first came to Guatemala in 1953 by invitation of the archbishop. This organisation established university residences, a school for social workers, another for domestic servants, a day nursery for the children of market women and a workers' club. All these institutions were financed by the growing number of members, almost all of them belonging to the richest and most conservative families in Guatemala. In 1973 the charismatic renewal movement was added.

There has not been as much interest in socio-economic development or in the social question in the cities as in the rural parishes. Quantitatively the parishes which measured their vitality by the number of sacraments administered and the number and extensiveness of religious groups predominated. There was the unusual case of a Guatemalan priest who was concerned about communist infiltration of the peasants and began his own radio programme, but without institutional support. Another priest, also Guatemalan, the parish priest of La Limonada, one of the fast-growing areas on the outskirts of the capital, also used the radio and television to spread his progressive ideas which were identified as 'communist'. The hierarchy tolerated both as long as they did not seriously threaten their relations with the upper classes. Presumably it was not bad to have a 'communist' parish priest as long as he was unsuccessful.

In general terms the Church was more interested and had more confidence in traditional activities. The schools, dispensaries and catechism took priority over any other new activity. This was as important for the national as for the foreign clergy. These traditional activities complemented the educational work in the capital to which a great concentration of resources and personnel was given. Approximately half of the Church secondary schools were in the capital. The other third were in the largely indigenous dioceses (Verapaz, Sololá, Huehuetenango, Quezaltenango), most of these educational centres being in Quezaltenango and Huehuetenango, as the former is the second city of the country and the latter the Maryknoll missionaries' centre of activity.

Another aspect of the educational emphasis in 1966 was the

proportion of students in Catholic schools and colleges. The Catholic centres had 7.4 per cent of the country's primary students and twenty-one per cent of secondary students. One third of all private secondary and teacher training educational centres was in Church hands. These facts not only show the concentration on education, but also the Church's emphasis on the upper rather than the popular sectors. Meanwhile the hospitals and clinics were nearer to the indigenous population.

CONNIVANCE WITH STATE TERRORISM

Behind the facade of Méndez Montenegro's civil government (1966–70) the United States put a counter-insurgence plan into operation with the direct collaboration of Colonel Carlos Arana in the eastern part of the country. Between 1966 and 1968 some 8000 people died, many of them as a result of the bombardment of their villages. The operation was directed by officials of the United States army. One of them organised paramilitary groups made up of landowners to collaborate with the army in the capture of presumed subversives. These groups later resulted in the *Mano Blanca*, a paramilitary organisation responsible for thousands of assassinations.

When Arana assumed the presidency in 1970 a second wave of terror was unleashed with the help of 32 000 police trained as a result of a public security programme of AID. Between 1970 and 1971, 7000 people disappeared or were assassinated, the majority by the *Mano Blanca*. In the first three years of the presidency of Arana 15 000 people died. When he left the presidency Arana joined up with a right-wing terrorist group which acted not only for political but also for economic reasons.

The bishops remained silent in the face of the repression of those years. Although the communist threat caused violence and deaths, the bishops, led by Monsignor Mario Casariego since 1964, considered that the Church was fulfilling its evangelising and charitable mission. Lack of respect for legitimate authorities would provoke more insecurity and in particular would jeopardise the Church's position of power. The hierarchy remained imprisoned by the anti-communism which had led it to oppose the reformist regime of Arbenz, uniting its efforts to those of the United States government. However, since the arrival of foreign clergy a slow awareness of the unjust living conditions of the vast majority of Guatemalans had developed.

In the Church, however, there was no unanimity about relations with the anti-communist government. A group of university students questioned the vision of the bishops in 1967. As in Honduras the social training courses based on the social doctrine of the Church were welcomed in these restless surroundings. The courses began with students of the most important Catholic colleges. Soon there were followers in all the departments. In the college holidays of 1966–7 various groups of students went to work in rural areas. The group in the capital, called *Cráter*, went public in May 1967 protesting about repression. The document was backed by forty-five university students. Its author had to flee to Mexico. In August one of the priests of the movement had a unique contact with one of the leaders of the guerrilla movement (FAR) who questioned him on the reformist line of the Catholic Church. When they knew national reality better, the university students proposed two alternatives; one reformist and the other revolutionary. In the beginning of November 1967, at a clandestine meeting, they decided to found a Christian-inspired guerrilla movement in co-ordination with that already existing, which they continued to view with distrust. The movement was discovered through the indiscretion of one of the participants, frightened by the radical nature of the option. The information passed from the local superior of the Maryknoll missionaries to the United States ambassador and through him to the government. The information also came to the government through Archbishop Casariego. The Maryknoll religious were expelled from the country with the consent of their superior and the archbishop. Some of the students involved fled to Mexico. The movement did not flourish, its members scattered and the matter was forgotten.

The archbishop outlined his position in a pastoral letter condemning the use of the adjective Catholic in any movement which damaged the principle of authority or promoted violence. But his rejection went further when he warned that some sectors might utilise the adjective Christian to advocate political ideas opposed to the government.

The hierarchy remained divorced from violence. One of the characteristics of the Guatemalan Church has been the lack of clear and decisive episcopal direction. The lack of cohesion and co-ordination of the episcopate extended to the entire Church, in which work continued regionally without any common goal. Perhaps the most scandalous was the silence in the face of the continued waves of state violence. For example in 1971 when a group of Catholics and

Protestants including some bishops, priests and ministers asked the State publicly to change direction as a matter of justice, one of the auxiliary bishops of Monsignor Casariego 'in the name of the Catholic Church of Guatemala' accused them of 'interfering in politics, of speaking without sufficient knowledge and of assisting a group of evil-doers.' The foreigners who signed the declaration were expelled from the country, the nationals received threats. The bishop of Verapaz had to leave the country on one occasion. The government asked the episcopal conference to take care that the clergy did not interfere in politics. Meanwhile immigration procedures for the foreign clergy became stricter. The bishops were made responsible for the actions of their respective clergies. Some of them took on this obligation with great rigour, threatening to expel the rebels.

The committed priests, religious and laity tried many ways of socially advancing the dispossessed, especially the indigenous. Almost all of them were learning the bitter lesson of being called communists or of experiencing the inefficacy of the developmental scheme stifled by exploitation, oppression and violence. Most of the priests assassinated since 1976 had spent many years working on this type of advancement project. All of these were victims of State terror.

The Medellín documents gave a new horizon to this pastoral effort, to which the conferences of religious contributed considerably. However, the denunciation of injustice was left aside as the majority of them were foreigners and subject to the arbitrariness of the military and ecclesiastical authorities in relation to their residence permits. In spite of that, in the 1970s a growing number of pastoral workers dared more and more to run the risk of preaching the truth of the gospel with regard to national reality.

In the very difficult circumstances which followed the 1976 earthquake, it became evident that Church forces were divergent and lacking in ideological clarity. The Church tended to the victims promptly but without a coherent plan of action; for some it was an act of charity, for others a humanitarian act and for a few a form of solidarity with the poorest, who had been those most affected. In any case, it was a brief experience of Church unity for two months centred around Caritas. This organisation and the bishops tried to monopolise Church aid, but the most committed group did not accept that line and abandoned Caritas.

The dissidents organised the Christian Committee (el Comité Cristiano), comprising different Christian groups who for many years had been working for the liberation of the people and particularly of the indians. Subsequently the only assistance for the earthquake victims was channelled through Caritas and the said committee, as the government contributed nothing. The committee continually asked the bishops to state their position on the situation, given that since the earthquake, poverty, hunger and social inequality had become more evident. The group did not have enough force to pressurise the hierarchy but the occasion favoured it. The people perceived oppression and injustice more clearly, which gave rise to a general uneasiness and a desire to hear the voice of the Church. Another important factor was the absence of the archbishop. This circumstance gave some bishops the opportunity to achieve the consensus of the conference to publish 'United in Hope' (*Unidos en la esperanza*).

In this document injustice and exploitation are denounced and violence, the so-called economic boom and the unjust distribution of land are confronted openly. The bishops recognised the existence of institutionalised violence 'so that it is not strange to perceive a silent cry issuing from millions of men asking their pastors for liberation which they cannot find anywhere. But repression comes quickly and many years ago we entered what has come to be called the frightful spiral of violence. Subversion follows oppression, repression follows subversion and thus gradually the atmosphere becomes more and more exasperating and the bloodbath which our country suffers is of an insufferable nature'. Likewise they clearly recognised that 'the basic needs of our people are very far from being satisfied as they ought . . . we must make it absolutely clear before God and men: the accumulation of land in a few hands to the detriment of the vast majority of the inhabitants of a nation is a sin of injustice which cries out to heaven'.

In the letter attention was also drawn to church disunity, the disillusion of many and the urgent need for an all-embracing pastoral approach. The more traditional and conservative sectors exerted pressure for a boycott on the distribution and knowledge of the letter. In a short while the letter was forgotten, reaching only a few groups who were inspired by more concerned pastoral workers.

The socio-economic situation denounced in 'United in Hope' gave rise to great activity in urban and rural areas. The right to organisation, to collective bargaining and pay increase were sought. In the countryside this struggle led to the demand for lands and avoidance of further dispossessions and evictions, to the recent peasant organisation and the repeated protests about the working conditions of the labourers and migrant workers of the southern coastal plateau. In all of these struggles there were priests and religious and many of the struggles were possible because of the social and community development projects of the previous decade, and were facilitated by the parochial platform. Persecution of the Church soon followed. This persecution was part of the general repression of the movement and the popular organisation.

PERSECUTION

The Church took part in the condemnation and popular protests about the massacre of Panzós where the army and the landholders of the area assassinated more than 140 indians in cold blood in 1978. The presence of the Church in the protests had an impact, though in a different way, on the organised popular sectors, the bourgeoisie and the army. The presence of one sector of the Church was co-ordinated by the so-called Committee for Justice and Peace (Comité Pro Justicia y Paz). The army responded accusing these sectors of agitation among the indian peasants of the north and of participating in subversive acts. Archbishop Casariego delegitimised this Christian and Church presence.

Repression against the Church had begun in 1977. Pastoral workers, catechists, delegates of the Word, and any Christians were assassinated. Persecution was directed against the ecclesial body, including the priests. The bishops of Verapaz and Zacapa were accused of being communists in anonymous leaflets from the extreme right. The same accusation, which was as good as a death sentence, was levelled at many Christians. Some of the accused were expelled from the country. But very many Christians were assassinated for their faith.

The wave of terror and persecution which from 1977 on began to touch the clergy and pastoral workers caused division among the bishops. This division was evident in the diversity of stances regarding the massacre of Panzós. Thus while some bishops were accused of being communists, others became open defenders of the military regime and State terrorism. Among the latter were Archbishop Casariego and some of his auxiliaries. In the episcopal conference it was endeavoured not so much to maintain unity as to prevent differences from reaching the public. The situation came to a climax when some bishops presented their resignations when faced with the impossibility of dealing with the archbishop. On this occasion in June 1979 the Vatican accepted only the resignation of the Jesuit bishop of Quezaltenango.

In the first six months of 1980 the State directed repression against the sector of the Church which had most openly adopted a stance in favour of the oppressed and which had dared to denounce structural sin and institutionalised violence. On 1 May Conrado de la Cruz Schmit, a native of the Philippines, religious of the Immaculate Heart of Mary congregation, and parish priest of Tiquisate, was obliged by armed civilians to enter a vehicle in the capital after a demonstration. He was not seen again. On 12 May Walter Woordeker, a Belgian and religious of the same order, was assassinated in his parish of Santa Lucía Cotzumalguapa, Escuintla. A few weeks later on 4 June José María Grau Cirera, a Spaniard and member of the Sacred Hearts congregation, was shot ten times in the back. He had worked for ten years in the guerrilla zone of Quiché, where many catechists had been taken from their houses and assassinated in front of their families. Two teachers accused of being subversives had been assassinated. Grau Cirera celebrated Mass in Nebaj for them. The Dominican sisters and the Marists were threatened for having attended the Mass. The assassination of Cirera occurred later. The body was abandoned and was only discovered by the neighbours after three days. On 10 July Faustino Villanueva, a Spaniard and religious of the same order was killed after fifteen years of work in the Quiché area. He was assassinated in his parish office presumably for being a witness to army repression against the indigenous communities.

In those same months the government launched a campaign of slander and death threats against the Jesuits, who had published a document themselves when the bishops failed to speak out. Two weeks later demonstrators who had peacefully occupied the Spanish embassy were assassinated. Black lists began to appear signed by clandestine organisations behind which the security corps hid.

In November 1976, before these assassinations and outrages, a Maryknoll missionary, Guillermo Woods, who had worked for seven years in the jungle area of Huehuetenango, was assassinated. He had bought lands to sell at a low price to poor peasants. The fertility of the lands contributed to the success of his enterprise. His work upset the landlords. When he transported some wounded to the nearest hospital he was accused of helping the guerrillas. In his defence he said that Christian charity obliged him not to make distinctions between people. A little later, in November 1976, when he was taking off from a small airport in Quiché soldiers machine-gunned the petrol tank of his light aircraft. The army hid the aeroplane but the Maryknoll missionaries found evidence of the accident. Four other North Americans died with him.

On 30 June 1978 the parish priest of San José Pinula, Hermógenes López, was machine-gunned. He had been receiving death threats for a year for defending the right of the peasants of his parish to water, for protecting small dairies and for preventing the conscription of youths.

In 1981 the State continued to assassinate priests. In that year alone six more were killed. In February 1981 Juan Alonso Fernández, a Spaniard and Sacred Hearts religious, was assassinated. At that time he was parish priest of San Andrés in El Petén. Previously he had spent seventeen years in Quiché. Seeing the need to return after the first assassinations he had offered himself to help in the northern region of the diocese, the region of most conflict. On 14 May Carlos Gálvez Galindo, a Guatemalan priest of Técpan, was assassinated in his sacristy. He had actively denounced military repression in his parish. On 2 July Marco Tulio Marusso was killed near Quiriguá by a paramilitary group. In his will he had written, 'If I am assassinated, I wish to be buried as a witness against government violence'.

On 28 July 1981 Stanley Rother, parish priest of Santiago Atitlán, was assassinated by persons unknown. For fifteen years he had been working in the area, having been sent by the diocese of Oklahoma. On 4 August the Jesuit Carlos Pérez Alonso, a Spaniard, disappeared on leaving the military hospital. On 17 September John D. Troyer, also a North American, was assassinated and on 14 February 1982 James Miller. The persecution of such members of the Church is a chapter which still remains open in Guatemala.

This chapter was translated by Mary Harris.

12 The Martyrdom of the Salvadorean Church

Rodolfo Cardenal

The Church emerged from the liberal crisis with very good relations with the State and with the landholding coffee-planter classes, despite the fact that the break in relations in the nineteenth century was violent, though not as violent as in Guatemala.

The State established a type of space suitable for the development and preservation of religion. The Church ended up submitting resignedly, compromising the faith in order to preserve and increase that space which it considered indispensable. In this way the Church ended up submitting to the State, afraid of never again recovering its privileges and institutional rights which had been astutely manipulated by the official lay civil power. Otherwise the Church would have had to declare itself in open rebellion, but it opted for the first alternative, playing the part of preserver of the established order. The second alternative was institutionally impossible.

THE TRADITIONAL CHURCH

From the alliance of the Church and State there emerged a very traditional Church, one of the characteristics of which was the lack of leadership and definite pastoral outlines. The exception was always the archdiocese of San Salvador. The bishops in El Salvador, as in all of Central America, have been clear symbols of the presence of the local Church and the stances they have adopted indicate one of the means by which the Church has exercised its influence on society. In El Salvador all social forces have for a long time known and recognised that the social force of the Church is rooted in the archdiocese and in the groups which assist it in other dioceses, and that the real mouthpiece of the Salvadorean Church has always been the archbishop of the capital.

Within the traditional Church the figure of the bishop has always been separate and distant from the body of his diocese or from its most significant groups, of which the bishops have not had, and do not have, the power of convocation; likewise the bishop has played a major part in serious conflicts with relatively important groups of his priests and pastoral workers who have tried to follow the pastoral line of commitment to the poor, a marked line in the archdiocese in recent decades.

The absence of a pastoral approach and of ecclesial direction has led to a negative type of social influence, that is, it has preserved the traditional order directly or indirectly, effectively it has maintained the prevailing socio-political order. It is true that on some occasions some bishops have denounced the abuses of the landholders and the army, but on most occasions they have made common cause with both, through action and omission, sanctioning with their silence or presence important public actions, from blessings of all types of buildings to the taking of power by unlawfully elected presidents.

This traditional Church which persists up to the present day in almost all of the dioceses of the country has given more importance in its doctrinal declarations and its messages to judgements on ideologies (communism, marxism, liberation theology) than to the urgent nature of the actual situation; more to the shortcomings and dangers pertaining to any historical action, particularly to the popular organisations, than to the urgent misery of reality; more to the abstract ideological purity in which it is expressed than to the service of the world which, given its historic character, is not lacking in ambiguities and dangers. Outside the archdiocese the pastoral approach has been marked exclusively by the administration of the sacraments with some timid attempts at modernisation in the sacramental approach beginning with the charismatic movement. However, there have always been small groups of priests and religious following the outlines defined by Vatican II and Medellín. These groups have been formed and have worked without the support of the bishops and at times in open opposition.

This Church has not been able to form a compact unity, but rather has defined itself negatively by not allowing itself to be inspired by the innovative trends of Vatican II, Medellín and Puebla. Urban middle-class groups who have seen the defence of their bourgeois interests in the traditional Church belong to this type of Church. Some of these Catholics have often been seen publicly abandoning the Church or seeking refuge in some Protestant sects who have removed the social dimension from the faith.

Within this traditional Church there are also those well-intentioned Christians who still possess a dual vision; they have advanced, perhaps, in some strictly religious areas, but without any social implications. Here one finds the charismatic movement and other similar movements, which without basis and without the will and knowledge of their members are effectively supported by reactionary and conservative interests.

In this form of Church existence there is a lack of specific cohesion and historic consciousness. Church existence is more or less what it has always been, adding secondary modifications to be up to date. Its social influence has been almost nil and formally negative because it has sanctioned and religiously justified the established order.

In the countryside, where the majority of the population live, the prevailing ideological system applauded the right of a few to decide on the life and death of others and that power was projected onto divinity. The system of exploitation inverted its logic of death into an appearance of life. Death was presented as life, like a friend who liberated, and, thus, divine. The peasant died surrounded by his relatives and friends, rosaries, scapulars, statues of saints and prayers seeking his salvation, a salvation which was not assured because it depended on ethical conduct.

The predominant concept of salvation promised a home above, in heaven, 'and there we said that there were altars, there all the saints were well and truly alive, that when we arrived there we were going to be with them. That we were not going to eat, we were not going to drink, but we would just see the Lord with all the saints. That there we were going to be singing, praying and praising the Lord, finally without any suffering of this life. Happy, because we had already suffered'. Sufferings derived directly or indirectly from domination or exploitation were tolerated as they implied a compensation beyond history. In this way, civil and ecclesiastical power achieved a consensus which gave them indisputable power for centuries.

This dualist concept reflected the social dualism characteristic of a society with classes. God sent death because the destiny of each one was the result of his will; all were marked from their birth to their death. Rebellion against this destiny was considered a grave sin which seriously endangered individual salvation. God's plan was equivalent to considering the social order as something natural.

The after-life was reduced to an individual problem of joy or suffering based on the reward-punishment binomial. The peasants' analogy between God-father-judge and landholder-boss-last-word is significant. The peasant confronted these powers individually. A significant part of social legitimacy revolved around the threat of hell. Thus the salvation ethic was doubly reinforced with the theme of condemnation-hell. In effect, if the promise of eternal joys was not sufficient to maintain silence, the pains of hell acted as a powerful reinforcing factor.

The vast majority of the population lived denying reality, and their lives were an apprenticeship for death. The road towards eternal life only passed through the natural and the necessary, falsely converted into divine will. The politico-religious command 'to save the soul' was observed as one accepted the 'will of God', the basis of morality. Salvation of the soul depended on fulfilling the eternal divine law, preserving the natural order and prohibiting the disturbance of it. The commandments took on a normative value and their transgression implied sin (a situation of condemnation) and their observance no sin (a situation of salvation). The usual sermon gave full meaning to the sin-condemnation-hell trilogy.

Observance of the commandments was evident in a dual structure, the world of the sacred and the world of the profane. In the profane world actions were prohibited, passivity being demanded; while in the sacred world positive actions were required to obtain salvation. Actions in the material world and their potential efficacy had been stripped of their importance in favour of the spiritual world ruled by vertical God-man relations.

Passive activity in the sacred implied active passivity in the profane; therefore the will of God consisted of abandoning the affairs of men. Although the commandments tried to bring order and harmony to social relations, they did so individually. Rites, especially the sacraments, were considered privileged means with regard to salvation and were directed towards ensuring the total sense of existence and indirect action, through recourse to divine action, in an immediately uncontrolled world.

Sacramental practices were the unifying link between the peasants and the Church which presented itself as administrator of the sacred and its official representatives as experts in the sacred. Since liberal reform, the parish priests' income came largely from the administration of the sacraments.

Behind each rite there was suffering. That is, any utilitarian rite cost money and its efficacy was assured by its costs. Suffering was presented as the key to happiness. Consequently, suffering was undergone in profane activities and actively sought in the sacred.

Another important value of the rites consisted of the expression of feelings (love) in relation to the divine. The expression of love assisted salvation. Thus, the utilitarian value of the rite was provided by the suffering and the love liable to be recompensed. In this way the world of the sacred was converted into a factor which promoted active passivity.

All of these aspects were synthesised in the archetypal model of Jesus. Jesus was the archetypal model because he fulfilled divine will within the dual version of the commandments and the law in their widest expression. Jesus became a model opposed to social change, as suffering was the principal duty of this life, and death the final result of the suffering. Jesus synthesised these two concepts wonderfully, hence the great significance of the suffering Jesus. Even the risen Christ was still a Christ who brought death and who saved only when there was resignation in the face of oppression. The rulers saw the other face of this same Christ, one who was reigning and glorious. But this was not so simple. The popular images of Jesus suffering reproduce the features of the dominator more than the dominated. This archetypal reality whose repetition brought salvation, the supreme end of existence, immutable for decades, made something safe of history. Rebellion had been excluded because the archetypes were created by God himself, creator of the world, and who is at the end of all when this suffering passes and one arrives at eternal salvation.

This cosmic vision and the resultant type of religiosity have continued up to the present day in almost all the dioceses of the country, except for the archdiocese and some well-defined sectors of the other dioceses.

THE ARCHDIOCESE BEGINS ITS JOURNEY

The archdiocese remained structured in a determinative form during the long archepiscopate of Monsignor Luis Chávez (1939–77). Monsignor Chávez was an archbishop who was very close to the people in his ministry, open, with a very characteristic prudence, but without any paralysing fear of what was new. He provided many pastoral projects to bring the archdiocese up to date. First he promoted Catholic Action and similar groupings, but he also quickly concerned himself with the establishment of co-operatives and the social secretariat. He supported the media of social communication in the archdiocese, the press and radio. He attended to the educational needs of the poorest, promoting the foundation of parish schools. A constant concern of Monsignor Chávez's was the promotion and training of lay people to make up for the shortage of clergy and make effective the presence of the Church in society, especially in social, family and university spheres.

He was very faithful to pastoral visits and saw them as a special moment for coming into contact with the people of God. Year after year he went out to travel through the parishes of the extensive archdiocese. He gave of his best to bring out an all-embracing ministry. He often adopted stances on the situation in the country and made Christian diagnoses of the situation in more than fifty pastoral letters. From the outset he concerned himself with the training of clergy, building and endowing a good seminary with the help of the Jesuits. In its better times priests from all of Central America were trained in this seminary. For the most gifted young priests he obtained opportunities for the continuation of their studies abroad.

In 1937 he was accused for the first time of being a communist for defending the barbers (who wanted to raise their prices) and from then on he declared his stance in every national crisis. In 1944, for example, he risked his life defending those persecuted in an abortive *coup d'état*. During the 1970s he defended the peasant organisation as far as he could and tried to prevent the approaching repression. He defended the clergy against the attacks of the government and the right, though at times he personally was not in agreement with what he considered too extreme. For that, however, he drew attacks and criticism upon himself.

Monsignor Chávez, with more than words, pushed the archdiocese forward with great ecclesial fidelity and conviction, even amid the risks and obscurities which accompanied the new approach. He led the archdiocese to flourish contrary to the reservations of the former allies of his predecessors, to the opposition of the rest of the bishops and of the nuncio. The attacks by the press were continual and increasingly more aggressive up to the end of his archepiscopate. They recurred particularly when he put the weight of the institution on the side of justice and the poor. On innumerable occasions Monsignor Chávez showed signs of being a man of simple faith in the Spirit of God. His prudence was proverbial, but also his decisiveness and his courage.

Vatican II passed unnoticed until Medellín. Until then very few were concerned about the council. But the options of Medellín provoked a significant debate within the social and ecclesial sphere. It was then necessary to study the Council to sustain the affirmations of Medellín firmly. The prevailing anxieties were crystallised in a very well-attended pastoral week in which, after much discussion, the conclusions of Medellín were promoted. The episcopate did not participate in the week, in spite of having convened it. As the conclusions were not to their liking, they delegitimised them with their authority.

This episcopal opposition was not sufficient to halt the new trend which Medellín had introduced. At opposite ends of the country centres for peasant advancement were founded. The pastoral experiences of Suchitoto, Tecoluca and Aguilares began to have an impact on the archdiocese. To those rural experiences were added others of a suburban nature in the metropolitan zone of the capital, especially Zacamil and Ilopango. An itinerant pastoral team came to a clear break with the traditional sacramentalist scheme. The celebration of the Word took the place of the parish mass. Mass attendance in the rural parishes dropped dramatically. The same happened with the practice of confession and other old practices such as novenas and first Fridays.

The more anxious clergy of the archdiocese, supported by the bishops, sought points of reference in Riobamba, Choluteca and in the Latin American Pastoral Institute. Some began to introduce delegates of the Word and give courses in the advancement centres; others proceeded more slowly and applied themselves first to becoming acquainted with parochial reality, experiencing the joys and contradictions of popular religiosity. In both experiences, there resulted a rapid identification between the parish priest and his people, discovering each other's riches and limitations. For parish priests who adopted this line Paulo Freire's book, *Pedagogy of the Oppressed* was decisive. Experience showed that working together involved a mutual and reciprocal demand; the people demanded increasingly more of the priest and he found himself pressed to broaden his horizons continually.

The general feeling among the clergy was one of crisis; the outlines which were sure and well known began to topple one after the other. One frequently heard it said that the people had lost the faith on account of a wave of materialism. It was a critical moment of loss of the former ecclesial and priestly identity. The traditional roles of priests and bishops were severely questioned. Some abandoned the ministry.

The crisis developed when the believers began to assert themselves in the Church. Their policies affected the hierarchy and the powers of this world who began to be questioned. The people spoke of exploitation and frauds. The dominant groups warned of the danger from the outset and began to point out those to blame for the disorder, describing them first as Third Worldists, trendies, hippies and later even came to call them communists and subversives, which was equivalent to sentencing them to death. The bishops of the archdiocese were the first to be attacked for permitting the clergy to take these options. When attacks through the media were not sufficient, the next steps were the expulsions of foreigners, threats, and finally the assassination of the national clergy.

After 1970 the archdiocese made a great effort to produce a consistent pastoral line. After the failure of the first pastoral week on account of blocking and condemnation by the episcopate, another was organised solely for the archdiocese in 1976. That week was carefully prepared in the parishes, and with the active participation of the growing base Christian communities. The week reaped the fruit of the recent urban and rural pastoral experiences. In that new light the pastoral work of the archdiocese was evaluated. From this week there emerged clearly the need to intensify evangelisation, placing special emphasis on accommodating popular religiosity to the demands of liberation, enabling local communities to train their pastoral workers and promote the integral liberation of all Salvadoreans.

The personal prestige of Monsignor Chávez and his pastoral line also supported by his successor, Monsignor Romero, unified the clergy at times in an impressive manner. Individually the parish priests, in effect, gave varying emphases to the actual ministry, basically continuing the sacramental emphasis, but on the whole the diverse tendencies which existed did not prevent the priests from giving the impression of a united sacerdotal body. With few exceptions of very traditionalist priests who could not be assimilated in the archdiocesan body of priests, the vast majority tried honestly to place themselves in the ecclesial centre. There also existed a more radical group, but in basic communion with the two archbishops and their sacerdotal body. This more radical group, a source of tensions, was the driving force behind the rest of the clergy.

The archdiocesan clergy, because of their basic unity and the leadership of the two archbishops, were an obvious social force which surpassed the actual realisations of many of their members. The people identified with these priests and felt that this Church was theirs. There was an awareness of a new form of Church and priest. The change, however, was not easy, nor was it free from ambiguities.

The religious clergy were for the most part foreign (some seventy-five per cent approximately at the end of the 1970s) and largely concentrated in urban education, although important pastoral work was also being done. The dedication to education, however, ceased to be exclusive since the archepiscopate of Monsignor Chávez who removed the nuns from their colleges in the capital to entrust them with vacant rural and suburban parishes. Traditionally education has been geared towards the wealthier classes of the metropolitan zone but in the most important educational centres there were important changes in the 1970s, a greater integration of religious formation and analysis of national reality, the democratisation of the student body and the transformation into training centres predominantly for the lower classes. Then the bourgeoisie and the upper middle class founded their own educational institutions.

After the progressive transfer of the nuns from the colleges to the rural parishes, they began to work in the parish ministry, especially in forming base Christian communities and as pastoral workers. The nuns have acquired an enormous credibility both for their actions and for the constancy they showed in the face of persecution. The pace of change among the religious has varied according to the congregation except for the Jesuits and those congregations more committed to parish work, where it has been much more rapid. Since 1980 the religious, and again the nuns in particular, have rendered valuable and irreplaceable services with a view to humanising the war. The religious as a body have done their utmost to attend materially and spiritually to the hundreds of thousands of displaced and refugee victims of the armed conflict. Since 1986 they have made a tremendous effort to serve those parishes abandoned through lack of parish priests and situated in the zones of conflict.

The social assistance ministry has not been abandoned. In 1980 there were twenty-three bodies working in dispensaries, orphanages, places of refuge, nutritional assistance and so on. In that year also five organisations were working in ministry to the sick.

THE BELIEVING PEOPLE SET OUT

The celebration of the Word took possession of the rural parishes in an irrepressible way, awakening the community awareness of the peasants. That new awareness was evident in the return to the Eucharist, but as a community celebration. The index of mass attendance rose again considerably, but not so the practice of confession. However, in the other sacraments the community dimension and social commitment appeared strongly. The celebration of the Word rapidly spread thanks to the missionary consciousness of the delegates and the catechists. With this movement the bible was given back to the people.

The increase in *cursillos* afforded the peasants a new theoretical apparatus which helped them to understand their social situation better. These bible courses introduce the figure of Moses and the situation of Exodus. Moses became the archetype because of the tremendous strength inspired by his feat of liberation. Further, he became a figure to be emulated because of his struggle, as related in the bible, with foreign political forces. The most significant fact was that the image of Christ could be finally compared with another in view of the construction of the kingdom of God. It was shown how both fulfilled the Word of God in accordance with their historic circumstances, liberating the people and building the kingdom.

The preaching and movement of the delegates gave rise to a structural, demythologised and scientific understanding of social reality and the possibility of interpreting the historical dynamics as class history. Religious and sociological categories such as exploitation and violence were used equally. Then class struggle was spoken of explicitly. This step was fundamental for the acceptance of categories of scientific and structural analysis. It was so fundamental that preaching in any other sense would radically impede the progress of the delegates.

The hard and conscientious pastoral work of the parish priests and religious mined the traditional ideology of the peasants and gave them analytical instruments. At the same time it allowed them to apply the category of social sin to reality. In this way they understood violence as an inherent reality in the history of salvation. Nevertheless the attraction of violence was not directly induced by pastoral workers as some, including some bishops, have tried to lead one to believe. It fittingly arose from the peasant's contact with the Word of God. What the pastoral workers did was put the bible in their hands and afford them indispensable knowledge for reading and interpreting it. The great force was rooted in the extreme situation of injustice and oppression. Thus, in the history of salvation they found a powerful parable of their own history.

For the first time innovation was introduced in history. The peasants grasped various situations, structured them coherently up to a certain point starting from oppression, observed their various forms and consequently took up the possibility of opening up to the analysis of their own reality and more conscious action regarding it. In this way they overcame localised and spontaneous perspectives. The opening up was permitted by the clash of archetypes, but it was only one form of opening up. Agrarian organisation and its analysis raised the levels of understanding of reality.

The training obtained on the parish *cursillos* facilitated the distinction of the kingdom of God from any human realisation, but without human activity ceasing to be necessary anticipation of the kingdom of God on that account. Therefore, the millenarianism characteristic of such movements did not result. However, there were masked millenarianisms that were difficult to overcome. The existence of such millenarian trends, also evident in some groups and organisations of a marxist character, indicates an attempt to channel despair when faced with the political and economic crises of the Salvadorean countryside.

The deepening of the political crisis, the influence of the urban intellectuals who brought a filtered scientific analysis and the actions of the peasants themselves made the rise of the peasant organisation possible. Now the image of Jesus and that of other biblical personages ceased to be a model of any imitation and came to be understood as an incitement to recreate their attitudes and profound options regarding life and death, in terms of the dominant sectors. Consequently it was not possible to move spontaneously from Gospel-inspiration to political action.

The peasant organisation spread rapidly throughout the country between 1972 and 1975. Peasant groups united with the urban organisations and they controlled the city streets. The dominant sectors began to ward off the danger with every means within their reach, military deployments, propaganda campaigns in the media, intensification of espionage networks in the country and city, imprisonment, tortures and assassinations. However, the repression, instead of halting the organising movement made it advance even more, obliging it to perfect its methods of struggle.

The new consciousness showed that exploitation was not considered ahistoric. Exploitation and its concrete methods were discussed. The system was demythologised. The social structure was considered dichotomic and factions and sectors were distinguished.

The State was no longer considered a neutral entity to approach seeking protection, but was seen as a coercive instrument of the dominant class. The radical solution was in the suppression of the capitalist system and the construction of socialism. Political action and training courses investigated these expositions.

Pastoral work left the ground prepared for the appearance of this peasant organisation. This, for its part, once begun, took advantage of the parochial structures to spread and consolidate whereupon it created ambiguities difficult to resolve between the Church and the organisation and conflicts between both institutions. In spite of that, in the archdiocese all possible was done to prevent repression from befalling the organised peasants. The Church in general and the parishes in particular served as protection.

The influence of the gospel on the leaders of the organisation was clear. From this influence sprang the desire to give one's life for others. The peasant organisations began with a great mysticism that was at first fundamentally Christian, then Christian-revolutionary and finally revolutionary-Christian. Each step involved a crisis of growth for the peasant organisation and for the parishes where it operated. The process was not a rejection of the gospel, nor of the Church nor of the parish, but the conquest of ideological and organisational autonomy on the part of the peasants.

The gospel and its mysticism resulted in the culmination of organisation. The mysticism of those organised was impressive and disconcerting. The euphoria and organisational mysticism increased as the organisation made its power felt in opposition to the dominant classes. Joining an organisation was considered a conversion of a religious type, but the fullness of the same was only reached in the organisation. The revolutionary approach did not consist of addressing the obvious problems, but rather the class interests which were not immediately perceived. A class interest involved caring for others and being capable of risking one's life for it. Here there was a mystical experience which was not contrived in any way.

In addition to the Christian faith there was a profound faith in socialism. First both professions of faith occurred together, but later the second took precedence over the first. The experience of political conversion took possession of the peasants like a passion, understood as a tendency of life to react intensely. The greatest emphasis of political life came from the risk with which one lived and the heroic connotations which it entailed. The organisation generated new realities at the individual level, demanding the change of attitudes and morality.

After 1975 the importance of lay urban middle-class movements like the *cursillos de cristiandad* and the Christian Family Movement declined. Some of the members of these movements worked in bodies with great social influence such as the Interdiocesan Social Secretariat, the Justice and Peace Committee, in educational works of Christian inspiration and so on.

THE CHURCH OF MONSIGNOR ROMERO

Monsignor Oscar Romero succeeded Monsignor Chávez amid general uncertainty because he was a recognised bishop of the traditional Church. The spiritual honesty of his manner and the persecution which increased at the time of his taking over the archepiscopate were more powerful than his previous traditional approach. Monsignor Chávez handed over the authority of the archdiocese to him when he could no longer do anything against the attacks on the Church and the repression unleashed against the peasant organisation and urban movements. Contrary to what was expected of him, Monsignor Romero in an unsuspected way promoted and strengthened the line defined by Monsignor Chávez. That was possible because he encountered an archdiocese which was already prepared, directed and decided. When the two archbishops are compared, differences in their ways and manners are found but the closeness to the people, openness to what was new and the decision to direct, with risks, the progress of the country united them both closely. However the fundamental factor in understanding their action was persecution, as that sealed the authenticity and credibility of the pastoral approach of the archdiocese during the 1970s.

During his three years as archbishop Monsignor Romero became the Christian conscience of the country, a conscience which criticised the outrages and violence produced by unjust structures and gave hope and strength to the masses. He was the natural leader of the clergy of the archdiocese and even beyond it. He unified the diocesan clergy and, to a considerable extent, the religious, the lay pastoral workers and the vast majority of the people. He became an international Church figure in a manner unknown until then. His actions went far beyond the boundaries of the strictly ecclesial, acquiring a tremendous social influence. His Sunday homilies were the radio programme most listened to, both by those who followed him and those who criticised him.

Monsignor Romero was a pastor close to all Salvadoreans. He approached the people in his visits to the communities, the poor approached him in the archbishopric and the cancer hospital where he lived. But all the social forces of the country also approached him. It is impressive to confirm in his pastoral diary how journalists, diplomats, political parties and government employees, the military, members of the bourgeoisie and of the popular organisations, workers and peasants, students and rectors of the universities, victims of repression, priests, international agencies and so on went to him. This abundance of callers indicates an archbishop open to all, kind and understanding with all, but at the same time firm and clear in telling all his gospel message.

In this way Monsignor Romero became, without trying to, the centre of the life of the country. In the moments of conflict in which it fell to him to live, these social forces, even those who attacked him, felt the necessity of going to him. Monsignor Romero became necessary to console and enlighten, to mediate and to help, to bring antagonistic social and political forces into contact.

In his conversations he was always clear and firm. With the representatives of the right wing forces whom he clearly denounced in his homilies he was respectful and appeared hopeful of being able to change them, of being able to convert them to the gospel. With the representatives of the popular organisations and the politico-military groups whom he defended in public in their just demands, he was open and very demanding in private. To all who suffered he appeared a merciful pastor without exception.

Monsignor Romero was a pastor accessible to all social sectors, disposed first to hear and later to direct, to teach, thus exercising his magisterial function in a very unusual way. It can be affirmed without fear of exaggeration that the entire country passed through Monsignor Romero and through the archbishopric. Likewise, Monsignor Romero was a man of dialogue. He promoted it himself and practised it continually, learning, taking an interest, reflecting and always maintaining his liberty to proclaim his evangelical and ecclesial message. This availability and accessibility led to the affection which the people showed publicly. They recognised him and they continue to recognise him as their pastor.

On the pastoral level Monsignor Romero dreamed of a ministry for the archdiocese along the lines of Vatican II, Medellín and Puebla. That is, he wanted a ministry rooted in evangelisation and in the preferential option for the poor, a pastoral approach which would meet the most serious problems of the country. Therefore he insisted strongly on the formation of ecclesial communities and pastoral workers on the one hand, and on the other, on defending the right to life of the Salvadoreans.

As pastor he understood that he must promote a united ministry and encourage all the pastoral workers to form a single ecclesial body. Given the national situation, pastoral unity was not an easy matter, as there existed tendencies to ignore the said reality or become involved in it without sufficient ecclesial identity. He was concerned particularly with the synthesis of historic commitment and ecclesial identity, especially after October 1979 when political polarisation reached one of its extremes. Therefore he came forward to have dialogue with the representatives and the most important nuclei of the two tendencies. With the most recalcitrant of the first tendency he failed; but with the rest he succeeded in maintaining enough unity within an all-embracing ministry, at least avoiding the more scandalous contradictions. With this second tendency he could always maintain frank and open dialogue, in spite of the differences in perspectives and criteria.

Monsignor Romero brought the Church into the centre of the popular struggle. The Church could not ignore that which had sprung up under its shadow and had been urged on by it. But now it had to recognise the autonomy of the popular organisation. The problem then was how to maintain autonomy, but at the same time be present. Monsignor Romero expressly asked the popular organisations and politico-military groups to formulate as soon as possible a plan of government 'which comes from the people and which presents itself to the people in order to unite the people in these organisations'. The role of the Church in this project was one of service, illuminating technical areas from the gospel point of view and watching over the human and religious interests of the people. Romero wanted the plan to be made public as soon as possible so that the people would know what these organisations were offering as opposed to what Christian democracy and the United States were offering.

Monsignor Romero had serious reservations about the use of violence by politico-military groups, but he was always prepared to act as good Samaritan. He was also pastor to those who were organised. He gave humanitarian assistance and put the Church infrastructure at their service.

For him the popular organisations were an important social force to be reckoned with. And furthermore they were a beginning in renewal of the social and economic order in which he put his hopes, despite their obvious limitations. They were also Salvadoreans who wanted the good of the masses and many of them, furthermore, were Christians.

Contrary opinions did not frighten Monsignor Romero. What made him nervous was the lack of dialogue and openness, the lack of trust and honesty. For the rest, he considered it interesting to discuss different points of view. It was a way of enriching oneself in order to take charge of situations later.

For all that, Monsignor Romero was a bishop who suffered conflict and attack. To some traditional ecclesial sectors he was the cause of all the country's ills, but to the people he was simply their pastor. The tensions within the episcopal conference grew to the point where Monsignor Romero was left in isolation. The nuncios were also against him and in favour of the other traditionalist bishops. This obliged him to present himself in Rome to give information and bring awareness about the real problems of the country. These journeys to Rome were not very successful, as the vision of the nuncios and the other bishops always prevailed. Monsignor Romero was seen in Rome as a suspicious and untrustworthy bishop. On several occasions thought was given to replacing him.

CONFLICT WITH THE TRADITIONAL CHURCH AND PERSECUTION

The traditional Church, together with the more right-wing sectors of society, always viewed the innovative paths of the archdiocese with foreboding and suspicion. In fact, although Monsignor Chávez was respected by the other bishops, his pastoral lines were never accepted. The episcopal conference distrusted the archdiocese. Within that conference suspicion fell on one of the auxiliary bishops of Monsignor Chávez, Monsignor Arturo Rivera who at that time was considered 'the red bishop'. For that reason he was not allowed to succeed Monsignor Chávez in the archdiocese.

This suspicion and distrust regarding the archdiocese was continually intensified as the archdiocese opted more clearly for the poor and favoured the popular organisations. It is true that when persecution began the bishops presented themselves as united in two messages, one in March 1977 and the other in May of the same year, defending the Church, denouncing the outrages and calling on the government to put an end to repression. But regarding the themes of conspicuous social interest, the public order law and the legislation and justification of popular organisations, the bishops were clearly not united. In the archdiocese the incompatibility of Monsignor Romero with his auxiliary bishop who eventually withdrew from ecclesiastical office further increased. As Monsignor Romero adopted more radical stances the other bishops attacked him silently, finally denouncing him before the Holy See in various documents, some of them unbecoming and contemptible.

The nuncios could not unite the episcopate and even less bring it into line with Vatican II, Medellín and Puebla. Their attitudes in brief but significant public appearances, their presentations in diplomatic and governmental circles, their absences from popular and priests' circles have forged an image of obstruction and attack on the line of the archdiocese and of favouring the other bishops. Likewise they clearly supported the State thesis in relation to the Church. The differences between Monsignor Romero and the nuncios are well known. The nuncios clearly tried to have him relinquish his pastoral options for the sake of building unity on a traditional base.

Repression of the people and persecution of the Church were added to intra-church conflict. Both had a logical and chronological order at the end of 1976. Peaceful demonstrations were violently dissolved by the security and military corps leaving countless injured and dead. They violently cleared the churches and other places where protests were made against the growing repression and justice was demanded. There were repeated and bloody military operations; unpunished machine-gunning of pedestrians; selective assassinations of national and local political leaders, especially of trade unionists and organised people. The number of assassinations increased and went unpunished.

The Church was persecuted at institutional and personal level. Ten priests were assassinated (Rutilio Grande, 12 March 1977; Alfonso Navarro, 11 May 1977; Ernesto Barrera, 28 November 1978; Octavio Ortiz, 20 January 1979; Rafael Palacios, 20 June 1979; Alirio N. Macías, 4 August 1979; Cosme Spezzotto, 14 June 1980; Manuel A. Reyes, 7 October 1980; Ernesto Abrego, 23 November 1980; Marcial Serrano, 28 November 1980), one deacon (José O. Cáceres, 25 July 1980), four nuns (Ita Ford, Maura Clark, Dorothy Kazel, 2 December 1980; Silvia Arriola, 17 January 1981), one lay missionary (Jean Donovan, 2 December 1980) and Monsignor Oscar Romero, archbishop of San Salvador, on 24 March 1980. Some forty priests were seriously threatened, expelled from the country or tortured; all the Jesuits were threatened with death twice, in 1977 and 1980. Many Christians of the base Christian communities were threatened, searched, tortured, harassed and even assassinated in their capacity as Christians. Liturgical celebrations were obstructed. Attacks by the media were innumerable and intense. There was physical violence against the ecclesiastical institutions, the Catholic colleges; the Catholic radio was victim of various bomb attacks and systematic interferences; priests' and religious houses were searched and attacked with bombs and machine-guns; the same happened to churches and houses of lay collaborators. Likewise there was military occupation of churches, violations of the Eucharist and sacred vessels. But the steadfastness of the clergy in the face of this persecution between 1977 and 1982 had an impact on national consciousness and gave great credibility to the Church.

In this persecution and repression the Church found its historic place of solidarity with the people, learning and concretely expressing their faith. Repression and persecution were the same thing, though each had a different form. As the Church took part in the historic process, in the same measure it was also persecuted. The Church was persecuted by hatred of justice, but that hatred really, though indirectly, stemmed from hatred of the faith. It was persecuted equally because it was considered a community of the poor whose very lives were threatened and denied. Persecution sought those who promoted the Kingdom, simultaneously destroying the Kingdom of God and all it stood for. The years of persecution fostered Christian virtues which would have been difficult to achieve in any other way, that is, humility, solidarity, fortitude in suffering and hope against hope.

THE CHURCH AFTER PERSECUTION

After these years of repression and ten years of persecution the Church is decimated. Its human resources have been impoverished and its creative experiments reduced. A considerable part of the Church is terrified, a fact which has reduced proximity to the poor, along with its commitment and clarity regarding the denunciation of injustice.

To this weariness has been added the war since 1980. All that has led to many Christians' disregarding the situation of conflict in their

Christian capacity. These Christians have sought refuge in the practices and understanding of an individualistic and introverted faith. Likewise the ecclesial body has lost strength in the service of the option for the poor and therefore has reduced the social influence of the Church.

The Church which Monsignor Romero left was a more evangelical and Salvadorean Church. That Church was profoundly different, but in a very simple way. It was closer to Jesus and the poor rejoiced for that. But for the traditional sector, that Church was an object of suspicion and from this has come to a greater or lesser extent the involution which pervades the Salvadorean Church at the moment. What was evangelical for Monsignor Romero is considered with foreboding and fear by those who dominate the Church today.

The real reasons for the suspicion are neither the limitations nor the real shortcomings of this new form of Church existence; besides, the shortcomings can be minimised and in any case they do not rule out the positive aspects of a Church of the poor. The Church is afraid on account of the costs which the model urged by Monsignor Romero involved. This Church, although unified, produced a terrible intra-church division and in a very radical way because it originated in God Himself, in the very gospel of Jesus and in the poor. The new manner of existence for the Church was uncomfortable because of insecurity. Its new social place among the poor, the relations with the State and the bourgeoisie, previously held as natural interlocutors, and, on the other hand, the creativity arising from the base of that same Church, resulted in a very uncomfortable situation for all.

Faced with this uncomfortable situation created by the Church of Monsignor Romero, the economic and military powers have renewed the invitation to the traditional Church to become the defender of western Christian civilisation once more. Sponsoring and financing pentecostal and fundamentalist sects, it is endeavouring to neutralise the Church born of the inspiration of Medellín and Monsignor Romero. Furthermore, a direct attack persists in the form of threats, defamations, expulsions, kidnappings, tortures and assassinations of thousands of Christians throughout the country. If demands for commitment to liberation are added to the costs, the involution which has taken place will be understood.

Involution is taking place with regard to the fundamental contents of Vatican II, Medellín and Puebla. In latter years there has been increasing disagreement with canon law and the papal magisterium. There has been renewed insistence on the intrinsic importance of the institution as such, attempts being made to strengthen and unify it. There is no disposition to risk the institutional for the good of the kingdom of God again. Increasingly less has been risked. There has been pressure not to provoke the government unnecessarily, to seek good relations which would favour or guarantee the good functioning of the institution. In opposition to the supremacy of the people of God centralism and authoritarianism have increased. The people of God have once more been made recipients of the action of the hierarchy, with the subsequent demand for unilateral obedience from the faithful. Likewise a tendency has arisen to depend on ecclesial movements almost blindly submissive to the hierarchy, abandoning and even attacking the critics.

The option for the poor has been doctrinally turned back and pastorally abandoned to a considerable extent. In the face of the new trend of transforming history with optimism and confidence there is now an insistence on control and doctrinal and administrative security. There is a tendency to make the people of God excessively dependent and not to favour or value their own creativity. This is clearly seen in the policy of training pastoral workers and in particular seminarians. Their training is academic and pastorally insufficient but the hierarchy prefers this to the risk of a possible deviation or contamination based on Vatican II, Medellín or Puebla.

In these latter years an exaggerated distrust has developed towards liberation theology although little is known about it. Attempts have been made to replace it with another theology which approaches liberation from a doctrinal and conceptual point of view, but not according to the signs of the times, which would demand an historic response.

The episcopal conference is at last united functionally with a single voice and presumably with greater social power. In this way possible divisions have been hidden and the prophetic voices in the episcopate have been moderated. In any case, the Vatican is attempting to depend on some bishops who are docile to its directives, distrusting the bishops who try to exercise their autonomy. The appointments of new bishops, which have increased in number recently, have been made according to these criteria.

There has been a movement away from an evangelical and prophetic attitude to another ethic, important in itself, but which tends to deprive denunciation of its sharpness, diluting it into universal principles. There is a tendency to pursue an excessively political attitude which weighs up the pros and cons too much for the

Church and not so much for the people of God. Furthermore, there is a tendency to weigh up what is said and done, and on account of that the Church has become too easily biddable.

There has also been an increase in ecclesial triumphalism in judging the evils of society and the marxism of revolutionary organisations, and even in condemning capitalism and the doctrine of national security as if the Church had no part in them through its actions and omissions. The great truths about justice, peace and human rights are proclaimed doctrinally, without being accompanied by consequent practice or at least without massive and decided practice corresponding to the evils which are denounced.

In the same way the actual conflict is judged ideologically. The tragic condition of the country and the revolutionary movements are similarly judged. When marxist elements are found in them they are judged as extremely evil. The dangerous aspect of this procedure is not the analysis or judgement of FMLN (Frente Farabundo Martí de Liberación Nacional), or the criticism of its faults or its real ills, but the fact that the tragic situation in the country passes into second place. The supposed neutrality and equidistance cannot signify effective impartiality towards the fundamental fact of poverty and oppression. The basic calculation of this attitude is ultimately that the Western democratic and Christian world would be a world which must be preserved at all costs because that would be the best world for the Church. Fear and weariness have paralysed ecclesial expansion and organisation. There has not been, for example, a single pastoral letter analysing the overall problems of the country in the past seven years. The Church at present appears to know well what it does not want: prolongation of the war, continuation of the dehumanising capitalist system, the absolute triumph of FMLN, but it has not clearly expressed what it positively does want.

The most significant fact in the promotion of the laity was the growth of the Church starting with its natural bases which resulted in many local base Christian communities. From the early 1970s until about 1982, the base Christian communities were sufficiently broad to constitute the majority of the Church. The primary factor in the base Christian communities was the characteristic awareness of having overcome the alienating aspects of traditional popular religiosity. They rejected not what was popular, but rather the separation of religious values from the real and distressing problems of life which, furthermore, they discovered opposed popular Christian religiosity. The transcendence was possible through the conscientising and liberating evangelisation which, coming from the bible and in particular from the gospel, discovered the demands of the Christian and of life went hand in hand. It also rediscovered in the people a series of ideological and organisational values pertaining to Christian faith and capable of critical examination and the transformation of society.

The Church of the poor, with less splendour than in the times of Monsignor Romero, with the moderation imposed by the passage of the years, and with the weight of persecution, continues to be, however, the road to travel. Despite what has happened in the past the Church of the poor has set in train a movement to a large extent historically irreversible. At doctrinal level the ecclesial option for the poor has been made commonplace and necessary, together with what it involves: the description and analysis of historic reality and its causes, the demand for solidarity with the poor and defence of them by the Church, the legitimacy and necessity of a theology of liberation.

The base Christian communities have continued and grown in spite of experiencing grave external difficulties, persecution, internal incomprehension, and on being dismissed, without proper analysis, as a marxist, anti-hierarchical popular Church. They continue to work with great liturgical and pastoral creativity, they commit themselves to their brothers and to the processes of liberation with increasingly more maturity and continue to give witnesses and martyrs. Maintaining the necessary presence of Christians in the political revolutionary process they have grown in understanding of what the Christian contribution to them should be, the defence of legitimacy and justice. But they have also introduced Christian spirituality, they have humanised the revolutionary processes and rendered them less dogmatic. This maturity proves that the Church of the poor has the capacity to face the future in a Christian way and that involutions are not necessary for it.

This chapter was translated by Mary Harris.

13 Elegy for the Murdered Bishop

Italo López Vallecillos

His words were swords that sliced the night.
No longer young but grey-haired and erect,
He was a match for storms and destined death.
Workers crowded to his Sunday cathedral Mass –
Office clerks, sweet-sellers, fruit-sellers,
Hucksters and charwomen, mothers with baskets
At their feet and a baby snuggled at a breast.
Stately with a staff, he moved among them:
The poor people's bishop in the crowd.

He talked to families from far coasts
And mountains, listening, whispering advice
Or a blessing to ease the loss of a son
Picked up by the National Guard, gone for good
In graveyards of the military dictatorship.

He owned nothing and made the powerful afraid.
He shed the purple cape, gold rings, the lace
Laid on the liturgy by tradition. He wore black
With a cross at his neck where Christ spoke
To Pharisees and merchants in the temple.
Some wondered at the way he turned towards
Ordinary people. They muttered over linen
At mealtime and chorused a loud warning
That danger bristled around this plain man
Who wandered through a midnight of bayonets.

During a sham reception in the nunciature
For the President of the Republic, it was said
He was a subversive push-buttoned by Jesuits
Getting orders from Moscow. A tight-strapped
Officer warned of the need to watch him,

To teach by silencing the scandal of his voice.

Some, afraid, sidled near him and said, 'Excellency,
Tread softly. The church is filled with suspects.
Barefoot. Reeking, It's not right to say Mass
Outside in the street.' Unfluttered, he just read
From the gospel and said scripture is more subversive
Than marxism. He had nothing new to say to anyone,
A man without plots or schemes or plans. All he had
Was the gospel and Jesus for all those banished
From abundance in the slums and zones of misery.
His voice deepened in crowds swept by a living word.
His bell tinkled. His enemies slid past like snakes.

He was a loved symbol, a pillow for tired heads.
Letters flooded in and told of abuse everywhere,
Handkerchiefs came wrapped around tears and blood
Spilt in the latest murder by police and curs.

At last, sick of his voice, they planned his death
With a twelve-calibre shotgun, its shot poisoned.
They mapped the route of his small Volkswagen,
Watched him walk into church where they knelt
At a Mass in memory of a woman from their own class.
They waited, hidden until the Eucharist, then fired –
A sure, single shot that finished him.
He crumpled slowly with nuns around him
And terror spread, engulfing the country.

The news went out. People were quiet but the blow
Of his death was a reverberation around the world.
The voice of the voiceless sounded over and over
Like an earthquake spreading to far, Vatican pulpits.
Yankee sorrow touched papal prie-dieus and the rooms
Of cardinals where faith lies filed in folders.
The voice of the voiceless – a voice from a small
Country no more than a strip held by fourteen volcanoes,
Where tourists buy parakeets and parrots
In yellow cages, fluttering to America.

In a sense, the Pope condemned the crime.
Archbishops and cardinals came from everywhere
As the cathedral opened to take the bishop's body.
Bit by bit, the peasants came in small groups –
Women, workmen, children of the cold and workless
Who rose early to huddle at street-corners.
Slum-dwellers left flowers on the steps he had climbed.
The plaza filled in an alliance of life and death.

Solidarity was lavished over the dead bishop
Carried by priests for the last ritual.
No government representative was at the *Te Deum*.
This burial had no protocol. Ambassadors
Kept prudent and quiet as girls sang hymns
And enemies waited again, spying and armed
When a voice cried out his banned name and bombs
Exploded as shots pierced morning's brightness.

It was death again. Men and women murdered
At the church door. Terror rampant and tears
Pouring again as fresh grief was scattered
At the very moment of the bishop's burial.

Then ugly silence. Chaos until the *barrios*
Watched and guarded over his tomb, a bishop
Defamed, mocked, immolated yet still speaking
Out in the desolation of a civil war.
He was a bright sword raised in the gloom,
An eternal conscience from within the people,
Within the wheat breaking out of the earth.
He was a simple man saying hour after hour:
Stop the repression! I beg, ask, order you.
Stop the repression! Stop the repression!

Translated for Silvia López by James Torrens SJ and adapted by Seán Dunne

Part Four
The Catholic Church, Revolution and Counter-Revolution in Latin America

14 Fidel Castro, the Catholic Church and Revolution in Cuba

Margaret Crahan

In November 1959 over one million people gathered in Havana, Cuba, for a national Catholic congress. In a country long regarded as having the weakest Catholic Church in all of Latin America, the turnout was remarkable.[1] The message the organisers wanted to communicate was clear: namely, that Fidel Castro was not the only one capable of turning out massive numbers of supporters.[2] A further objective of the meeting was to express Catholic support for social justice within a framework of liberal capitalism while rejecting communism.

As José Ignacio Lasaga, a leader of the lay organisation Agrupación Católica Universitaría phrased it:

> Liberal capitalism allows there to be a few proprietors in the face of a multitude of dispossessed. Communism, and in general all totalitarian socialist regimes, converts all persons into the dispossessed, since there exists only one proprietor, that is, the State. An ideal social order would be one that permits all persons, in one or another form, to feel as if they were proprietors, in the fullest sense of the word.[3]

Lasaga's speech was greeted with shouts of 'Cuba sí, Communismo no!' and before the congress concluded, a resolution condemning totalitarianism was passed.[4] Such action was stimulated by fear among Catholics about the direction of the revolution.

More than twenty-six years later some six thousand Catholics gathered in the Cathedral of Havana and the adjoining plaza for the inauguration of the Encuentro Nacional Eclesial Cubano (ENEC), the first public meeting since 1959. Planning for ENEC began in the spring of 1979 in an effort to adapt to Cuban conditions the recommendations of the Latin American bishops' conference in

Puebla, Mexico, in January of that year. That meeting had reaffirmed the Catholic Church's commitment to socio-economic justice, peace and human rights. Strong emphasis was also placed on the need to focus on evangelisation to accomplish social change. This was, in part, a response to preoccupation by the hierarchy over the increasing political activism of the clergy in some countries. The Cuban clergy and laity were the least politically active and many of the changes initiated by Vatican II (1962–5) and Medellín (1968) had yet to be incorporated. In 1979 the Catholic Church in Cuba was still essentially pre-conciliar and pre-revolutionary. Between 1979 and 1986 the Church made a monumental effort to modernise and position itself to reassume an important role in Cuban society.

To do this the Catholic church held preparatory meetings at the parish, diocesan and national levels all over Cuba for five years. These gatherings revealed a strong desire on the part of Cuban Catholics to reassess their historical heritage and current status theologically, pastorally and ideologically. Out of this came a plan of action that became the focus of discussion at the 1986 meeting in Havana. One hundred and eighty-one bishops, priests, nuns, brothers and laity representing all sectors of the Church met to adopt a course of action for the future. Emphasis was placed on the need for the Catholic Church to be open, committed to dialogue, participatory, and forgiving. It was emphasised that the Church was not seeking a privileged position within Cuban society, but rather the necessary space to accomplish its mission, that is, to communicate the Word of God and thereby impart faith. Cuban Catholics, it was asserted, would no longer be satisfied simply to survive. Instead, they were ready to re-think and come to terms with their past, recognise their errors, transform pastoral structures and renovate their faith in order to fulfil the evangelising mission of the Church. Catholics wanted to be a symbol of communion for all Cubans. The meeting itself was considered an intermediary step, the end product of five years of reflection and the initiation of a new phase that would revitalise the Church internally and make it more capable of bringing Cubans together to promote a just society characterised by truth and love.[5] It was also a symbol of the re-emergence of the Catholic Church from the margins of Cuban society.

ENEC was repeatedly described by participants as the culmination of an arduous process of change on the part of the Church to make it more Cuban and more responsive to the needs of Cuban society. Special emphasis was placed on the desire of the Church to reach out to those within the Church for whom religion had become simply a ritualistic formula, and to those who had fallen away from the faith or who had no faith at all, and regarded the Church with suspicion. Assurances were given that the Church desired to help heal breaches among all Cubans, encourage greater solidarity and integrate the Church into the process of creating a more equitable society. The meeting witnessed the admission of past errors, of seeking and offering forgiveness, and accepting the reality of a marxist-leninist government. ENEC did not signal an embrace of marxism, but rather suggested that it was better for the government and Church to co-operate for the common good in an atmosphere of mutual respect than for each to try to undermine the other. The Church continued to reserve to itself the role of critic of public morality and made clear its rejection of scientific materialism.

ENEC revealed that the Catholic Church while willing to work with the government for the common good, continued to regard marxism-leninism as antithetical to the Christian nature of Cuban history and culture. Hence, while the Cuban Catholic Church has changed substantially since 1959, it continues to reject strongly a materialistic explanation of life. Nevertheless, there is a desire to insert the Church into Cuba's socialist society. This desire was forged principally out of the experience of the Cuban Church since the onset of the Castro revolution and was made possible, in large measure, by the modernisation of the international Church since the second Vatican Council (1962–5).

The principal weaknesses of the Catholic Church[6] in Cuba in the mid-twentieth century, according to ENEC, were the absence of an integrated pastoral strategy, concentration of personnel in urban areas, particularly in Havana, and the lack of a broad vision of Cuban reality, particularly with respect to politics. Indifference to political and socio-economic injustice was criticised.[7] The lack of an overall pastoral strategy was not uncommon in the pre-Vatican II Catholic Church. Such absence, however, was compounded in Cuba by dependence on foreign theological developments and personnel and by the urban concentration of church personnel and institutions. Throughout the twentieth century approximately 85 per cent of church personnel and institutions based in Havana were engaged in private secondary education.[8] The majority of priests and religious taught in schools that catered to middle- and upper-class students. Pastoral work was limited, in spite of the fact that beginning in the 1920s the Catholic Church had begun to focus on social problems via the organisation of such groups as the Federación de Juventudes Católicas (1928), Agrupación Católica Universitaría (1931) and Acción Católica (1932). While social action was one of the objectives of these groups, prime emphasis was placed on combating the inroads of Protestantism, secularism, and marxism and on reinforcing Catholic identity particularly among urban youth, the traditional source of religious vocations. The upshot was that these organisations tended to insulate Cuban Catholics from debates over how best to achieve societal change, thereby reinforcing the image of the Church as indifferent to political struggle. Hence, in spite of the fact that by the 1950s Acción Católica had some 30 000 members and was espousing increased ecclesial attention to Cuban problems, particularly the plight of the rurual population, such efforts had limited impact.[9]

While the 1950s were a period of increasing activism for Catholics, the focus was principally on the internal revitalisation of the Church coupled with charitable work to ameliorate some of the consequences of rural and urban poverty.[10] Catholic activists were preoccupied primarily with reforming existing political, economic and social structures, rather than radically changing them. Furthermore, there was no agreement on specific strategies to accomplish change, nor were most Catholics willing to support a reformist agenda. They were, in fact, just beginning to question the status quo when the revolution occurred. Nor did the Cuban hierarchy have a clear social justice agenda. In the late 1950s the bishops publicly proclaimed their neutrality in the struggle between the Twenty-sixth of July Movement and the forces of Fulgencio Batista. In 1956 Cardinal Manuel Arteaga proposed a peace plan that was essentially ignored by both sides. Subsequently, the bishops limited themselves to criticising the insurrectionary forces for having taken up arms, and Batista for repression. Nevertheless, eight priests joined the guerrillas in the mountains.[11] In the cities, some Catholic youths served as messengers, raised money, gave out leaflets and organised strikes as well as demonstrations in support of the Twenty-sixth of July Movement. Such activities were not, however, sufficient to eliminate the image of the Catholic Church as a bulwark of the status quo, if not of Batista personally.

While Catholic sentiment was largely anti-Batista, Catholics did not feel prodded by their faith, nor by the majority of the clergy, to engage in political and ideological struggle. Hence there was a tendency for church people to remain on the margins of the conflict. While the majority welcomed Batista's fall, they were not receptive to the onset of a radical revolution. Rather, they wanted a multiparty western-style liberal democracy that would promote increased economic prosperity.

In short, the Cuban Catholic Church was unprepared for the challenge of a socialist revolution. It lacked a theological and ideological base, as well as the organisational flexibility to cope with wide-ranging political and economic changes. Hence in early 1959 Archbishop Enrique Pérez Serantes of Santiago who had intervened on Castro's behalf in 1953 was warning the revolutionary leadership to beware of 'utopian egalitarianism'.[12]

Anti-revolutionary sentiments within the Church grew in the spring of 1959 with the government's proposal of a unified curriculum for public and private schools and an extensive programme of agrarian reform. Some Catholics feared that the new curriculum would diminish the quality of private education and promote marxist indoctrination. Many church people had hoped that the Castro government would allow religious education to be resumed in public schools and provide financial aid for parochial schools. Failure to do this was regarded by some as proof of an anti-religious bias on the part of the government.[13]

The position of the Catholic Church on Castro's agrarian reform programme was initially somewhat ambiguous. While in March 1959 the hierarchy officially welcomed the proposed legislation, some leaders of the influential lay organisation, Agrupación Católica, publicly condemned it. In June the Jesuits organised a meeting of sixty-two clerics at Belén, Fidel Castro's alma mater, to discuss the proposal, as well as the general direction of the revolution. The Franciscan Ignacio Biaín defended the agrarian reform programme, as well as the revolution, but the majority of the clerics were critical. The meeting served to reinforce fears that the government was anti-clerical and anti-religious and thereafter denunciations of Castro from pulpits all over the island increased.[14] This served to stimulate counter-revolutionary sentiment and activities among the laity and particularly within such organisations as Agrupación Católica and among Catholic high school students. In pre-Vatican II Cuba, fear of socialism and support for the sanctity of private property were generally unquestioned and such sentiments predisposed Catholics to oppose the revolution.

In a report to the Latin American bishops' conference in Puebla, Mexico, in 1979, Cuban Catholics described their Church in 1959 as 'profoundly marked by conservatism and anti-communism. Although it exhibited sectors with liberal and social democratic tendencies ... it was predominantly a conservative church'.[15] This was the situation when the one million Cubans gathered in Havana in November 1959. The turnout was largely the result of the increasing radicalisation of the revolution, the collapse of the traditional political parties and the incorporation of opponents of the revolution into such organisations as Agrupación Católica.

Late 1959 also witnessed frequent charges that the Castro government was planning to establish a national church. While this allegation was denied by the Cuban hierarchy such rumours helped encourage a siege mentality among Catholic clergy and laity.[16] Some church leaders, including Manuel Artimé of Agrupación Católica, began organising counter-revolutionary groups, some of whose members later became involved in the 1961 Bay of Pigs invasion.[17]

Throughout 1960 the Catholic bishops were increasingly critical of the revolution. In May of that year Castro's former defender, Archbishop Enrique Pérez Serantes, declared 'we cannot say that communism is at our doors for in reality it is within our walls, speaking out as if it were at home'.[18] There followed a series of pastoral letters by the Cuban bishops questioning the legitimacy of the Castro government and the revolution. A prime reason for the challenge was the bishops' belief that since Cuba was a Catholic country a marxist revolution was contrary to the island's history, culture and values. The revolution was strongly criticised for not having a spiritual conception of life, and not recognising the dignity of the person. Finally, the prelates publicly announced that in any conflict between the US and the USSR over Cuba, they would align themselves with the former.[19]

By 1961 relations between the Catholic Church and the Castro government were tense. While the revolutionary government adopted no anti-religious laws, its increasingly marxist orientation convinced many Catholics that they were under attack. Combined with increasing social turmoil and fear of a US invasion this encouraged many clergy and laity to leave Cuba. Church schools which had been the prime institutional basis of Catholic influence lost students, teachers and income. Some schools were raided by the government looking for counter-revolutionary arms caches. After the failed CIA organised Bay of Pigs invasion on 17 April 1961 the government ordered all private schools closed, as well as the headquarters of Agrupación Católica. This precipitated an exodus of church people from the island. Of the approximately 723 Catholic priests in Cuba in 1960, 70 per cent of them left by 1963, while 90 per cent of the 2225 male and female religious left. Some 8 per cent of priests and religious were expelled by the government for allegedly counter-revolutionary activities.[20]

The nationalisation of schools was defended by the government on the grounds that many of these institutions had been used to organise the uprising that was to have accompanied the Bay of Pigs invasion. The present Executive Secretary of the Cuban bishops' conference, Monsignor Carlos Manuel de Cespedes stated in 1970 that:

> Many priests actively supported the counter-revolutionary movements that arose, especially after the summer of 1960, and that culminated in the Bay of Pigs invasion in April 1961. I don't know how much, but I am certain that counter-revolutionary meetings were held on church property, and that some priests urged Catholics to take part in counter-revolutionary activities and to go into exile.[21]

A 1969 survey of Catholic parishes in Havana estimated that over 50 per cent of their members had left Cuba.[22] Such attrition, together with the loss of clergy and religious, resulted in the closing of some churches and disbanding of Catholic organisations. Pro-revolutionary church people were generally unwelcome within the Church and hence they tended to drift away. The Catholic Church turned in upon itself and became a refuge for the disaffected. The failure of the Catholic Church in Cuba to develop a theology and pastoral strategies rooted in Cuban conditions, its dependence on foreign personnel and their opinions, the urban concentration of clergy and religious, and the focus on elite education all contributed to the Church's appearance as a foreign bourgeois institution. As such, it was easily threatened by a nationalist revolution aimed at radically changing the status quo. While Christianity was a strong cultural presence in Cuba, the Catholic Church as an institution was considerably less strong. Its failure to penetrate rural Cuba facilitated the consolidation of support for the revolution in the countryside. Its long-term identification with the bourgeoisie also opened the way for its utilisation as a base for the counter-revolution.

The abandonment of Cuba by a substantial proportion of the middle and upper class in the early 1960s depopulated the Church and left it a skeleton of its former self. As such, it was in no position to influence the course of the revolution and was increasingly marginal to it. The development of Catholic social doctrine before 1960 did not provide a basis for a socio-economic programme competitive with Castro's. While church leaders criticised the revolutionary government's actions, it did not offer any specific alternatives. Hence, the Church was relatively powerless in the face of the momentum generated by revolutionary change. Buffeted by the ferment in Cuba, the Catholic Church opted to be a witness to the revolutionary process rather than a participant. This attitude began to change in the late 1960s and was officially abandoned at ENEC in 1986.

As early as 1962 some of the priests and religious who fled Cuba began to return, as well as a few foreign clerics.[23] The loss of clerical personnel created some opportunities for increased lay participation, but this was more common in the Protestant churches than in the pre-conciliar Catholic Church. Furthermore, active participation in one's church was cause for suspicion, as religiously motivated counter-revolutionary bands continued to roam the Escambray Mountains in the mid-1960s. With the imposition of universal military service, some church youths and seminarians who resisted the draft were impressed into Unidades Militares de Ayuda a la Producción (UMAP), forced labour battalions. In addition, priests and Protestant ministers suspected of counter-revolutionary activities were also sentenced to UMAP where they served alongside common criminals, pimps and homosexuals. The shock of doing manual labour alongside individuals they would not normally come into contact with disturbed church people. For some it precipitated a re-evaluation of their beliefs, for others it caused a reassertion of quietistic views. Upon their release a few church people were received by their churches as martyrs, while others were regarded askance. Public criticism of UMAP was sufficiently strong that it was disbanded in the late 1960s.[24] Since then some individuals have been imprisoned for draft evasion, primarily Jehovah's Witnesses and Seventh Day Adventists.

Discrimination against active church people in schools and the workplace also occurred, prompting some to leave the Church or Cuba. While senior government officials, including Fidel Castro, denied that such discrimination was officially sanctioned, at the local level the tradition of anti-religious sentiment combined with marxist antipathies limited active church peoples' opportunities. It also reinforced the Church's inclination to turn in upon itself. In a 1972 analysis of religious life in Cuban parishes some Catholics criticised religious practices as being too focused on insulating them from the 'evil spirit of the outside world' and 'preserving the forms and values of a counter-society'.[25] Such attitudes, together with discrimination, did not encourage energetic responses to the situation of the Catholic

Church in Cuba. Nevertheless, by the late 1960s there were increasing calls from within the Church for reforms in accord with Vatican II and clarification of the Church's role in a socialist society.

While the majority of Catholics continued to maintain a witnessing posture, vocal minorities called for a revitalised Church capable of inserting itself into the revolutionary process. At the same time the Castro government was increasingly desirous of building alliances with change-oriented movements, including church groups. Within the Catholic Church, youths pressed for greater participation, as well as more openness to the revolution. According to Acción Católica leader, Mateo Jover, this required a rethinking of the Church's mission in the modern world, revamping of clerical and lay education, and the development of mechanisms to allow the Church to reinsert itself into Cuban society.[26] In addition, younger Catholics pressed for greater lay participation in all aspects of church decision-making. There was, however, considerable debate over how best to achieve change within the Church, as well as dialogue with the government.

Some lay activists felt that the Church needed to establish its credibility by acknowledging its role in the counter-revolution and praising the government's accomplishments, particularly in health and education. Others felt that it was imperative for the Church not only to work with the government for the common good, but also to reassert the Church's role as a moral legitimator by criticising the government whenever necessary. Still others felt that there should be no *rapprochement* with the government. The hierarchy disagreed and opted for a tightly controlled strategy of *rapprochement*. As a consequence, on 10 April and 3 September 1969, two pastoral letters were issued. They called for the end of the US trade embargo of Cuba and urged Catholics to support the government's developmental programmes and to respect the positions of atheists.

Both letters served to improve relations with the government, but they also precipitated discord within the Church. Some Catholics felt that the letters should have been more supportive of the revolution, others that they should have been more critical, while still others felt that they should not have been issued at all. The debate resulted in Rome sending a representative to Havana in October 1969 to meet with approximately 200 clergy, religious and lay leaders. While some issues concerning lay participation were resolved, there was no substantial increase in lay input into ecclesial decision-making.[27] The formulating of church policy with respect to the revolution and relations with the government was left firmly in the hands of the hierarchy. At this juncture the bishops appear to have been intent primarily on *rapprochement* with the government rather than reasserting the Church as a major actor in Cuban society.

The government of Fidel Castro was receptive to the hierarchy's initiatives. In 1971 at the First Cuban Educational and Cultural Congress notice was taken of the Catholic Church's increasing involvement in social justice issues throughout Latin America. Only those sects that were considered obscurantist or counter-revolutionary were criticised.[28] This referred to the Jehovah's Witnesses and Seventh Day Adventists whose members refused to serve in the military or send their children to public schools. The government, as a consequence, mounted a campaign to discourage Cubans from belonging to those groups and went so far as to jail those who refused military service. Catholics, on the other hand, were praised for their growing tendency to co-operate with ideologically diverse groups to promote the common good.

In 1975 the government's official policy on religion was spelled out in Article 54 of the newly drafted Constitution. It stated that:

> The socialist state, which bases its activity and educates the people in the scientific materialist concept of the universe, recognizes and guarantees freedom of conscience and the right of everyone to profess any religious belief and to practice, within the framework of respect for the law, the belief of his preference.
>
> The law regulates the activities of religious institutions.
>
> It is illegal and punishable by law to oppose one's faith or religious belief to the Revolution.[29]

Catholics welcomed having the government's position on religion clearly stated. A representative of the Cuban Conference of bishops claimed that the Church was reassured to have the right to choose one's own beliefs confirmed.[30] The rector of the Seminary in San Carlos, Father José Manuel Meyares, held that 'it is extremely . . . consoling to see . . . all types of coercion and discrimination against believers . . . proscribed'.[31] A seminarian felt that the constitution recognised that Christians had a contribution to make to Cuba as a nation. A fellow student added that Article 54 'created the conditions for the full exercise of religious freedom'.[32]

The basis for Article 54 was elucidated at the First Congress of the Cuban Communist Party in December 1975. It held that the promotion of a scientific view of the world was secondary to the need to construct a new society through the efforts of 'believers, non-believers, members of religious orders and atheists'. Since the creation of a new society required the participation of all Cubans, church people had to be incorporated into the revolution. Furthermore, it was recommended that historical and dialectical materialism be disseminated in such fashion so as not to offend individual religious beliefs.[33]

The 1978 Communist Party Platform reaffirmed liberty of conscience, and freedom to worship within the law, but condemned the utilisation of religion to undercut the revolution and socialism. Believers and non-believers had equal rights and social responsibilities. Coercion and isolation of believers were condemned.[34]

Fidel Castro himself stated in an 11 October 1977 speech to the Jamaican Council of Churches that he felt that there 'are no contradictions between the aims of religion and the aims of socialism'.[35] At the same meeting Castro also asserted that no revolution as thorough-going as the Cuban had had so few conflicts with churches. This he attributed to the astuteness of church leaders, the increasing number of progressive Christians and the desire of the Cuban government not to encourage the feeling that the revolution was an enemy of religion. Castro did, however, hold that it was essential for materialist atheism to be taught in the schools.[36] Hence, marxism had a clear advantage over religion in the formation of Cuban culture and normative values.

In addition, while Catholic leaders such as the present Archbishop of Havana, Jaime Ortega Alamino and the former papal nuncio Cesare Zacchi feel that religious freedom is today guaranteed in Cuba, they also believe that there remain vestiges of anti-religious sentiment and discrimination.[37] In addition, Cuban church people complain that they cannot engage in mass evangelisation because of lack of access to the media and public auditoriums and stadiums. Proselytisation in the streets is also prohibited.[38] Archbishop Ortega, among others, has complained that Mass cannot be said in homes or meeting rooms in new communities and housing developments which have been built without churches.[39] Since the only schools available are public, church people would also like to see a lessening of the emphasis on materialist atheism in the curriculum.[40]

The chief restriction, however, continues to be the exclusion of believers from the Communist Party and the Union of Communist Youth. This denies them positions of influence in the government and armed forces and substantially reduces their input into public policy formulation. It is also difficult for active church people to gain senior positions in the universities, although there is greater openness in the arts.

In recent years the government has emphasised that discrimination against church people is contrary to official policy. In July 1984, during the visit of Jesse Jackson to Cuba, Fidel Castro appeared with him in the pulpit of a Methodist church in Havana, surrounded by leaders of virtually all the religious denominations in the country. This event, which was covered by the Cuban media, helped reduce prejudice against church people among the general public. Shortly thereafter the government established an Office of Religious Affairs as a department of the Central Committee of the Communist Party. According to its head, José Felipe Carneado, the office was intended to facilitate church–state exchanges and to discourage discrimination against church people in schools, workplaces and neighbourhoods. He also held that 'not long ago, we co-existed separately', and 'now we have the possibility of living together, exchanging ideas, hearing the difficulties the churches encounter. We are co-operating together and we aim to make our differences disappear'. He attributed the change principally to the government's sense that the Catholic Church had demonstrated 'a readiness to participate in our reality, to accept the revolutionary process'.[41]

The interest of the government in *rapprochement* with the churches was symbolised by the publication in Cuba in late 1985 of the book *Fidel y la Religión*, based on interviews of Castro by the Brazilian Franciscan Frei Betto. Estimates of the number of copies sold in Cuba have ranged from 600 000 to 1 000 000, clearly making it a bestseller. According to the Archbishop of Havana Jaime Ortega Alamino, the volume 'brought the subject of religion out of a somewhat taboo, reserved area', as well as giving religion 'a new space in the life of the country'. He further expressed the hope that the new atmosphere would allow the Church 'to fully promote its values throughout Cuban society'.[42] The prelate did not, however, expect any rapid changes, but rather the gradual development of a new relationship.[43]

The year 1985 witnessed the initiation of a formal dialogue between the Cuban hierarchy and the Castro government. The conversations dealt largely with such questions as the Church's access to the media, elimination of anti-religious language from school textbooks and the end of employment discrimination. According to the executive secretary of the Cuban bishops' conference, Monsignor Carlos Manuel de Cespedes, the government was partially motivated by its belief that the churches could promote greater ethical and moral values among Cubans.[44] The need to reduce corruption and venality in Cuba was a frequent theme of Castro's speeches in 1986 and 1987, as well as a pre-occupation of the Third Communist Party Congress in early 1986. In addition, civil and ecclesiastical officials have noted an upsurge of religious feeling among Cubans, in part, because of increasing dissatisfaction with a materialist explanation of life and the values it promotes.[45]

Many observers believe that the Cuban government is also motivated by a desire for greater legitimacy internationally, particularly in the rest of Latin America, where the Catholic Church and some Protestant denominations have been major forces for change since the 1960s. Reflecting a common interpretation a foreign diplomat resident in Cuba stated that, 'Castro is offering more religious freedom in return for a patina of respectability that the government will get through good relations with the Church'. On the Church's part, he felt that the bishops were 'playing it very cleverly, and apparently with a good deal of support from the Vatican'.[46] International support has also increasingly come from the United States bishops' conference.

In January 1985 a delegation consisting of the head of the United States Catholic Conference (USCC), Bishop James W. Malone, Archbishop Patrick W. Flores of San Antonio and Cardinal Bernard Law of Boston, together with Monsignor Daniel Hoye and the Reverend David Gallivan, visited Cuba at the invitation of the Cuban hierarchy. In addition to meeting with church officials they also met with Fidel Castro at his invitation. They discussed the need for regular dialogue between Cuban civil and ecclesiastical officials, as well as the necessity of ending discrimination against church people. Castro, while admitting that historical circumstances had resulted in discrimination, asserted that it was not government policy. The US clerics concluded at the end of their visit that the greater communication between Church and State in Cuba was a hopeful sign.[47]

Subsequently, in September 1985 and in September 1987, delegations of Cuban bishops visited the United States principally to consult with their counterparts. They also met with some representatives of the Cuban-American community, as well as the State Department's Assistant Secretary for Inter-American Affairs, Elliott Abrams, and the then National Security Advisor, Robert C. McFarlane. With

Abrams they discussed the facilitation by the USA of entrance visas for some political prisoners whose release had been requested by the US bishops during their January 1985 visit.[48] It was also reported that the bishops asked that the US economic embargo of Cuba be lifted and that the name of the Voice of America's Radio Martí be changed as it was an affront to Cuban national sentiment.[49] In 1987 the Cuban bishops again visited the United States appearing intent on generating international support for the revitalisation of the Church, as well as improving relations with the Castro government and reducing the US–Cuban tensions. Such actions were the outcome of the formal process of internal reflection undertaken in 1979 which culminated in the 1986 Encuentro Nacional Eclesial Cubano.

The meeting reflected, according to Bishop Pedro Meurice of Santiago de Cuba, the growing realisation that 'the renovation of our Cuban church in the light of Vatican II was the only way to live within our socialist context'.[50] In addition, there was a sense within the Cuban Catholic Church that a thorough-going internal revitalisation was necessary in order to discharge the call of the Latin American bishops' conference at Puebla, Mexico, in 1979 for an intensification of the evangelisation of the modern world. Hence, ENEC emphasised renewal, greater lay participation, dialogue with all Cubans, and the increasing spread of the gospel. Evangelisation would not, according to ENEC, result in ideological competition between Church and State, for Catholicism was a religion, not an ideology. Nor was Catholicism antithetical to socialism. Rather ENEC affirmed that the Church could function under any political and ideological system. In fact, believers had a responsibility to participate in the development of any society and promote the pursuit of the common good. In doing so, the Catholic Church assumed a critical attitude towards all systems and socio-political structures.

Of particular concern to the Church were such societal deficiencies as duplicity, lying, fraud, theft, lack of care of social property, workers' irresponsibility, abortion, sexual licence and abuse of alcohol. The Church's task was, as a consequence, to promote moral regeneration. Beyond that, it also felt responsible for promoting peace, disarmament, conservation of the environment, the proper utilisation and distribution of consumer goods, international justice, a new international economic and social order, and greater East–West understanding. The means to accomplish this were considered to be reconciliation and dialogue.[51] In reasserting a role for itself in Cuban society, the Catholic Church was proposing that it serve not so much as a moral legitimator of a particular regime or political and economic system, but rather as an enunciator of broad moral principles. Hence, it was not attempting to recapture its more traditional position within Cuban society, but rather carve out a new, less obviously painful, one.

A prime challenge to such an effort was to bridge the gap between traditional Cuban culture, in which pre-conciliar Christianity was a major force, and contemporary Cuban culture which is heavily influenced by marxism-leninism. To do this the Church, according to ENEC, must conserve, purify and develop the gospel message embedded in traditional Cuban culture and deal prophetically with the new cultural reality. This requires the Church to promote Christian love to stimulate societal reconciliation, dialogue and unity, in order to enrich the new Cuban lifestyle with values rooted in the gospel and to reinforce human dignity and national identity. Thus the Catholic Church must reach out in pursuit of mutual understanding and ultimately mutual perfection.[52] Such conclusions reflect the reassertion of certain basic elements of Catholic faith and social doctrine including the centrality of the gospel message of peace, love and justice and the historical notion of the ultimate perfectability of all individuals, if not of all systems. The latter is an essential difference from the marxist view of the ultimate perfectability of the communist system. Hence, the Catholic Church in Cuba continues to retain a somewhat more individual view of perfectibility than the marxists.

On the first anniversary of ENEC, the Archbishop of Havana, Jaime Ortega Alamino, assessed the Cuban Church as alive, open to dialogue, desirous of participating in society, and capable of accomplishing its mission in a socialist country. The image of a static Church, inflexible and habit-bound was, he felt, fading away. While problems remained, there was, at the grassroots, increased concern for the Church's contribution to remedying Cuban social problems through co-operation with believers and non-believers alike. While the Archbishop admitted that the ideal of achieving a Church without privileges and not discriminated against had yet to be achieved, he felt that there were positive developments that suggested an increased role for the Church in Cuban society. In short, the internal revitalisation of the Church had contributed to greater acceptance of it by the Cuban government and people. What was notable in the Archbishop's homily was the confidence expressed in the capacity of the Church and of Catholics to contribute substantially to the building of a better socialist society.[53] It was a vision of a transcendent church rooted in faith.

This suggests the degree to which the image of the Catholic Church in Cuba today has changed in the minds of its leaders as well as of the faithful. No longer is it considered to be a refuge from change, nor a bulwark of the status quo. Since 1959 it has, by virtue of a very painful exodus of priests and religious, become Cubanised in terms of its personnel. In addition, it has developed a strong sense of national identity, which has led it publicly to support the Cuban government's position on the need for a new international economic order, on third world debt and a number of other issues. The Church, once fearful of socialism and marxism, now holds that it can contribute to societies moulded by both. Furthermore, the Church claims it can contribute to the perfecting of socialist societies and appears eager to do it.

The simple fact of making such a claim marks the emergence of the Catholic Church in Cuba from its marginal position of the past twenty-five years. Full participation depends on its achieving the proposed internal revitalisation, as well as the willingness of the Cuban government to accept competition. For while Catholicism is not an ideology, it does demand the ultimate loyalty of the individual, as does the Cuban revolution. Hence, the realisation of the role which the Catholic Church in Cuba now projects for itself requires not only that it undergo profound changes, but also that the government do so. Both will be enormously difficult and hence the future role of the Catholic Church in revolutionary Cuba remains unclear, albeit a greater role than in the recent past.

NOTES

1. In 1960 church sources estimated that 70–75 per cent of Cubans were nominal Catholics, the lowest percentage in all Latin America. Protestants claimed three to six per cent of a total population of approximately 7 500 000. The Jewish community reportedly numbered 12 000 with most residing in Havana. Practising Catholics, defined by the Church as individuals who attended services four or more times a year, were thought to constitute only five to eight per cent of nominal Catholics. Other indices of loyalty to or involvement in the Catholic Church such as reception of the sacraments and participation in religious instructions or church groups were also low as compared to most other Latin American countries. Nevertheless, Christianity was a

pervasive cultural presence, which helped mould normative values, as well as ideology. Religious appeals, as a consequence, helped mobilise some one million Cubans in late 1959 as political and social ferment grew in Cuba in the face of an increasingly radical revolution.

2. Claude Julien, 'Church and State in Cuba: Development of a Conflict', *Cross Currents*, XI, 2 (Spring 1961) p. 188.
3. Mariano Errasti, 'La noche mas luminosa de la historia de Cuba', *La quincena*, V, 23–4 (diciembre de 1959) p. 55.
4. Alfred L. Padula, Jr., 'The Fall of the Bourgeoisie: Cuba 1959–1961' (Doctoral dissertation, University of New Mexico, 1974) p. 459.
5. Monsignor Adolfo Rodríquez, 'Discurso Inaugural de ENEC pronunciado por Mons. Adolfo Rodríguez, Presidente de la Conferencia Episcopal de Cuba, en Nombre de los Obispos Cubanos', and 'Breve Reseña Histórica de la Evangelización en Cuba', Encuentro Nacional Eclesial Cubano (ENEC), *Documento Final* (Miami: Instituto de Estudios Cubanos, 1987) pp. 7–19, 31; Maria Rosa Lorbés, 'Encuentro Nacional Eclesial Cubano: una Iglesia fiel a Cristo y a su pueblo', *Paginas*, XI, 77 (mayo 1986) pp. 10–11.
6. Because of space limitations and the predominance of the Catholic Church, this Chapter will focus on that institution rather than on the Protestant churches, Jewish community or Afro-Cuban religions.
7. ENEC, *Documento Final*, p. 29.
8. François Houtart and Andre Rousseau, *The Church and Revolution* (Maryknoll, N.Y.: Orbis, 1971) pp. 113–14.
9. A 1957 survey of 400 rural families by Agrupación Católica revealed that 42.34 per cent had inadequate housing with only 3.26 per cent having running water and 63.97 per cent were without indoor sanitation. Only 7.27 per cent had electricity. Disease was endemic among the rural population with 36.10 per cent having suffered from parasites; 13.25 per cent from typhus, 30.93 per cent from malaria, and 13.99 per cent from tuberculosis. Illiteracy was 43.09 per cent and 44.11 per cent never attended school. Only 52.1 per cent identified themselves as Catholics and over half of these (53.5 per cent) said they had never laid eyes on a priest. This latter statistic reveals the degree to which rural Cuba was unevangelised.
10. In 1955 the Catholic Church had approximately 250 charitable institutions and programmes in Cuba. These included 58 hospitals and asylums. In 1987 there were 8 such institutions, which included several old-age homes and a leprosarium. Hospital facilities and asylums are now maintained by the government. ENEC, *Documento Final*, pp. 28–9; *Anuario Pontificio, 1987*.
11. ENEC, *Documento Final*, p. 30.
12. Claude Julien, 'Church and State', p. 187.
13. Padula, 'The Fall', pp. 441–5.
14. Ibid., pp. 143, 453–4.
15. Maria Teresa Bolívar Arostegui *et al.*, 'Cuban Christians and Puebla', *LADOC 'Keyhole' Series*, 17 (Washington: United States Catholic Conference, 1980) p. 41.
16. Julien, 'Church and State,' p. 188.

17. Padula, 'The Fall', p. 166.
18. As quoted in Julien, 'Church and State', p. 188. For the original Spanish text of the pastoral letter, see Enrique Pérez Serantes, 'Por Dios y Por Cuba', 16 May 1960 (Santiago), in Ismael Teste, *Historia Eclesiástica de Cuba*, V (Barcelona: Artes Gráficas Medincelli, 1975) pp. 562–8.
19. Conferencia Episcopal de Cuba, 'Carta Abierta del Episcopado al Primer Ministro' (4 December 1960); Enrique Pérez Serantes, 'Ni Traidores, ni Parias' (24 September 1960); 'Roma o Moscu' (November 1980); 'Con Cristo o Contra Cristo' (24 December 1960); Teste, *Historia Eclesiástica*, V, pp. 603–6, 569–72, 572–7, 585–90.
20. Houtart and Rousseau, *Church and Revolution*, pp. 122–4; Leslie Dewart, *Christianity and Revolution: The Lesson of Cuba* (New York: Herder & Herder, 1963) p. 165; Padula, 'The Fall', pp. 491–2; Interview IH4714111. In 1973, 1974, 1975, 1976, 1979 and 1984, I conducted some 80 interviews of Cuban church people on the island, in Spain, and in the United States. Some interviewees in Spain requested anonymity and hence all interviews are identified by letter and number only.
21. Carlos Manuel de Cespedes as quoted in Antonio Benítez Rojo, 'Fresh Air Blows Through the Seminary', *LADOC 'Keyhole' Series*, 7 (Washington, D.C.: United States Catholic Conference, nd) p. 53.
22. Mateo Jover, 'The Cuban Church in a Revolutionary Society', *LADOC*, 4, 32 (April 1974) p. 27.
23. Houtart and Rousseau, *Church and Revolution*, pp. 124–5.
24. Raimundo Garcia Franco, 'Pastores en la U.M.A.P.: Diálogo en la U.M.A.P.', MSS (10 February 1966) p. 108; Juan Clark, *Religious Repression in Cuba* (Coral Gables: University of Miami, 1985) pp. 21–3; Interviews IM5771112; IH4701181; IH377221.
25. Cuban Christians for Socialism, 'How Christians in Cuba See Their Future', *LADOC 'Keyhole' Series*, 7, p. 77.
26. Jover, 'The Cuban Church', p. 23; El Equipo Diocesano de Jovenes de Camagüey, 'Estadística Socio-religiosa de la Diocesis de Camagüey', MSS (1967) pp. 19–21; Jim Wallace, 'Christians in Cuba', *Cuba Resource Center Newsletter*, III, 1 (April 1973) p. 7; Interview IM5771112.
27. Antonio Benítez Rojo, 'Fresh Air Blows Through the Seminary', p. 4; Cuban Christians for Socialism, 'How Christians in Cuba See Their Future'; Episcopal Conference of Cuba, 'Pastoral Letter', 10 April 1969, *LADOC 'Keyhole' Series*, 7 (Washington: United States Catholic Conference, nd), pp. 4, 76–7, 46–9; Houtart and Rousseau, *Church and Revolution*, p. 124; Wallace, 'Christians', pp. 4–5; Interview IM5771112.
28. National Congress on Education and Culture, 'Declaration, April 30, 1971', *LADOC 'Keyhole' Series*, 7, p. 51.
29. *Constitution of the Republic of Cuba* (Havana: Instituto Cubano del Libro, 1975) p. 30.
30. Interview IH67328.
31. José Manuel Meyares as quoted in Elmer Rodríquez, 'Cuba: Who

Said There is No Religious Freedom in Cuba?', *Prensa Latina Feature Service*, 168 (1 May 1977) pp. 2–3.
32. Ibid.
33. Center for Cuban Studies Archives, D 888, 'Resolution on Religion: First Party Congress of the Cuban Communist Party' (December 1975) p. 35.
34. Partido Comunista de Cuba, *Plataforma Programática: Tésis y Resolución* (Havana: Editorial Ciencias Sociales, 1978) pp. 100–2.
35. Fidel Castro, 'There Are No Contradictions', *Granma Weekly Review* (20 November 1977) p. 5.
36. Ibid, pp. 3–9.
37. D. P. Noonan, Interview with Jaime Ortega Alamino, Archbishop of Havana, July 1982, xerox, np; Bolívar Arostegui, 'Cuban Christians', pp. 45–6; 50.
38. Harry Genet, 'Cuba: The Church Finds Its Role in a Socialist State', *Christianity Today*, 23 (21 December 1979) p. 40; Herbert Meza, 'Is There Freedom of Worship in Cuba? An Eyewitness Report', *CELEP*, IV, 3 (October 1977) p. 59.
39. Noonan, 'Interview . . . Ortega', np.
40. John Hogan, 'Reflections on a Visit to Cuba', *Origins: NC Documentary Service*, 9, 7 (5 July 1979) p. 110.
41. Joseph B. Treaster, 'Religion in Cuba: Castro Now Eyes It Less Coldly', *New York Times* (20 May 1985) p. 4.
42. William R. Long, 'Cuba and Church – A Thaw Starts', *Los Angeles Times* (12 April 1986) p. 31.
43. Ibid.
44. Ibid.
45. Since 1979 the Catholic Church has reported an increase in the number of baptisms, church marriages and funerals, as well as an upsurge of popular religiosity. Don Shannon, 'Church's Impact on Latin Affairs Helps Its Position in Cuba', *Los Angeles Times* (25 May 1986) pp. 1–28.
46. Long, 'Cuba and Church', p. 31.
47. United States Catholic Conference (USCC), National Catholic Office for Information, 'Bishops See Hope for Improvement in Church-Government Relations in Cuba' (28 January 1985) p. 1.
48. 'Statement by Delegation from Cuban Episcopal Conference', *United States Catholic Conference News* (16 September 1985) p. 3.
49. 'Moving Towards Reconciliation: Church–State Relations in Cuba', *Cuban–American Bulletin* 3, 3 (December 1985) pp. 1–2.
50. Bishop Pedro Meurice as quoted in Eve Gilcrist, 'Cuban Catholic Encuentro Calls for Evangelism, Dialogue', NC News Service (27 February 1986) p. 3.
51. ENEC, *Documento Final*, pp. 94–7.
52. Ibid., pp. 99–100.
53. Monsignor Jaime Ortega Alamino, 'Homilia Pronunciado por S.E. Mons. Jaime Ortega Alamino, Arzobispo de La Habana, en el Primer Aniversario de la Celebración del Encuentro Nacional Eclesial Cubano' (18 February 1987) Havana, Cuba, pp. 1–4.

15 Continuity and Change in the Mexican Catholic Church

Soledad Loaeza-Lajous

Relations between Church and State have followed an irregular pattern in independent Mexico (1821), alternating between periods of sharp conflict and of collaboration. After the wars of independence, anticlericalism took hold as a powerful political tradition, despite the fact that some of its most notable leaders, Miguel Hidalgo and José María Morelos, for example, were priests. Opposition to the Catholic Church has been one of the characteristic traits of the modernising Mexican elites, who have seen the ecclesiastic institution and the values it upholds as being the main obstacles to change.

The prolonged instability of the nineteenth century in Mexico had its origins in the hostility between Church and State. The 1910 Revolution heightened the differences and the scars these left can still be seen in the Constitution which has been in force in Mexico since 1917. The bloody Cristero War (1926–9) was the flaring up of tensions caused by the policies of the revolutionary State intended to secularise society. This conflict ended at the same time as the formation of the official party, which has governed the country since then. So that the so-called 'agreements' between the Church and the State formed part of a general policy of stabilisation. For more than thirty years, between 1936 and 1970, Church–State relations developed within the framework of a *modus vivendi* which consisted in not enforcing the anticlerical laws in the Constitution in exchange for collaboration in maintaining social order.

However, since the early 1970s, important changes have occurred within the Catholic Church and the Mexican political system. These have become apparent in a growing pressure for the revision of the previous agreements. The severe economic crisis which Mexico has been experiencing since 1982 has contributed very significantly to increasing the pressures on the State to grant the Catholic Church its juridical identity which the present laws deny it. The most important problem raised here is whether a modification of this nature constitutes a political retreat or a step forward in the political modernisation of the country. Whatever the answer to this dilemma may be, a new stage in Church–State relations in Mexico is about to commence. Developments in recent years indicate that history will no longer be the main factor determining the characteristics of these relations. Instead the needs of a pluralist society and of the political system will be decisive in this evolution.

THE CATHOLIC CHURCH IN MEXICO, AN ESSENTIAL POLITICAL ACTOR

In general terms, studies carried out on the subject of the Church in Mexico tend to underline its role as a predominantly cultural agent. From this viewpoint, the conflicts between Church and State, especially in the twentieth century, have been analysed as resulting from differences generated by a process of modernisation; in other words, from the clash between traditional values defended by the ecclesiastic structure and the modernising values encouraged by the State, or those which, broadly speaking, are associated with social change. Without wishing to lessen the cultural importance of the Church, we are emphasising here the role it plays as a political actor. From this perspective, the Church's cultural function is more instrumental than essential given that it upholds its position within the power structure.

In order to analyse the importance and the significance of a religious organisation in a particular society, we must look at the concept of secularisation which is one of the most important aspects of a modernising process. Taking that concept as a starting point, we can formulate a general hypothesis regarding the political role the Church has played.

Throughout Mexican history, the Church has occupied an important position in the political power structure. This is because, in the first place, in Mexico the social values associated with the Catholic tradition continue to thrive within the dominant culture, and secondly when there have been periods of stability in Church–State relations, that stability has been based on a fundamental ideological convergence. The perpetuation of these social values would imply that, despite the change which modernisation has brought about, the process of secularisation in Mexican society has not been achieved completely. This phenomenon has provoked the politicisation of the religious factor, one level of which is the institutional structure, that is to say, the Church as an organisation.

The process of secularisation has two dimensions, institutional differentiation and the rationalisation of human behaviour; in a secularised society 'action is organized efficiently, because it is considered possible to calculate and control action and the situations in which it takes place. Human behaviour obeys rules established rationally and no longer incalculable and magical forces and powers'.[1]

Despite the fact that there is a relatively close link between the rationalisation of behaviour and institutional differentiation, the timing of these two developments is not necessarily the same. Therefore, in recently modernised countries, there exists the tendency for institutional differentiation to precede rationalisation. This disparity can produce the 'crises of values' which arise in societies in the process of changing.[2] On the other hand, the disparity can be explained by the fact that institutional differentiation may be the result of decisions taken by political authorities, as occurred in Mexico in the second half of the nineteenth century, when the liberals came to power.

The rationalisation of behaviour, that is, the transformation of values and attitudes, is, on the other hand, much more difficult to bring about, because modifications on that level attack structures deep within society and their effects are only discernible in the long term. The set of values associated with tradition tends to prevail so long as no alternative arises. In Mexico, on only two occasions has the State tried to carry out organised secularisation of social values and attitudes: in 1932 with the Revolution's first educational plan, which proposed explicitly to impose a set of social values distinct from Catholic ones, and in 1934, when socialist education as it was called was introduced into primary schools,[3] in accordance with the radical policies of President Lázaro Cárdenas. Both attempts ended in resounding failure.

In Mexico a very obvious disparity exists between the two dimensions of secularisation, which can be explained as much by the persistence of tradition as by the use made of it by the elite groups in power in the periods of stability in order to consolidate an authoritarian structure of political domination. So true is this that even though social organisation in Mexico revolves around civic institutions whose legitimacy is fed by rational sources of power, none the less, the dominant values in society are directly linked to the Church's sources of spiritual power. This is one of the factors which define the Church's position as a political actor.

The deep rivalry between Church and State may be explained from this perspective. And it has not been resolved by the ideological complementarity which (between 1880 and 1910 and from 1940 to the present day) has finally formed the basis of their reconciliation. The nature of the opposition separating these two institutions which are central to social life in Mexico is more political than, as each one claims separately, strictly ideological. For so it is that 'when two bodies assert their authority over the same individuals, problems of supremacy necessarily arise, in fact each one of them would like to be the only one to rule'.[4]

There are some constants in relations between Church and State in Mexico. Essentially, these are the fight for control over education and the debate on the legitimate extent of the State's authority. However, topics for discussion have varied with time. In the nineteenth century the fundamental differences concerned the secularisation of authority and, consequently, of the social organisation. In the first third of the twentieth century, the conflict found expression around the question of the relationship between the individual and the State, while in the last twenty years the area of disagreement has once again centred on the Church's social role. In this history, periods of confrontation have been followed by periods of 'equivocal complicity'[5] and of critical support, which would be the characteristic of the present era.

THE CONFLICT BETWEEN LIBERALISM AND THE CATHOLIC CHURCH IN THE NINETEENTH CENTURY

The politicisation of the Catholic religion which occurred after Independence (1821) was caused, first of all, by the need to create a lay system of symbols which would be the basis of the brand new Mexican nation. The primordial though perhaps unexpected effect of the spiritual conquest of Mexico was to create a basis of social solidarity which became the starting point for defining a national character. The politicisation of religion in Mexico is undoubtedly linked with the involvement of religious elements in the myth of the birth of the nation. The Catholic religion served first to justify the Spanish presence in Mexico and then it became the support of an anticolonialist and pro-independence ideology. For during colonisation an authochthonous system of symbols had developed, with the Virgin of Guadalupe as its central symbol, an indigenous invocation of the Mother of Jesus which became the cornerstone of the nation's history.[6]

The conflict between Mexican nineteenth-century liberalism and the Catholic Church can also be seen as a product of incompatibility between the political consensus which was attempting to develop liberalism and the religious consensus which was defending the Church. The origins of this hostility were the same as elsewhere: the authoritarian and anti-democratic nature of the ecclesiastical organisation in opposition to the aspirations of the Liberal State, and the essential disagreement as to the origins of authority, which takes us back to the influence of the Enlightenment and the French Revolution on Mexican Liberal circles, one of the central hypotheses of which is that governments rule according to principles derived from social observation and not from the precepts of a revealed religion.

Consequently, one of the original aims of Mexican Liberals was to limit the social effects of the Catholic religion. To achieve this they concentrated their efforts on extending education so as to create a community of values which would be the basis of a wide national consensus. From the Liberals' viewpoint, the type of education given by the Church was one of the fundamental obstacles to their objectives of prosperity and progress, because, according to them, Catholic culture fostered resignation, submission and obedience, all attitudes adverse to change. As a consequence, secularisation was invariably an important aspect of their political programmes, in particular the laïcisation of education, since this was a way of depriving the Church of its strongest instrument of influence and of social control. The Liberals' programmes for secularisation attempted to separate civil and ecclesiastical authorities. Their main objective was institutional and functional differentiation, and in the area of education the diffusion of the values held by Liberal groups of the time: individualism and private property. It was a question of offering an alternative to the Catholic Church's corporatist tradition and also of depriving it of strength as a social institution so as to make religion an exclusively individual phenomenon.

These policies of limiting the Church's social competence produced serious conflicts, a civil war and foreign intervention, because, to resist the Liberal offensive, the ecclesiastical organisation had recourse to the influence it exerted on the society of the time. Its ability to respond, expressed by organising and supporting a Conservative party, was based on the great advantages it had at its disposal, as opposed to a relatively disorganised Liberal party which lacked the structural and doctrinal coherence of its adversary. The memory of the Church's active opposition to Liberal policies, and of its open intervention in the political confrontations of the nineteenth century, has remained alive in the collective mind, and it has served to nurture the official rhetoric which denies the Church any formal legitimacy as a centre of social organisation.

The privatisation of the religious phenomenon which the Liberals pursued posed very serious problems, which went beyond decisions of an exclusively administrative type, since the Catholic religion was, and still is today, inextricably linked with the dominant culture. As an essential support to the colonial society, the religion imposed by the Spaniards had been the favoured means through which Mexicans had been introduced to Western culture. The Catholic religion had become a basic element of social cohesion and an essential channel for the syncretism that underlies a distinct Mexican identity. The religious consensus had been crucial in consolidating the structure of colonial domination, and consequently, it had permeated social attitudes deeply. The conservative party's only strength lay in this identification of the Catholic religion with social cohesion and national integration. From this stemmed its opposition to freedom of worship and educational freedom which it considered a mortal risk for the extremely fragile national unity, threatened from within by major social differences and from without by a powerful and ambitious Protestant neighbour, the United States.

Nonetheless, the association of the Church and the Conservative party, with the French intervention which began in 1860, placed a question mark over their nationalistic loyalties which it took almost a century to remove. Likewise, the role which the Church played later during Porfirio Díaz' dictatorship (1884–1910), heightened the image of the Church as an anti-democratic and anti-lower-class institution. This idea has lasted even to the present day and has been aggravated by the alliances it established with the counter-revolutionary opposition after the events of 1910. Moreover, during the nineteenth century, the Catholic Church also maintained very close links with the upper and middle classes, which reinforced the paternalist ideology it was supporting.

The Catholic Church's reconciliation with Liberalism took place within the framework of the general political stabilisation of Porfirio Díaz' dictatorship. He attempted to depoliticise religion and neutralise the Church as a potential source of conflict. Instead of destroying it, he knew how to make use of it by integrating it into the power structure, once he recognised the value of the capacity for social control Catholicism could exert. Thanks to this policy, the Church recovered part of the social ground it had lost in previous battles. A situation was then created in which the Church enjoyed a *de facto* freedom which was the result of a political agreement, made outside the limits of the anticlerical laws of the 1857 Constitution. In exchange, the State obtained the co-operation of the ecclesiastic authorities.[7] This pattern in Church–State relations would recur after the post-revolutionary stabilisation.

THE CHURCH DURING THE REVOLUTION

One of the first victims of the Revolutionary fighting was the Catholic Church. This was on account of the complementary support it had given to the Porfirio dictatorship, and also because the movement of 1910 began as a struggle for the restoration of the Liberal modernisation project of the previous century.

The outbreak of the conflict with the State was inevitable. For, among other reasons, many Liberals considered that one of the principal deviations of the Porfirio regime from the 1857 Constitution had been its reconciliation with the Church. Besides, in 1911, the Partido Católico Nacional (National Catholic Party, PCN) was formed, which had little in common with the Conservative party of the previous century, except for its alliance with the ecclesiastical authorities. Its position was that of the encyclical *Rerum Novarum* of Leo XIII. It consequently supported certain important demands for social reform which had been the starting point for a very significant Catholic activism among the incipient working class, which had led to the formation of some unions. The question which set this PCN against the early revolutionaries was that of the rights of the Church, but the definitive rupture occurred in 1913.

In the first months of that year, the instigator of the revolutionary movement, Francisco I. Madero, the president of the republic at the time, was deposed and assassinated in a *coup d'état* led by General Victoriano Huerta. The latter attempted to set up a military dictatorship. The PCN had been vigorously involved in the opposition to Madero, and now joined this counter-revolutionary movement. It collaborated with the Huertista movement and then became the political and sworn enemy of the revolution. This alliance explains the anticlerical virulence of the 1917 Constitution which was formulated by the triumphant revolutionary faction. It was no longer a question of merely reviving the anticlerical provisions of the Liberal Constitution of 1857, but of preventing the Church from ever recovering its social strength, which had allowed it to contribute significantly to the counter-revolutionary mobilisation.

The 1917 Constitution, therefore, denies juridical identity to the Churches, and political rights to religious ministers. It establishes obligatory lay education in all the country's primary schools, whether public or private. It prohibits the setting up of religious orders, denies them the right to own property, and lays down a series of norms for the functioning of these organisations which amount to open intervention by the State. The ecclesiastical authorities rejected this document the day after its publication in a declaration that was accompanied by a call for the mobilisation of Catholics to fight for its abolition. By acting in this way the Church placed itself outside the new regime.

Nevertheless, the predictable conflicts which the enforcement of the law brought with it did not arise until ten years later. Among other reasons this delay was caused by the necessity to resolve the struggles for revolutionary hegemony, and to stabilise state administration. In 1924, President Plutarco Elías Calles (1924–8) initiated a very ambitious plan for modernisation. As is obvious, one of the first targets for attack was the Catholic Church which he considered a major obstacle to the implementation of his project. The result of this policy of imposed secularisation was a bloody war which lasted three years. It was basically rural people from the centre of the country who fought in this war, defending their religion while at the same time fighting to gain their demand for land rights which the revolutionary State had not granted.

From a general viewpoint the Cristero war (1926–9) was a struggle between modernity and tradition, between social change and passivity. But it can also be seen as part of a more general contradiction between society and a State determined to broaden the scope of its authority. President Calles was concerned first to consolidate the autonomy of the State. To achieve this, he thought it indispensable to ensure that it had the symbolic self-sufficiency to impose the revolutionary consensus emanating from the triumph of one faction. The realisation of an objective of this nature provoked confrontation not only with the Church, but also with numerous liberal middle-class groups who took action to defend the rights of the individual against the authoritarian State.

From the outset of the conflict, Calles insisted that the Church was a political enemy of the Revolution whose downfall was necessary to stabilise the new regime. For its part, to defend itself, the Church resorted to the principles of Mexican liberalism of 1857, so long its sworn enemy. It was aiming to obtain the support of those Liberals who remained loyal to the principles of individual freedom and political independence. In this way, the Church succeeded in extending the reach of its own cause and in adding its interests to those held by people who, though not religious, did agree with opposing authoritarianism.

The 1929 agreements which brought an end to the armed conflict, and formed the basis of the *modus vivendi* which was to govern Church–State relations for more than half a century, were very similar to the agreement that had prevailed during the Porfirio era. The laws were not abolished. They would simply be applied with 'benevolence'. In practice this became a non-application which gradually led to a modification in the Church's real position. The Church laid down its weapons but did not renounce its fundamental opposition to the revolutionary State. During the 1930s their relationship continued to be unstable, since Catholics did not renounce anti-authoritarian resistance. What is important is that in a process parallel to the monopolisation of political power carried out first by Calles and later by Lázaro Cárdenas (1934–40), the lay organisations dependent on the Church continued to gather strength quietly, and became an alternative area of involvement for those who rejected State authoritarianism. In critical times, this infra-structure of involvement could serve to oppose the State.

THE CATHOLIC CHURCH IN THE CONTEXT OF LIMITED MEXICAN PLURALISM

The politicisation of religious power – of which the institutional structure is just one level – is determined not only by the persistence of traditional values. It is also determined by the significance possessed in a society like that in Mexico by the function of social cohesion, normally brought about by the religious factor. In this case, two elements highlight its importance as an agent of social cohesion: the close connections between Catholic symbolism and the myth of the nation, and the internal heterogeneity and fragmentation of Mexican society. As a result the political importance of the religious organisation arises not so much from one group's desire for power as from the nature of the political system and of society.

The history of the Mexican Catholic Church in the post-revolutionary period, and more particularly since 1940, shows that its political involvement is determined mainly by the ways in which power is organised and exerted in society, rather than by the degree of the population's religiousness or by the class structure.[8]

Since its consolidation in the 1940s, the Mexican political system has shown two characteristic traits which allow it to be defined as an authoritarian regime: concentration of power and limitation of political involvement.[9] The first of these can be seen in a limited political pluralism. Unlike democratic systems where social pluralism can be expressed in an almost unlimited political pluralism, the authoritarian regime restricts the number of participators struggling for power. In the Mexican case, access to political power is reserved to members of a dominant party which is closely allied with the State – the Partido Revolucionario Institucional (Institutional Revolutionary Party, PRI), founded in 1929 – and to members of the civil service; but the limited Mexican pluralism also includes other participators who intervene in political life as pressure groups, and who represent special interests. They do not seek to exert power directly but to intervene in the decision-making process. A typical example is the employers' organisations. Some authors consider that the Mexican Catholic Church, too, plays the part of a pressure group, because, like specialised economic or trade union organisations, it attempts to influence governmental decisions which concern it, though not to replace the political authorities. Its interest and objectives would be limited: to assure itself of special legal treatment, economic privileges and the possibility of intervening in education.[10] However, in the last ten years, the Church has clearly shown that its aims are much more general than those indicated above.

On occasion, and regarding certain questions, it has acted as a pressure group; but since it is a point of reference for the majority of the population and hence forms a very important centre of social contact, it is difficult to affirm that it represents a limited social group.

Besides a very marked concentration of power, limited pluralism implies a restricted number of channels through which social demands may be voiced. From this arises the second general characteristic of the authoritarian regime: the reduction and limitation of political participation to the electoral arena, or to that of organisations controlled by the State itself. In Mexico, the main party incorporates organisations of craftsmen and of urban and rural workers in the state authority's own interests and not, as official sources maintain, to ensure their political participation. They are included so as to neutralise their effect. Historically, this phenomenon has reduced the credibility of trade unions and parties as bodies that really represent the interests of their affiliated members. The Mexican regime has never adopted a single-party doctrine and neither has it rejected the formula of pluralist democracy. But opposition parties have not succeeded in developing as autonomous organisations, capable of challenging the strength and omnipresence of the official party. Moreover, the State's authoritarian and controlling nature, and its need to base its legitimacy on the control of the large social groups, has resulted in a marked intolerance towards any tendency to independent political organisation.

Parallel to the strictly political organisations, the authoritarian regime permits the existence of social organisations that are relatively independent of its power. These would be difficult to suppress given their economic importance (the employers' organisations), and their influence, rootedness and legitimacy within society (the Catholic Church in Mexico). They are allowed to exist because they maintain political neutrality, especially in normal times (professional colleges and mutual benefit societies), or because they do not present a threat to the monopoly of power held by the State. In authoritarian regimes, these types of organisations which are not specifically political may fulfil some of the functions belonging to political parties. The Church in Mexico has assumed this role; it does not put itself forward as a political alternative, but it does represent certain interests, it participates through education in the formation of elite groups,[11] it supplies ideological guidelines, it forms opinion and it constitutes a means of mediation between the State and society. The Church in Mexico has the characteristics of a 'parapolitical' institution.[12] Up to now no opposition party has attained either the level of presence or social credibility which the Church enjoys as a social centre independent of the State.

The Mexican Church's strength may be measured by the virtual universality of Catholicism in Mexican society and by the persistence of the values associated with that tradition, which form the predominant social code. But to these ideological functions must be added the 'logistic functions'[13] of social structuring which the Church carries out through parishes, schools, pious associations, lay organisations and charitable works.[14] These form a whole background of support for the Church's activity. The importance of this organisational network lies in the fact that it provides a great mobilisation potential which is the Church's political capital. In the last twenty-five years, this potential has been used for various ends and in varying degrees; at local and national level it has been used as a trump card in negotiations with the State. But to reach that stage, the Church first followed a strategy which helped it recover fully.

THE RESTORATION OF THE CHURCH IN MEXICO: FROM SUBORDINATION TO AUTONOMY

In the years following the Cristero War and Cardenist radicalism, two crucial phases stand out in Church–State relations in Mexico. The first of these, from 1940 to 1970, was a time of collaboration. Then followed a second phase which can be described as one of critical support by the Church for the State. This evolution was the product of changes within both the Church and the political system.

THE POLICY OF GRADUAL ADVANCE, 1940–70

In 1940, a long period of social stability commenced in Mexico. This grew out of the consolidation of the political system, brought about by the revolution of 1910, and a process of sustained economic development. It was also the starting point of a new stage in Church–State relations. From an historical perspective, the armed conflict of the Cristero war from 1926–9, and the instability of the 1930s were the Church's response to attacks by revolutionary governments who proposed to limit its power. Once this period of institutional re-adjustment ended, the Church found a formula for entry into the political system which allowed it to become an integral part of that system. Through reconciliation with the State, the Church managed to adjust to the prevailing conditions and have harmonious relations with all the political institutions; and from then on its activities within society developed under the banner of collaboration with the State.

This process of functional adaptation by the Church to the political system could seem surprising given the anticlerical limitations of the revolutionary governments. However, when stability, or as President

Manuel Avila Comacho would say in 1940, 'the consolidation of the revolutionary conquests',[15] became the government's top priority, the ecclesiastical hierarchy accepted the solution of reintegration offered to it. And, due to its own prudence and a gradualist policy, it succeeded in recovering the position of the power which radical groups of the revolutionary elite had wanted to take away from it.

From the point of view of the group in government in the early 1940s, the Church's reintegration was no longer considered a threat. Rather, it was seen as an instrument to be used; the revolutionary elite believed the struggles of the previous years had weakened the Church considerably and they also thought the monopoly of power was firmly established in their hands. Nevertheless it had not been possible to completely destroy the Church's social presence. Consequently, after 1940, Mexican governments opted to incorporate it within the system, conferring on it the function of supporting the framework of ideological domination. This policy, which at first could seem astute, was based on the supposition that the State's position of control had reduced the Church's autonomy, and that the confrontation of previous years had neutralised its political capability.

For its part the Church derived great benefits from the reconciliation. The *modus vivendi* relied more and more on the non-enforcement of the laws relating to the Church. And in this climate of tolerance the Church flourished. It showed an intense capacity for recuperation and expansion which permitted it to secure a sound position and to a certain extent restore its independence *vis-à-vis* the State.

The State's strategy after 1940 to reintegrate the Church within the structure of social dominance was, to a certain extent, similar to that adopted by Porfirio Díaz during his dictatorship. On the one hand it recognised the part the Church plays in society in maintaining unity and orientating individual behaviour. But, on the other hand, it attempted to prevent any interference by the Church in the political sphere. In other words, its social presence was tolerated, even encouraged, but at the same time, the State retained legislation which denied it any juridical identity and which hung over it like Damocles' sword, serving as a constant reminder of the limits of tolerance.

The contradiction inherent in this strategy lay in the fact that when the Church was given its head in an area as fundamental as social control, the door was necessarily opened for it to develop purely political activities. So the persistence of legal limitations on the Church's social activity did not mean there was any real obstacle to the restoration and expansion of ecclesiastic structures, even when the ambiguity of its position caused it to be in fact in a subordinate position in relations with the State. Moreover, as maintaining social order became an important requirement for the unhindered exercise of authoritarian power, the Church gained importance as a political entity and its collaboration with the State became essential.

As the Catholic religion is a subculture whose essential elements act as a frame of reference for the majority of the population, its inclusion as a legitimate component in the social consensus served to strengthen the nationalist consensus which was to underlie political stability. The traditional values defended by the Church – unity, order, social peace and conformism – were not incompatible with the nationalist and liberal rhetoric which the political powers adopted after 1940. By collaborating with the political authorities, it regained its legitimacy as a socialising agent. In spite of the repeated declarations of political neutrality which the ecclesiastical authorities made during the 1940s and 1950s in this regard, there is no doubt the Church was already playing a very significant political part in the legitimisation of the existing order. It is for this reason that the 1940–60 period seems to be a phase of equivocal complicity in Church–State relations. During those years the Church gained advantages from the implicit support it received from the State, and these in time would allow it to increase its own autonomy. In that period the ecclesiastical hierarchy was stressing that both the political and religious powers had the same mission in Mexico: to preserve and promote national culture against external attack, which in those years basically meant international communism. In fact, the area of ideological agreement between Church and State was anti-communism. Between 1940 and 1960 this became in Mexico an authentic national crusade in which the Church participated only and directly while the State took part in a more indirect and irregular way.

Apart from this, there was not much the Church could do then. Rather than set itself up as the voice of some social or political groups, as it had done to a certain extent during the Cristero war, it concentrated in this period on defending its own interests. Its aim was probably to secure a basis of power which would later enable it to exercise functions of social leadership. In this sense, the particular conditions under which the Mexican Church was working show from a broader historical perspective how it had taken the option of gradual recuperation, a prudent and gradualist strategy which would bear much fruit in the long term. So at that time the Church acted as a pressure group with a limited area within which to work. The areas of its active interest were limited to private education, so that even its socialising work was restricted in terms of social groups, since only the bourgeoisie and some middle-class sectors could afford those schools. Despite the fact that a minimal percentage of the population attended these schools, the Church played an important role through them in forming elite groups. Besides, its alliance with these social groups helped it to strengthen its position in the power structure. The criticisms it made laid claim to the civil rights of Catholics as such. Some, in particular the Jesuits, protested against the legal prohibition which prevented them from actively intervening in public in the civic guidance of Catholics. But these are only isolated examples. In any case, the policy of gradual advance which the Episcopacy followed in those years required a patience that was amply rewarded by the unexpected rapidity with which the ecclesiastical structure was re-established.

Stability allowed the Church to recover at an impressive rate from the destruction caused by the Cristero war. During the month of July 1946, fifteen new parishes were founded and up to 1960 their number continued to increase, as did the number of seminaries, convents and educational institutions run by religious orders. The number of priests and nuns also increased considerably. As a result in 1959 the Church's position in Mexico was one of the most favourable in Latin America,[16] – a surprising phenomenon if we take into account both the immediate background and the continuance of the anticlerical legislation, as well as the fact that in some countries in the area the Catholic religion had official status.

In spite of the growth in population, which rose from 20 million in 1940 to 35 million in 1960, the number of inhabitants per priest decreased slightly from 5439 in 1940 to 5289 in 1960.[17] This proportion stayed relatively constant in the following years. In absolute figures, the number of priests grew from 4220 in 1940 to 6466 in 1960[18] and to 8451 in 1968.[19] But the most impressive figure is that relating to religious sisters who in 1945 numbered 8123 and in 1960 19 400.[20] It should also be pointed out that during these years there was a significant influx recorded of foreign religious (mostly Spaniards) into Mexico, and that in 1963 these represented more than 16 per cent of religious active in the country, of whom more than 17 per cent were in positions of authority and more than 30 per cent were involved in education.[21]

To counteract the 'bad influence' of the secular media which was exposed to 'exotic doctrines', the Church threw itself into publishing in a very important way. Although the religious press had never actually disappeared, from the time of the reconciliation it received a considerable boost. Likewise, stability encouraged the rebuilding of lay organisations and the reorganisation of Catholic militants under ecclesiastical authority.

A CHURCH FACING SOCIETY

During the 1960s, the behaviour of the Mexican Catholic Church altered. The stability of the previous period had allowed it to strengthen its position because of a strategy which was a reaction primarily to the demands of its relations with power. The change that occurred in the following years consisted in the importance it attributed to its relationship with society. One of the effects of that change has been a higher political profile on the part of the Catholic Church in Mexico.

This presence and open participation by the Church in public affairs, which is relatively new, should be examined by starting from the convergence of two parallel processes. In the first place, the politicisation of the ecclesiastical institution in this period was the outcome of changes occurring within it. The most concrete expression of these changes was the appearance of two opposing sides in the Mexican clergy. One of these was progressive, close to the positions held by the political left, and the other was conservative, although no less politically active because of that. Secondly this phenomenon was also a response to the policy of reform followed by the governments of Presidents Luis Echeverría (1970–6) and José López Portillo (1976–82), which broadened the terms of the political debate and the boundaries of the power-game.

A central aspect of the equivocal complicity of the earlier period was that it allowed the Church to maintain its credibility as a body independent of the State, in spite of its collaboration. Although there is a lot of information testifying to the alliance between governmental and ecclesiastical authorities,[22] the contacts were always informal though close. The State never renounced the anticlerical tradition to which it claimed to be heir. Nor did the Church back down in its fundamental opposition to a State which, from its point of view, infringes some of the essential rights of the individual: freedom of education, belief, expression and association. Starting from this basic difference of opinion regarding the legitimate range of State influence on social life, the Mexican Church has since 1917 been elaborating a tradition of acting as society's protector, a tradition which goes beyond ideological discrepancies. From this perspective, a policy of reform which attempted to recognise and allow for social demands would strengthen the Church's presence and its intervention in the struggles for power. Moreover, the electoral reform which has been the cornerstone of the gradual liberalisation in Mexican political life in the last twenty years corresponds to the tactics used by the Church in Mexico since the 1930s; to show opposition to the State by using the power of the vote. Following the Cristero defeat and with a pontifical recommendation,[23] the ecclesiastical authorities definitively rejected violent methods and insisted that Catholics should protect their interests by exercising their right to vote.

Between 1970 and 1982, the Mexican political system underwent certain adjustments which tended to absorb those social changes produced by economic growth. In this way it resolved the crisis of legitimacy which the students' movement of 1968 had precipitated. At that time, the power structure became more complex; new channels opened up through which social demands could be voiced. Trade union and party organisations sprang up which were relatively independent from the State. Self-criticism was imposed as the sign of the political times. The right to social protest was recognised, provided it was expressed through institutional channels. The critical press prospered and the means of expression increased, especially those of the middle-classes. The aim of these changes was to widen the boundaries of tolerance within the system by strengthening the opposition parties and so to guide protest through the electoral process, and in this way to channel any demands which, under adverse circumstances, might have a disruptive effect.

To achieve this, López Portillo's government introduced important legislative reforms to increase the credibility of the electoral process and to encourage this form of participation. Although this liberalisation was essentially directed at political organisations, the Church benefited enormously from these modifications since it possessed a doctrinal and structural coherence which was much superior to that of the majority of social organisations.

CHANGES WITHIN THE CHURCH

The Mexican Church's new attitude regarding society was also the outcome of significant changes which occurred within it during the 1970s. From this point of view two reasons, at least, explain the Church's political reactivation: the first is that the existence within the Catholic Community of a progressive wing linked with popular social movements and organisations made it necessary for the more moderate sector to publicly express the Church's official position on the most diverse subjects. The second reason is that the activities of left-wing Christians, who were expressing the political potential of popular religiousness, led governmental authorities to pay more attention to the ecclesial body. In addition, it may be supposed that these activities were used by the ecclesiastical authorities in their own negotiations with the State; on the one hand the hierarchy undertook to control the Christian left and, on the other, the governmental authorities allowed it to deal with such matters autonomously. The immersion of the Catholic community – the clergy in particular – in social reality provoked the outbreak of significant internal ideological differences. This contrasted markedly with the uniformity which had characterised the Church since the 1930s.

The Church's circumstances in Mexico caused it to lag behind in those changes which occurred in Catholicism after the Second Vatican Council.[24] The first effects of the 'aggiornamento' were not felt in Mexico until 26 March 1968, when the Mexican bishops gave as much publicity as possible to a pastoral letter on the country's development and integration. This document is a critical analysis of the country's social and economic situation, its internal instability, marginality and the civic poverty in society; to attack those evils it puts forward a 'democratic programme or plan' which could allow a solution mid-way between 'individualistic liberalism and totalitarianism'. But the most important thing about this message was that for the first time since 1926, the Mexican bishops officially assumed a position of social commitment and leadership.[25]

The brutal repression by the Government of the 1968 students' movement produced widespread political tension which forced the Mexican Episcopate to slow down its impulse towards active social commitment. But the longings for it by the clergy which the letter on integration and development had opened up intensified after the second CELAM conference. This took place in Medellín, Colombia, in August 1968, and is considered a central event in the history of the Catholic Church in Latin America.

According to the summing up documents, at that meeting:

> The Latin American Church directed her attention on man (note: not on the Church) in this continent which is living a decisive moment in its historic development.... She recognizes that throughout her history, not all her members, whether clergy or laity, were always faithful to the Spirit of God. On considering the present time, she gladly acknowledges the dedication of many of her children and also the fragility of her own messengers; She respects the judgement of history on those shining lights.... This shows we are on the brink of a new stage in the history of our continent, full of yearning for total emancipation, for freedom from all servitude, for personal maturity and collective integration. We perceive here the first signs of the painful birth of a new civilization.[26]

Subsequently, these documents were interpreted in many different ways; the most disturbing of these developed three years after the conference into a liberation theology. In Mexico, Medellín had very clear disruptive effects: the contradictions in which members of the episcopate became involved, the high rate of defection among priests, the doctrinal and ideological differences which gave rise to the formation of opposing groups and the uncertainty among the faithful.

The Medellín documents examine 'institutionalised violence', the privileges of minority groups and the oppression of the large social groups. From them came what is called the 'opción por los pobres' (the option for the poor), which in Mexico gave rise to the formation in 1972 of groups like 'Sacerdotes para el Pueblo' (Priests for the People) and 'Cristianos por el Socialismo' (Christians for Socialism). These rejected capitalism and committed themselves to the construction of socialism; from then on the Comunidades Eclesiales de Base (base Christian communities) also became widespread.

Throughout the 1970s, the presence of these left-wing Christian groups was very striking. For, although they did not constitute a majority section of the Church, their aim was to spread the new message and to mobilise the consciences of Catholics. Despite their influence having been felt even in some workers' organisations – for example, the Frente Auténtico del Trabajo (the Authentic Front for Workers) – the Christian left-wing has never become more than a minority, which, according to one of its instigators, has changed from being 'minimal' to being a 'respectable minority'.[27] It should be mentioned that this group has avoided alliances with political parties although many of its members are affiliated to one party or another.

The changes which took place within the Mexican Catholic Church can be illustrated by the transformations that occurred in two very important religious orders: the Society of Jesus and Opus Dei. One of the events which most disturbed the Mexican Catholic community was the decision by the Jesuits to give up their traditional mission of educating the elite, in order to direct their activities to the most needy groups. From the early 1970s, the Jesuits reestablished the tendency they had of becoming a focus of theological reflexion and social and political organisation. Many of them set themselves up in the poorest districts of the cities where they acted in the defence of the needy. In some cases, their activities placed them in situations which were uncomfortably close to those of violent organisations such as the Liga 23 de Septiembre (the 23rd September League).[28]

At the same time as this displacement process was taking place among Jesuits, Opus Dei was also gaining in importance in Mexico. In the last fifteen years it has expanded its educational activities considerably and it represents the conservative wing of Catholicism.[29] The number of its members is not as important to Opus Dei as is their quality (it is estimated that there are around five thousand members in Mexico). This is because its mission is to assume the leadership of society. The importance which Opus has acquired in Mexico can be measured by the number of educational institutions it has in its charge and by the number of prominent people connected with it; so much so that in May 1983, Alvaro del Portillo, the president of Opus, was welcomed to Mexico with great celebrations among ex-students of institutions run by Opus Dei.

Faced with all these changes in the balance of power within the Church, the ecclesiastical authorities have consistently reacted cautiously and with restraint. The only official condemnation of minority tendencies was an echo of the one issued by the Vatican against Lefebvrism. But generally at this time, only some of the outspokeness and declarations made by left-wing bishops and priests caused disapproval among the leaders of the episcopate. Faced with the pluralisation process in Catholicism throughout the world in the 1970s, the Catholic Church in Mexico adopted the relatively tolerant position dictated by the Vatican, without modifying its traditional dependence. Its first official reaction to the swing to the left which seemed to be inexorably taking over the ecclesial body was the document on Christian commitment in the face of social and political options, December 1973. This reflected both the views of a powerful section of the Church, who rejected the radicalisation of CELAM and Medellín and who adhered to the social doctrine of 'Tercerismo' (a third force): neither individualist liberalism nor totalitarianism. From that moment on, differences became more specific and apparent at various levels, but up to now, in all cases of conflict, the institution has prevailed. Dissident groups are not repressed directly. They are deprived of authority and, as a result, they dissolve, as happened in the case of the two organisations founded in 1972. Neither Sacerdotes para el Pueblo (Priests for the People) nor Cristianos por el Socialismo (Christians for Socialism) were condemned by the hierarchy; they ceased to exist 'because their members took that decision'. The weakness of these Christian left-wing movements makes it plausible to think that 'the fate of the Christian left is linked in one way or another to the political and social left in the continent: their destinies are parallel, if not the same'.[30] The same could be said of the right: the strengthening of Conservative tendencies encourages Catholic Conservatism. However, the fact that the Christian left is a minority heightens its dependence on organisations with similar ideological attitudes, whereas Catholic Conservatism gains autonomy from its own strength. In conclusion, it can be said that, in general terms, the moderate position has prevailed among the Mexican clergy, a political moderation which implies obedience to the Vatican's official positions and criticism of the Mexican State from an anti-authoritarian stance, not far from that held by the Democratic right. In April 1976, the Assembly of the Mexican episcopal conference issued a document entitled Fidelidad a la Iglesia (Fidelity to the Church) which proposed ending the divisions.

According to this document, ideological differences had caused two large groups to be formed: one which rejected change and was considered conservative and traditionalist, and another which was supported by the progressives who were of the opinion 'that the Church is advancing slowly' and were demanding more deep-seated transformations. Fidelidad a la Iglesia invited people to reflect on the Vatican II documents and to reconcile the two ideological extremes in one intermediate position, under the Church's maximum authority, accepting it 'as it is': an attitude of reconciliation – which does not reject social commitment, provided it occurs under the authority of the ecclesiastic hierarchy – and which has received the support of the majority of Mexican Catholics.

THE CATHOLIC CHURCH DURING THE MEXICAN CRISIS OF THE 1980s

In January 1979, Pope John Paul II travelled to Mexico to inaugurate the Third General Conference of the Latin American Episcopal Council, CELAM. However, history still influenced every current political or religious consideration. The Pope's presence in this country could not be presented as an official visit since Mexico does not have diplomatic relations with the Vatican, and also because if he had been considered an official guest, the State would have been obliged to act as host.

John Paul II provoked an extraordinary interest and enthusiasm among all social classes. The religious fervour of large sections of Mexican society reached its highest level ever on that occasion, encouraged by the overwhelming nature of the tributes to Pope Wojtila and by the Pontiff's own personality. The success of the trip was complete in terms of the Church's capacity for mobilisation. Each public act carried out by the Pope in the city of Mexico and in the provincial cities he visited became a mass meeting in which the expressions of faith also implied a defiance of public authority on the part of the ecclesiastical authorities, the clergy and in general of all those taking part. There is no doubt that the stances which the Church has adopted since then with regard to the State and society are related to this success.

The Church's advances in the previous period were in some way co-ordinated with the State itself. In the 1970s, they had negotiated questions as fundamental to both as a new educational reform and family planning, and they had succeeded in establishing a type of informal concordat. The difference between those years and the following ones lies in the fact that after 1979 the ecclesiastical hierarchy began to act with increasing autonomy. It found support in the strength it had accumulated during the restoration process and in the loss of popularity of the traditional political organisations. This phenomenon in particular strengthened the Church's image as the defender of society at a time when the civil authorities had to face severe criticism provoked by Mexico's worst economic crisis in living memory.

The end of President López Portillo's government (1982) came in the middle of a stormy political climate in which all the power groups seemed to be confronting the authority of the State. Having maintained more than forty years of sustained growth and having promised a prolonged period of prosperity due to oil, the State now seemed incapable of honouring the excessive commitments it had taken on abroad as well as the demands of a constantly increasing population. In those conditions, re-adjustments in the power structure began to take place. These have continued during the last five years and are the result of fierce criticism of the State's authority. They are also the result of governmental policies which have tended to limit the State's responsibilities and the areas of its competence.

The Church has not remained detached from this course of events. On the contrary, after 1982, the ecclesiastical authorities made public the unanimous decision of the bishops to take up their duty of 'highlighting and denouncing' society's problems. In reality, this has meant a widening of their interests to include all spheres of contemporary life, from inflation to nuclear power plants, and the open involvement of bishops and priests in giving guidance to voters. This contrasts with the previous period when the Church only offered opinions on problems concerning education or social customs.

The political repercussions of the economic crisis, evidenced basically in votes for the opposition parties, in particular for the Partido Acción Nacional (Party for National Action), the voice of Mexican conservatism, have favoured political activism within the Catholic Church, which has brought into operation its organisational infrastructure so as to become associated with the demands of electoral democracy. In doing this it has abandoned the earlier policy of collaboration, and offers the State only critical support.

Mexican priests have fully adopted the role of social leadership which they have been seeking for years, and in doing so, they have succeeded in establishing links with a variety of political forces. In the backward areas of the country they have agreed to support the claims of left-wing political organisations, while in the richer areas they have become associated with groups and organisations of the right. The common ground is the fight against the State's arbitrary actions, and the defence of citizens who are at the mercy of decisions taken by an authoritarian public power.

All the social legitimacy which the Church has does not, however, change the realities that it must take into account in long-term planning. The political strength of the Mexican Church is inversely related to the weakness of independent political organisations, capable of performing the functions which it has fallen to the Church to carry out in the authoritarianism of Mexico. In this respect, the significance, for the Church, of the democratisation process does not lie in an increased freedom of action but in the fact that it would probably produce a depoliticisation of the religious factor.

NOTES

Fragments of this article were previously published in 'Notas para el estudio de la Iglesia en el Mexico contemporáneo'; Martín de la Rosa y Charles A. Reilly (Coords.), *Religión y política en México* (Mexico: Siglo XX1 edns., 1985) pp. 42–8; 'La rebelión de la Iglesia', *Nexos*, 78, junio de 1984, pp. 11–17 and 'La Iglesia católica mexicana y el reformismo autoritario', in *Foro Internacional*, El Colegio de México, vol. XXV, 2 (octubre–diciembre 1984) pp. 138–64.

1. Karel Dobbelaere, 'Secularization: multidimensional concept', *Current Sociology*, 29, 2 (Summer 1981) p. 17.
2. More than thirty years after the first studies on modernisation were undertaken, the first critical evaluations of this viewpoint have been initiated. One of the most interesting of these is that by S. N. Eisenstadt, who states that cultural continuity was consciously assimilated by the elite groups in power, with the aim of minimising the violence of the dislocations caused by accelerated change. See S. N. Eisenstadt, *Tradition, change and modernity* (New York: John Wiley & Sons, 1973).
3. The then Secretary of State Education, Narciso Bassols declared: 'It is not enough to have abandoned the direction and rhythm of the Porfirio era. We must be able to propose new formulas for spiritual direction to put in their place. A Society which has not managed to create new forms of culture, of political solidarity and of economy . . . is always threatened by the old ways of life', in Antonio Luna Arroyo (ed.), *La Obra Educativa de de Narciso Bassols. Documentos para la historia de la educación pública en México*: declaraciones, discursos, decretos, tesis y acuerdos (Mexico: Patria, 1934) p. 237.
4. A Haurion, 'Démocratie et forces religieuses', in A. Audibert, A. Bayet, B. E. Brown *et al.*, *La laïcité*, vol. VI (Paris: Presses Universitaires de France, 1960), pp. 23–42.
5. This idea of 'equivocal complicity' has been elaborated by Guy Hermet to describe the relations between the Church and Franco's dictatorship in Spain in the period following 1965–6, when the Church was attempting to separate itself from the State without losing the material and juridical advantages it derived from its association with it. Guy Hermet, *Les catholiques dans l'Espagne franquiste. Les acteurs du jeu politique*, vol. 1 (Paris: Presses de la Fondation Nationale des Sciences Politiques, 1980) p. 359.
6. 'To rally the Creoles, *castas* and Indians against Spain, (they) proclaimed what was essentially a fiction, the myth of a Mexican nation,

which was the linear heir of the Aztecs. In practice, however, the insurgents fought behind the banner of Our Lady of Guadalupe. Both these symbols had emerged through the growth of Creole patriotismo. Now employed to justify independence, they flowed together to form a nationalist ideology which evoked an idiosyncratic blend of Marian devotion, antiespañolismo, and neo-Aztecism . . .'. David Brading, *The Origins of Mexican Nationalism* (Cambridge: Cambridge Latin American Miniatures, Centre of Latin American Studies, University of Cambridge, 1985) pp. 55.

7. '. . . Porfirio Díaz, in his desire for unity, obsessed as he was by the North American expansionist threat, wished to govern at a level above the frictions. . . . A relatively free Church, whose bishops would appreciate the service granted by the President, would contribute to national unity, by giving support to the Government'. Jean Meyer, *La Cristiada México* 3 vols, vol. 2 (Mexico: Siglo XXI edns, 1973) p. 44.
8. An analysis of the roles played by the Churches in limited pluralist regimes leads to the conclusion that religious organisations play a similar political role in all these regimes, even if the social structures of the countries in question differ markedly. (Compare, for example, Mexico and Spain under Franco.) See Guy Hermet, 'Les fonctions politiques des organisations religieuses dans les régimes à pluralisme limité', *Revue Française de Science Politique* 23 (1973) pp. 439–72.
9. Juan Linz developed the analytical model of the authoritarian system to explain the case of Spain under Franco; see his article 'Una teoría del régimen autoritario. El caso de España' in Stanley G. Payne (ed.), *Política y sociedad en la España del siglo XX* (Madrid: Akal, 1978) pp. 205–63. Subsequently, many authors used this model to examine the Mexican situation; see, among others, Susan Kaufman Purcell, *The Mexican Profit-Sharing Decision: Politics in an Authoritarian Regime* (Berkeley: University of California Press, 1975) and Rafael Segovia, *La politización del niño mexicano* (Mexico: El Colegio de Mexico, 1975).
10. See for example, Otto Granados Roldan, *La Iglesia católica mexicana como grupo de presión* (Mexico: UNAM, 1981) Cuadernos de Humanidades, no 17.
11. The Mexican Church's eventful history during the first half of the twentieth century has concealed the enormous importance of its role in the education of economic, political and, of course, social elites. The educational policies of the Mexican State and, in general, its commitment to the lower classes gave rise – especially after 1940 – to the Church concentrating its activities on private education, intended for the upper and middle classes, the privileged recruiting ground of Mexican elite groups. This specialisation in social groups is highlighted in the middle level. Studies carried out on Mexican elites concentrated on university education as a variable for the identification of these privileged groups, overlooking secondary education and the crucial distinction between private and public schools at this level.
12. See G. Hermet, 'Les fonctions politiques', p. 440.
13. Hermet, 'Les fonctions politiques'.

14. According to data supplied by the archbishopric in Mexico, in 1979 92% of the population called itself Catholic. The pastoral centres in the Country (dioceses, prelatures, apostolic vicariates, parishes, missionary posts and churches), added up to 6018, with an average of more than 10 000 inhabitants, and there were 361 kindergartens, 1552 primary schools with 586 850 pupils, 952 secondary schools with 237 764 pupils and institutes of higher education, with almost sixty thousand students. The church also provided health services in 167 hospitals, 205 dispensaries, two leper colonies, 127 asylums, 174 orphanages, 162 marriage guidance centres, and 208 research centres (Teresa Gursa, 'Censo: 60.6 milliones de mexicanos son católicos', *Uno más uno*, 9 de octubre de 1981).
15. 'Discurso del Gral. Manuel Avila Comacho, al protestar como Presidente de la República ante el Congreso de la Unión, el 1 de diciembre de 1940', Cámara de Diputados, XVI Legislatura, in *Los presidentes de México ante la nación, 1821–1966*, vol. IV (Mexico: Imprenta de la Cámara de Diputados, 1966) p. 149.
16. See Isidro Alonso, *La Iglesia en América Latina* (Madrid and Freiburg: Feres, 1964) pp. 208–9 and 214–15.
17. Rutilio Ramos, Isidro Alonso and Domingo Garre, *La Iglesia en México Estructuras eclesiásticas* (Freiburg and Bogotá: Feres, 1963) p. 88.
18. I. Alonso, *La Iglesia en América Latina*, p. 208.
19. Manuel R. González, *La Iglesia Mexicana en cifras*, (Mexico: Centro de Investigación y Acción Social, 1969) p. 100.
20. I. Alonso, *La Iglesia en América Latina*, p. 214.
21. M. González, *La Iglesia Mexicana en cifras*, p. 165.
22. Besides taking part in joint public acts such as the inauguration of the Plaza de las Americas of the Basilica in Guadalupe in 1952, over which the president at the time, Miguel Alenán, presided, the episcopate collaborated with the State by inviting Catholics to support decisions on foreign policy or health campaigns. A study on the lower-class districts in Mexico city shows, for example, that the negotiating ability of the PRI to take steps to obtain public services assures it the support of the parish priest in the community which benefits, despite the fact that the latter might consider himself closer, ideologically speaking, to the Partido Acción Nacional. (Susan Eckstein, *The Poverty of Revolution. A Study of Social Economic and Political Inequality in a Center City Area. A Squatter Settlement and a Low Cost Housing Project in Mexico*, thesis, Columbia University, 1972, pp. 271 et passim).
23. See for example, Pius XI's Exhortation to Mexican Catholics to fulfil their civic duties and not ignore either their right to vote or their right to form political parties ('Carta apostólica sobre la situación religiosa en México', *Christus* (1937) 18, pp. 228–399). From then on, the Mexican clergy have religiously carried out this stipulation of the Pope, and each election time invite their parishioners to vote.
24. Martín de la Rosa, 'La Iglesia católica en México: del Vaticano II a la CELAM III', *Cuadernos Políticos*, 19 (enero–marzo de 1979) 88–104.
25. 'Carta pastoral del episcopado mexicano sobre el desarrollo et integra-

ción de país', *Christus* (1968) 390, p. 397.

26. A brief historic summary of the CELAM in Enrique Dussel, *De Medellín a Puebla: Una década de sangre y esperanza, 1968–1979* (Mexico: Edicol, 1979) pp. 49–82. Claude Pomerlau deals with the internal changes in the Mexican Church in 'The Changing Church in Mexico and its challenge to the State', *Review of Politics*, 43 (1981) 450–559.
27. De la Rosa, 'La Iglesia católica en Mexico', pp. 101–2.
28. In some cases, this radicalisation ended in violence because members of the clergy were victims of the anti-guerrilla struggle. At least this is the mostly widely held explanation of the deaths of Fr Rodolfo Aguila Alvarez in Chihuahua and Rodolfo Escamilla in Mexico City, in the early months of 1977. Both were involved in work to promote and support independent social organisations in lower class districts. Their deaths were never properly explained.
29. Opus Dei came to Mexico in 1949. Among the institutions it supports are: Escuela Cedros, Escuela Mexicana de Turismo, Residencia Universitaria Panamericana, Universidad Panamericana, Instituto de Capacitación y Adiestramiento de Mandos Intermedios, Escuela Superior de Administración de Instituciones, Instituto Panamericano de Empresa. From the beginning of 1970 onwards, there was much talk of the increase in the influence of Opus in Mexico and of its presence in the upper levels of public administration. See Oscar Hinojosa, 'El Opus Dei avanza en la conquista del poder en Mexico', *Proceso*, 343 (1983) pp. 39–53; Jesus Ynfante, *La prodigiosa aventura del Opus Dei* (Paris: Ruedo Iberico, 1970).
30. De la Rosa, 'La Iglesia católica en Mexico', p. 103.

16 The Call to do Justice: Conflict in the Brazilian Catholic Church, 1968–79

Leonard Martin, CSsR

When the military took over the government of Brazil in 1964, the Catholic bishops, as a body, welcomed the new regime as the saviour of the country from communism, from the corruption of elected politicians and from inflation. History, however, taught the bishops a sharp lesson.[1] Scenes such as the following recounted by Cardinal Arns of São Paulo began to multiply. He tells how, one morning, two ladies came to see him in his office. The younger of the two put a ring on the table in front of him and said: 'This is my husband's wedding ring. He disappeared ten days ago. I found it this morning on the door-step. What does it mean? Is it a sign that he is dead, or is it a message that I should continue looking for him?'[2] Seminarians, priests and nuns began to be included among those who were arrested, tortured and killed.[3] The bishops began to change their minds. Far worse than the *threat* of communism was the *reality* of arbitrary arrest, torture and systematic state terrorism at the service of international capitalism. Corruption in public life continued. Inflation increased. The Second Vatican Council also took place, nudging the Catholic Church in Brazil into a new awareness of its nature and its mission. Change was on the way, and with it came conflict. What we hope to look at here are some of the changes and some of the conflict.

I. PARADIGM SHIFTS IN THE BRAZILIAN CHURCH: 1500–1968

The Catholic Church came to Brazil with the Portuguese explorers in 1500. Ever since, it has been the dominant religious tradition, even though, in recent times especially, a great variety of other religious traditions is also to be found. During the four and a half centuries which preceded the period we hope to examine, the Catholic Church in Brazil underwent a number of changes which we might characterise as 'paradigm shifts'.[4] In my own view, two periods of relative stability can be discerned, each followed by a period of conflict as alternative ways of being Church are tried out and compete with each other.

Allowing that dates in this sort of context are at best fairly accurate approximations, the first period of stability, or 'normal ecclesiology', would be roughly from 1500–1750, the period of Luzo-Brazilian Christendom, a form of medieval Christianity relatively untouched by the concerns of either the Protestant or Tridentine reforms. This paradigm of Church began to be challenged around 1750 as Enlightenment ideas and a certain form of liberalism began to filter through to Brazil. The Jesuits were expelled. Clerics became actively involved in politics both parliamentary (for example, Fr Feijó) and revolutionary (Fr Caneca, who was eventually hanged). A liberal paradigm of Church was being tried out. Before it could gain predominance, however, it began to be challenged, from about 1850 on, by a new way of being Church which can be characterised as neo-Tridentine Romanised Catholicism.

The appointment of Roman-trained bishops and the opening of seminaries in Brazil were two very important factors in the development of this paradigm. A great deal of conflict accompanied its emergence, and the famous 'Religious Question', in the early 1870s, which saw the jailing of two bishops,[5] is but one rather dramatic incident. With the coming of the Republic in 1889 and the separation of Church and State, it was 'romanised' Catholicism which flourished and became the dominant paradigm in a new period of relative stability between, roughly, 1920 and 1950. The high-point of this Neo-Christendom paradigm was the alliance between Cardinal Leme of Rio de Janeiro (the then capital of Brazil) and President Getúlio Vargas.[6]

From 1950 on, this paradigm also began to be challenged. Movements such as Catholic Action[7] and MEB (Movimento de Educação de Base)[8] began to give lay people a new awareness of their place in the Church and in society, while the foundation of the CNBB (the National Conference of the Brazilian Bishops) in 1952 also exercised a modernising influence. These tendencies towards reform and renewal were to receive the seal of approval from the Second Vatican Council, 1963–5.

The reason I have found this historical overview necessary as an introduction is because vestiges, to a greater or lesser extent, of these historical paradigms and battles are still to be found during the period we are studying. Further, it is helpful to remember that much of so-called 'popular religion' is, in fact, a form of colonial Catholicism, a battered survivor of many paradigm conflicts.[9]

II. THE CHURCH OF THE TWO CHRISTENDOMS

The first paradigm of Church active during the period 1968–79 is what we will call Paradigm One: the 'Church of the Two Christendoms'. At the beginning of the period, it is the paradigm that was dominant, although it was already under threat from the other paradigms we will treat of later. It is a way of being Church that operates out of a world-view that is basically medieval, and is marked by what J. B. Libânio terms the 'moment of the OBJECT'.[10]

On the one hand, it is a Church with its roots deep in the type of Catholicism brought to Brazil by the Portuguese at the time of the colony (1500–1822). It is strongly marked by tradition, in that it is handed on from one generation to another, and by popular piety: by devotion to the saints, by 'promessas' (promises made and fulfilled in exchange for favours from the saints), by long pilgrimages, and by certain penitential exercises.

On the other hand, it is the Church of Neo-Christendom: of what Brazilian scholars tend to call the 'romanisation'[11] process of the late nineteenth and early twentieth centuries. Its clergy, trained in seminaries developed along the Tridentine model, tended to wear the soutane wherever they went, and, especially in the interior, to become an authority figure alongside the mayor and the doctor. There was a strong emphasis on orthodox doctrine and on defending the Church from outside enemies: the Communists, the Protestants and the Spiritists. A great deal of the priest's time was devoted to administering the Sacraments: to saying Mass, to baptising, to marrying couples (many of whom would already have been living together as man and wife because of the scarcity of priests) and to hearing confessions. Popular piety continued to play an important part, though the older colonial devotions tended to be substituted by newer, imported ones such as the Sacred Heart, the Miraculous Medal, and Our Lady of Perpetual Succour. The older colonial 'irmandades' (a type of confraternity) found themselves competing with newer organisations such as the Apostolate of Prayer, the Vincent de Paul Society and the Legion of Mary. Salvation, in this scheme of things is seen, fundamentally, as saving souls for an after-life.

Because of its medieval world-view, this paradigm tends to have a static view of the cosmos, of society and of the Church, as well as a highly stratified and hierarchical one. Each person is placed in the order of things into which he or she is born. The Church is understood along the model of the perfect society composed of two classes, the clergy and the laity, the former with the task of teaching, sanctifying and ruling, the latter with the obligation of being instructed, sanctified and ruled. One of the favourite Scripture texts, especially among the better-off adherents to this paradigm when the plight of the less fortunate is brought to their attention, is: 'The poor you shall always have with you'. The poor are poor because it is God's will, and they are sanctified by patient suffering. The favoured strategy for dealing with the poor is giving alms.

The writings of Dom Antônio de Castro Mayer, who was bishop of Campos, Rio de Janeiro, during the period we are examining, provide a good example of the mind-set characteristic of this paradigm. In the pastoral letters which I have examined, his attitude is clearly authoritarian and paternal. The pre-supposition is that he is the one who knows and that his 'dear children' are precisely that, children, who should not be disturbed in their simple faith or confused, and who need to be protected from 'erroneous and dangerous interpretations' of the documents promulgated by the Second Vatican Council.[12]

His resistance to the reform movement in the Church clearly manifests itself in his opposition to the *cursilho*[13] which at the time was exercising a strong modernising influence in the Brazilian Church. He insists that the Church is an unequal society in which the pastors have the power to command, and he notes with horror that, within the *cursilho*,

> there is a tendency, evermore accentuated, to conceive of the Church as a totality whose members are distinguished by function and not precisely by dignity, and consequently there is a tendency to level all the members of the Church to the same dignity. Accordingly, on laying down the obligations (within the Cursilho) of priests and laity, the manner of writing is such that it avoids underlining the superior state which in the Church belongs to the clergy.[14]

Here we have in conflict not just two different visions of the Church but two different visions of the world. Castro Mayer's vision is aristocratic, where social prestige comes from the fact of belonging to a particular class. The *cursilhistas*, on the other hand, have a modern 'bourgeois' and technological vision of the world in which prestige comes from one's function and competence in society.

Castro Mayer was firmly rooted in the Church of Neo-Christendom which understood itself as an institution divided into two classes: those who command and those who obey. He sensed that if people are really all equal in dignity then the scheme of things with which he was familiar and with which he could cope would crumble, not only in the Church, but in society as well.

III. THE CHURCH REFORMING AND RENEWED

The second paradigm which emerges during the period under review may be called Paradigm Two: the 'Church Reforming and Renewed'. It is a Church whose world-view is that of the modern world. In Libânio's terminology, it is the 'moment of the SUBJECT'.[15] The knowing subject comes to the fore. Science, history, evolution, socio-economic and political development and democracy become key words. Inter-personal community and pastoral planning are preferred models for Church organisation. In a world 'come of age' the laity begin to clamour for a 'Church come of age' where at least the more educated among them can participate in resolving the problems facing the Church, if not democratically, at least bureaucratically.

The approach which this paradigm adopts towards the poor is very different from that of the first paradigm, and is indeed one of the key points of conflict between the two. For this second paradigm of Church, the giving or receiving of alms is considered degrading. Poverty begins to be understood as a justice issue. The solution looked to on the level of the individual is that of promoting human rights, while on the socio-economic level, the preferred strategy is development aid. It is in this context that the famous story of the fish is told. If you give a poor man a fish, he will eat it and come back tomorrow hungry. If, however, you give him a rod, and teach him to use it, he will be able to catch fish for himself every day. According to development theory, people and countries are poor, not because it is God's will – as medieval Christianity would have tended to believe – but because they are backward, lazy and uneducated. Once they start working, once they are educated, once they catch up on the developed world, poverty will disappear, human rights will be respected and all will be well.

Many factors contributed to the growing support for this paradigm within the Brazilian Church in the late 1960s and early 1970s. The opening words of Vatican II's Pastoral Constitution on the Church in the Modern World: 'The joys and the hopes, the griefs and the anxieties of the men of this age, especially those who are poor or in any way afflicted, these too are the joys and hopes, the griefs and anxieties of the followers of Christ' (G.S.1),[16] served to focus Church attention on the problems raised by the modern world. This concern with social justice was reinforced by Paul VI's letter *Populorum Progressio* published in 1967,[17] and even more so by the Medellín document of the Latin American bishops published in 1968.[18]

Official documents such as these were important because they gave official sanction to the knocking down of the huge defensive walls which the Counter-Reformation mentality had erected around the Church to protect it from Protestants and from the modern world. Even more importantly, they encouraged the members of the Church to get to know the challenges faced by the modern world and to get involved with its problems. This new awareness had within it seeds of conflict both within the Church itself and between the Church and the militarily controlled State.

One of the factors of great importance in the modernisation process was the development of the CNBB.[19] It provided the bishops with a forum for dealing with the very real differences that existed between them and gave them some experience of dealing with conflict in a democratic rather than authoritarian way. It also made possible the attempts at pastoral planning at national level which have become so much part of the Church's life-style in Brazil. Further, it provided a structure whereby the views of the bishops could be expressed authoritatively and rapidly at times of crisis, something which was to prove increasingly important.

Gradually, the official Church in Brazil took on the role of being the *voice of the poor*, speaking out for those who were deprived of any say due to the social and economic situation in which they found themselves. The bishops began talking *on behalf* of the poor and of those whose human rights were being disregarded. The emphasis was on reform, both of the Church and of society, and on the shaping of a new elite both clerical and lay which would serve the masses instead of manipulating them.

This development has to be understood in the context of the political situation of Brazil at the time, where the ideology of national security[20] held sway and where 'relative democracy' under the tutelage of the military meant, for many people, both inside and outside the Church, imprisonment, torture and/or death or exile. The gradual distancing of the institutional Church from the 1964 military coup which it had first welcomed became inevitable as proof of repression and mistreatment could no longer be ignored. Simultaneously an increasing number of bishops became acutely aware of the rapid rate at which the poor were becoming poorer.

Censorship of the media had spread a cloak of silence over the excesses of the regime. Since the bishops were one of the few groups sufficiently organised to survive in this situation, they began to break the silence and speak out. At national level, worthy of special note are *A Pastoral Communication to the People of God*,[21] published in 1976, and *Christian Demands on a Political Order*,[22] published in 1977. Such statements were to a large extent possible because a great deal was already going on at regional and grassroots level. Examples of this were two famous documents published in May 1973. One by the bishops and major superiors of the north-east of Brazil, echoing the words of the Lord to Moses in Exodus 3:7–10, was called '*I Have Heard the Clamour of my People*',[23] the other, by the bishops of the centre-west, was called *The Marginalization of a People: the Cry of a Church.*[24] The former started from the presupposition that the people had been reduced to silence, or at most to groanings, by years of oppression, so the religious authorities took it upon themselves to speak to 'Pharaoh' on behalf of those who had no voice of their own. These Church leaders, seeing and hearing the misery of their people decided to speak out *on their behalf* to those who were oppressing them. The bishops went armed not only with their theology, as they might have done in earlier times, but also with the results of sociological and economic studies to strengthen their case. Since it was a document *about* the people, but directed *towards* the civil and military authorities, little effort was made to render it intelligible to the former.

This document was important because it broke the silence that enshrouded the misery of the people. Its limitation, however, was that it was the discourse of one elite (ecclesiastical and scientific) to another elite (military, economic and political) about a third party: the ordinary people.

In this sense, the document of the bishops of the centre-west provides an interesting contrast. This document is directed to all of goodwill, and specifically 'to those who are marginalized by our society'. Since it is written by pastors and 'doctors' of theology and of the social sciences *for* the people, a certain effort is made in some passages to simulate the language of the people, as in the opening dialogue,[25] or at least to use images to illustrate the points being made. The following paragraph will give us something of the flavour of this effort with its recourse to images that lose nothing of their forcefulness for being at the same time biblical and contemporary.

> The Church is that people who meet to proclaim with the most intimate certainty: 'we are the Church'. ... That people who, together with others, struggle for the cause of a new society, of a new way of living together with others. All those who struggled are the seed of a new world, which is prepared even to rot in the soil of life (Jn. 12:24), but which rejoices in the certainty that new ears of corn will be born for the making of a new world. Up to now, in this world of money and of profit, in this world that functions like a machine for manufacturing the marginalized, these our people were a seed abandoned, a brick thrown away. But they will be the seed that will sprout and the brick that will build the world of tomorrow.[26]

The limitations of these undoubtedly modern and progressive documents were perceived bit by bit and gradually it was admitted that the people themselves, speaking in their own language, are excellent authorities on the problems arising from the poverty they live. Many bishops, priests and pastoral agents came to realise that their role was not to interpret the groans of the people to the elite that was oppressing them, but rather to help the people to put into their own words what their life-experience was teaching them. It was discovered that a first step towards liberation is to learn to speak for oneself.

In short, a new ecclesial SUBJECT was beginning to emerge. In Paradigm One, only certain authorised people were entitled to speak, the others had to listen respectfully, to learn and to obey. In Paradigm Two, the base was broadened a little to allow certain qualified lay people also to speak. A further move was on the way, however, that can be discerned in Pastoral Letters such as *On Puebla's Paths*,[27] published under the name of Dom José Brandão de

Castro, bishop of Propriá, and one of the signatories of '*I Have Heard the Clamour of my People*'. The popular and informal language of the letter is the first thing to note. The second is its structure. Of 23 pages of text, 17 are devoted to a statement of the situation in which the people of the diocese of Propriá live. This statement, however, is not the result of a scientific survey carried out by sociologists, it is rather made up of extracts taken from reports sent in by the various communities and couched, to a large extent, in the language of the people themselves.

Dom José's concern is not so much to talk himself about the conditions in which his people live as to provide them with a platform from which they can themselves speak. He insists on the dialogue nature of this letter. It is only after he has listened attentively to what others have to say that he makes his own contribution. He characterises the situation unveiled by the people as being 'anti-Christian' and states that the preferential option of the Church of Propriá is for these people:

> who are obliged to sell their labour for almost nothing; who produce, and yet have no real place in society; who suffer and moan forgotten by the plans of officialdom.[28]

It is worth observing that, in this letter, the ordinary people have conquered the right to speak and to be heard at least in relation to one subject on which they are experts: the misery they have to put up with. When it comes to interpreting the situation theologically, however, it is left to the bishop to speak. A further step needs to be taken so that the people become subjects not only of sociological discourse, but of theological discourse as well. Dom José shows himself aware of this need when he reiterates the support of the local church for the policy adopted by the diocesan bulletin and newspaper. The diocese supports:

> the writings of our popular poets, their hymns and their poetry – these are the means of communication of our oppressed people – as it also supports the writings and all the aids for evangelization which are being born from the experience with the oppressed of our Diocese.[29]

In view of these developments, it was only a matter of time before significant elements within the Brazilian Church at all levels began to suspect that the newly modernised Church, treading the path of reform and development, was inadequate for the challenges facing it. For one thing, in spite of dramatic economic development, the human rights situation deteriorated, especially during the Médici Government (1969–74). As well as that, the promised narrowing of the gap between rich and poor failed to materialise. The rich grew richer and the poor grew poorer and more numerous. It began to dawn on certain people that there is no point in providing rods and training in their use if the trainees are then sent to fish in a polluted river where the fish are either diseased or dead. It began to dawn on them that they were poor, and getting poorer, not because God wanted it so, and not because they were lazy and uneducated, but because the rich countries and their local allies needed it so in order to continue rich. The theory of dependence was born, and along with it a commitment of many, inside and outside the Church, to work to overthrow the social and economic *structures* which condemn millions to slow death by starvation and disease so that others can live in unimaginable luxury.

A new paradigm of Church was beginning to emerge.

IV. THE LIBERATING CHURCH OF THE PEOPLE

Paradigm Three, the 'Liberating Church of the People', is a way of perceiving the Church which owes a great deal to the conciliar concept of the Church as the People of God.[30] It is also a way of talking about the Church that ecclesiastics who subscribe to either of the other two paradigms find disconcerting and even threatening. When lay people speak of the Church in the context of Paradigm One: the 'Church of the Two Christendoms', they almost invariably are referring to the clergy and religious. 'They' are the Church. In the modernised Church of the second paradigm, the 'them and us' vocabulary is softened somewhat as a controlled participation is permitted to some of the more 'trustworthy' laity along the lines of the model of 'relative democracy' greatly favoured by the Brazilian military dictatorship. In the third paradigm, however, people say quite freely: '*We* are the Church', and if it is our Church, we are entitled to expect that our priests and our bishops will defend our interests and not those of the people and structures who thrive at the expense of our misery and in total disregard for the gospel values of justice and fraternal concern. It is not a question of setting up a lay people's Church independent of the clergy – as is sometimes suggested[31] – it is rather a question of insisting on the need for the priests and bishops to share more closely the life, the hopes, the privations and the struggles of their people. It is seen as just as important for the bishop to be in communion with his people as for the people to be in communion with their bishop.

This third paradigm of Church is profoundly concerned with social issues. It considers its world-view to be post-modern (it belongs to the 'moment of the SOCIAL',[32] to return to Libânio's terminology), and is searching for models of society and the Church which go beyond liberal, representative democracy (whether 'relative' or not). Such models would hopefully open up to all, and not just to an economically or culturally privileged elite, possibilities of genuine participation and fraternal communion.

This paradigm is not content simply to give alms to alleviate the worst excesses of poverty, nor is it content with piecemeal reforms which benefit a few while masking the mechanisms that generate impoverishment. A radical dismantling of sinful structures is called for, so that a more just and fraternal society may be constructed.

This way of being Church is marked by a preferential option for the materially poor, not simply as a question of strategy, but because such a preferential option is perceived as an integral part of the Church's nature and mission. In this paradigm, the poor are no longer seen as mere objects of apostolic or pastoral concern. It is no longer a Church *for* the poor, but a Church *of* the poor, a Church in which the poor feel at home and have a privileged place, a Church in which they are at once evangelisers and evangelised. Here there is no need for anyone to speak on their behalf. They have conquered a space in which they are free to utter their own word and rehearse the shape of a Church that does justice to its own members.

It is in the context of this paradigm that emerges the model of Church that has come to be known as the base Christian community.[33]

V. UNDERSTANDING THE CONFLICT BETWEEN PARISH AND BASE CHRISTIAN COMMUNITY

One of the most radical changes to occur in the Brazilian Church between 1968 and 1979 was in the way the parish structures were modified. In some places, the base Christian communities (henceforth referred to as CEBs) became the fundamental nuclei of completely restructured parishes, while in other places they were ignored, discouraged and even banned. The various paradigms of Church operative during our period, and which we have already looked at sketchily, provide us with a framework for perceiving more clearly what was going on.

We have identified, so far, three fairly distinct paradigms. The next step is to identify the various wings within each paradigm with its corresponding model of parish.

At this stage, perhaps the best way to proceed is by means of an example: the prelacy of Miracema do Norte, in the interior of the state of Goiás. In the early 1970s, a great deal of the parish work followed the model of the 'desobriga' (visits by the priest to the many isolated communities scattered through the bush). This would be an example of Paradigm One:One (P 1:1): the Church of Luso-Brazilian Christendom. According to this mentality, an enormous territory – one of the parishes I worked in covered an area of 18 700 square kilometres – is entrusted to a priest and he is responsible for the sacramentalisation of the inhabitants of that region, which is then called a parish. The priest normally lives in the principal town of the municipality, and several times a year, he visits the scattered communities of the 'sertão'. The trip would normally be done by jeep or mule, though sometimes also by boat. Especially in the early 1970s, the routine followed would have been along the following lines.

The priest would arrive towards dusk and would be welcomed by the owner of the house where he would stay and by the people from round about. This would often involve an elaborate ritual with fireworks and galloping on horse-back, in strict formation, the last kilometre or so to the house. Once the reception was over, the owner of the house would lead the priest and his guide to the nearby stream to wash. Then came dinner. The men sat at the table, the women ate afterwards in the kitchen. Then work began. There was a 'reza' (prayers, usually the Rosary) and a sermon, followed by confessions which would often go on past midnight. The few hours of sleep in the hammock pass quickly, as by four o'clock the women are already at work in the kitchen. By five o'clock, the day's work has already begun. The priest notes the names of those who are to be baptised – one of the first steps towards lay ministry was when this task was taken over by a lay-helper! – and when all is ready, Mass begins, usually celebrated in the shade of a tree out in the yard. Then come the weddings and the baptisms. The activities would usually go on till about eleven o'clock, when there would be time for lunch and a brief rest before heading off for the next house at around one o'clock to begin things all over again.

The social structure on these isolated farms, even to this day, is predominantly patriarchal and the religion of these people tends to be traditional and family-centred. They are baptised, get married before the priest, occasionally go to confession and communion at the time of 'desobriga', but their level of religious instruction is minimal.

As the ecclesiologies of Vatican II and Medellín began to influence the priests who did the 'desobriga' their aims and methods perceptibly changed.

During a 'desobriga' in which I participated in the prelacy of Miracema, in the municipality of Itacajá, in June 1978, the sacramentalist emphasis of the earlier part of the decade had practically disappeared. The traditional 'reza' continued, as did the celebration of the sacraments of penance, baptism, matrimony, and of the eucharist under the tree in the yard. But now, the emphasis was on *evangelisation*: in the preaching, in the preparation for the sacraments, which before was practically unheard of, and in meetings held, especially with the men, to discuss the problems of the place, and especially land problems, which, within a few years were to become particularly violent in that region.[34] Another difference worth noting was that while previously the criterion for choosing the house for Mass was the ability of the owner to feed the people who would turn up, the criterion now was whether the house belonged to people who participated in a Christian community that came together regularly to celebrate the weekly liturgy of the Word, and one of the chief aims of the 'desobriga' now was to train and encourage the leaders of these communities. Indeed, a second day was added to each visit with this particular aim in mind.

From one point of view, one of the advantages that came from these people being abandoned for so long is that they began the transition from Paradigm One to Paradigm Three without having to suffer the intermediary crises and conflicts. Neither the reforms of Trent nor of Vatican II had reached them. Their first experience of any sort of systematic evangelisation was in the context of the social and communitarian model of the Liberating Church of the People.

The transition in many other parts of Brazil was not, however, so peacefully achieved. In places where the Neo-Christendom style of Church (P 1:2) had been successfully implanted it was not so easily displaced. The model of parish that corresponds to this wing of Paradigm One is highly centralised and clerical. In the words of Medina and Oliveira, it is that parish:

> in which the parish priest, juridically nominated by the bishop, administers the sacraments, organizes and determines the parochial activities, bases his authority exclusively on his juridical investiture, and does not share it with the faithful, not even with those most closely linked to the parish activities. The only limit on the parish priest's power is his subordination to the bishop. The parishioners can exercise no control over decisions to be taken. They confine themselves to carrying out the tasks and activities thought of and decided upon by the parish priest. The function of the parish priest, therefore, institutionalized itself as that of boss and administrator and not as pastor.[35]

This is the model of parish in which initiatives come from the top down and power is concentrated in the hands of the cleric. It is a highly institutionalist system and resistant to change. The fundamental role of the laity here is to obey. Law and order are values highly prized, and legitimacy is sought in a selective appeal to tradition. Though this model is firmly but gently rejected by Puebla,[36] it continued to exist in many parishes throughout Brazil during the period in question.

Paradigm Two: the 'Church Reforming and Renewed' is perhaps the one which gained most practical support in the period between Medellín and Puebla. In this case as well, two wings can be discerned: elitist-technocratic wing (P 2:1) and a democratic-communitarian wing (P 2:2). As far as the parish is concerned, the two wings would have in common their focus on *modernisation*, with its emphasis on development, secularisation, personalism and community. Both would be reformist in ecclesiology and politics, favouring gradual and irenic changes which avoid conflict. While they would frequently be agreed as to their objectives, the methods they would choose tend to differ.

The parish along the model of P 2:1 has certain distinctive characteristics. Firstly, it tends to distinguish between the (ignorant) masses on the one hand, and the minority of committed believers (an enlightened elite) on the other. Secondly, efficiency is highly valued. Thirdly, planning is considered very important. Fourthly, among the elite, there is a strong tendency to secularisation and with it a disdain for the popular religiosity of the ignorant masses.

The type of planning typical of this model is pyramidal, with decisions coming from the top down. The elite on top (those who know) decides for the mass of parishioners (those on the bottom who do not know) which are the parish's priorities, what its objectives and which are the means to be used. The social scientists are invited to study the lives of the people. New value is given to the life-situation as a factor in pastoral action, but in this type of planning the ordinary people (the masses) are merely an object of study, and do not participate as subjects in the analysis of their reality. The main defect in this type of pastoral planning, elaborated by the few to be executed by the others, is that it does not work, as can be seen from dioceses or parishes where it was tried. People who are not consulted in the process of elaborating a plan are unlikely to interiorise the objectives outlined and, consequently, are not inclined to sacrifice themselves achieving them.

If we look at the liturgical reform favoured by this model, we find that it tends to imitate European patterns which grew out of the needs of the French and the Dutch rather than out of the needs of Brazilian culture. Processions, saints, candles are all marginalised in this type of reformed parish. The enlightened elite feels itself obliged to demystify and demythologise the confused and superstitious religion of the masses.

The parish council, as it was implanted in certain places, is an example of this reform of the type P 2:1.[37] Often, the decision to form a council was the parish priest's, and the members were chosen and nominated by him. It is a modernising institution in that it permits greater participation of at least some lay people, and in that it favours a more efficient administration of the parish, taking advantage of the technical talents, for example in the financial area, of the council members. The authority of the parish priest, as the one in charge, is, however, carefully safeguarded.

The reform of a parish along the lines of P 2:2 follows a line that is more personalist and communitarian, and is less technocratic. It is a fairly ecclesio-centric model, though it has a definite openness to the problems of the world of its day. Suspicious of authoritarianism, it is influenced by political and economic theories of democracy, development and progress. It seeks to develop structures in the Church which would promote greater equality, liberty and brotherhood and greater participation on the part of its members. The parish priest is no longer the 'owner' of the parish. He becomes more a co-ordinator of a great variety of activities. He still exercises an amount of control, but in a much more indirect manner.

The lasting strength of this model has been its emphasis on community as the basis for parish life. Indeed, I have argued elsewhere[38] that the model of basic community proposed by Medellín is that of P 2:2. By way of summary, we can say that the model of parish here proposed is that of a confederation of base Christian communities. It emphasises the communitarian aspect, it insists on ecclesial communion and, in general, understands 'base' as the base of the ecclesial pyramid.

During the long journey from Medellín to Puebla, Paradigm Three: the 'Liberating Church of the People' appeared. One of the factors which facilitated its emergence was a changing perception of the meaning of the word 'base'. For P 2:2 'base' refers primarily to the 'base' of the Church, while in the P 3, it refers to those who are not only at the base of the Church but also at the base of society: the poor, those who are marginalised socially and politically. Indeed, there are those who are quite insistent that it refers only to those.[39]

Once again, two wings within this third way of being Church can be distinguished, P 3:1: the secularist-marxist wing, and P 3:2: the participation-communion wing.

Because of its nature, P 3:1 did not tend historically to produce a model of parish, though it had immense impact of parish life. It was the expression of two very strong tendencies: secularisation and an option for the creation of a better world. It was a movement which tended to diminish the importance of doctrinal differences between the members of the various Christian churches on the one hand, and between Christians and non-Christians, especially marxists, on the other, in the context of a process which emphasised unity in the realisation of a task assumed in common. It was weak on institutional structuring and tended to instability. Its members were ruthlessly persecuted by the military, especially after 1964, and it never received whole-hearted support from the main body of the Church.[40]

The great strength of P 3:1 was its sensibility to the Brazilian situation, the priority it gave to praxis, and its commitment to the radical changing of unjust social structures. Its secularism, which tended to slacken its ecclesial bonds, was one of its weak points. Another was its intellectualised marxism which easily led to an elitism which manipulated the religiosity of the people while despising it.

The emergence of the type of parish which welcomed the base Christian communities was a clear sign of the growing strength of P 3:2. A number of factors facilitated this growth. Firstly, there was a rediscovery of the value of popular religion: of processions, of statues, of the non-verbal in human expression and communication. This functioned as a counter-balance to the secularisation trend already referred to and which tended to a certain elitism on the one hand and to increase the alienation of the ordinary people on the other. This discovery was on the part of the priests and pastoral agents. Secondly, there was the discovery of the bible by the ordinary people, the discovery that the bible belonged not only to the church-institution but also to the church-people. The contribution of Carlos Mesters to this is worthy of mention.[41] His writings, in popular language and full of images, helped the members of many CEBs to conjugate those two fundamental elements: their own lives and the bible, to develop a whole methodology for confronting the challenges of life with the demands of faith. A third factor was the growing awareness of the need for Christians to be involved politically and of the potential political strength of the CEBs. For the Christians of the CEBs there is no dichotomy between faith and politics. They assume their religion as a constitutive element of the political action of the people and not as a stage to be superceded as in the rationalist-marxist interpretation. As Clodovis Boff puts it, 'Politics is not something added on to faith, it rather flows from it'.[42] The people see the situation they are suffering in the light of their faith. From this confrontation arise ethical demands, some of which are political.

From our rapid survey of the variety of models of parish and even of base Christian communities to be found during the period we are examining, it is not surprising that a great deal of conflict is experienced between neighbouring parishes, where the parish priests in question adopt radically divergent policies, or within parishes, where one group favours one model, other groups their own preferences. Conflict there is in plenty, but creativity also abounds. Base Christian communities are undoubtedly a threat to certain models of parish which concentrate power and which limit participation. However, to those parishes which are prepared to risk ample participation they tend to bring the blessings of robust communion.

VI. CONCLUSION

A Church marked by immense vitality is perhaps one way to describe the Catholic Church in Brazil during the period between Medellín and Puebla. It is a Church disturbed by the call to do justice. The story of the various paradigms is, in a sense, the story of how various people and groups perceived that call and sought to answer it. It is a Church in which the lay people are more and more discovering their rightful dignity and role and where priests and bishops are discovering the excitement and challenges of being servants of the people rather than their lords. It is a Church that, in spite of persecution from without and of dissent and conflict from within, managed to keep alive in the hearts of many people, especially among the oppressed and down-trodden, the hope that their salvation, their liberation is at hand.

NOTES

1. Cf. Thomas C. Bruneau, *The Political Transformation of the Brazilian Catholic Church* (New York and London: Cambridge University Press, 1974) pp. 177–216, for his treatment of the origins of the conflict between Church and State at this period.
2. Dom Paulo Cardenal Evaristo Arns, 'Prefácio', in *Brasil: Nunca Mais* (Petrópolis: Vozes, 1985) p. 11.
3. Cf. CEDI (Centro Ecumênico de Documentação e Informação), 'Repressão na Igreja no Brasil: Reflexo de uma situação de opressão 1968–1978', in *Cadernos do CEAS*, n° 60 (março–abril de 1979) 56–78.
4. The theory of paradigms relied on in this chapter is a development of the theory elaborated by T. S. Kuhn in *The Structure of Scientific Revolutions*, 2nd edn, enlarged (Chicago and London: University of Chicago Press, 1975), and an adaptation of it to ecclesiology, following up a suggested application of the theory in Avery Dulles, *Models of the Church* (Garden City, New York: Doubleday, 1974) pp. 26–30. My adaptation of paradigm theory to ecclesiology and its use in the analysis of the Brazilian Church is to be found in Leonard Martin, CSsR, *Rumos da Igreja no Brasil: o Método de Paradigmas como Instrumento de Análise das Mudanças entre Medellín e Puebla* [Thesis] (Pontifícia Universidade Católica do Rio de Janeiro, 1980).

   As far as the history of the Church in Brazil from 1500–1900 is concerned, two volumes of the history of the Church in Latin America brought out by CEHILA are of particular importance: *História General da Igreja na América Latina: História da Igreja no Brasil: Ensaio de Interpretação a partir do povo. Primeira Época*, Tomo II. (Petrópolis: Vozes, 1977), and *História General da Igreja na América Latina: História da Igreja no Brasil: Ensaio de Interpretação a partir do povo. Segunda Época: A Igreja no Brasil no século XIX*, Tomo II/2 (Petrópolis: Vozes, 1980).

   A further two articles, both by the same author, which shed some light on historical paradigm shifts are Riolando Azzi, 'Elementos para a História do Catolicismo Popular', in *Revista Eclesiástica Brasileira*, 36 (março de 1976) pp. 95–103, and 'A Igreja do Brasil na Defesa dos Direitos Humanos', in *REB*, 37 (março de 1977) pp. 106–42.

5. Cf. Antônio Carlos Villaça, *História da Questão Religiosa no Brasil* (Rio de Janeiro: Francisco Alves Editora, 1974).
6. For an overview of the situation in the first half of the twentieth century, see Ralph Della Cava, 'Igreja e Estado no Brasil do Século XX: Sete Monografias Recentes sobre o Catolicismo Brasileiro, 1916–64', in *Estudos de CEBRAP*, n.º 12 (abril–maio–junho de 1975) 5–52.
7. In 1983, *Revista Eclesiástica Brasileira* published two articles to commemorate the Golden Jubilee of Brazilian Catholic Action which are worth referring to: Dom Marcelo Pinto Carvalheira, 'Momentos Históricas e Desdobramentos da Ação Católica Brasileira', in *REB*, 43 (março de 1983) pp. 10–28, and Scott Mainwaring, 'A JOC e o Surgimento da Igreja na Base (1958–1970), in *REB*, 43, pp. 29–92.
8. Cf. Emanuel de Kadt, *Catholic Radicals in Brazil* (London and New York: Oxford University Press, 1970).
9. Cf. José Comblin, 'Para uma Tipologia do Catolicismo no Brasil', in *REB*, 28 (março de 1968) pp. 46–73. This article, published at the beginning of the period we are reviewing, provides evidence of a growing awareness that Catholicism in Brazil is far from monolithic, that it is indeed made up of a complex mosaic of different traditions.
10. J. B. Libânio, SJ, *Formação da Consciência Crítica: 1. Subsídios Filosófico-Culturais*, 3rd edn (Petrópolis/Rio de Janeiro: Vozes/CRB, 1982) pp. 33–58.
11. Cf., for example, Pedro A. Ribeiro de Oliveira, *Religião e Dominação de Classe: Gênese, Estrutura e Função do Catolicismo Romanizado no Brasil* (Petrópolis: Vozes, 1985).
12. Dom Antônio de Castro Mayer, bispo de Campos, *Carta Pastoral: Considerações a propósito da aplicação dos documentos promulgados pelo Concílio Vaticano II* (São Paulo: Editora Vera Cruz, 1966) p. 4.
13. Although founded before Vatican II, and in spite of its name 'Cursilhos de Cristandade', the *cursilho* in Brazil was a reform movement in the spirit of the Council. Cf., for example, the book by the founder, Dom Juan Hervas, *Os Cursos de Cristandade: Instrumento de Renovação Cristã* (Lisboa: Secretariado Nacional dos Cursos de Cristandade, 1965), also an unsigned article, 'A História dos Cursilhos no Brasil', transcribed from the official organ of the movement, *Alavanca*, of December 1971, in *SEDOC*, vols 6–62 (julho de 1973) cols 75–82. For a critical study of the movement in Brazil, cf. Otto Dana, *Os Deuses Dançantes: um Estudo dos Cursilhos de Cristandade* (Petrópolis: Vozes, 1975).
14. Dom Antônio de Castro Mayer, 'Carta Pastoral: Cursilhos de Cristandade', in *SEDOC*, vols 5–61 (junho de 1973) col. 1496.
15. Libânio, *Formação da Consciência Crítica*, pp. 59–83.
16. Council documents are quoted in the version of Walter M. Abbott, SJ (ed.), *The Documents of Vatican II* (London and Dublin: Geoffrey Chapman, 1966).

17. The English version is published by the Catholic Truth Society (London: 1967).
18. Second General Conference of Latin American Bishops, *The Church in the Present-Day Transformation of Latin America in the Light of the Council: Conclusions*, 3rd edn (Washington DC: Secretariat for Latin America, National Conference of Catholic Bishops, 1979).
19. The standard work on the origins and early development of the National Conference of Bishops, at the moment, is Gervásio Fernandes de Queiroga, *CNBB – Communhão e Responsabilidade* (São Paulo: Paulinas, 1977).
20. For a critical approach to this ideology, from a Christian point of view, see José Comblin, *The Church and the National Security State* (Maryknoll, New York: Orbis Books, 1979).
21. CNBB, *Comunicação Pastoral ao Povo de Deus*, 3rd edn (São Paulo: Documentos da CNBB/8, Paulinas, 1977).
22. CNBB, *Exigências Cristãs de uma Ordem Política* (São Paulo: Documentos da CNBB/10, Paulinas, 1977).
23. Bispos e Superiores Religiosos Maiores do Nordeste, 'Eu Ouvi os Clamores do meu Povo', in *SEDOC*, vols 6–66 (novembro de 1973) cols 607–29.
24. Bispos do Centro-Oeste, *Marginalização de um Povo: Grito das Igrejas* (no publisher, 6 de maio de 1973) Cf. also in *SEDOC*, vols 6–69 (março de 1974) cols 993–1021.
25. Bispos do Centro-Oeste, *Marginalização de um Povo*, p. 3.
26. Ibid., pp. 39–40.
27. Dom José Brandão de Castro, CSsR, bispo de Propriá, *Nos Caminhos de Puebla: Carta Pastoral* (Propriá: 1979).
28. Ibid.
29. Ibid.
30. Chapter 2 of the Dogmatic Constitution on the Church, *Lumen Gentium*, goes under the title 'The People of God'.
31. Bonaventure Kloppenburg, OFM, *The People's Church: A Defense of my Church* (Chicago: Franciscan Herald Press, 1978) represents an interesting example of the work of a theologian who, through his writings, did much to promote the shift from P:1 to P:2, and who then dug in to resist with all his might the further shift to P:3.
32. Cf. Libânio, *Formacão da Consciência Crítica*, pp. 84–102.
33. The bibliography on this phenomenon, as it emerged in Brazil, is quite extensive, even if we confine ourselves to the period we are examining. The early 1970s saw the articulation of the Basic Ecclesial Communities in Brazil as a decidedly ecclesial phenomenon. This is best exemplified by the series of national encounters which began in 1975. Six took place, in Vitória in 1975 and in 1976, in João Pessoa in 1978, in Itaici in 1981, in Canindé in 1983 and near Goiânia in 1986. The documentation associated with these meetings has been published by *SEDOC* Vitória (1975) vol. 7 (maio de 1975). This material is also to be had in book form: *Comunidades Eclesiais de Base: uma Igreja que Nasce do Povo* (Petrópolis: Vozes, 1975). Vitória (1976): vols 9–95 (outubro de 1976) and vols 9–96 (novembro de 1976). João Pessoa

(1978): vols 11–115 (outubro de 1978) and vols 11–118 (janeiro–fevereiro de 1979). Cf. also J. B. Libânio, 'Igreja que se Liberta: 3° Encontro Intereclesial de Comunidades de Base', in *Síntese* (N.F.), n° 14 (setembro–dezembro de 1978) pp. 93–110. Itaici (1981) vols 14–144 (setembro de 1981). Canindé (1983): vols 16–165 (outubro de 1983). Cf. also Frei Betto, *CEBs, Rumo à Nova Sociedade: o 5° Encontro Intereclesial das Comunidades Eclesiais de Base, Canindé, julho de 1983.* (São Paulo: Paulinas, 1983) for an account of the meeting in reasonably popular language. For an account of the style of liturgy developed by these communities, see Leonard Martin, CSsR, 'Um Povo que Reza com os Pés: os Gestos e Símbolos das CEBs no 5° Encontro Intereclesial Canindé', in *A Vida em Cristo e na Igreja*, n° 59 (setembro–outubro 1983) pp. 1–7.

For a more detailed bibliography for the development of base Christian communities in Brazil, 1968–1979, see my *Rumos da Igreja no Brasil*, p. 285 note 249.

34. The Catholic Church's pastoral involvement in conflicts over the right of ordinary people to live on, to own, and to work the land became more and more pronounced over the years. In the mid-1970s, the National Conference of Bishops published two studies as an aid to those involved in this particular form of pastoral action: *Pastoral da Terra*, Estudos da CNBB/11 (São Paulo: Paulinas, 1976), and *Pastoral da Terra: Posse e Conflitos*, Estudos da CNBB/13 (São Paulo: Paulinas, 1977). The Pastoral Commission for Land was set up in 1975, and to commemorate its ten years of activity a useful little book was produced, a collection of articles which reflect on the theological and ecclesial significance of such a pastoral initiative: Comissão Pastoral da Terra, *Conquistar a Terra, Reconstruir a Vida: CPT – Dez Anos de Caminhada* (Petrópolis: Vozes, 1985).
35. C. A. de Medina and Pedro A. Ribeiro de Oliveira, *Autoridade e Participação: Estudo sociológico da Igreja Católica* (Petrópolis/Rio de Janeiro: Vozes/CERIS, 1973) pp. 43–4.
36. 'All this is a process, in which we still find broad sectors posing resistance of various sorts. This calls for understanding and encouragement, as well as great docility to the Holy Spirit. What we need now is still more clerical openness to the activity of the laity and the overcoming of pastoral individualism and self-sufficiency' *Puebla* #627. The rejection of this P 1:2 model of parish is even more clearly stated a few lines further on: 'But we still find attitudes that pose an obstacle to the dynamic thrust of renewal. Primacy is given to administrative work over pastoral care. There is routinism and a lack of preparation for the sacraments. Authoritarianism is evident among some priests. And sometimes the parish closes in on itself, disregarding the overall apostolic demands of a serious nature' *Puebla* #633. Note: the document is quoted in the following edition: Third General Conference of Latin American Bishops, *Puebla, Evangelization at Present and in the Future of Latin America: Conclusions*, Official English Edition (Slough: St Paul Publications, 1980).
37. Cf. my *Rumos da Igreja no Brasil*, p. 248.

38. Ibid., pp. 249–52 for a discussion of this question.
39. Cf. Leonardo Boff, OFM, *Eclesiogênese: as comunidades eclesiais de base reinventam a Igreja* (Petrópolis: Vozes, 1977, p. 18); Clodovis Boff, OSM, 'A influência política das Comunidades Eclesiais de Base (CEBs)', in *SEDOC*, vols 11–118 (janeiro–fevereiro de 1979) col. 806, and also Alvaro Barreiro, SJ, *Comunidades Eclesiais de Base e Evangelização dos Pobres* (São Paulo: Loyola, 1977) p. 21.
40. Cf. De Kadt, *Catholic Radicals in Brazil*, and also Charles Antoine, *Church and Power in Brazil* (Maryknoll, New York: Orbis Books, 1973).
41. Carlos Mesters' writings are numerous. A good introduction to this thought on the role of the bible in the Church's life is a relatively recent collection of his essays: *Flor Sem Defesa: uma explicação da Biblía a partir do Povo* (Petrópolis: Vozes, 1983).
42. Clodovis Boff, 'A influência política das Comunidades Eclesiais de Base', col. 802.

17 The Catholic Church and Politics in Chile

Brian H. Smith

INTRODUCTION

Since the mid-60s the Chilean Catholic Church has had to adjust its pastoral strategies to three very different political regimes – reformist Christian Democratic (1964–70), Democratic Socialist (1970–3), and authoritarian military (1973–). While there has been a major attempt by the hierarchy to promote an 'evangelical-pastoral' strategy of Church influence in society since the last years of the Christian Democratic era (from 1968 on), others have continued to characterise the Church by including traces of a 'neo-Christendom' approach and an emerging 'liberation theology' model.[1] These contrasting models for Church action in society are a reflection both of the socio-political challenges to the Chilean Church in a rapidly changing society and the varying interpretations of those challenges made at different levels inside the Church. In this chapter I shall examine how Church leaders have interpreted the political context in each of the three eras in Chile since the early 1960s, what adaptive strategies they have taken in each period, and what the consequences of such strategies have been both for society and the Church itself.

THE CHURCH DURING THE RISE AND DECLINE OF CHRISTIAN DEMOCRACY (1964–70)

After Independence (1810) and up until the early twentieth century, the Chilean Church (like its national counterparts in the rest of Latin America) followed a 'Christendom' strategy of influencing society. This entailed a close alliance with upper-class landed elites and a structural linkage with the State (whose policies heavily reflected the interests of these same groups). Clerical salaries and expenses of Church schools were paid by the State, the Church tacitly supported the existing social order, and it relied on its influence with landed elites and the Conservative Party to protect and promote Christian values and interests in society.[2]

In the late nineteenth and early twentieth centuries, however, the power of the Conservative Party and its prime supporters, the landed gentry, was declining with the emergence of urban middle (and small working) classes who were predominantly secular, and even anti-clerical, in orientation. This resulted in the erosion of some Church privileges in society (control over civil registries, cemeteries and so on), and in the period after World War I finally resulted in a formal separation of Church and State (1925) after a political coalition (the Liberal Alliance) representing the interests of these new groups gained executive power (1920). This separation, however, was handled relatively peacefully in comparison to much of the rest of Latin America due to moderate leadership on both sides and intricate negotiations between the Vatican and the new liberal coalition government.[3]

After the separation of Church and State in 1925 the bishops (with strong encouragement from the Vatican) distanced the Church officially from its traditional close alliance with the Conservative Party and from upper-class landed elites. The Chilean hierarchy (also with Rome's blessing) authorised in 1931 the establishment of Catholic Action programmes to train lay men and women from the emerging urban middle class in the social principles of Catholicism elaborated by Pope Leo XIII (*Rerum Novarum*, 1891) and Pope Pius XI (*Quadragesimo Anno*, 1931). Many of these Catholic leaders engaged in new Church-sponsored efforts to help the poor, and also became the founders of new political parties – the Falange Nacional in 1938, and its successor, the Christian Democratic Party (Partido Demócrata Cristiano, PDC) in 1957.

Throughout the 1930s, 1940s and 1950s, however, these reform efforts in Church and society affected only a minority of the population. The majority of Catholics did not belong to Catholic Action or participate in any of its new social action programmes and continued to vote for the Right. Moreover, the Conservative and Liberal parties still exercised sufficient veto power in Congress to block major structural changes in society, especially land and tax reforms.

However, in the early 1960s this neo-Christian strategy (significant Church social action coupled with application of Church social teachings in politics through cadres of committed middle-class laity) became dominant among significant numbers of Church leaders and laity alike. The context which precipitated this was a sharp decline in the Right's electoral strength and the image of the new Christian Democratic Party among many (both in Church and in society at large) as the only political movement capable of stopping the Socialist and Communist Parties who were gaining ground electorally in the late 1950s and early 1960s. Amidst growing fears of a leftist victory in the 1964 presidential election, centrist groups came to dominate policies in both Church and politics with tacit 'crisis support' from conservatives in both sectors bent on stopping the Left at any price.

By 1962 statements of the hierarchy began to focus more on structural rather than individual moral causes of poverty (personal egoism, laziness and so on). While denouncing both marxist and *laissez-faire* capitalist solutions, they urged such major economic changes as land and tax reforms, more investment in consumer rather than luxury goods, and an end to the flight of private capital out of Chile.[4] In addition, Church-sponsored pastoral and social programmes in poor areas expanded, aided significantly by the influx of foreign Church support into Chile (mission personnel and money). Such projects included new labour unions in rural areas, educational and technical training programmes for peasants and workers, and low-income housing co-operatives.[5] Increasing numbers of Catholic laity from both the middle and working classes participated in these projects giving the Church a new image as a significant and consistent force for social change.

One result of such a neo-Christian approach to society by the Church was a major ideological and structural boost for the Christian Democratic Party. The moral weight of the Church was definitely behind reform but explicitly against marxism, which meant that Catholics in a two-person race were practically under moral obligation to vote for the PDC presidential candidate, Eduardo Frei, in 1964 rather than the only other viable candidate, Salvador Allende, supported by a coalition of communists and socialists. Frei won easily with 56 per cent of the vote. Moreover, those lay leaders who remained active in the Church's pastoral and social programmes so identified with the PDC that as the party began to undergo internal ideological conflicts in 1967 these spilled over into pastoral programmes (especially among youth) causing severe polarisation within the Church. When upper-income Catholics (who had supported Frei in 1964 primarily as a way of stopping Allende) became disillusioned with his administration this was becoming a definite liability, since it was clear the Left might surpass the PDC and win the next presidential election in 1970. In fact, some Catholics in leftist sectors of the

PDC bolted from the PDC in May 1969 and formed a new party (MAPU) that subsequently announced support for Salvador Allende in the approaching 1970 election.[6]

In the face of all of these events the hierarchy in 1968 began a shift away from a 'neo-Christendom' strategy to an 'evangelical-pastoral' approach to Church-society relations. They de-emphasised the importance for the Church of carrying out social projects on behalf of the poor, since the PDC government was doing this more effectively and on a grander scale. Their public social statements, while still urging structural rather than personal moral solutions to poverty, did not rule out more radical changes than those espoused by Christian Democrats and did not reiterate Church condemnations of marxism. Finally, they authorised the formation of new Church structures at the neighbourhood level – base Christian communities – to concentrate primarily on the religious formation of lay Catholics in all social classes through such activities as bible study, shared prayer, preparation for sacramental worship, and lay leadership training in each of these areas. While these CEBs (varying in membership from 20 to 50 persons) were to include in their focus some commitment to justice as well, this was to occur not so much through Church sponsorship of socio-economic projects as through the active engagement by CEB members in secular service organisations in their communities or at the regional or national levels.[7]

Hence, with the approaching 1970 election, the hierarchy placed the Church in a more neutral political position without sacrificing its official commitment to further social change on behalf of the poor. Simultaneously the bishops urged a more exclusively religious emphasis in Church ministries. They felt this would not only be a prudent choice for the short run, given the uncertainty of the political context, but in the long run keep the Church freer of the negative consequences of partisan politics and also provide it with more credibility as it focused on its primary mission – religious evangelisation of all.

Both Cardinal Silva and the president of the episcopal conference during the 1970 presidential campaign declared that the Church favoured no party or candidate, and that clerics should not publicly support any political ideology or movement. Cardinal Silva's remarks, made on national television six weeks before the election, also stressed that the Church wanted to be a home for all Chileans regardless of political persuasion and thereby provide a source of unity for the country.[8]

The Left (Popular Unity coalition – UP) for its part played down its traditional anticlerical sentiments as the election approached, made overtures to the progressive Christian vote (accepting MAPU – Movimiento de Acción Popular Unitaria, United Popular Action Movement – into its electoral coalition), and included in its platform commitments to religious freedom and respect for traditional constitutional processes during a transition to socialism. In the closely-contested election on 4 September 1970 Salvador Allende, the UP candidate, won a plurality of 36.2 per cent, while the candidate of the Right, Jorge Alessandri, gained 34.9 per cent and the Christian Democrat, Radomiro Tomic, 27.8 per cent (with 1.1 per cent of the ballots blank or void). Moreover, the Left's support among practising Catholics in Santiago jumped from 10 per cent in 1964 to 22 per cent in 1970.[9] Severe political tensions with the Left were thus avoided by Church leaders during the campaign and, in turn, overtures to Catholics clearly paid off for the Left in such a close election.

THE CHURCH AND A MARXIST COALITION GOVERNMENT (1970–3)

The new political party neutrality of the official Church that characterised the last two years of the Frei regime and the 1970 electoral campaign carried over into the new marxist coalition administration. During the delicate six-week transition period (after the popular election in early September and before congressional confirmation of the new president in late October), there were efforts by the CIA and the Chilean Right to prevent Allende's becoming president through illegal and even violent means. The Catholic bishops spoke out clearly during this time in favour of constitutionalism, refused to denounce Allende, and thus contributed to an atmosphere propitious for dialogue between the UP and the PDC which resulted in Allende's confirmation in Congress on 24 October. Moreover, during the first two and a half years of Allende's presidency, on several occasions the Episcopal Conference issued public statements supporting continued structural transformations in the economy favouring the poor (without specifically endorsing the UP) and denouncing such tactics of the irresponsible opposition as black market profiteering, the accelerated export of capital, and sabotage.[10]

The UP administration, in turn, during this period respected its commitments to respect constitutional processes (including religious freedom), and also accepted an additional split off from the PDC into its ruling coalition in 1971 (MIC – Movimiento Izquierda Cristiana, Christian Left Movement). Allende even increased state subsidies to Church-sponsored schools and universities (originally legalised in the mid-1950s by conservative coalition governments) to provide more educational opportunities for low-income sectors of the population.[11]

During the last six months of the UP government, however, Church–State relations became strained. The administration increasingly found it difficult both to control sectors of its own coalition advocating increased societal polarisation and to maintain social order amidst growing violent opposition by the Right. The regime, unable to reach a compromise with the PDC in 1972 over conditions and limits on the state sector of the economy, also continued to carry out nationalisations without congressional approval. All of these events worried the bishops, and on several occasions in 1973 they urged both government and opposition to observe the law and to compromise with each other.

Most damaging for its relations with the Church, however, was the administration's announcement of an educational reform bill affecting private schools. Soon after the stalemated parliamentary elections in March 1973 (in which the Left gained enough – 44 per cent – to prevent its congressional opponents from reaching a two-thirds majority sufficient to impeach Allende, but not a majority of its own), the administration introduced a proposal to set up a National Unified School system (ENU) requiring all public and private schools to adopt an ideology of 'socialist humanism' under state supervision. The Catholic bishops for the first time squarely confronted the regime, and publicly denounced ENU for not respecting pluralism and parental consultation (as promised in the UP's 1970 platform regarding education). The proposal, also criticised by the military and all the opposition parties, was quickly withdrawn.[12]

Moreover, some sectors at lower levels of the Church firmly opposed to Allende's policies – parents of Catholic school children, rightist and some PDC students in Catholic universities, those in control of parts of the Catholic media (especially Fr. Raúl Hasbún, director of the news department at the television station of the Catholic University of Santiago) – all bitterly clashed with government supporters in words or in street demonstrations during the last six months of Allende's term. The hierarchy, however, who articulated the official position of the Church, after the withdrawal of ENU in late March, did not use their public moral influence to undermine the regime or to encourage sedition. Right up to the military coup on

11 September, while criticising illegality and violence from whatever source, the bishops continuously supported a constitutional solution to the political stalement. Cardinal Silva himself personally attempted twice to promote effective negotiations between the administration and the PDC during Allende's last six weeks in office.[13]

Thus, while Church–State relations were strained during this final period, they never broke down. The hierarchy never ceased trying to promote dialogue and compromise among opposing political factions and refused, just as they had done in the post-election period in 1970, to legitimate those preparing to overthrow the constitutional system. The Church's freedom, moreover, except for the brief ENU episode, was never threatened by the Allende administration.

While this critical aspect of the 'evangelical-pastoral' strategy (partisan political neutrality and moral support for justice and freedom) was realised by the hierarchy during the Allende years, the other half of the strategy – sacramental preparation and religious formation of laity in small base communities at the local level of the Church – encountered serious problems. While there was no attack on CEBs by the Left while in power, mounting politicisation of society (combined with increased mobilisation efforts by all political parties) practically consumed the interests and energies of all Chileans. Political parties held meetings precisely at the times CEBs met – evenings and Sundays, the only times Chileans had free from work. Mass attendance fell off dramatically during these years with regular practice (once a month or more) among Catholics in Santiago declining from 32 per cent in 1970 to 20 per cent in 1973. Bible study, lay leadership and catechetical training programmes also did not attract significant numbers of participants.[14]

In addition, those CEBs that did function often became polarised internally along party lines, as small-group religious discussions quickly turned into political debates with biblical themes interpreted in the light of current political struggles. Some members of the lower clergy guiding CEBs – especially in working-class areas – insisted that participants be both Christian and revolutionary in their commitments. They and others formed a clerically-dominated movement, Christians for Socialism (Cristianos por el Socialismo, CpS) which included about 300 of the 3000 priests in the country, especially those who were foreigners. CpS supported socialism as the only valid option for Christians, urged their parishioners to vote for leftist parties, and frequently criticised the bishops publicly for not more definitely backing Allende. CpS and an affiliate clerical group, called 'the 200', also openly advocated the construction of a radically new Church, more independent from the bishops, more actively committed to socialism, with critical decisions made at the CEB level, and controlled by the laity and a married clergy.[15] These positions of CpS and 'the 200' clearly reflected a 'liberation theology' strategy, and radically departed from the bishops' 'evangelical-pastoral' approach both in its socio-political and religious implications.

All of these developments inside and outside the Church both short-circuited the growth of religious activities at the local level and precipitated a serious breakdown of Church unity and discipline. The bishops finally issued an official condemnation of CpS (begun before, but not completed until just after, the coup) for seriously challenging episcopal authority, undermining Church unity, and attempting to re-establish close ties between the Church and political parties (this time, the Left).[16]

Hence, an 'evangelical-pastoral' strategy was not effective at the local Church level during the Allende years. The political context created cross-pressures on most laity too severe for them to find time for pastoral activities, and for CEB participants in many working-class areas (clergy and laity alike) it was practically impossible to separate religious and partisan political commitments.[17]

THE CHURCH AND THE MILITARY REGIME (1973–)

Church reaction to the military coup of 11 September 1973 was a mixture of relief and cautious concern. Most clerical lay leaders at all levels of the Church, although not openly hostile to the UP, were glad that the chaotic political and economic situation characterising the last months of Allende's regime was over.[18] As the military junta began to suppress or severely limit all major forms of political and social expression (media, political parties, unions, neighbourhood associations), the hierarchy in addition to relief with the restoration of order also wanted to preserve the institutional freedom of the Church both to carry on its religious mission unimpeded and to offer humanitarian aid to those in trouble after the coup. As a result, the bishops did not clearly and forcefully denounce violations of human rights perpetrated on a grand scale from the first moment of military rule. Their words, while urging moderation by the new government, were cautious and tacitly offered it moral legitimacy.[19]

In exchange for this cautious support, the junta allowed the

Catholic Church – in co-operation with leaders from the Lutheran, Greek Orthodox, Anglican, Methodist, Baptist and Jewish communities – to set up soon after the coup emergency relief programmes for foreign refugees and for Chileans suffering the brunt of the repression. An ecumenically sponsored National Committee to Aid Refugees (CONAR) helped approximately 5000 foreigners leave Chile safely by February 1974. Another ecumenical organisation – the Committee of Co-operation for Peace (COPACHI) – quickly established offices in 22 of the 25 provinces, and between late 1973 and December 1975 offered legal aid services to prisoners and to workers arbitrarily dismissed from their jobs. In its two years of existence, during mounting torture and forced disappearances, it initiated legal actions for more than 7000 persons in Santiago alone who were detained, tried or who had disappeared, and it defended an additional 6000 workers fired for political reasons.

Moreover, as the junta moved to curb inflation (600 per cent per annum at the time of the coup) by severely cutting social services and depressing wages, COPACHI expanded its activities to provide health and nutritional assistance. By late 1975 it had treated 75 000 patients in its clinics in Santiago's shanty-towns, and was providing hot lunches for more than 30 000 pre-school-age children suffering severe malnutrition throughout the country. It had also provided assistance to 126 small self-help enterprises in cities and to 10 rural co-operatives for small farmers.[20]

As during the early and mid-1960s, the major source of financial support for such Church-sponsored social programmes came from abroad. After 1973, however, such aid came not only from Catholic Church sources in the North Atlantic countries (CIDSE – International Co-operation for Development and Solidarity – in Western Europe, Catholic Relief Services in the US), but also from Protestant and secular agencies as well – the World Council of Churches in Geneva (the major monetary contributor to COPACHI), the US National Council of Churches, and the US government's Inter-American Foundation.[21]

Throughout the first two years of military rule, while the hierarchy as a group remained ambiguous about government policies in their public statements,[22] tensions between Church and State mounted steadily due to the work of COPACHI and the activities of some local Church leaders in working-class areas. COPACHI quickly became the most reliable source of information on what was happening throughout the country, and its reports provided the outside world (including the media and human rights organisations in Europe and the USA) with first-hand testimonies of human rights violations in Chile. Some of its full-time professional staff (over 300 in 1975) also had previous connections with leftist parties (especially MAPU, MIC and the Socialist Party). Moreover, rectories and convents in shanty-towns became places of refuge for those seeking to escape arrest and subsequent torture or arbitrary execution. With the assistance of those closely associated with COPACHI, priests and nuns enabled countless numbers of Chileans to exercise their right of political asylum in foreign embassies and thus leave the country unharmed.

All of these activities angered the government and, in addition to vilification of COPACHI in the pro-government media, many of its lay and clerical members and associates suffered harassment and arrest. In late 1975 General Pinochet also pressurised Cardinal Silva, chairman of COPACHI's board of directors, to close down the organisation on the grounds that it was a 'means whereby Marxist-Leninists were creating problems threatening the civil order'.[23]

The Cardinal acquiesced in December 1975, but the following month inaugurated a new organisation to carry on comparable humanitarian services – the Vicariate of Solidarity – under the exclusive control of the Catholic Church. It quickly established regional offices or affiliations in 20 of the 25 provinces, and over the next five years provided legal, health, nutritional, and employment services to about 900 000 Chileans (180 000 annually). On average, one of every 60 persons in the country received some form of assistance by the Vicariate each year from 1976 through 1980.[24]

After 1975, although there were some improvements in the economy, these did not significantly benefit the majority of Chileans who are poor. Inflation decreased dramatically amidst forced austerity measures (from 600 per cent per annum in 1973 to below 40 per cent per annum in 1979), new loans from private foreign banks soared to nearly $3 billion annually in 1980, exports increased (especially in agriculture), and foreign reserves totalled more than $1 billion in 1980. Manufacturing, however, declined sharply after drastic tariff reductions and unemployment remained chronically high (13 per cent in 1980 and over 20 per cent by 1983). Wage increases continued to be pegged lower than price rises, diminishing purchasing power of the poor by almost one-half between 1973 and 1980. Moreover, health and housing expenditures by the government were cut back and union activities remained severely restricted.

In light of these continued high social and economic costs imposed on workers the Vicariate of Solidarity (like its predecessor, COPACHI) has continued a wide range of service programmes for the poor. By 1980 in Santiago (where one third of the national population is located) it was sponsoring a network of community organisations that included: (1) 74 community health clinics, assisting annually more than 22 000 patients; (2) 160 feeding centres providing daily hot lunches for over 13 000 children and adults; (3) 105 cottage-industry centres administered by unemployed men and women; (4) 74 artisan and handicraft projects run by prisoners to gain income for their families; (5) 68 housing committees to pressurise the government to provide needed services in shanty-towns (water, sanitation, electricity) and protect slum dwellers from evictions by private land speculators. These services helped about 154 000 in the capital city in 1980 – or 1 out of every 23 residents.[25]

Moreover, all of these programmes were organised from the bottom up by local residents themselves, many of whom were new participants in CEBs. They emerged out of CEB-sponsored meetings where citizens formed committees, elected leaders and decided on the most effective tactics to alleviate the worst effects of malnutrition, sickness, unemployment, and scarce housing in their neighbourhoods. Vicariate of Solidarity personnel provided encouragement and technical expertise for such associations, but did not dictate agenda or control the leadership.

The Vicariate also served as a major conduit of foreign assistance for many of these Church-sponsored projects at the diocesan and neighbourhood levels. Although domestic contributions to the Church increased significantly in the late 1970s ($1.2 million in 1978) in proportion to what they were in 1974 ($155,000), these still only covered a very small part of the costs of the Church's social programmes. Ninety-three per cent of the financial and material contributions to the Chilean Catholic Church for its social agenda in 1978, for example, came from foreign Catholic, Protestant, and governmental agencies in the North Atlantic countries, much of it channelled through the Vicariate.[26]

As with COPACHI, however, the Vicariate and its supporters in local CEBs angered elements in the government and its supporters. Verbal attacks began to appear in the media (almost entirely controlled by the government or its allies) by 1977, charging that the agency was harbouring marxist sympathisers and taking foreign money to support political dissidents in Chile. Various diocesan affiliates of the Vicariate were raided, rectories and convents in low-income areas continued to be closely watched, and local CEBs working closely with the Vicariate harassed. Although such repression against the Church subsided for a time it was renewed again in 1980, and again in early 1983 when several foreign clergy working with CEBs in shanty-towns were expelled.[27]

Most bishops in the last seven years have shifted their own perspective on regime policies. Caution and ambiguity in episcopal statements changed to sharp and clear criticisms of the government after mid-1976 when some high-level Christian Democrats were expelled and several progressive bishops publicly humiliated by members of the secret police (DINA) at Pudahuel airport upon returning from an international pastoral meeting in Ecuador. These events, coupled with a formal suppression of the PDC in early 1977, finally awakened the majority of bishops to the systemic dangers both to the Church itself and to society at large created by the regime. Since 1976 the Episcopal Conference has released over a dozen major statements criticising such policies as continued use of torture and arbitrary detention, lack of adequate investigations into the causes of the disappearances of over 15 000 Chileans since the coup, refusal to set an effective amnesty policy for thousands of Chileans in exile abroad, failure to provide for significant public participation in critical national decisions, and economic strategies whose costs weigh disproportionately on the poor.[28]

Despite the significant array of services provided by expanding structures of the Church at the national, regional and local levels since 1973 and the shift since 1976 by the hierarchy to a more prophetic denunciatory position in face of systemic repression, the actions and words of the Church have not had any appreciable effect on the regime. Church-sponsored social programmes have provided an important respite from the worst effects of repression for a good number of Chileans and some structural space in which they can meet and keep alive hopes for a better day. Neither these actions nor the critical statements of the bishops after 1976 precipitated any moderation in government policies, however. Political repression and libertarian economic policies continued, and the living conditions of the majority who are poor have further deteriorated in the absence of effective public social services.

The repercussions for the Church itself, however, resulting from its new strategies since the coup have been multidimensional. First of all, once again the institutional Church is officially sponsoring a whole range of social services for the poor but now on a greater scale and for a more prolonged period than in the early 1960s. Begun as emergency programmes and envisioned as short-term efforts, these have become institutionalised and are now seen as absolutely essential by thousands of Chileans who depend on them for survival. The recent economic depression in Chile begun in 1982 and worsening in 1983 has made it unlikely that such services by the Church can be curtailed in the near future in favour of more strictly religious activities.

Secondly, such expanded social commitments have reinforced the Chilean Church's heavy dependence on foreign sources of monetary and material support. Given the current economic crisis there is no way that the Church will be able to generate adequate internal support in Chile to approach financial autonomy from external religious and secular (including governmental) aid.

Thirdly, both of these aspects of the Church's current position – expanding social commitments, and heavy dependence on foreign private and public support – have exacerbated its relations with the government and its major supporters. The junta and its allies in the media and business do not consider the public criticisms of some government policies by the bishops as part of the latter's responsibilities to support justice and human rights. They view such statements as having a partisan political purpose – namely, to weaken the regime in the face of its foreign and domestic opponents. They view the social action of the Church not as humanitarian service but as sectional political action, since they believe such activities are aiding government opponents and offering foreigners a 'trojan horse' inside Chile whereby they can meddle in its internal affairs and attempt to subvert the government.

Such criticisms by regime supporters have been translated into action. In addition to cyclic harassment of Church projects and vilification of clergy and laity alike, the government has also attempted on several occasions (unsuccessfully) to cut off some of its foreign funds and has substantially reduced public subsidies to Catholic universities and schools.[29]

Upper-income Catholics, most of whom have supported the junta, have not only been reluctant to contribute financially to the Church's new ministries, but also have diminished their participation in its sacramental and other religious activities since 1973. Some have given support to reactionary movements such as the Society for the Defense of Tradition, Family and Property (TFP) that has challenged episcopal authority even more vehemently than did CpS, and which has been equally condemned by the hierarchy.[30]

Hence, on the socio-political front, the Church since late 1973 has not been able to pursue successfully an 'evangelical-pastoral' strategy. Aspects of a neo-Christian approach have reappeared (that is, direct Church administration of extensive social services) out of economic necessity, since there are no secular agencies effectively serving the basic needs of the poor in which individual Christians can work and from which they can seek aid. Moreover, although the hierarchy believe they are being politically non-partisan and that their prophetic words and active support for the Vicariate are nothing more than part of their moral obligation to alleviate suffering and promote justice, those with power in contemporary Chile (inside and outside the government) view such a position as heavily partisan. Moreover, they have taken action to limit the Church's freedom – something never even contemplated by the previous marxist regime which believed in the Church's basically non-partisan and humanitarian public position.

On the religious front, however, the 'evangelical-pastoral' strategy has been more successful since the coup than during the Allende years. Whereas in the early 1970s when most Chileans had no time for the Church, in the last ten years participation has dramatically increased. Regular Mass attendance in Santiago has more than doubled from 20 per cent in 1973 to 42.8 per cent in 1979. Participants in CEB-sponsored activities such as bible study, preparation for the sacraments, and shared prayer in small groups have all risen significantly. By 1975, for example, it was estimated that already there were over 20 000 active adult participants in CEB religious programmes, and by 1978 an additional 10 000 teenagers were active in these and other CEB activities for youths.[31]

Some of these new participants in CEB religious activities also take part in the various social service programmes of the Church at the local level affiliated with both CEBs and the Vicariate. A survey in Santiago in 1977, for example, of 319 women engaged in Church-sponsored soup kitchens in shanty-towns found that while only 4.7 per cent of those helping to prepare the food also participated in some religious function of the local CEB, 55.8 per cent of those with top administrative responsibilities in these *comedores* did.[32] While this indicates a wide division between the social activists and those who pray, it also shows that there is a small but significant group (especially those with leadership skills) who are combining a commitment to justice with an active religious faith – the ideal form of a Christian life outlined in Latin American Church pronouncements such as the Medellín (1968) and Puebla (1979) documents, and encouraged by the Chilean bishops themselves in the 1968 and 1969 guidelines for CEBs.

An additional sign of vitality in the CEBs is the large number of non-clerics who exercise effective leadership roles. The responsibility for both the social and religious functions of CEBs for the most part is in the hands of women, lay and religious, and some married men. Bible study, catechetical training, and prayer groups, as well as preaching, administering baptism, distributing the Eucharist and officiating at weddings are all now carried out by women religious and lay women due to the chronic shortage of priests in Chile (2200 for over 10 million Catholics in 1979).

Almost one-half of the approximately 5500 nuns in Chile, heeding the call of the hierarchy in the late 1960s to become more involved in direct pastoral work, have been the ones most responsible for training new lay leaders and nurturing the growth of CEBs. Many have also been given administrative functions over entire parish territories when no clergy are in residence. By 1976, 80 of the 750 parishes throughout the country (10.7 per cent of the total) were under the exclusive control of such nuns. Although not ordained, they are performing many priestly functions (except granting absolution and saying Mass).[33]

Lay women have begun to exercise many similar religious responsibilities as the nuns (except administer parishes and officiate at weddings). Their greatest impact has been in the area of training children and adults for receiving the sacraments. By 1975 over 100 000 women catechists had received a two-year biblical and doctrinal training from nuns. They were then given responsibilities to prepare over 100 000 additional parents to teach religion in their own homes, thus reaching approximately 400 000 persons.[34]

Although male participation in religious activities in Chile (as elsewhere in Latin America) has traditionally been quite low, since the coup more lay men are participating in CEBs since the Church is now a more visible and credible institution in their neighbourhoods. By 1979 there were 167 married men functioning as deacons who, after several years of special theological and pastoral training, acted as ministers for baptism and weddings and shared preaching responsibilities with priests.

All of this new vitality in CEBs, although an indication of important success for the religious dimension of the hierarchy's 'evangelical-pastoral' strategy in the last decade, is also fraught with some problems. Many of the Church's new adherents (as mentioned earlier) participate only in social projects sponsored by the CEBs in collaboration with the Vicariate. Most of them for years prior to the coup, while baptised, had very little contact with the Church and some were active in leftist parties. While this is understandable, and even exciting given the potential for the Church, it also means that the process of full evangelisation among them will be slow. Moreover, if the social context changes in the direction of a more open political system and a sounder economy before these new adherents are drawn more fully into the religious life of the CEBs, they may withdraw from the Church again since they will be able to fulfil their social agenda elsewhere.

A second, and perhaps more serious, problem is the new attitudes about the nature of the Church that are emerging in CEBs and among lower clergy, women religious and laity closely associated with them. Several of the issues actively promoted by Christians for Socialism and 'the 200' in the early 1970s have not disappeared, but have penetrated the mentality of contemporary local Church leaders due to their social and pastoral experiences since the coup.

During interviews in 1975 with 186 leaders at different levels of the Chilean Church, I found that while over three-fifths of the bishops (62.5 per cent) felt that there was no place for liberation theology methods in the Church, many leaders at the local Church level thought otherwise. Well over two-fifths of the priests (46.4 per cent), and nearly one-half of the nuns (48.5 per cent), disagreed, and many said they were trying to combine in their work in CEBs the teaching of religion with a critical reflection on political and social problems.[35] Many of the local leaders, while not active in, or even sympathetic to, CpS, had become radicalised by the severe repression of the military regime. The longer such repression continues (now fifteen years), the greater likelihood that such attitudes will deepen and even spread among local CEB leaders.

Corroborating this evidence of a 'liberation theology' orientation was a cluster of other parallel attitudes close to those of CpS and 'the 200' manifested by these same respondents in 1975. Regarding the scope of Church membership, only one-third of the bishops expressed preference for a sectarian model emphasising the necessity of a profound commitment by all members even if this would entail a smaller but more vital community. Over three-fifths of the priests (62.5 per cent), over three-quarters of the lay leaders (78.5 per cent), and nearly nine-tenths of the nuns (87.9 per cent) chose precisely this kind of Church model which is closer to a Protestant approach than to traditional Catholic preferences for universality of membership with varying degrees of commitment and participation.[36]

In addition, seventy per cent of the hierarchy felt that Church decisions should be made by themselves alone, perhaps after some consultation with local Church personnel. Over one-half of the nuns (51.5 per cent), however, and close to two-thirds (64.7 per cent) of the lay leaders stated that decisions should be reached through dialogue across all levels of the Church or be made by representatives of CEBs with the bishops.[37]

Finally, there were very divergent views between bishops and lower leaders regarding the question of who should be eligible for priesthood. While 60 per cent of the hierarchy were against married men becoming priests, over three-quarters of the nuns (78.7 per cent) 80 per cent of the laity, and over 80 per cent (81.9 per cent) of the priests felt this was either a possibility, or even one of the most necessary changes needed in the Chilean Church. Moreover, while less than ten per cent (6.8 per cent) of the bishops supported the ordination of women as priests, over one-fifth of the priests themselves (22.2 per cent), over two-fifths of the laity (43.2 per cent), and more than one half of the nuns (51.5 per cent) viewed this as desirable, given the many priestly functions women were already successfully performing.[38]

Ironically, the very decentralisation of Church structures and the delegation of more responsibilities to local leaders (especially non-clerics), while furthering the religious success of the hierarchy's 'evangelical-pastoral' strategy, has also precipitated a radically new ecclesiology (theology of the Church) among local leaders. This ecclesiology is not only closely identified with a liberation theology strategy of Church influence in society (whereby the Church acts as a partisan political force with and for the poor) but also implies a smaller, more homogeneous, democratic, declericalised, and sexually egalitarian institution. This kind of Church is diametrically opposed to official Catholic teaching and discipline presently upheld by Rome and the hierarchy, and was rejected by the Chilean bishops when they condemned Christians for Socialism ten years ago.

At present local Church leaders, given their all-consuming efforts to meet the social and spiritual needs of their people in a severely depressed economy and repressive political system, do not have the time or the energy to push this new religious agenda vigorously with the bishops. If and when the social context changes, however, and these leaders focus their exclusive attention on religious issues these competing strategies will in all probability be frankly discussed with the hierarchy. Whether the dialogue will result in mutual growth and accommodation, or in confrontation as happened with CpS, will depend on the honesty, openness, and good sense of both higher and lower leaders in the Chilean Church.

CONCLUSIONS

The Chilean Church has significantly shifted the fulcrum point of its strategy of relating to society and fulfilling its religious mission over the past half-century. It has definitely rejected the traditional Christendom approach, and in so doing no longer identifies so closely with the interests of State nor of upper-class groups. It has shifted towards a more long-term strategy of influence, especially focusing its evangelisation efforts among the majority of poor whom it long neglected prior to the 1930s. In so doing in recent years it is relying less on specialised elite approaches (such as Catholic Action circles for the educated) and more on widespread penetration of the masses through small base communities run by non-clerics, many of whom are poor. It has also over the past twenty years given significant moral and institutional support to structural change in society, and no longer speaks, or relates to, the causes of poverty in personal moral terms.

While the bishops have officially endorsed an 'evangelical-pastoral' position for the church over the past fifteen years – (1) non-partisan moral support for justice, and (2) primary attention to religious training – this strategy has to date met with limited success. The hyperpoliticised context during the Allende years short-circuited the second, or religious, dimension of this strategy, while the authoritarian context since 1973 has created a situation in which support for justice and human rights is quickly interpreted in partisan political terms (and thus rejected) primarily by those to whom such moral appeals by the bishops have been addressed – namely, those with dominant political and economic power in the Pinochet regime.

An additional complication since the coup has been the role of economic and social safety-nets forced upon the Church due to active repression and unbenign neglect of the poor by the military government. An aspect of a 'neo-Christendom' strategy has had to be readapted by the Church out of necessity – institutional support for a significant array of social services for the needy. Being financially unable to perform this role, and not given any significant aid by the government to do so, the Church has become heavily dependent on foreign assistance (including public aid) which, in turn, only exacerbates relations with its own highly nationalistic and suspicious government.

While such social services have attracted to the Church many who would not otherwise come – and thus enhances the potential for the Church to make its religious message credible to them – overlapping participation in both social *and* religious activities has not advanced except among a minority of extremely committed CEB members. The integration of social and spiritual dimensions of Christian faith will take some time among those long neglected by the Church and not accustomed to share in its sacramental life. The problem facing Church leaders – who yearn to pursue a strictly 'evangelical-pastoral' strategy, but also do not wish to weaken the fragile allegiances of their new adherents nor shirk their humanitarian responsibilities in a very difficult economic crisis – is how to manage a mix of social and religious services without attracting more persecution by pro-government forces and without diverting the institutional energies of the Church away from its primary religious mission.

Finally, whether the hierarchy wants it or not or is even fully aware of the situation, a 'liberation theology' strategy is growing at the lower level of the Church. It cannot be avoided given the severe repression of the regime which has politically radicalised many local clerical, religious and lay leaders. It is they, not the hierarchy, who have borne the brunt of the government's oppression of the poor with whom they live. For them – as for Christians for Socialism in a different era – the processes of evangelisation and political liberation are intimately related, and must be integrated in any effective pastoral action that has credibility among the working class.

Moreover, the delegation of many ecclesiastical responsibilities to local CEB leaders and participants has created in them not only a deeper love for the Church but a new vision for its future. They are forming a new Church that is very different in style, composition, and decision-making than the traditional Roman model. Although doctrine and discipline have not changed in the Vatican nor at the episcopal level, the pastoral practice of CEBs in Chile has *de facto* changed the Church's approach to community, authority, ministry, and sexual equality. This is the most profound long-range consequence for the Chilean Church entailed in pursuing an 'evangelical-pastoral' strategy. How its implications are to be worked out remains to be resolved.

NOTES

1. The 'evangelical-pastoral' strategy of Church action in society (prominent in the Final Document at Puebla and in the majority of pastoral letters of episcopal conferences in contemporary Latin America) stresses the promotion of religious unity within the Church, the building of effective small base Christian communities (*comunidades eclesiales de base* – CEBs) for prayer, catechesis, bible study, and sacramental worship, and the non-involvement of the official Church in party politics while supporting social justice through the words of clergy and personal action choices of laity in the secular world. The neo-Christian model (prevalent among clergy and laity formed in Catholic Action circles from the 1930s through to the mid-1960s and closely associated with the formation of Christian Democratic parties) has emphasised the training of cadres of committed Catholic laity (primarily in the middle classes) to apply the Church's social teaching in reformist politics and economics, and also has stressed the use of the institutional resources of the Church (money, personnel, buildings) by clergy and laity to carry out direct social action services on behalf of the poor. The 'liberation theology' approach (characteristic of many leaders and participants in the new base communities (CEBs) of the Church in Central and South America) focuses on the need for the Church to place its moral influence officially behind contemporary political liberation movements among the poor, and for groups of Christians to reflect and act on the social implications of their biblical faith by also supporting such movements. The best description and analysis of these and other relevant models of Church strategy has been done by Daniel H. Levine, building on the work of Ivan Vallier and Thomas G. Sanders. See Levine's, *Religion and Politics in Latin America: The Catholic Church in Venezuela and Colombia* (Princeton: Princeton University Press, 1981) pp. 131–41, 304–12.
2. This 'Christendom' strategy was based on the assumption that Chile was a 'Christian' society (since 90 per cent of the population were baptised Catholics), and that the most influential political structures of the time (the State and the Conservative Party) and social groups (the landed interests) would both support the institutional Church and make sure that Christian policies dominated the rest of society. For a further description of this traditional model of Church-society relations in Latin America, see Levine, *Religion and Politics in Latin America*, p. 305 and Ivan Vallier, *Catholicism, Social Control and Modernization in Latin America* (Englewood Cliffs, NJ: Prentice-Hall, 1970) pp. 71–2, 74.

3. For a description of these negotiations and the resulting terms of separation (mutually acceptable to both Church and State), see my *The Church and Politics in Chile: Challenges to Modern Catholicism* (Princeton: Princeton University Press, 1982) pp. 70–81.
4. Conferencia Episcopal de Chile, 'La iglesia y el campesinado chileno', *Mensaje* (Santiago) 11 (May 1962) 185–94A; 'El deber social y político en la hora presente', *Mensaje* 11 (November 1962) 577–87.
5. Smith, *The Church and Politics in Chile*, pp. 111–15.
6. Ibid., Table 5.2, p. 108.
7. The ingredients of this 'evangelical-pastoral' strategy are found in the following documents of the episcopal conference: 'Chile, voluntad de ser', *Mensaje* 17 (May 1968) 190–7; *Orientaciones pastorales I*, Chillán, May 1968 (Santiago: Imprenta Alfonsiana, 1968); *Orientaciones pastorales II*, La Serena, June 1969 (Santiago: Typografía San Pablo, 1969).
8. Cardinal Raúl Silva Henríquez, 'Iglesia, sacerdocio y política', 20 July 1970, and 'Carta de Mons. José Manuel Santos Presidente de la Conferencia Episcopal de Chile (CECH) a algunos dirigentes campesinos de Linares', Valdivia, 19 May 1970, both in *Documentos del Episcopado: Chile, 1970–1973*, edited by Bishop Carlos Oviedo Cavada (Santiago: Ediciones Mundo, 1974) pp. 10–15, 23–5.
9. Smith, *Church and Politics in Chile*, Table 6.1, p. 130.
10. Ibid., pp. 182–96.
11. Public subsidies, for example, to the Catholic University of Santiago by 1973 covered 80 per cent of operating costs, as compared to 60 per cent at the end of Frei's presidency. Ibid., p. 189.
12. Ibid., pp. 197–8.
13. Ibid., pp. 201–5.
14. Ibid., pp. 261–2.
15. Ibid., pp. 234–47.
16. Ibid., pp. 253–7.
17. While those Catholics with rightist views also tried to combine religious and political commitments during the Allende years, they did not disturb the hierarchy as much, since, claimed the bishops in their condemnation of CpS these were not 'crystallized in organized groups' as was CpS, did 'not entail militancy on the part of priests and religious', did not 'propound a distinct doctrine or vision for the Church', nor 'oppose the ecclesiastical hierarchy in the same measure'. Episcopal Conference of Chile, 'Christian Faith and Political Activity', 81, in *Christians and Socialism: Documentation of the Christians for Socialism Movement in Latin America*, edited by John Eagleson (Maryknoll, NY: Orbis, 1975) p. 217.
18. In 1975 I interviewed in Chile 186 Catholic leaders, including all 30 active bishops, 41 priests working among different social strata in 18 of the 23 dioceses, 31 priests in a random stratified sample in Santiago, 33 women religious acting as pastoral leaders of CEBs among different social classes in 7 dioceses, and 51 lay men and women participating in CEB's in urban areas (mainly in Santiago). I found that 70 per cent of these leaders (including 89 per cent of the bishops, 76 per cent of the

priests, 51 per cent of the nuns, and 65 per cent of the laity) felt that the military coup was necessary in September 1973. A great many said they were relieved at the time with the re-establishment of social order, but added that they never dreamed that the military would act so repressively, and definitively disapproved of what had transpired since the coup. Smith, *Church and Politics in Chile*, Table 7.2, p. 210, and pp. 211–13.

19. Two days after the coup Cardinal Silva and the Permanent Committee of the Episcopal Conference issued a public statement decrying the spilling of 'blood of civilians and of soldiers', and asked for 'respect for persons fallen in battle', including Allende himself. The statement called for 'moderation toward the vanquished' and for 'no needless reprisals'. It also, however, affirmed the 'patriotism and selflessness' of the military junta, and asked all citizens to co-operate with them so as to 'return soon to institutional normality'. 'Declaración del Señor Cardenal y del Comité Permanente del Episcopado Chileno', Santiago, 13 September 1973, *Mensaje* 22 (October 1975) 509.
20. El Comité de Co-operación para la Paz en Chile, 'Crónica de sus dos años de labor solidaria', Santiago, December 1975, 21 pp (mimeographed); US Congress, House, Subcommittee on International Organisations of the Committee on International Relations, 'Prepared Statement of José Zalaquett Daher, Chief Legal Counsel, Committee of Co-operation for Peace in Chile', *Chile: The Status of Human Rights and Its Relationship to U.S. Economic Assistance Programs*, 94th Congress, 2nd session, 1976, pp. 57–65.
21. For statistical information on foreign support to Church-sponsored social programmes during the first two years after the coup (over $25 million), see Smith, *The Church and Politics in Chile*, pp. 325–7 (esp. Table 9.2, p. 326).
22. In both 1975 (April) and 1974 (September) the Episcopal Conference issued documents that included criticisms of such repressive policies as 'arbitrary or prolonged detentions' and the use of 'physical or moral constraints during interrogations'. In neither document did the bishops explicitly acknowledge the widespread use of torture and arbitrary executions that were occurring during the two years after the coup. Moreover, in the second document, entitled 'Gospel and Peace' (September 1975), the hierarchy thanked the military for 'freeing' the country 'from a Marxist dictatorship which appeared inevitable and would have been irreversible', and they renewed their confidence in the 'spirit of justice of our armed forces'. Los obispos de Chile, 'La reconciliación en Chile', *Mensaje* 23 (May 1974) 196–8; Comité Permanente del Episcopado de Chile, 'Evangelio y Paz', *Mensaje* 24 (October 1975).
23. *Chile-América* (Rome) 3 (November–December 1975) 41.
24. *Vicaría de la Solidaridad: quinto año de labor, 1980* (Santiago: Arzobispado de Santiago, 1980) p. 15.
25. Ibid., pp. 67, 87, 111–13.
26. Smith, *Church and Politics in Chile*, Table 9.2, p. 326.
27. Since the coup many foreign clergy have been expelled or left under

pressure. Some had been active in CpS but many were forced out simply because they were carrying out humanitarian services to those persecuted by the regime. Between 1973 and 1979 there was a loss of 378 foreign priests in the country, precipitating a net decline of 11 per cent in the total clergy. Smith, *Church and Politics in Chile*, Table 9.3, p. 332.

28. These documents are summarised in Smith, *The Church and Politics in Chile*, pp. 305–11.
29. Ibid., pp. 320–2, 328–9.
30. In 1976 TFP published a 450-page book (*La iglesia del silencio en Chile*) in which it excoriated almost all the bishops and a decisive part of the clergy purportedly for having been soft on marxism during Allende's term and for having undermined traditional Christian respect for private property. The book claimed the hierarchy to be in heresy and called for open resistance to them by Chilean Catholics. Although small in number, TFP had wealthy supporters and some members well placed in government, education, and the media after the coup. The hierarchy responded swiftly by excommunicating all who collaborated in writing or disseminating the book. 'Declaración del Comité Permanente', *Mensaje* 25 (July 1976) 316.
31. Renato Poblete, SJ, Carmen Galilea W. and Patricia van Dorp P., *Imagen de la iglesia de hoy y religiosidad de los Chilenos* (Santiago: Centro Bellarmino, 1980) p. 38; Smith, *Church and Politics in Chile*, p. 340.
32. Cristián Vives, 'La solidaridad: una forma de evangelizar y participar en la iglesia' (Santiago, Centro Bellarmino, 1978) pp. 22–3 (mimeographed).
33. Katherine Ann Gilfeather, MM, 'Women and Ministry', *America* (2 October, 1976) pp. 191–4.
34. Enrique García Ahumada, FSC, 'Nuestra catequesis actual', *Mensaje* 26 (November 1977) 657–61.
35. Smith, *Church and Politics in Chile*, Table 2.3, p. 32.
36. Ibid., Table 2.5, p. 46.
37. Ibid., Table 2.4, p. 41.
38. Ibid., Tables 9.5 and 9.6, p. 344.

18 The Catholic Church and State Tension in Paraguay

Andrea O'Brien

April 1987 will be remembered as important in the history of Paraguay, at least for the government announcement that, after more than thirty years in force, it was lifting the state of emergency or 'estado de sitio'. This measure, which had always been religiously renewed every six months, gave special powers to the police and the army. Its ending made international headlines, but during that same month of April other less reported but significant events took place in Paraguay and they will be the focus of this chapter.

Ever since he came to power in 1954, it has been the custom of General Alfredo Stroessner to give a lengthy address at the opening of parliament on the first of April each year. 1987 was no exception. His car arrived at the congress building surrounded not only by motorcycle and horse guards but accompanied by vanloads of heavily armed soldiers. His address to the government party deputies (Colorado members, many of them sporting the red colour that gives them their name) and to diplomats (including the papal nuncio in a white cassock) lasted the best part of a hundred minutes. In the long, narrow hall the interruptions of applause became notably less frequent as the speech progressed. At the end the chairman thanked the President in one sentence and the session closed without further ceremony, the General returning to his palace up the road.

The content of this year's speech was fairly standard. Much of it was taken up with figures of expenditures, products and roadworks. There were fewer ideological statements than on many previous occasions. In a country which had seen the closing down of the major opposition newspaper *ABC Color* in March 1984 and of Radio Nanduti (due to 'atmospheric' interference) at the end of 1986, the only reference to this area was a warning not to confuse 'freedom of expression with freedom to defame' or to express 'antisocial impulses'; the general also criticised 'newspapers drenched in pessimism'. There was the by now customary self-praise of the regime as a 'genuine democracy' and a 'friend of the ballot box', a country where 'the people are the soul and the brain of our democracy'. Yet about a fifth of the Paraguayan people are in exile in Argentina and it is well known that to get a good job in the civil service and even more so in the army, one has to be able to prove that all one's immediate relatives are members of the Colorado party. Hence 40 per cent of the population are officially members of that party and many of them believe its rhetoric. Their fidelity is their ticket to minor favours of all kinds, such as a bed in hospital or getting through the red tape of some official permission. With most of the Liberal opposition party in exile, the elections every five years are of interest only to see what wing of the Colorado party has most influence.

Since one of the definite attractions of the dictatorship has been the version of social and political stability it has provided, Stroessner's speech included plenty of reference to the tragedies of Paraguay's long history of turmoil before 1954. There were forty-four presidents in the eighty-five years before his coming to power, and that period included the terrible War of Triple Alliance which killed some 90 per cent of the male population. Hence Stroessner could boast: 'we have put behind us completely the times of anarchy and backwardness. There is peace and order under the rule of law . . . there is no terrorism nor any serious social or political crisis'. This is a familiar message echoed again and again each evening at 8.30 when *La Voz del Coloradismo* takes over practically all radio stations for a special programme. The exception is the church-run Radio Caritas which is itself often the object of attack in this broadcast as an 'instrument of the left and of terrorism'. This nightly propaganda programme makes free and frequent use of the word 'communist' to dismiss international critiques of the Stroessner regime: 'there will be no communism in Paraguay: we live in peace'. It also indulges in personal and bitter attacks on individuals especially in the worlds of communication and the Church.

The President's speech contained only one, somewhat solemn, reference to the Catholic Church:

> The national government, inspired by the Christian and patriotic roots of our people, always offers its collaboration to the Roman Catholic and Apostolic Church, the official religion of the State. . . . The people raises its faith in God with gratitude for the peace that makes possible its spiritual enrichment.

All this is a rhetoric that conceals more than it reveals, because this longest dictatorship in Latin America seems to be entering one of its several phases of tension with the Church in Paraguay. What is more, there seemed to be a certain white-washing going on by the government, partially in view of a possible Papal visit in 1988. The visit, which took place in May 1988, did provide the archbishop with such an opportunity. As a result, the Church is in a special position of strength at the moment. These few pages aim only to show how the blandness of General Stroessner's reference to Catholicism was undermined by other words and deeds even within that same month of April, and that, as Paul Lewis claimed in his scholarly study of *Paraguay under Stroessner* (Chapel Hill, 1980), the Church still provides the only real if inconstant opposition to the regime.

In fact every decade of the Stroessner period has seen a major confrontation between the Church and the regime, in which so far the regime has emerged as the clear victor. In the late 1960s various priests on the staff of the recently-founded Catholic University were either exiled or physically beaten, so that even the conservative archbishop of the time excommunicated the chief of police. In the mid-seventies some ten religious, mainly Jesuits, involved in the Ligas Agrarias Cristianas or peasant co-operatives were expelled from the country and their organisation destroyed. After each of these defeats the Church tended to go silent or to tone down the stridency of its declarations on justice. But the situation of 1986–7 would seem to be moving towards another increase of church–state friction after another decade of relative quiet. Encouraged by the church role in Haiti and in the Philippines and counting on the desire of the government to keep its Catholic image as untarnished as possible in view of a Papal visit, a new boldness of church critique seems in evidence. But on the government side covert pressure is being brought against rural catechists, for instance; these are lay volunteers who are key agents in the upholding of faith in the people. Since many of them are teachers, they are being warned that they will lose their jobs if they continue this ministry on the side. The government's real fear is over the social content of the education offered and that it may wake up deprived peasants to their real situation and just rights.

Apart from the constant hidden tensions, an obvious public expression of the new spirit of conflict by the Church happened in

May 1986. As a result of the killing of peasants who had taken over unoccupied land and of the arrest of trade unionists, and finally of the attacks by police on the congregation at a special Mass for justice, the church authorities took the unprecedented step of calling out all the priests and religious of the capital for a procession-demonstration. Their master-stroke was to make it a silent procession carrying the statue of the Virgin of Ka'akupe. Led by Archbishop Rolón and with all the religious provincials in the front line, the procession walked through the centre of Asunción. The police were powerless to interfere, because whatever one felt about attacking church leaders, it would be unthinkable to seem irreverent to the most important statue in the nation's history. Subsequently, the students of the national seminary announced a similar religious demonstration to protest against 'popular' repression; somewhat naughtily, they timed it to coincide with the appearance of Paraguay in the world cup football opening round, thus forcing the police to miss the match as well!

Later in 1986 another symbolic and public expression of tension occurred. It is customary for each of the main religious congregations to hold a special Mass and vigil at the shrine of Ka'akupe on the Marian feast of December. Each group comes for a period of the night. Soldiers were present at this event in 1986 and if any of the various preachers through the night seemed to speak of injustice or the social gospel in anything other than innocuous terms, the security forces lined up so that all the members of that congregation had to walk from the altar in single file past rows of menacing bayonets.

By far the most important Church move in 1986 was that it launched a call to national dialogue. This meant an invitation from the Church to those in political and intellectual life to come together to reflect on the state of the country and on its roads into the future. It was born of the feeling that some such process of listening and sharing was urgently needed to allow people to find hope. It was also surely influenced by the age of the dictator, now in his mid-seventies; even though he sought and got another term of office in 1988, he cannot last for ever and there is much genuine worry about what might happen after his demise. The initiative of the Church was welcomed by everyone except by the government party and its officials. They have continued to side-step the invitation, saying that either there was no need for it, or that the church authorities were 'useless idiots', disobedient to the Pope and meddling in politics. In spite of this boycott, the dialogue has gone ahead and has been a source of unity for many people in Paraguay's cultural leadership – academics, journalists, trade unionists and so on.

Against this sketched background of 1986, another series of seemingly minor events in April 1987 assume new significance as indicators of the relationship between Church and State in Paraguay. The President's speech, as already mentioned, had been delivered on 1 April. On 10 April the weekly church newspaper called *Sendero* (and subtitled Organo de la Conferencia Episcopal Paraguaya) carried an article by Ismael Rolón, the Salesian who has been Archbishop of Asunción and leader of the hierarchy since 1970. Entitled 'Precisiones en torno a la democracia paraguaya', it could not be other than a reply to Stroessner's speech of the previous week. Even though he never mentioned the President directly, the whole thrust of the archbishop's article seemed to argue in a contrary direction. He spoke of the twisting of the word 'democracy' by politicians who will tolerate no opposition and resort to personal threats against their critics. According to Rolón, democracy should mean serving the good of the whole people through rulers chosen in open elections. Without those traits, said the archbishop pointedly, one merely had 'manipulation and dictatorship', where 'one confuses the party with the people'. Often, he added, those who control security 'turn the State into their private property, like a family plantation, reducing the citizens to serfs and to people of an inferior class'. He ended by saying that the Church was committed to the creation of a 'more just and more fraternal society' and that through education and spiritual formation it was hoped that 'new men could raise up a new Paraguay'.

Three days after the appearance of that article a confrontation occurred between the 'new men' and the old 'security'. A few hundred theology students, both seminarians and young religious, announced that Monday of Holy Week would be for them a day of fasting in solidarity with a peasant leader on hunger strike in prison after a series of evictions in a zone called Tavapy. As part of this day they planned to hold a Stations of the Cross in the street outside the national seminary. But their procession got less than fifty yards outside the gates when it was attacked by police in riot gear. The peasant-made bare cross was broken, knocking its crown of thorns to the ground. Some thirty of the students were injured by batons, two fairly seriously, before they retreated behind the gates to continue the Stations with the police now only feet away. At the end of the ceremony the Rector took a loud-hailer and said, 'I now give a blessing to all here present but especially to the policeman who struck me'. At this point also one of the students advanced to the line of police to hand back one of their helmets that he might easily have kept as a trophy. It was roughly received but the crown of thorns was not returned to them.

The next day Archbishop Rolón issued a particularly strong statement asking if the lifting of the state of siege were merely a 'piece of theatre', and he went on to take up the accusation of 'subversion' sometimes levelled at the Church and at him personally. If the word implied violent revolution, that was not the way of the Church. But in its Latin origin *sub-vertere* could mean to change from below and in this sense yes, the Church was struggling for justice for the oppressed. He ended by referring to the possibility of a papal visit to Paraguay (an occasion welcomed by *La Voz del Coloradismo* as a great encounter between an anti-communist country and an anti-communist Pope). We will make sure that he knows the truth, said the Archbishop.

Other reactions to the Stations of the Cross incident took various forms. On the evening of the event itself, several interviews on the independent radio station Primer de Marzo denounced the irreverence of an assault on such a religious act during Semana Santa. Others spoke of the Catholicism of the government officials as being of the 'Lord, Lord' and even 'Pope, Pope' variety but never listening to the situation of the poor. On the following day the Colorado party daily, *Patria*, made no mention whatever of the confrontation. Instead it launched an attack on the Catholic station, Radio Caritas, for not reciting the St Francis prayer for peace each day, as it was accustomed to do when a Franciscan priest was its director. This seems a perfect example of corrupt and hypocritical propaganda in view of the fact that the same Franciscan was expelled from Paraguay, or at least not allowed to return from a visit abroad. *Hoy*, another pro-government newspaper, carried a first editorial saying that any critics of Stroessner are critics of the truth and of the fatherland, but it did give a quarter page report of the confrontation in fairly neutral tone.

The Stations episode may have been minor but it is typical of the conflict of interpretations of religion that can be found in many countries of Latin America, where it is increasingly transparent that the powerful are in more danger than the poor of retaining a religiousness of mere form and devoid of real faith. In so far as they 'use' the Church for its rituals, they are shielding themselves from any gospel of liberation and erecting an idolatrous god who is the defender of their own security. In this respect General Stroessner is fond of a distinction between 'good' and 'bad' priests; he used it in his Christmas message last year. Good priests nourish the passive pieties of the people but bad priests use religion to interfere with society, disturbing the people with leftist notions of justice and upheaval.

The Church in Paraguay has its own mixture of such good and bad priests. Some of the bishops are decidedly 'bad', not only Archbishop Rolón but in a particular way Bishop Mario Medina who is the editor of a monthly called *Nuestro Tiempo*, which gathers together many of the journalists ousted from the banned *ABC Color*. Started in 1985, this periodical has been consistently critical of all the stances of the dictatorship and it brings to light many of the issues that the government would prefer to suppress. Its particular focus has been on the struggle of land rights by peasants, on the erosion of human rights by the security forces, and on the various ways in which the regime denies press freedom. It is hardly surprising that *Nuestro Tiempo* is not sold openly on the usual newstands but available by private contact.

What seems to characterise the Church in Paraguay now is a wide spectrum of agreement among these 'bad' men and women of the Church, who probably make up the majority of clergy and religious in the country. They are not advocating revolution – which would seem futile in any case – but they are choosing a road of slow preparedness for a different future. Their strategies include the 'national dialogue', the creation of various religious-based communities of reflection, a speaking out from solidarity with the poor and oppressed, and an alertness to the abnormality of what can pass for normal in this long-lived regime. For instance, letters are opened entering and leaving the country; there are more government informers than primary teachers; contraband corruption is omnipresent; poor conscripts in the army are used as house-boys by wives of the officers; each line of the capital city's bus system is owned by a particular general; control of all sporting clubs is in the hands of the Colorado party. And so on.

Of course there are Catholics who think that Stroessner and his regime are justified because the country has found stability and peace, and these supporters, reluctant or vehement, can be found in rich and poor alike. But many of the Catholic leaders as well as the more vocal and committed among the younger generations, lay and religious, remain opposed to the price being paid each day for that 'peace'. This chapter has sought to present some of the evidence for this spirit of opposition and resistance in recent times. One thing is certain. The Church remains a vital presence of hope in an increasingly uncertain situation and it can expect to play a crucial role when the moment of real change comes.

POSTSCRIPT

The thirty-four-year-old dictatorship of General Alfredo Stroessner was ended on 3 February 1989 by a *coup d'état* led by General Andrés Rodríguez. Amid claims of widespread intimidation, General Rodríguez was elected President of Paraguay on 1 May 1989 while the Colorado Party won a majority in Congress.

19 The Catholic Church, Human Rights and the 'Dirty War' in Argentina

Emilio Mignone

During the 1970s, the Argentinian republic experienced a period of political violence which continued up to the establishment of the constitutional government on 10 December 1983.[1]

To a large extent as a reaction to the repeated interventions by the armed forces and consequent military dictatorships, there emerged certain groups – principally the Montoneros (Guerrilla fighters) and the Ejército Revolucionario del Pueblo (the People's Revolutionary Army, ERP) who developed tactics of urban and rural guerrilla warfare.[2]

This provoked severe suppression, both during the *de facto* regimes of Generals Juan Carlos Onganía, Roberto M. Levingston and Alejandro A. Lanusse (1966–73), and the brief Peronist constitutional period (1973–6), particularly from the time of María Estela (Isabel) Martínez de Perón's presidency which commenced on 10 July 1974.

As emerges from serious impartial studies, at no time did the subversive groups come to constitute a threat to the country's institutional stability nor to its armed forces, although initially they did find support among sectors of the youth. A real 'war' never existed. The guerrilla episodes were made up of attacks on police and military units – in all cases repelled – kidnappings, surprise assassinations and the planting of bombs. An attempt at rural guerrilla warfare in Tucumán was quickly thwarted. Towards the end of 1975, due to the discovery of the military commands, the operative ability of the combating centres had been destroyed and their headquarters identified and infiltrated. They were only able to carry out isolated acts of violence and they had lost the support which they could have relied on at a different time.[3]

On 24 March 1976 the armed forces overthrew the constitutional government – for the sixth time since 1930 – and took charge of governing, assuming absolute power, without any limits whatsoever.

To this end they issued a series of institutional acts, modifying the country's constitution.

This new *coup d'état* had certain characteristics which differentiated it from previous ones, significantly affecting the development of events. On this occasion, the armed forces not only took the decision in an institutional manner, with the express approval of their higher ranks, but also they decided to rule the nation as an institution. It involved a government directly controlled by the armed forces, who shared the governmental duties among their members, maintaining the balance between the three branches (army, navy and air force) and establishing an internal mechanism of filling vacant posts. It was not a personal dictatorship, supported by the armed forces, as in the classic cases, but a military dictatorship.

Moreover, the armed forces were determined to remain in power for as long as necessary – no doubt for several decades – until a new political, socio-economic and cultural structure would be established which would carry on their principles and would accept the permanent guidance of the military power. In other words it was the total application of the so-called doctrine of national security.[4] To this end, General Jorge Rafael Videla, a member of the first military junta, and the first *de facto* president, constantly repeated: 'the Proceso de Reorganización Nacional (Process of National Reorganisation) – as the regime called itself – has aims but no deadlines'.[5]

A third element is linked to this which is directly related to the theme of this article. The armed forces, together with the express vote of the Generals, Admirals and Brigadiers (airforce generals) approved the application of a system of clandestine repression of present and potential dissidents. Essentially, this action consisted in the forced disappearance of individuals. The military decided not to use the legal process to judge suspects nor to apply the death penalty which existed in the penal code. The number of untried prisoners, even though it reached 8000 at the most intense period, was small in comparison with the total number of victims. As a document from the Centro de Estudios Legales y Sociales (Centre of Legal and Social Studies) states, 'the principal characteristic of the adopted system, which distinguishes it from other similar ones in Latin America, is the almost total secrecy of procedures. To this end, the arrest of individuals, followed by their disappearance, and the refusal to recognise the responsibility of intervening organisations, practised in thousands of cases throughout that extensive period, is the key instrument in the method conceived and used by the government of the armed forces to act against suspects and dissidents. It is the practice of State terrorism on a large scale which includes, among other elements, the indiscriminate use of torture, the concealment of information, the creation of a climate of fear, the marginalization of the judicial power, the uncertainty among families and the deliberate confusion of families'.[6]

This procedure was applied against thousands of citizens, principally youths. The report by the Comisión Nacional sobre la desaparición de Personas (National Commission on the Disappearance of People, CONADEP),[7] records, duly documented, 8960 cases of 'disappeared persons', but their number is, without doubt, much higher. The estimate varies, I believe, between twenty and thirty thousand. To this must be added the several thousand assassinations in public and the tens of thousands of those tortured, harassed, robbed and exiled.

It involved, as the Cámara Federal de Apelaciones en los Criminal de la Capital Federal (Federal Chamber of Appeal in Criminal cases in the Federal Capital) stated at the trial of the ex-members of the military juntas, a *criminal plan* conceived and executed by the armed forces, bringing all the State's resources into play to that end. The Argentinian republic had never suffered a systematic violation of fundamental human rights in that way, systematically and coldly carried out by the State, bringing terror to the population and leaving citizens defenceless. And the most serious aspect from a Christian view point is that this real genocide was committed while invoking God's holy name and claiming that by acting in that way they were defending the Catholic Church and Western Christian civilisation.

To emphasise the homicidal intention of the military dictatorship and its conception of who were considered dissidents and suspects, it is relevant to quote two statements by General Jorge Rafael Videla. In 1975, when he was acting as Commandant in Chief of the Army during the constitutional regime, on the occasion of the eleventh Conferencia de Ejércitos Americanos (Conference of American Armies), Videla said: 'if needs be, all the people whose deaths are necessary to bring about security in Argentina will have to die'.[8] When he was already *de facto* president, Videla stated: 'a terrorist is not just someone with a gun or a bomb. But also someone who spreads ideas that are contrary to Western and Christian civilization'.[9]

THE ROLE OF THE CATHOLIC CHURCH

In the context described, I will attempt to analyse in this piece of work, the role played by the Catholic Church during the military dictatorship (1976–83) and in particular by its Episcopate[10].

The presence of Catholicism in the Argentinian Republic is important and originated with Spanish colonialisation initiated in the sixteenth century. About 85 per cent of a population of 32 million inhabitants claim to adhere to that belief, although those practising are much fewer. A high number of Catholic congregations and institutions exist, particularly in the educational field and not only the religious but also the social, political and cultural influence of the Church and that of its hierarchy is notorious. The diocesan and auxiliary bishops number close to a hundred. As will be seen in due course, the link between the State and the Catholic Church, has, in turn, very deep historical roots.

The first fact I wish to point out is the intimate relationship between the episcopal cupola (inner circle), especially the members of the military vicariate, and those responsible for the coup of 24 March 1976.

Monsignor Adolfo Tortolo, who died in 1986 after a long illness, was in 1976 the Archbishop of Paraná in the province of Entre Ríos; the president of the Conferencia Episcopal Argentina (Argentinian Episcopal Conference) and the Vicar of the Armed Forces. On account of his previous actions in the diocese of Mercedes in the province of Buenos Aires, he was a close friend and adviser to the members of the first military junta, General Jorge Rafael Videla and Brigadier Orlando Agosti, natives of that city.

Tortolo was closely linked with the events which preceded the coup of 24 March 1976 and he could not have been unaware of the repressive methods which the armed forces had decided to use. The night before the military revolt, two of the leaders of the conspiracy – General Jorge Rafael Videla and Admiral Emilio Massera – met with the heads of the episcopate in the main offices of that organisation. On 24 March, the three members of the military junta held a long session with the Archbishop of Paraná, the president of the episcopal conference and the military vicar, according to a report the following day in *La Nación* newspaper. On leaving the interview, Tortolo stated that 'although the Church has its specific mission, there are circumstances in which it cannot avoid taking part even when problems which are usually the specific order of the State are involved'; hence the 'positive co-operation' with the new government, the product of a military rebellion against a constitutional regime freely elected by the people.

To stick strictly to the truth, the *coup d'état* was announced beforehand by some bishops, among them Tortolo. On 23 September 1975, in a homily given in the presence of General Roberto Viola, Monsignor Victorio Bonamín, Vicar of the Army, wondered 'will Christ not wish someday for the armed forces to go beyond their normal function'. And on 29 December of the same year, during a lunch in the Cámara Argentina de Anunciantes (Argentinian Chamber of Advertisers) in the Plaza Hotel, Monseignor Adolfo Tortolo prophesied that a 'process of purification' was approaching.

My wife and I had close dealings with Tortolo for many years when we both were active in the Juventud de Acción Católica (Youth of Catholic Action) in Luján city in the diocese of Mercedes. Tortolo was then acting as vicar general of that diocese. For that reason, he was one of the first people we approached for help when, on 14 May 1976, a group of men belonging to the armed forces entered our house in Buenos Aires city in the early hours of the morning and took our daughter Mónica, then aged 24, with them. We never heard anything about her again. Mónica had been added to the list of thousands of those arrested – and disappeared. The authorities always denied her arrest, but we have established that she was a prisoner in the Escuela de Mecánica de la Armada (Navy School of Mechanics), where without doubt she was savagely tortured and then assassinated. More than 4000 people suffered the same fate in that sinister establishment, among them two French nuns, Sisters Alice Domón and Léonie Duquet. The bodies of those assassinated were thrown out of planes belonging to the armed forces into the Plata river and the Atlantic ocean. Mónica's crime was collaboration, along with the other young people who were arrested and disappeared that same night, in a slum in a suburb of Buenos Aires, working for the human, religious, social, cultural and political advancement of its inhabitants with whom she was identified.

I saw Tortolo in July 1976. He told me he received hundreds of reports every day, but that nothing could be done. A little later I met him again against his wishes, with a group of parents of young people who had been arrested and had disappeared. He avoided any commitment and blocked the possibility of further interviews. On 14 October 1976, while disappearances were happening by the hundred every day and the orgy of blood unleashed by the military was at its height, Tortolo declared to reporters: 'I do not know, I have no reliable proof that human rights are violated in our country. I hear about it, I listen to it, but I am not convinced.' Of course, he was lying. No informed person – military personnel, politicians, bishops, ambassadors, journalists, managers, social and working-class leaders – was unaware of what was happening.

THE MILITARY VICARIATE

The conduct of the members of the military vicariate is one of the most lamentable aspects in the scene of the relationship between the Catholic Church and State terrorism.

Although since the days of colonisation, Argentinian armies could call on Catholic priests for the spiritual attention of their members, it was in 1957, during the *de facto* government of General Pedro E. Aramburu, that a military vicariate for the armed forces was established, through an agreement with the Holy See. It was established that the military vicar would be a bishop designated by the Pope, in agreement with the President of the Nation. The first vicars, Fermín Laffite and Cardinal Antonio Caggiano, at the same time Archbishops of Buenos Aires, did not pay much attention to this duty. On the other hand their successor in 1968, Adolfo Tortolo, appointed during General Juan Carlos Onganía's military dictatorship, dedicated himself to the indoctrination of the Army Corps.

Tortolo was succeeded by Monsignor José Miguel Medina, appointed in 1982, at the height of the military dictatorship. Medina resigned his post as Bishop of Jujuy and dedicated himself full-time to his task.

On 21 April 1986, Pope John Paul II, through the apostolic constitution 'Spiritual Militia', raised military vicariates to the status of dioceses with military jurisdiction, logically including the one in Argentina (there are 12 in America, 9 in Europe, 3 in Africa, 3 in Asia and 2 in Oceania). Since then Medina has been the bishop of the armed forces, with jurisdiction over military personnel and their families and with the authority to set up seminaries.

I believe that from what the Argentinian experience shows, this decision by the Holy See constitutes an extremely serious mistake. The military bishops and chaplains, incorporated into the armed forces with military rank and all its prebends, are assimilated rapidly into its mentality, they submit to its discipline and cause this condition to prevail over their priestly nature. And we know well that 'no-one can serve two masters'.[11]

During the clandestine repression, the military bishops and

chaplains publicly and privately justified the torture, assassinations and abuses by the armed forces, exempting its members from moral responsibility. They even developed a supposed doctrine with that meaning.[12] In my book referred to at the beginning of this chapter, I have furnished an appreciable quantity of documents, statements and testimonials which prove beyond doubt this assertion.

From among hundreds of cases, that of the army vicar, Bishop Victorio Bonamín must be pointed out. He refused to see me when I went to ask for his help on account of my daughter's arrest and disappearance. He had his secretary tell me that he did not become involved in situations about prisoners, 'disappeared persons' and unemployed so as not to interfere with the actions of the armed forces. Clearly military discipline had prevailed over his condition as a minister of Christ – who was persecuted and who exalted the persecuted. He set himself up, moreover, as a violent exponent of blood, death and hatred, sacrilegiously mixing sacred values with more spurious interests and servilely giving adulation to the military authorities.

THE EPISCOPATE

Three sectors must be distinguished in the Argentinian episcopate. First, the small group who acted decidedly in favour of the enforcement of human rights, composed of Jáime de Nevares, the Bishop of Neuquén and one of the presidents of the Asamblea Permanente por los Derechos Humanos (the Permanent Assembly for Human Rights), Jorge Novak, Bishop of Quilmes in the province of Buenos Aires and the director of the Movimiento Ecuménico por los Derechos Humanos (The Ecumenical Movement for Human Rights), Enrique Angelelli, Bishop of La Rioja, assassinated by the armed forces in a simulated traffic accident on 4 August 1976; and Miguel Hesayne, Bishop of Viedma in the province of Río Negro, a member of the Asamblea Permanente por los Derechos Humanos.

Secondly, a nucleus of prelates aware of the crimes being committed but whose actions went no further than private gestures or pressure within the Church. With the risk of being unjust through omission, I believe that the following must be included in this: Vicente Zaspe, from Santa Fe, Alberto Devoto, from Goya; Jorge Alcides Casaretto from San Isidro, in the province of Buenos Aires, Justo Laguna from Moron in the province of Buenos Aires,

Jorge Kemerer, from Posadas Misiones, José Marozzi, from Resistecia, Chaco, Carlos Ponce de León from San Nicolás de los Arroyos in the province of Buenos Aires (who also died in a suspicious car accident on 11 July 1977) and Manuel Marengo from Azul, in the province of Buenos Aires.

The remainder of the bishops, that is to say the majority, decidedly supported the military regime and many of them took an aggressive stance against human rights' organisations and the victims of state terrorism. The management of the episcopal conference, made up of archbishops from the most important and central dioceses, compelled that body to take up positions incompatible with the Gospel. In my book I quote abundant public statements by cardinals and bishops which summarise that identification which was also apparent from its practice. The following must be mentioned among these: the two cardinals, the archbishop of Buenos Aires, Juan Carlos Aramburu and the archbishop of Córdoba, Raúl Primatesta; the archbishop of La Plata, Antonio José Plaza, who acted as police chaplain in the province of Buenos Aires and justified torture and assassinations; Antonio Quarracino, former bishop of Avellaneda, ex-president of CELAM and the present archbishop of La Plata; Jorge Mayer, archbishop of Bahía Blanca; Jorge Manuel López, the present archbishop of Rosario, Santa Fe; Octavio Nicolás Derisi, rector of the Catholic Pontifical University of Santa María in Buenos Aires; Desiderio Collino, from Lomas de Zamora; Italo Di Stéfano, archbishop of San Juan; Guillermo Bolatti, archbishop of Rosario, deceased; Carlos Mariano Pérez, the retired archbishop of Salta; Ildefonso María Sansierra, archbishop of San Juan, deceased; Jorge Carreras, bishop of San Justo, deceased; Juan Rodolfo Laise, from San Luis; León Kruk, from San Rafael, Mendoza; Rubén di Monte, from Avellaneda and others whom I omit.

As I explained earlier, the heads of the Catholic Episcopate were duly informed of the plans to overthrow the constitutional regime and to establish a military dictatorship for a prolonged period of time, followed by a new political, economic and social order. At those lengthy meetings, at the critical time of the fundamental decisions, a complete examination of the situation and of the effects which would follow from the repressive method adopted must have been carried out. It could be foreseen that the victims' relations and friends would desperately seek the bishops' intercession, as, in effect, occurred.

The agreement reached emerges clearly in the light of events. The regime would have a free hand in its repressive action and would count on the support of the episcopate, in exchange for its alleged defence of 'Western and Christian civilization', and the consolidation of the Church's privileges.

The attitude of the majority of the episcopate and the influence of the cupola of the episcopal conference, decided the position taken by the body regarding state terrorism, set up by the military dictatorship.

The Argentinian episcopate made a purely political choice. It allied itself with the temporal power, renouncing the words of the gospel, which required the prophetic renouncement of crimes and those responsible for them, and the active assistance of victims, even with the risk of persecution. The episcopate knew the truth and hid it, for the benefit of the government of the armed forces. Between God and Caesar, it chose the latter.

It does not escape me that a different decision would also have had political implications. But it is not human criteria but the gospel which must guide the action of Bishops. 'As pastors', John Paul II said when inaugurating the Puebla Conference 'you have a vivid awareness that your principle duty is to be teachers of the truth. Not a human, rational truth but the truth which comes from God, which brings with it the principle of the authentic liberation of Man: *And you will know the truth and the truth will make you free* (John 8: 32); that truth which is the only one to offer a solid basis for an adequate praxis.... Those who are familiar with the history of the Church know that at all times, there have been admirable figures of bishops, profoundly pledged to the promotion and valiant defence of human dignity. They have acted always in line with the mandate of their episcopal mission, because for them, human dignity is an evangelical value which cannot be depreciated without greatly offending the Creator.... It is not from opportunism nor from a desire for novelty that the Church is a defender of human rights. It is from an authentic *evangelical commitment* which, as happened with Christ, is a commitment to those most in need.'[13]

In May 1976 as a result of its twice yearly meeting, the episcopate issued a document in which it indicated in general terms the illegitimacy of kidnappings and assassinations, but then it set out a lengthy exoneration of the regime, which it did not directly accuse. It is as if the crimes were committed by persons unknown, or by the forces of Nature, when the whole country knew their source. In short, it was playing the same game as the dictatorship in the tactics of denying its responsibility for the criminal events.

The following year, on 7 May 1977, when families of victims of the clandestine repression were bringing pressure to bear on the bishops, that body issued the most complete of its documents on the subject, entitled *Reflexión cristiana para el pueblo de la patria* (Christian reflection for the people of the fatherland). In the chapter on 'Hechos Observados' (Observed Facts), it tells of the reports it received, without assuring their credibility and it reiterated their incompatibility, in the case of their being correct, with Christian doctrine. The text is also accompanied by expressions of cordiality, understanding and excuses towards the authorities.

In 1982, when the military dictatorship was in its decline, the episcopate published a book of documents intended to justify its controversial action regarding the violations of human rights, which was beginning to be discussed. In the second edition of that work, a communication dated 26 November 1977 is included, which was kept secret until that moment and in which the bishops stress the seriousness of the reports they receive and the disrepute which maintaining a position of supporting the regime means for them.[14]

From that time on, a series of conversations took place between members of the Comisión Ejécutiva de la Conferencia Episcopal (the Executive Commission of the Episcopal Conference) – usually at publicised lunches – and the *de facto* president Videla and other members of the military hierarchy. The episcopal conference – which never wanted to meet representatives of human rights organisations any more than Cardinals Aramburu and Primatesta did – allowed intelligence officers in to their meetings to explain the anti-subversive activity.

Later events show that the episcopate resolved, in 1978, even though the disappearances, torture and assassinations continued, perhaps on a lesser scale, to make a fresh start and to speak no more about the matter. As I said before, between the gospel and the political powers, it opted to maintain ties with the latter even though it was at the cost of the Lord's commandment. The bishops did not say as Peter and John: 'We cannot but speak of what we have seen and heard', nor did they address the authorities as they did: 'Whether it is right in the sight of God to listen to you rather than to God, you must judge'.[15] They did not dare to report on those responsible despite knowing who they were, nor to indicate with gesture or action the seriousness of the crimes committed. They feared the consequences of a split or conflict. They abandoned the poorest and most crushed among their congregation: the disappeared persons.

A disappeared person is a totally abandoned one. The armed forces kidnap him with impunity; they isolate him and prevent him from knowing his whereabouts; they cover his head with a hood; they torture him to the limit of his strength; they harass him; they insult him; they humiliate him and after days, months, years, they coldly and cowardly murder him, not allowing him to die with his parents, brothers, sisters, friends. Finally they hide the body, preventing a time of mourning. I am thinking about my daughter, Mónica, and her friends who suffered that calvary. And about Jesus, who was also abandoned. It is the expression in Psalm 22, which is repeated in Mark and Matthew: 'My God, My God, why have you forsaken me?'[16]

The position of the Bishops became obvious when, in April 1983, the Comisión Ejecutiva de la Conferencia Episcopal (The Executive Commission of the Episcopal Conference) was the only institution which found the so-called final document of the military junta acceptable. With this declaration, the armed forces were attempting to close off the possibility of any investigation and they were justifying the genocide action, giving up as dead the thousands of disappeared persons. The reaction against it was unanimous and was expressed even in the *Osservatore Romano* and in the Vatican. Pope John Paul II, in St Peter's Square on 4 May 1983, made an unequivocal condemnatory reference to that fateful report, which was rejected by churches, political parties, organisations and individuals from all walks of life.

I recall the episode of St Ambrose using the pulpit in Milan Cathedral against Emperor Teodosius' crimes. A similar act on the part of Cardinal Aramburu in Buenos Aires would have, in my opinion, stopped the genocide, or at least have saved the lives of thousands of people. Clearly the Episcopal body rejected the idea of creating an ecclesiastical institution, like the Vicaria de la Solidaridad (the Vicarate of Solidarity) in the archbishopric of Santiago de Chile, leaving the victims and their families abandoned and the human rights organisations, which were accused by the prelates of being communists, without protection.

I accept the possibility that there was a risk that such action would not change the course of events. But that is not the question. The mission of pastors of the Christian flock, in accordance with the Master's example, does not consist of guaranteeing results, but of bearing witness to the truth, even at the cost of life itself.

It could be objected that it is not fair to lay the responsibility for what happened on the episcopate, when other equally important sectors of society, like the political leaders and the Jewish organisations also kept quiet. I do not attempt to defend them and it will be for others to carry out that analysis. But it is important to indicate very clearly that, in the circumstances in which the coup of 24 March 1976 took place, only the Catholic hierarchy was in a position to exert a decisive influence. The military regime was trying to base its action on the defence of Christian values and it could not have survived an open criticism by the bishops.

This omission has been recognised by several bishops. 'When all this ends', Archbishop Vicente Zaspe said to me in 1977, 'the Episcopate will be held up to ridicule'. 'There is a need for an examination of the conscience of the Argentinian church', indicated the Bishop of Neuquén, Jáime de Nevares, on 9 April 1984, 'regarding its attitude during the military dictatorship.'[17] 'Our accusation was not always accompanied by any moves, by concrete actions', bishop Justo Laguna said on Vatican radio on 3 June 1984.

The Vatican and Nuncio Laghi

To appreciate the role of the Holy See and the Pope in the events which took place in Argentina during the military dictatorship, the limitations of the universal government of the Church must be taken into consideration. His Holiness the Pope cannot take over the functions of the national episcopate.

In the light of this circumstance, I do believe that the attitudes of the papacy were important. Hardly had the military coup taken place than reports and requests for intervention began to arrive in Rome, particularly via the Argentinian Cardinal Eduardo Pironio, the then Prefect of the Sagrada Congregación de Religiosos e Institutos Seculares (the Sacred Congregation of Religious and Secular Institutes). I am only going to refer to those of a public nature since I am unaware of the private actions there may have been, while the Vatican does not open up the files.

The first action was that by Paul VI, who, towards the end of 1976, on receiving the credentials of the ambassador of the military dictatorship before the Holy See, Rubén Blanco – the brother of the vice-rector of the Argentinian Catholic University – addressed only the Argentinian people. He added that the disappearances and assassinations needed an adequate explanation and he issued a warning to the episcopate, which the latter – as will be seen further on – did not heed. 'The Argentinian Church', he said, 'must not maintain any privileges. She must be content with being able to serve the faithful and the civil community, within a climate of serenity and security for all.'[18]

John Paul II, in turn, on three occasions, referred publicly to the problem of the disappearances in Argentina: on 30 August 1980, in St Peter's Square, on 4 May 1983 in the same place on the occasion mentioned before and at the end of that year when addressing the diplomatic corps. The curious thing is that, on each occasion, the Argentinian Cardinals Aramburu and Primatesta and other bishops tried to scale down the nature of the Holy Father's allocutions, claiming that he had not said what, literally, was interpreted. On two occasions, one in Porto Alegre, Brazil and the other again in St Peter's Square – my wife being with them the second time – the Madres de Plaza de Mayo (the Mothers of May Square), managed to exchange a few words with John Paul II.

However, on the two visits which John Paul II made to Argentina, in 1982 and 1987, he refused to meet with the human rights organisations, giving as a reason a shortage of time. I think also, from impromptu comments expressed to journalists during his flights, that the Pope has not understood – or does not wish to understand – the special nature of military repression in Argentina, and the particular cruelty and cynicism of the method used in the disappearances carried out in the name of God.

Another aspect which has aroused interest in the international press is the role of the nuncio, Pio Laghi, who remained in Argentina almost throughout the period of military dictatorship. His name turned up in 1984 – when he had already been transferred to Washington DC – on being included in a list of 1351 people linked with the repression, drawn up by CONADEP. He was accused of having interviewed a prisoner in a secret detention camp in Tucumán. I have carried out a personal investigation on this subject, which I relate in my book and I have come to the conclusion that it cannot be proven that, on the occasion of his journey to that city in June 1976, he saw that person, of whose good faith, however, I have no doubt. There was surely some mix up.

But, from my point of view, that matter is of little consequence. What is important is to analyse his overall behaviour.

From this viewpoint, Laghi's actions were irregular. He opened the doors of the nunciature to receive reports on the victims and, on many occasions, he listened to the families' stories. Sometimes his reaction was hard against the military regime. At other times, he attempted to excuse them. That happened to me personally several times. He lacked coherence and I think he is subject to sudden mood swings and is erratic. He used to appear fearful, despite the fact that in his situation – as I pointed out to him one day – he need not have been, and when all comes to all, the shepherd must give his life for his sheep. He helped many people to leave the country, especially ex-prisoners, but he never managed to lessen the rigidity of the illegal repression nor to locate one person who had been arrested – and had disappeared. He knew everything that was happening but his public addresses exalted the military regime, and he was on unnecessarily close terms with its highest members. Faced with the errors of the episcopate, he did not take, in my understanding, the necessary steps to urge them on or to make up for them. He gave out communion to military personnel whom he knew – so he revealed in private – were directly responsible for torturing and assassinations, even of priests.

HISTORICAL AND DOCTRINAL CONDITIONING FACTORS

What reasons explain the behaviour of the Argentinian Episcopate, so different from the cases in Chile, Brazil, Bolivia and Paraguay, to mention but a few?

The first cause lies in the tradition of dependency on the State which the Argentinian Catholic Church, in particular the episcopate, has had since colonial times. As is known, during the Hispanic period, by virtue of successive pontifical bulls, the Holy See granted the Spanish monarchy the so-called Real Patronato (Royal Patronage) through which the said monarchy, except in the distribution of the sacraments, had all-embracing powers, from proposing the appointment of bishops to setting up a village hospital, authorising a parish, a mission or a chaplaincy.

After Independence (1810–16), national governments considered themselves to have inherited this 'Patronato'. The Argentinian constitution of 1853 – *still in force* – retains that clause and recently in 1966, by virtue of an agreement with the Holy See, the Argentinian government ceased intervening in the appointment of bishops. Article 2 of the fundamental law establishes that 'the federal government supports the Roman Catholic apostolic religion'; Article 67, paragraph 15 orders Congress 'to promote the conversion of Indians to Catholicism'; Article 76 determines that the president of the nation must 'belong to the Roman Catholic apostolic communion'.

In practice, the State's contribution to the religion is small, although the contribution to private schools – 80 per cent Catholic – is substantial. The serious aspect of this is that those who receive the State's assistance are the bishops directly. At the height of the military dictatorship, founded on terror, the episcopate had the ill-fated idea of negotiating and obtaining, among other privileges, a state salary for each diocesan and auxiliary bishop, equivalent to 70 per cent of the income of a state judge, also special retirement terms for them, a salary proportionate to that of a civil servant for seminarians and even a grant towards a new house for the archbishop of Buenos Aires, Cardinal Juan Carlos Aramburu. Who could then prevent an image growing among the people of an episcopate which was well-disposed towards the government of the armed forces on account of these unwarranted and inopportune prebends?

There is no doubt that the first constitutional reform to take place in the country will abolish these anachronisms. I have proposed, meanwhile, that the Church take the lead and renounce such privileges and economic advantages, organising its support from the contributions of the faithful. It will only be fulfilling a mandate from the Second Vatican Council. 'The Church', the *Gaudium et Spes* constitution of 7 December 1965 says, 'uses temporal means when her own mission requires it. She does not, however, place her trust on privileges granted by civil power; moreover, she will renounce the exercise of certain acquired legitimate rights as soon as she sees that their use may tarnish the purity of her testimonials or that new conditions in life require other dispositions'.[19]

The second aspect concerns doctrinaire teaching. The vast majority of Argentinian bishops have had a conservative training which they have not managed to overcome and which, very often, they transform into a kind of national Catholicism, inherited from Spain. For this reason, when a regime like the military one presents itself as a crusader of the Faith they join up fervently. To that is added the feeling of security the dictatorship offers them, isolation from society's real forces, intellectual mediocrity, and provincialism.

That attitude showed in Puebla where the episcopal delegates defended the military dictatorship, holding that the doctrine of national security did not apply. All this also explains the universal discredit of the episcopate with the exceptions I indicated earlier.

The Argentinian episcopate found it difficult to adapt to pluralism, to a modern democratic society. But that is another story which, in due course, I will tell.

THE PERSECUTED CHURCH

The most striking thing about what happened in Argentina is that the episcopal complacency already described took place in the midst of the only bloody persecution which the Catholic Church has suffered in the history of Argentina

It is the incomprehensible case of an episcopate which denies its martyrs, hands over to a temporal authority the faculty of deciding on the orthodoxy of its faithful and persecutes Christians – priests and laity – who try to defend the dignity of the human being and the rights of the people.

Let us look at the facts. In the investigation I carried out to write my book – which may be improved on by other authors – I have confirmed that two bishops – Enrique Angelelli from La Rioja and Carlos Ponce de León, died in 1976 and 1977 respectively, both in car accidents, which without any doubt whatsoever were arranged intentionally. The first case has been proven in a judicial court and is particularly dramatic. It concerns a prelate who had developed an ecclesiastical community along the lines set out by the Second Vatican Council and the Medellín Conference and was defending the rights of the people. He was hated by the military, who after persecuting his followers for years decided to have him disappear. In spite of all the evidence, the episcopal conference continued to support the hypothesis of an accident, which nobody believes.

As I estimate it, 16 priests were assassinated by agents of the armed forces or have disappeared and are, undoubtedly, dead. Another 10 clerics were imprisoned for many years without judicial process and 11 were arrested and were tortured, harassed and concealed until their liberation. Between these and those exiled, the number reaches approximately one hundred.

Equally high is the number of committed brothers, nuns, seminarians and lay people who went through similar ordeals. This extended to the evangelical churches. For the moment, it is impossible to estimate the number. One congregation, the Fraternidad del Evangelio (The Gospel Fraternity) was exterminated.

Particularly well known are the incidents involving two French nuns of the Foreign Missions, Alice Domón and Léonie Duquet. They were arrested on 8 and 10 December 1977 respectively, for collaborating with the Madres de Plaza de Mayo and since then they have disappeared. It is known, however, that they were arrested under orders from Captain Alfredo Astiz, brought to the Escuela de

Mecánica de la Armada (Navy School of Mechanics), tortured and assassinated. In that same place were the two Jesuit priests, Orlando Iorio and Francisco Jálics who were freed after months of secret detention.

Early on 4 July 1976 three priests and two seminarians from the Pallottine order were assassinated in the San Patricio parish in Buenos Aires city. Although the episcopate and the nuncio had proof of who were responsible for the crime – agents of the Federal Police Force – nothing was done to investigate the incident.

Among the Christians who have disappeared, there is the well-known international Protestant theologian, an ex-rector of the National University of San Luis, Mauricio López; Elizabeth Käsemann and Patricia Anna Erb, both daughters of Evangelical pastors, from Germany and from the United States respectively.

And I cannot forget my daughter Mónica and her six companions, who lived for the poor, for human and religious advancement.

The Argentinian Catholic Church contains thousands of committed clerics, religious and lay people who were aware of the reality of the violations of human rights. It would be unjust if I began to list names, although I do want to indicate three outstanding examples. Fr Enzo Guistozzi, of the Pequeña Obra de la Divina Providencia (the Small Work of the Divine Providence), attached to the Asamblea Permanente por los Derechos Humanos (the Permanent Assembly for Human Rights); Fr Mario Leonfanti, a Salesian, attached to the Movimiento Ecuménico por los Derechos Humanos (the Ecumenical Movement for Human Rights); and Brother Antonio Puigjané, a Capuchin, and a follower of the Madres de Plaza de Mayo. The three were punished at the request of their respective bishops for these activities. The same thing occurred to a group of seven clerics from Buenos Aires city, headed by Monsignor Jorge Vernazza, who were living in the emergency shelters and who defended their occupants when the military dictatorship evicted 40 000 families in such conditions. Cardinal Aramburu admonished them for the stance they took.

Those well-known priests who did the opposite must not be forgotten, for their defence of torture and genocide or who carried on equivocal missions, such as Monsignor Emilio Crasselli, secretary to the military vicar, Fr Christian von Wernich and numerous chaplains to the armed forces, the police and the penitentiary service.

The episcopate, as I said, abdicated its doctrinal functions. The military became theologians, they delivered heretical speeches and penalised religious teachers in Catholic schools with the bishops' knowledge and tacit consent. 'This war', held Lieutenant Colonel Hugo Pascarelli on 12 June 1976 in the presence of General Videla and the military chaplains, 'does not recognise moral or natural limits. It is taking place beyond Good and Evil. It exceeds the human level. Not to see this is the greatest offence to God and to the Fatherland.'[20]

But I wish to end this article with something even more surprising. The gospel according to Admiral Emilio Massera, Commander in Chief of the Navy, which was preached to Father Orlando Iorio while he was hooded and handcuffed in buildings belonging to the Navy: 'You are not a guerrilla fighter', the officer interrogating him said. 'You are not in the violence, but you do not realise that by going to live in the shelter, you unite the people, you unite the poor and uniting the poor is subversion. Your mistake is having interpreted too literally Christ's doctrine. Christ speaks of the poor, but it is the poor in spirit and you have gone to live with the poor. In Argentina, the poor in spirit are the rich, who are those who are spiritually in need.'[21]

NOTES

1. The principal source of this chapter is my book *Iglesia y Dictadura – El papel de la Iglesia a la luz de sus relaciones con el régimen militar* (Buenos Aires: Ediciones del Pensamiento Nacional, 1986) 283 pages. There is an English translation of a revised edition: *Witness to the Truth – The Complicity of Church and Dictatorship in Argentina* (New York: Orbis, 1988).
2. See Richard Gillespie: *Soldiers of Perón – Argentina's Montoneros* (Oxford: Clarendon Press, 1982) 310 pages.
3. See Daniel Frontalini and Cristina Caiati: *El mito de la guerra sucia* (Buenos Aires: Centro de Estudios Legales y Sociales (CELS), 1984) 112 pages.
4. The Third General Conference of the Latin American Episcopate, meeting in Puebla, Mexico in January 1979, in the presence of John Paul II, issued a document which analyses in various places the objectives and contents of the doctrine or ideology of national security, its anti-Christian nature and the claim of military regimes of using it as a defence of so-called western and Christian civilisation. I quote some of those paragraphs.

   547, c: 'In the last years, in our continent, the so-called "Doctrine of National Security" has become established, which in fact is more an

Ideology than a doctrine. It is linked with a certain economic-political model, with elitist and verticalist characteristics which suppress full participation by the people. It even claims to justify itself in certain Latin American countries as a doctrine in defence of Western and Christian civilisation. It develops a repressive system in accordance with its concept of "permanent war". In some cases it expresses a clear intent for geopolitical protagonism. The Doctrine of National Security, understood as an absolute ideology, would not be in harmony with a Christian vision of Man as responsible for the realization of a temporal plan not of the State as administrator of the common good. It imposes, in effect, the tutelage of the people for elite power groups military and political, and it leads to a heightened lack of equality or participation in the results of the development.'

49: 'The ideologies of National Security have contributed to the strengthening, on many occasions, of the totalitarian or authoritarian nature of the violent régimes, from which have been derived the abuse of power and the violation of human rights. In some cases, they attempt to conceal their attitudes with a subjective profession of Christian faith.'

1262: '. . . .Assassinations, disappearances, arbitrary imprisonment, acts of terrorism, kidnappings, torture, extended throughout the continent, show a total lack of respect for the dignity of the human being. Some claim to justify them even as requirements of National Security.'

5. Lieutenant General Jorge Rafael Videla was sentenced in 1985 to life imprisonment by the Cámara Federal de Apelaciones de la Capital Federal (the Federal Chamber of Appeal of the Federal Capital), for his part in the crimes committed during the Military Dictatorship. The sentence was upheld by the Corte Suprema de Justicia de la Nación (the Supreme Court of Justice of the Nation).
6. Augusto Conte MacDonnell, Noemi Labrune and Emilio F. Mignone: *El secuestro como método de detención* (Buenos Aires: Centro de Estudios Legales y Sociales (1982) p. 6, cf. Emilio Fermín Mignone for CELS: 'Les déclarations abusives de disparitions, instrument d'une politique', in *Le refus de l'oublie – La politique de disparition forcée de personnes, Colloque de Paris, janvier, février 1981* (Paris: Berger-Lévrault, 1982) pp. 152–83.
7. The Comisión Nacional sobre la Desaparición de Personas (the National Commission on the Disappearance of People) was set up by the president of the Argentinian republic, Raúl Alfonsín, on 15 December 1983. It was presided over by the writer, Ernesto Sábato. Its principal objective was to obtain clarification on the disappearances which occurred during the military dictatorship of 1976–83. It produced a report entitled Nunca Más [Never Again] – *Informe de la Comisión Nacional sobre Desaparición de Personas* (Buenos Aires: Editorial Universitaria de Buenos Aires [EUDEBA] 1984) 490 pages with an addendum. There are translations in English (London: Faber & Faber 1986, 463 pages), French, Italian, Portuguese and German. 'From the enormous documentation gathered', Sábato says in the

prologue, 'it is inferred that human rights were violated institutionally and by the State through repression by the Armed Forces' (p. 8).

8. Quoted in *Clarín*, Buenos Aires, 24 de octubre de 1975.
9. Quoted in *The Times*, London, 4 January 1978.
10. Horacio Verbitsky: *La última batalla de la tercera guerra mundial* (Buenos Aires: Editorial Legasa, 1984) p.15.
11. Luke 16:13.
12. For a study on the theological background of this ecclesiastical position, see: Ruben Dri: *Teología y Dominación* (Buenos Aires: Colección Teológica y Política, Roblanco SRL, 1987) 436 pages.
13. John Paul II's homily on inaugurating the work of the Third General Conference of the Latin American Episcopate, 28 January 1979. In *Mensajes de Juan Pablo II en América Latina* (Ediciones Paulinas, 1979) p. 54.
14. *Documentos del Episcopado Argentino – Colección completa del magisterio postconciliar de la Conferencia Episcopal Argentina – Documentos del Episcopado Argentino* (1965–1981) (Buenos Aires: Editorial Claretiana, 1982) 479 pages.
15. Acts 4:19.
16. Mark 15:34; Matthew 27:46.
17. *Clarín*, Buenos Aires, 6 de enero de 1986.
18. *Caras y Caretas*, Buenos Aires, agosto de 1984.
19. Concilio Vaticano II: *Constitución 'Gaudium et Spes' sobre la Iglesia en el mundo* (Madrid: Biblioteca de Autores Cristianos 1968) no. 76 p.120.
20. *La Razón, Buenos Aires, 12 de junio de 1976.*
21. *Diario del Juicio*, Buenos Aires, 1985.

20 The Disappeared: A New Challenge to Christian Faith in Latin America

Patrick Rice

This chapter deals with the phenomenon of forced or involuntary disappearances in Latin America and the Caribbean, with particular reference to the response to this human drama of Christians and the Catholic Church in particular. The reality of the disappeared is one of the most poignant challenges to Christian faith that we face in today's world. Let me begin with a testimony from Guatemala describing a typical case of forced disappearance which I received over six years ago while visiting Ecuador. I was staying with the local superior of the Divine Word Missionaries, Father Neil Doogan from Donegal. Knowing of my work in the area of human rights, he commented that recently some women religious had arrived from Guatemala. They had to leave because one of their community had been disappeared some weeks previously. It was arranged that I visit their novitiate some distance outside Quito. In the secluded atmosphere of a traditional convent the sisters recalled the events of the fateful night. Their convent was on the outskirts of Esquipulas, a town in southern Guatemala very close to El Salvador and Honduras, and home to the most important religious shrine of Central America. Late at night the community was awakened by loud banging on the front door. The superior finally went to attend, but the men outside, one of whom was masked, demanded to see Sister Victoria de la Roca Aldana, an old Guatemalan nun who was having treatment for cancer. It was not very difficult for them to force their way in and they began to search the dormitories. Sister Victoria was dragged out of her bed and forced outside. The gang members tied the other sisters with sheets and bedclothes and bolted the door. They then sprinkled the hallway with petrol and set the place ablaze. Fortunately, the mother superior had slipped out earlier to follow the kidnappers and was pleading with them to release Sister Victoria. When she saw the convent on fire, she returned immediately to unlock the door and free the other nuns. All then struggled to put out the flames. As they were doing so they heard the sound of motors starting. Sister Victoria was taken away and never heard of again.

This testimony is an example of the many thousands of disappearances that occur in Latin America. There is a vagueness about the authors of the crime and the reasons for the act. There is total uncertainty with respect to the fate of the victim. The possibility that Sister Victoria may still be alive is extremely remote. But neither is there any concrete evidence that she has been murdered. The religious congregation to which she belongs decided not to initiate any formal legal proceedings. They put all their hope in the local papal nuncio who took up the case with the authorities. The government said it needed more details to investigate the identity of the kidnappers – but there was no more information available. The sisters quietly commented to me that Sister Victoria had been helping escaping refugees from neighbouring countries and they suspected her case was 'political'. The community also felt the masked assailant was probably a local police informer. The best advice the nuncio could give the nuns was to leave the country. They did so reluctantly.

A DEFINITION OF FORCED OR INVOLUNTARY DISAPPEARANCE

This is but one of many thousands of cases of disappearances that have occurred in Latin America since the mid-seventies. One could, on the basis of the information now available, construct a typology of the practice. This approach has been taken by the United Nations. The General Assembly first adopted a position towards the phenomenon in 1978.[1] The term 'forced or involuntary disappearance' comes from that resolution. It does not attempt a definition of the violation itself; it refers to reports from different parts of the world of persons who have been forcefully disappeared, and it then lists the causes:

- those cases may be the result of excesses committed by the police or security forces;
- they may be due to illicit actions;
- they can have their origin in 'generalised violence'.

It is quite clear that the ambiguity of this typology is deliberate so that the governments involved can always argue that 'generalised violence' is to blame. The usefulness of that historic resolution was that it brought about a debate in the international community on the problem. The UN is now prepared to accept that a case, which may first have seemed to be the result of delinquency, can in fact be part of a deliberate policy of the security forces. That ongoing discussion means that there is a general consensus among human rights organisations on the nature of disappearances. Another useful definition appeared in a recent study carried out by the Independent Commission for International Humanitarian Affairs which is presided over by the Aga Khan.[2]

According to that report the following elements are involved in the phenomenon of disappearances:

> There is a general framework of repression or intimidation and there are a series of actions or omissions by the security forces of people working under state surveillance, whereby the whereabouts of a person is concealed and their fate covered-up, while any official implication in the case is vigorously denied.

The Latin American Federation of Families of Disappeared-Detainees (FEDEFAM) has an even more precise definition. According to this approach, the crime is the concealment of the victim and his/her fate. It is not simply the kidnapping of someone, but the practice of concealing all information about the victim.

When we compare this practice to other flagrant violations of human rights, it becomes clearer what we are speaking about. An extra-judicial execution is the arbitrary deprivation of life by some security agent; torture is the administering of deliberate suffering or pain; illegal arrest is the privation of liberty; kidnapping, which is normally a private crime, is the privation of freedom for extortion or other reasons. The odds are that if disappearance is expertly carried out with full state complicity, it is usually difficult, if not impossible, to know afterwards what has happened to the victim. The practice may, in that sense, include all the violations mentioned but it can never be reduced to any single one without diluting its seriousness.

The most dramatic form that the practice can take is best illustrated in the report of the Presidential Commission established by President Raúl Alfonsín of Argentina in 1984.[3] After mentioning the existence of crematoria, the destruction of all evidence and the refusal of the military to come forward with information, the Commission was forced to concede that many cases of disappearances might well never be resolved.

The full importance of drafting a universally accepted definition of the practice can only be appreciated when one understands that within the legal system that prevails in Latin America, there is no way of charging those responsible until the crime is fully codified in law with the procedures for prosecution clearly outlined. The two codified offences that are closest to it, and often used, are illegal or arbitrary arrest and kidnapping. However, one can scarcely speak of illegal arrest when the victim, who has been taken by security agents, is never heard of again. In the case of kidnapping it is even difficult to show that such a group has had the victim in its power for extortion or other reasons.

It is evident then that where a campaign of disappearance is carried out there are many levels of responsibility: the unit or task forces that capture the people; the military bases or police stations that serve as clandestine detention and interrogation centres; cemetery facilities to dispose of the bodies; judges who are reluctant to investigate; authorities that permit the system to operate; military or counter-insurgent strategists who are behind it – and the media that prefer to keep silent about the wrongdoings.

It is impossible to come by exact numbers where disappearances in Latin America are concerned, so any statistical study of the phenomenon is limited. The number of cases that have been processed by the United Nations is relatively easy to establish, as are those that have been presented formally to the courts in the countries concerned. However, one has to resort to estimates in order to get a clear idea of the cases that have actually occurred. Many cases are not reported, like, indeed, the case cited at the beginning of this chapter. Numbers that are available have to be updated constantly. It is a common occurrence for a case which has been reported and favourably resolved to remain on the list. In 1984 when I visited Peru as part of an investigative mission, the local public attorney reported that his office had received over 700 cases in Ayacucho, but as some had been resolved, in the sense that the person involved had either been released or killed, they were revising the list. In each country, there are a number of documented cases on the one hand and estimated total figures of disappeared on the other. In the chart below, I give both numbers when available. I have also included details on when the practice began in a certain country and when it ended. The source for each statistic is listed and where none is available I have worked from my own documentation.[4]

Table 1: *The Disappeared in Latin America and the Caribbean*

Country	Documented cases	Total estimated	Commenced	Ended
Argentina	8 961[1]	20 000	1974	1982
Bolivia	142[2]	500	1967	1982
Brazil	71[3]	500	1966	1981
Chile	758[4]	2 500	1973	1984
Colombia	950[5]	2 000	1978	continues
Dominican Republic	10[6]	50	1980	unknown
Ecuador	6[7]	50	1984	continues
Guatemala	2 500[8]	35 000[9]	1960	continues
Haiti	—	12 000	1957	1986
Honduras	104[10]	200	1980	continues
Mexico	536[11]	850	1978	continues
Nicaragua	3 500[12]	3 500	1984	continues
Panama	15[13]	15	1968	1985
Paraguay	100[14]	200	1970	continues
Peru	2 500[15]	4 000	1983	continues
El Salvador	4 000[16]	7000	1977	continues
Uruguay	156[17]	156	1976	1980
Venezuela	120[18]	150	1980	continues
TOTAL	24 429	88 671		

The statistics shown in Table 1 give an estimate of 88 671 cases of disappearances in all Latin America during the last twenty years, of which practically one-third are fully documented. This figure is generally considered to be on the conservative side. Nobel Laureate Gabriel García Marqués in his address to the Swedish Academy in 1984 mentioned 120 000 cases.

The United Nations Working Group on Forced Disappearances offered other statistics in their 1987 report. Since 1980, the UN has presented 14 000 individual cases to the different governments. Considering the exacting procedural demands for an individual complaint to be filed by the UN, this figure is truly alarming and even though it is just the tip of the iceberg, it reinforces all we have been saying. The problem currently exists in thirty-nine countries of which eighteen are Latin American and the remainder are in Africa, Asia or the Middle East, with only one European country on the list (Cyprus). In other words, the phenomenon quite definitely concerns the Third World.

FORCED DISAPPEARANCES AND THE CONSEQUENCES

No other human rights violation has been found to have such a profound and lasting effect on the victim, the family and society itself, than forced disappearance.

The problem enters like cancer in a society. At first it is scarcely detected by the family of the victim, but as it persists and grows it spreads to corrode all of society, disseminating fear and terror particularly among the targeted groups. There is the constant uncertainty about the fate of the victim. There is the conviction that he/she is being subjected to all kinds of torture. There is the powerlessness to move the authorities to investigate the case. This paralyses the normal functioning of the social fabric of which the victim is a member. During the first year or two relatives may feel that a positive solution is imminent. It is felt that the person may be released or put into official detention. But, during the following years, the question focuses increasingly on his/her likely fate. There is no quietening the anguish experienced. If nature abhors a vacuum, as my science professor used to say, society finds it equally disturbing and turbulent. Forced disappearance creates a vacuum, a kind of non-existence if you wish, of someone who in fact does or did exist. This dynamic became very evident in Chile when the authorities began to destroy any public document, such as birth registers, that would testify to the legal existence of the disappeared. Such an individual, about whom inquiries are being made, does not even exist. Philosophers have pondered, and claimed for centuries, that the very concept of non-existence is unthinkable. The families and friends of the disappeared are consequently forced by the State and the authorities to fathom the depths of irrationality. They are often pictured as mad or insane as they make their rounds of detention centres inquiring for their loved ones. The relatives are presented with many types of plausible explanations.

> So and so has gone underground, he has eloped with some girlfriend or he does not even exist . . . the disappeared is the latest invention of the political opposition or of subversive groups to discredit the government.

Naturally, in such a context, the family concerned becomes alienated from society. The fear and force of public ridicule can be so powerful that the loss is not shared even with close friends. When these dimensions of the problem are taken into account we can appreciate how angry someone can become who is struggling with the forced disappearance of a loved one when he/she is asked to consider the victim dead or simply to forget all about the person. Certainly, it would be much easier to do that but that is impossible without definite evidence of death. Neither is it very reasonable to consider the victim missing for some months and alive in some secret location, or about to walk in the door at any moment. Those are the two extremes between which the family concerned has to work out a *modus vivendi* in order to survive in real life. In fact, each family seems to work out some type of solution, but all have the effect of prolonging the anguish and sense of loss. The most usual practice is that the personal belongings of the victim are kept in place as if nothing has happened. The person simply did not arrive home – that is the case when someone has been taken from somewhere other than home. When inquiries seem to be getting somewhere, a homecoming is quietly prepared for only to be postponed again as hopes are crushed. Families become hesitant about leaving their homes because the person may return and not have a key to get in. In Colombia I know one family that lived chained to the telephone because an anonymous caller sometimes rang to give information about their missing son. One day the daughter in the family discovered the truth.

The family had decided to call in the security forces to investigate. A detective arrived to check the telephone and attached a special device that would tap the mystery caller if he rang again. She entered the house when a man was working on the phone and his voice seemed familiar. She then realised it seemed to be identical to that of the mystery caller. The fact that he never rang again reinforced her suspicions. But the parody had gone on for well over a year and everyone was on the edge of breakdown when it ended. It was a life-line while it lasted, but it was also a most cruel form of torture.

In some situations the problem can become more manageable, when there is overwhelming indirect evidence pointing to the death of the victim. In that respect, Amnesty International published a most moving photograph on the cover of their report 'Disappearances in Peru 1985', depicting a rural wake with the clothes of the person laid out instead of the corpse. Such a funeral rite may seem absurd, but it is the way that the Ayacucho peasants have learned to respond to the phenomenon of disappearances. This does not resolve the problem. Speaking to some women whose husbands are disappeared in a community in the mountains of central Peru, I learned that they had decided to become widows. However, they could not carry out most of the customs which were expected of widows in traditional Quechua culture. They found themselves in a despairing situation. One woman searched so thoroughly for the body of her husband that she was affectionately referred to as *busca-cadáveres* (corpse-searcher).

Psychologists and psychiatrists who have studied the phenomenon explain the effects of the disappearance of a near relative or family member as a bereavement which never ends. There is a real parting and separation which is sudden and often violent. However, it is not definite and the situation becomes increasingly inconclusive. It has been further explained, particularly in Argentina where many of these studies have been made but where Freudian principles tend to dominate in psychiatry, that the leading consequence in the psyche of the near relative is its virtual breakdown in terms of motivation, symbolism and functions. The proper response therefore needs to be both personal and collective. The key to overcoming the paralysis and general disorientation of the relative is in fact his/her active incorporation into a local committee or association for families of disappeared. The energy that goes into the work helps the person to cope much better so that many of these studies speak of the therapeutic benefits that derive from active militancy in a human rights organisation.[5]

Special mention must be made of the effects on children and how they relate to disappearances. Here studies are still very much at an introductory stage for the simple reason that it is a problem which is currently working itself out. During the first months the absence of father or mother, or indeed both, can be explained: 'He has gone on an unexpected trip and could not say goodbye.' 'She is imprisoned and we cannot visit her.' 'He has gone to stay with some friends as some bad men were looking for him,' and so on. Children accept these types of explanations only for a short time. Even then they normally sense that something is being hidden from them and they begin to elaborate quietly their own explanations for the sudden separation of someone who evidently cared for them. Here, children normally explain these situations in terms of their own culpability. Communication with surrounding family members breaks down and concealment can become a feature of their behaviour. A Chilean organisation exclusively dedicated to child-care, has made important studies among the children of disappeared. They discovered that children normally need at some time to be with other children who are living the same drama so as to elaborate their social relationships.[6] They become more capable of handling questions such as references to their parents in school or at home. The advice that is normally given to adults is to explain to their children. At first they will find it difficult to assimilate, but in time they adapt. The damage which benevolent misinformation can do is incalculable in terms of a child's self-confidence and growth. It may seem the easy way out but is often more dangerous. Several cases in which I have been consulted come to mind.

One young mother desperately wished to know if we had been able to trace the whereabouts of her husband missing in Argentina for several years. Her most pressing reason was that she had been telling her young child that her father was imprisoned and could not write. The child convinced herself that she was to blame, and became withdrawn and depressed, showing little interest in school or play. The mother was tempted to forge letters to allay the child's doubts. She could have told the child that her father had been murdered by the military. To do that, however, she had to be sure that he was *not* alive. In the end, I realised that the hesitation of the mother to tell the truth had its roots in *her own attitude* to the disappearance of her husband; she simply could not believe it and preferred to fabricate a story than to face the anguish of the truth.

Another case concerned a young woman whose husband was disappeared. In fact, they had been picked up together by agents of the Argentine Navy. She was released after a few days while he remained in secret custody. The woman managed to escape to England with her four-year-old son. The child shared with his mother the campaign for his father's release which Amnesty International helped organise. However, after some years there was still no news. The family moved to Nicaragua where the mother began to work. With more recent developments in Argentina, she felt the moment had come to tell the boy that their search had been in vain and probably they would never see the father again. There was no dramatic change in his behaviour knowing that. However, sometime afterwards the grandparents came from Argentina to visit and they were absolutely convinced of the imminent return of their son. They were scandalised that the grandchild considered him to be dead. It was only after their holiday came to an end that the mother could begin to explain things again to the child, including the attitude of his grandparents.

Naturally, the family situation often becomes most desperate where the mother is the victim. In one case in Argentina, seven children were taken with their mother by the authorities. After several days of secret detention, the children were released. The mother was never seen again except for a sighting some months later in another camp. Her serenity at the time of final separation had meant at least that the last memory they had of their mother was of a woman quietly in command. Ten years of anguish have passed both for the father and his family. The children, however, 'have been marvellous and received some very timely professional help'. Some are now married but all are remarkable in the way they have adapted to an extraordinary and demanding situation.

It is not, however, sufficient that the truth of the situation be communicated to the children. They must be able to see as they grow up that forced disappearances are not condoned by society, and that the military responsible are prosecuted. The case of a Salvadorean woman who recounted her story for me five years ago in Costa Rica comes to mind. She had suffered torture, rape and the murder of her own father and young daughter at the hands of uniformed Salvadorean military. She escaped because she pretended to be dead after receiving a bayonet wound which split open a good part of her back. After she had concluded her testimony, we began to speak about the work of the Irish Franciscan Missionaries in El Salvador with whom she had worked as a catechist. Her young child was learning to speak and had listened very attentively to his mother. The child haltingly began to explain that when he grew up he would get a gun to kill the soldiers who had murdered his grandfather and his sister. I can only say the child was deadly serious in his words which were among the first he had learned. If society does not bring to justice those responsible for such crimes, then children such as we have seen can scarcely be expected to have much confidence either in state institutions or the legal system.

There are also moving cases where children themselves are the victims. There are nearly two hundred documented cases in Argentina where children were taken with their mothers or were born in clandestine custody and have subsequently disappeared. Many have been adopted illegally and reared mostly by military officers. Similar reports have been received from other countries and it is probable that the Argentine problem is just one of many.

Such cases are too numerous to mention. Each experience is a book in itself. There is one incredible case concerning a Peruvian child abducted with her Argentinian mother by police in Bolivia. The mother and her year-old baby were handed over secretly to the Argentine police. Their whereabouts was later traced to a secret camp in Buenos Aires which specialised in the repression of Uruguayan citizens. The father was Uruguayan but had been shot by the military in Bolivia. The child was 'adopted' with false identity papers by the very police officer who had 'done away' with the mother who was never heard of again. After practically ten years of endless searching by the grandmother, the child's whereabouts was discovered. After a short legal battle the grandmother recovered the child. It is one of the few victories we celebrate in the struggle against disappearances in Latin America.

What is involved for the victim in the case of forced disappearances as we know it? It means that, after abduction, the victim is immediately taken to a clandestine detention centre, a type of modern concentration camp, where he/she suffers the most cruel tortures. One can cynically describe these places as a torturer's paradise. They can carry out their brutal task without any limits whatsoever. The victim is totally in the hands of an interrogator who forms part of some counter-insurgent task force. Testimonies of survivors point to the extreme cruelty that is meted out to prisoners in such centres. At the same time, there are privileges and benefits given to certain prisoners. For instance, some are allowed to go back on the street, visit bars and restaurants, or their families. The few prisoners who receive such treatment are either actively co-operating with their captors, or are targeted for reasons that are never very clear. This peculiar mixture of torture, extortion and privilege is aimed at the psychological and ideological destruction of the victim's personality, personal beliefs and values. There is the constant hooding for months on end, immobility such as living and sleeping on a mattress, sessions of torture with electricity, beatings, hangings or exposure to cold, hunger, thirst, asphyxiation, blackmail and then secret transfer to some other centre or to an unknown destination. This process may end in death itself where the remains are disposed of in a crematorium, or by more primitive methods. This is the reality of life in a modern Latin American concentration camp.

The picture we have painted of what the victims go through is based on testimonies of the all-too-few survivors. In Argentina there are scarcely a few hundred who have spent over a year in secret detention and have survived. Fewer still are prepared to tell their story and go into the courts to give testimony. But some have done so and are the principal witnesses in the trials against military officers who have been responsible for disappearances. Evidently, there are many more whose stay in these centres have been shorter than one year and whose testimonies are also very important.

Today, we can say without doubt that there is a lot of information available on conditions and life in the secret prisons. We can conclude that the experience of forced disappearances is unique for the victim. It is very different from political imprisonment and kidnapping. There are no legal formalities. The victim immediately loses his/her personal identity and is recognised afterwards by a number or nickname. Torture is carried out according to a programme with a heavy emphasis on sensory deprivation and behaviour-modification techniques. This underscores the professional and 'scientific' nature of the whole operation.

The isolation is what many survivors in Latin America found most difficult to take. Prisoners are isolated, hooded, chained and subjected to constant blaring music. After several months of such treatment, where the only change is a visit to the toilet once or twice a day, it is almost impossible to remain sane. There is then no certainty or predictability about the future. When we understand the importance of social life in all dimensions of Latin American culture, we can comprehend how disorientating solitary confinement can be over a short period of time. Its effects over a longer time can only be aimed at the destruction of the person. In a visit to El Salvador in March 1987 we were told of a group of seventeen prisoners who had been held secretly in the basement of the Treasury Police headquarters for over two years. Almost a hundred political prisoners are still missing in Peru after the massacre in 1986 of over three hundred political prisoners. There were unconfirmed reports in 1988 that many were alive in secret detention in a navy base where they were undergoing a re-education programme – the euphemism used for such cases.

In the regular contact I have with many survivors, I must confess that they have been through such a deep traumatic experience that it is not very easy to be objective in one's judgements. Many have the same survivor complex characteristic of the Nazi death camp victims: 'Why me?' 'How do I judge my behaviour in captivity?' 'What can I do to speak for the rest?'[7]

Their experiences need to be studied and reflected on, and certainly they have a great deal to teach us. For example, *O Dia de Angelo* (Angelo's Day), a novel by Frei Betto, a Brazilian theologian who himself spent some years in prison during the late 1960s, is a masterly exposé of the inner search of a Christian in secret detention in Brazil.

By now the reader must realise that the phenomenon of forced disappearances, which might have seemed as one other violation of human rights, is much more complex. It really is a new sub-world that has intruded itself into Latin America. When we examine the relations of this problem with the state and official institutions, we can come close to the heart of the challenge it poses to Christian Faith.

FORCED DISAPPEARANCES AND THE STATE

As far as the authorities are concerned, the practice of disappearances is a reality to be concealed. Governments even deny systematically the existence of the disappeared, and allege that they have absolutely nothing to do with the victims. The armed groups that carry out the abductions operate with total freedom. If by some chance there are uniformed police at the time of a kidnapping, they quietly stand back. In many countries, these groups operate on an official basis and do nothing to conceal their identity as members of the security forces. The secret detention centres, some of which have a capacity for over a hundred detainees, may be located anywhere in a country – in military bases, in private houses, in police stations. Yet, for some mysterious reason, these places which are publicly known can never be discovered by the authorities. There is the further question of clandestine cemeteries, unmarked graves or common burial pits. Bodies are disposed of in many ways – sometimes with a 'no-name' identification on the grave, in an open ditch, thrown in the sea, or cremated. Yet the authorities, and in particular the judges, can never 'find out' about such activities. History repeats itself and it is just like in Nazi Germany: in the 1930s, the concentration camps did not exist even though people saw the trainloads of people, the exterminations were not happening, and the authorities maintained against all the evidence that there was no 'final solution' in progress. But the public anti-semitic and anti-communist preaching of the fascists underline the veracity of the Nazis' hidden actions. In a similar way, one has in Latin America virulent public campaigns against 'subversives', 'delinquents' 'terrorists', 'international communists', 'narcotic-terrorists' and so on, in all countries where forced disappearances are a common practice. It is all part of the doctrine of national security which is the ideological backdrop for human rights violations in Latin America.

This doctrine emphasises the role of the armed forces in combating all those who put the security of the State in jeopardy. It points out that in the nation there is a constant battle against the enemies and no quarter must be given. This doctrine, which was considered by the Latin American bishops as anti-Christian in 1978,[8] justifies the violation of human rights of all who can be branded as enemies. It creates the loopholes which the clandestine operation of forced disappearances needs in order to function in any country. The armed forces, in carrying out the role assigned to them by this doctrine, create paramilitary forces with unlimited power to organise counter-insurgency campaigns. Military jurisdiction means that civil judges are prevented from investigating arrests in army barracks. Under the pretext of national security, security forces invade homes without search warrants, arrest anyone considered suspect, and cover up the crimes of torture, homicide and forced disappearance. In practice, they become an omnipotent force which can harass, persecute and murder at will. If at some time they are prosecuted for these types of violations, they will argue, as in Argentina, that they were merely carrying out orders. There is a 'final solution' underway in countries where forced disappearances regularly occur.

Unfortunately, the national security argument is evident even in some Latin American constitutional democracies where the rationale used is the defence of democracy. Painfully, we have to accept, in Latin America at least, that civilian governments are no guarantee against continuing human rights abuses. Evidently, the strongest argument that can be used for such drastic forms of repression is the existence of certain groups who have resorted to violence to forward their political cause. One thinks of movements such as 'Shining Path' (Sendero Luminoso) in Peru, the Manuel Rodríguez Front in Chile, Farabundo Martí Liberation Front in El Salvador and similar groups in Colombia, Ecuador and Guatemala. It is normal for the authorities to apply the anti-terrorist argument in these circumstances as a rationale for a so-called 'dirty war'. Those who call for a moderate and restrained response are branded as wimpish. The most reactionary factions entrenched in the armed forces begin to take command. The results of recent Latin American history are there to be seen: thousands exiled, dead or disappeared.

INVESTIGATION OF DISAPPEARANCES

Under pressure from the human rights community, some governments have finally decided to investigate the whereabouts of the disappeared. This has usually occurred when there is a change of regime or of some leading military figure. The investigation may be entrusted to parliament, the judiciary, or to a special commission. Human rights organisations, each with an archive of cases, usually submit documentation to these bodies to facilitate their task. Some inquiries have done very valuable work revealing the dimensions of the phenomenon. Other investigations have worked more to conceal the practice of disappearances as has been the case in Honduras, Peru, Colombia and Guatemala. In successive investigations, such as the presidential CONADEP Commission in Argentina, which was presided over by writer Ernesto Sábato, and the National Commission, appointed by President Siles Suazo in Bolivia, the military have rarely co-operated. No official investigation has been able to answer to date, the question of families, 'What has happened to the disappeared?'

We have seen earlier some of the difficulties with respect to the administration of justice in terms of defining the practice, but the problems involved are immense and extremely sensitive. In Argentina where most headway in prosecuting the military has been made, the civilian government of Dr Raúl Alfonsín confirmed most of the judges who had turned a blind eye to the crimes of the dictatorship, arguing that the judicial system should not be interfered with – an opinion obviously not shared by these judges who meekly accepted all types of executive interference during the Videla dictatorship. When justice begins to finally move against the guilty, the cases are normally passed on to military courts and then, only on appeal, can the ordinary judicial system come into play. The military are never satisfied until a total amnesty decree is promulgated or some similar measure adopted based on questions of 'due obedience', 'abrogation of justice' (Uruguay) or that the prosecution time limit has been passed. Arguing the need for national reconciliation, these measures are taken and families are considered vindictive, living in the past or pursuing policies that deliberately destabilise democracy when they continue demanding truth and justice. Guatemala, Brazil, and Chile have closed all possible criminal proceedings for human rights violations through amnesty laws; Argentina and Uruguay had adopted similar policies by mid-1987.

THE INTERNATIONAL COMMUNITY[9]

We have seen how the UN has been actively involved in this problem since 1978 and has centred its efforts on getting official confirmation about the whereabouts of the disappeared. New ground was broken in UN procedures when it was accepted that the Working Group on Forced Disappearances could directly transmit the individual complaints received to governments. An urgent action mechanism has been created whereby a case can be presented to the authorities by the UN in the first few days after it has occurred.

The Inter-American Human Rights commission has used a similar method for many years. Within their own sphere of interest, UNESCO and the International Labour Organisation, the International Red Cross and international parliamentary organisations also take up the question of forced disappearances. Non-governmental organisations, such as Amnesty International, FEDEFAM, FIDH, Pax Christi and so on have been most active campaigning against this flagrant violation.

There is universal consensus that the practice of political disappearances goes against all principles of international law and the very concept of human decency. To date, however, international concern for this problem is almost exclusively expressed at the diplomatic level. Many human rights groups, above all FEDEFAM, wish to generate more urgency and resolution in the way the problem is being handled on an international level. There is a longstanding call to the General Assembly to declare forced disappearances a crime against humanity which must then be incorporated into national and international law. The families of the disappeared rightly demand that the problem be given the type of priority that is accorded to genocide, torture and apartheid. They hope that the UN will shortly adopt a Convention against forced disappearances, but world opinion must be informed and mobilised to pressurise governments to effect such an urgently needed programme. Disappearances, together with the practice of extra-judicial executions, are the challenge of our times.

Confronted by the phenomenon of forced or involuntary disappearances in Latin America, the Catholic Church might have been expected to proclaim the gospel and defend the most basic of all rights – the right to life. Although many church members have spoken out and given witness in defence of human rights, many bishops and clergy have remained part of the status quo. In order to comprehend this phenomenon, it is important to understand the peculiar historical role of the Catholic Church in Latin American society. That role began with the European conquest of the New World in the fifteenth and sixteenth centuries. The Spaniards and the Portuguese sought in Catholicism the formal justification for violent conquest and expropriation of lands and peoples. The Vatican entrusted to the countries of the Iberian Peninsula the mission to establish the Church all over Latin America and introduce the natives to its doctrines and practices. It must be stressed, however, that some of the clergy – and this point was made in the chapter by Peter Hebblethwaite – did intercede in a heroic way with the colonial powers in defence of the local people. Clergymen like Bartolomé de las Casas defended the rights of the indians and interceded on their behalf in Madrid.

However, the dissident voices of individual clergymen faded as the Church enjoyed the patronage and the largesse of the State in Latin America. The roots of the State–Church go back to the conversion of the Emperor Constantine and the establishment of Christianity as the religion of the Roman Empire. In Latin America, the State–Church emerged and this is even reflected in the architecture and layout of most Spanish American towns. The Church is generally found in the *plaza* (square) – the traditional centre of the urban community. Alongside the Church one finds the local government offices, the police barracks and governor's residence. Tradition usually demanded that all public civil ceremonies included the active participation of the head of the local church.

The influence of the French Revolution, the Enlightenment and the growth of liberalism during the nineteenth century challenged the place of the State–Church in society. Nevertheless, despite more recent developments which strongly advocated separation of Church and State in the wake of Vatican II, Catholicism continues to be the official religion in most Latin American countries with the exception of Uruguay, Mexico, Cuba and Nicaragua. But even in those countries just mentioned, the power of the Catholic Church is very noticeable.

The historical links between Church and State, which have turned Catholicism into a State–Church in most Latin American countries, have helped establish the mentality among many bishops and clergy that the Church is the spiritual guardian of the nation. The relationship is very intimate. In such circumstances, the hierarchy sometimes shares the opinions, prejudices and politics of the civil authorities even when state repression and terror are used to put down social and political unrest. In many Latin American countries, the Catholic Church has proved to be a very powerful political actor and has lent its considerable institutional weight to changing a regime. In the nineteenth century the Church experienced persecution at the hands of liberal governments. Mexico provides the best example of that phenomenon. However, in the latter part of the twentieth century, many members of the Catholic Church have been persecuted by regimes which have accused the Church of having changed sides in the social and political struggle. I will return to this later.

Getting down then to the question of disappearances and human rights violations, the general attitude of the hierarchical Church has been to uphold the official position in so far as the institution is close to the centres of political and military power. There is often a very special affinity between the military, higher clergy and the officer corps in particular. Both the Catholic Church and the armed forces are similar institutions in some respects, vertical in structure, dedicated, at least externally, to ritual. In fact, over the years the relationship has often grown so close that in most countries a bishop is assigned exclusively to the armed forces as chaplain-in-chief. The military relate directly to him rather than to the local 'civilian' church, so to speak.

On the question of disappearances, the authorities will often deny the existence of the problem to any clergyman who decides to take up cases which families have brought to him. And he may well believe the government without realising that he is being misled. Many bishops in Latin America have their hands tied due to the traditional role of the Church. It is a battle to convince some bishops that the political and human rights situation is not as they would like it to be. It is an ongoing task of human rights organisations to inform the hierarchy of what is really going on.

It is not surprising, when observing the reality of the different countries where disappearances and other human rights violations occur, to see that the predominant attitude of the Church (as an institution) is practically to ignore the problem or to be officially 'silent' about it. At some stage, a church may come to express concern and preoccupation about the situation, but it will not assume a committed position favouring the existing human rights organisations and the affected families.

If the majority of clergy tend to be non-committal at least in their public role, there is always a minority encrusted in the institution whose opinions are totally in accordance with the ideas, doctrines and practices of the armed forces. They are naturally the clergy who are part of the military as chaplains and bishops. This sector utilises a mixture of virulent anti-communism, right-wing Catholicism (tradition, fatherland and property movements, Spanish falangism, Bishop Lefebre and so on) and military camaraderie to endorse and promote public campaigns against 'subversion', the enemies of the fatherland, the traditional way of life, the Catholic Faith and defend the leading tenets of the national security doctrine.

Many people have written extensively on the renewal of the Churches that has been taking place in Latin America over the last twenty years. The Vatican Council and its teaching has certainly been the focal point for this renewal. From there ultimately sprang so many leading concepts such as the Church as People of God, the priesthood of the laity, dialogues with the modern world and with all philosophies, the separation of Church and State, the preferential option for the poor, critiques of militarism, capitalism and a re-evaluation of human rights. For so many generations Church teaching had been hesitant about many social and political issues and since the French Revolution it considered that any talk about human rights could be used to oppose the rights of religion or the Church. At Vatican II the key concept of religious freedom was re-emphasised. This has marked a turning point in the life and mentality of many Catholics.

In Latin America all these 'new winds', as Pope John XXIII called the changes introduced in the Church, were enthusiastically received and adapted to everyday life with the results we know. There has been an important renewal of the Church, its traditional role is being questioned, and there is the growth of theological reflection with liberation theology so that now people have begun to speak of two churches. The differences between the traditional Church and the Conciliar Church are indeed so great that, on a sociological level at least, there are two recognisable and contrasting churches present in society. The Second Vatican Council has given a tremendous boost to participation by the poor in the mainstream of the Church; there are thousands of chapels in poor communities where there were none before; religious congregations have begun to ration their attention to elite education while they give priority to popular education, late vocations are encouraged whereas a few years ago this majority sector of the population was ignored.

I title this position 'the believing Church' to use a phrase that can cover all positions that go from a very strict interpretation of the Church and renewal to a very broad and progressive view where some of the most radical sectors of the Church tend to situate themselves. However, all, even those with a most orthodox vision of Vatican II situate themselves principally as believers, men and women of faith, whereas those who espouse the traditional vision are concerned primarily with the ecclesiastical institution – and the military church, if the reader can accept that phrase, which is above all the military with religion as an appendix.

There is no doubt then that the believing Church is in general deeply concerned about human rights and in many cases is prepared to put aside institutional concern and risk church 'interests' in taking up a conflictive position with the authorities on human rights issues. This was quite clearly the case in Chile where the Archbishop of Santiago, Cardinal Silva Henríques decided in 1973 to establish a critical distance between himself and the Pinochet regime. Later, he created the Vicariate of Solidarity which worked under Church auspices but was totally dedicated to the defence of the people without inquiring of their religious practice. Since 1978, the Vicariate of Solidarity has been so identified with the struggle of the families of the disappeared that it has rented an office beside the cathedral in Santiago to the National Committee of Families of the Disappeared in the same Church building where it has its own offices. In contrast, we have seen in Argentina that the military Church has been to the forefront. Public expressions of the Church to the cause of human rights have been limited to a few bishops in dioceses very isolated from the political centre of the country.

In Central America and Brazil, the Church has taken up a very clear position on human rights. There are the testimonies of El Salvador's martyr-bishop, Oscar Romero, and Brazil's Archbishop Helder Câmara and Cardinal Arns, among many others. It was Archbishop Romero who advised the mothers of the disappeared to organise themselves into a committee which now carries his name. In Guatemala, the Church has become more supportive of the families of the disappeared. There is a similar process in Peru although in the areas where there is most repression, such as Ayacucho, the local church remains extremely reactionary and feudal. However, at the national level things are quite different and the Peruvian bishops conference has set up a special human rights office where people can come to bring their cases and can expect to be defended.

It is important to emphasise that the believing Church has become the victim of human rights violations including the practice of forced disappearances. In Argentina, ten religious were 'disappeared' by the military and have not been heard of again. The numbers of priests and religious disappeared in El Salvador, Guatemala, Colombia and Brazil are also high. The issue that Christians are victims because of their faith opens up the whole question of martyrdom. Some traditional writers consider that one cannot speak of martyrs in Latin America as Christians have not sacrificed themselves for the faith in itself, but rather in the defence of human rights or the people. The only modern martyrs by that definition would be in an atheistic country. Such an opinion is of dubious historical value and points to the divorce which still exists in some theology between faith and life. As one Latin American lay person puts it: no-one has ever been imprisoned for singing Christmas carols either in Russia or Latin America. If one were to endorse such an ethereal definition of martyrdom, it would be difficult to explain the death of Christ, the first martyr. The Vatican prefers to maintain silence on this question, as is typified by the case of Archbishop Romero murdered while celebrating mass. Christians in Latin America recognise him as a martyr but some prefer to ignore the circumstances of his death.

We have seen the many questions the issue of disappearances raises about the State, its institutions and politics. Now we are examining the challenge it poses to religion. Sooner or later, the phenomenon will oblige these societies to reformulate the very legal and institutional basis on which they are based so that such violations do not recur. Equally, at the religious level the phenomenon is not only disturbing but deeply questioning. A simple illustration will suffice: where do we situate the disappeared in the liturgy? Among the living or the dead? Should one celebrate Mass for a person whom we do not know to be alive or dead?

The traditional Church ignores such questions, the military Church is part of the problem and the believing Church is searching for answers.

The phenomenon of disappearances is one of the greatest affronts of our age, and certainly no-one interested in the well-being of the human race can ignore it, least of all the Church in its role as 'expert in humanity'. However, while disappearances are a plague to be eradicated, the movement of families of the disappeared has much to teach us.

The families of the disappeared have become a powerful moral force in Latin American society, calling for the changes that are necessary. The role of the family is vindicated and the inviolable nature of family relationships upheld. It is not unusual for a father or a mother, husband or wife, to abandon all their private concerns when a loved one becomes the victim of disappearances. A good example is the Horman family who searched for their son after he had disappeared in Chile. This was depicted brilliantly in the film 'Missing'. I met the family in the 1970s when they used to frequent Washington as a solitary lobby trying to get information about their son. No-one paid any attention to them. Jack Lemmon certainly did justice to the extraordinary growth and maturity which Mr Horman, a typical New York businessman, underwent as he searched for his son in Washington and Santiago.

Sometimes, the families of the disappeared are described as vindictive, disturbers of the public order, irreverent in their attitudes and all because of the insistence over the years on their demands. Some have even been called insane as is the case in Argentina with the movement 'Madres de Plaza de Mayo'. Others have been described as terrorists as the State Department branded the Archbishop Romero Mothers' Committee in El Salvador. Yet, they continue with their work because they know they are defending the most sacred right of all: the right to life in human dignity. The fact that the majority of the members of the movement are women and mothers who have discovered that they need to move out of the kitchen into the public arena to guarantee the defence of their children is one of the most moving and significant realities of modern Latin American society. That is not to say that these groups do not have their limitations, but certainly when the Church speaks of parental responsibility, the inviolability of the family and life itself, the families of the disappeared can be a very important ally.

The movement, organised in the Latin American Federation of Families of the Disappeared (FEDEFAM) of which I had the honour to be executive secretary for six years, is indeed unique. In conversation with UN experts on disappearances, Mr Hilaly (Pakistan) lamented to us that in other parts of the world such as Asia no movement existed. However, now it would seem that families in the Philippines have organised themselves in a group with the very meaningful name FIND. In Europe which has been witness to so many tragedies in the twentieth century, if families of the victims of war had organised themselves in the 1920s and 1930s to defend life and say 'never again', modern history could have been very different.

I conclude with this most hopeful of messages. In Latin America the families of the disappeared are quietly changing history. They have become a most determined and moving voice in defence of the right to life. This constitutes an authentic sign of the times which we Christians and our Churches need to support if the message of hope which is at the heart of the gospel is to come fully alive in our troubled world.

NOTES

1. RESOLUTION ADOPTED WITHOUT A VOTE BY THE GENERAL ASSEMBLY ON 20 DECEMBER 1978 ON DISAPPEARED PERSONS

The General Assembly,

Recalling the provisions of the Universal Declaration of Human Rights, and in particular articles 3, 5, 9, 10 and 11, concerning, *inter alia*, the rights to life, liberty and security of person, freedom from torture, freedom from arbitrary arrest and detention, and the right to a fair and public trial; and the provisions of articles 6, 7, 9 and 10 of the International Covenant on Civil and Political Rights, which define and establish safeguards for certain of these rights,

Deeply concerned by reports from various parts of the world relating to enforced or involuntary disappearances of persons as a result of excesses on the part of law enforcement or security authorities or similar organizations, often while such persons are subject to detention or imprisonment, as well as of unlawful actions or widespread violence,

Concerned also at reports of difficulties in obtaining reliable information from competent authorities as to the circumstances of such persons, including reports of the persistent refusal of such authorities or organisations to acknowledge that they hold such persons in their custody or otherwise to account for them,

Mindful of the danger to the life, liberty and physical security of such persons arising from the persistent failure of these authorities or organisations to acknowledge that such persons are held in custody or otherwise to account for them,

Deeply moved by the anguish and sorrow which such circumstances cause to the relatives of disappeared persons, especially to spouses, children and parents,

1. *Calls upon Governments:*

(a) In the event of reports of enforced or involuntary disappearances, to devote appropriate resources to searching for such persons and to undertake speedy and impartial investigations,

(b) To ensure that law enforcement and security authorities or organisations are fully accountable, especially in law, in the discharge of their duties, such accountability to include legal responsibility for unjustifiable excesses which might lead to enforced or involuntary disappearances and to other violations of human rights,

(c) To ensure that the human rights of all persons, including those subjected to any form of detention and imprisonment, are fully respected,

(d) To cooperate with other Governments, relevant United Nations organs, specialized agencies, intergovernmental organisations and humanitarian bodies in a common effort to search for, locate or account for such persons in the event of reports of enforced or involuntary disappearances;

2. *Requests* the Commission on Human Rights to consider the question of disappeared persons with a view to making appropriate recommendations;

3. *Urges* the Secretary-General to continue to use his good offices in cases of enforced or involuntary disappearances of persons, drawing, as appropriate, upon the relevant experience of the International Committee of the Red Cross and of other humanitarian organisations;

4. *Requests* the Secretary-General to draw the concerns expressed in this resolution to the attention of all Governments, regional and inter-regional organizations and specialized agencies for the purpose of conveying on an urgent basis the need for disinterested humanitarian action to respond to the situation of persons who have disappeared.

(UN document A/RES 33/173)

2. Commision Indépendant sur les Questions Humanitaires, *Disparus* (Paris: Berger-Levrault, 1986) p. 39.
3. Comisión Nacional sobre la Desaparición Forzada de Personas (CONADEP) *Nunca Más* (Buenos Aires: EUDEBA, 1985). English translation, London: Faber & Faber, 1986.
4. Figures are derived from the following sources:
   [1] CONADEP (Comisión Nacional sobre la Desaparición Forzada de Personas).
   [2] CNID (Comisión Nacional de Investigación de los Desaparecidos).
   [3] Com. Bras. Anis. (Comité Brasileiro por la Anistía).
   [4] Vicariate of Solidarity.
   [5] CINEP (Centro de Investigación Nacional y Educación Popular).
   [6] CEDEE (Comité Ecuménico Dominicano de Educación Ecuménica).
   [7] UN HRC (United Nations Human Rights Commission).
   [8] GAM (Grupo de Apoyo Mutuo por el Aparecimiento con vida de nuestros Familiares).
   [9] CDHG (Comisión de Derechos Humanos de Guatemala).
   [10] CODEH (Comisión de Derechos Humanos de Honduras).
   [11] CNPPDEP (Comité Nacional Pro-defensa de Perseguidos, Desaparecidos y Exiliados Políticos de Mexico).
   [12] CNDPDH (Comisión Nacional de Defensa y Promoción de los Derechos Humanos).
   [13] Com. Ds Hs (Comité Panameño de Derechos Humanos).
   [14] Comisión Ds Hs (Comisión de Derechos Humanos del Paraguay).
   [15] Ds Hs Fiscalía (Oficina de Derechos Humanos, Fiscalía General de la Nación.
   [16] Socorro Juridíco Cristiano.
   [17] Com. Inv. Congreso (Comisión Investigación de Congreso).
   [18] Diputados Congreso.
5. Amnesty International, '*Disappearances*', *A Workbook* (New York: Amnesty, 1981) pp. 109–18.
6. Reports of PIDEE (Protección a la Infancia Dañada por los Estados de Emergencia), (Santiago, Chile, 1986).
7. Eduardo Luis Dualde, *El Estado Terrorista Argentino* (Buenos Aires: Argos Vergara, 1983) pp. 145–87.
8. CELAM (Latin American Bishops Conference), Puebla, Mexico, 1978.

9. See Amnesty International, *'Disappearances', A Workbook*, and Commission Indépendant sur les Questions Humanitaires, *Disparus*, for fuller treatment of the subject.

21 Catholicism in Latin America: Conclusions and Perspectives

Dermot Keogh

Graham Greene, in his foreword to this volume, has written of the 'immensity of the changes' that have taken place in the Catholic Church in Latin America over the past sixty years. He was expected, as a convert to Catholicism, in the England of that time, to belong politically to the Right and support causes like that of General Franco's *cruzada* during the Spanish Civil War.[1] Although there remains a strong rightist Catholic tradition in Latin America – the resilience of which is often underestimated in Europe[2] – the last fifty years have been characterised by conflict and change.[3] But that change has been far from uniform, or unilinear. Professor Poulat has aptly chosen the metaphor 'terrain of manoeuvres' to capture that complex reality. The continued co-existence of the 'Church of the status-quo' and the 'believing Church' – to use Patrick Rice's terms – reflects the tensions that have led to fragmentation and change. During the 'dirty war' in Argentina in the 1970s where Patrick Rice and his wife Fatima were 'disappeared' for a time, the polarisation between the Constantinian model of Church and the model of the 'believing Church' was most in evidence. The identification of many of the higher clergy and hierarchy with the Argentinian military, so feelingly illustrated by Emilio Mignone, stands in contrast with the Christian opposition to militarism. The military in Argentina fought a war which was 'beyond good and evil'. They were assisted in the execution of that campaign against 'terrorism' and 'communism' by many members of the hierarchy who believed in the closest affinity between Church and State. The end justified the means.[4] But fundamental to the profound divisions within the Argentinian church was a conflict between rival ecclesiologies.

Each chapter has treated the divisions within the Catholic Church in Latin America. The struggle by the Church to distance itself from the State has been a feature of a Catholicism reacting to the liberalism of the nineteenth century. There was a clerical comfort with political conservatism which formed a bridge between colonial Latin America and twentieth-century oligarchical rule. The profundity of the present conflict within the Catholic Church in Latin America is traceable to a religion which has ceased to play its traditional role in society. The traditional alliance between conservatism and Catholicism has been challenged by the new theological visions so ably presented in this volume by Jon Sobrino, Rodolfo Cardenal and Enda McDonagh. There has been a rediscovery of the central biblical message – that the Good News was a message of liberation for the poor.

In historical terms, the relatively sudden shift by large sections of the Latin American church in support of a preferential option for the poor has evoked charges of betrayal and treason from sections of that society which have traditionally looked towards clergy to legitimise existing political structures. As a consequence, the violence against the Catholic Church and other churches in many countries has been acute. This is particularly true of Central America. Rodolfo Cardenal has chronicled the violence against lay and clerical groups who have opted for the poor and for social change. Christian engagement in societies of great inequality has resulted in widespread repression. The attempt to stereotype such work as political activism rather than pastoral engagement is rejected by many Latin American theologicans: 'It is necessary to defend the minimum', Archbishop Oscar Romero of San Salvador once told the Brazilian theologian, Leonardo Boff, 'which is God's greatest gift – LIFE'. Rooting pastoral action in that fundamental principle, many Latin American theologians stand in the same tradition as the great Dominican preacher and defender of the Indians in colonial times, Bartolomé de las Casas.

From Vatican II to Medellín, Puebla, and beyond, the Church in Latin America has struggled and divided over competing pastoral strategies based on differing interpretations of what is meant by a preferential option for the poor. CELAM has played a central role in the development of new directions for the Catholic Church in Latin America. François Houtart has argued that CELAM – once an agency for change in the 1950s and 1960s – has become a force in support of the 'new restoration', With over 800 bishops in Latin America, representing over 40 per cent of all Catholics, the future pastoral orientation of CELAM is a matter of major concern for the universal Church. But if CELAM continues to move towards a more conservative stance, the danger of the Brazilian hierarchy uncoupling itself from the former organisation is a recurring possibility. With over 300 bishops in Brazil, CELAM could only sustain such a departure with difficulty.

It might have been expected that the pastoral problems of Latin America would have been understood at the Vatican in the 1980s much better than in previous decades. In the pontificate of John Paul II, the Vatican has paid very full attention to that part of the world. There have been frequent papal visits. However, a populist pontificate is no substitute for the development of coherent policies towards the individual Latin American countries and regions. Peter Hebblethwaite has suggested that Pope Paul VI saw the necessity for giving latitude to the local churches and national hierarchies of the world. That was a recognition of pastoral particularisms. It still competes for attention at the Vatican long after the pontificate of Paul VI. The Cardinal Secretary of State, Agostino Casaroli, had been allowed to develop a subtle eastern European *ostpolitik* for the Vatican. A similar diplomatic and pastoral strategy towards the complex world of Latin America might also have proved worthwhile. But it was not allowed to happen. Faced with pastoral diversity in different parts of the world, there is growing evidence that some elements in the Vatican favour greater centralisation. The temptation to develop a global policy is real. Some see this as 'the new restoration' or as the universalisation of the Polish model of Church. There may be a temptation to interpret the papal role in Latin America as a strategy of containment.

Papal visits have yielded some results. The 'shuttle diplomacy' of Pope John Paul II has served to bring the social problems of Latin America to the immediate attention of the papacy. The response has been supportive of the 'preferential option for the poor'. The radicalism of the papal social message – reflected in John Paul II's speeches in Brazil – has received less attention internationally than the 'cases' against individual liberation theologians. The insensitivity with which Archbishop Romero was received in his final visits to Rome before his assassination has offended many Latin Americans. He felt that he had not had an opportunity to explain his case, so great was the misrepresentation of his position and views, to the Vatican.

After one particularly bruising audience, Romero found himself being consoled by Cardinal Baggio – a man with whom he would not have appeared to have had that much in common. Therefore, there appears to be a certain incongruity between the content of papal speeches and the response at the Vatican – in certain quarters – to the pastors who live with the realities of state repression and persecution. It is incumbent upon the Vatican – where there are bitter divisions in the Catholic Church – to be well informed on all topics, personalities and pastoral problems. The Cardinal Secretary of State ought to be the chief adviser to the Pope in matters of such delicacy involving issues of Church and State. But that has not always been the case in recent years. The resulting confusion and acrimony has not been particularly edifying. This must be avoided in the future.

The revolution that has taken place in theological thinking in Latin America over the past thirty years has challenged the Vatican to modernise and provide creative pastoral leadership. That is a particularly difficult role for the Papacy to adopt after centuries of interpreting events from a uniquely southern European perspective. Today the eastern European experience has been added but that has not proved sufficient to enable the Vatican to come to terms with the role of pastoral and theological leadership from the third world which was once the mere object of history. Of course, there is the fundamental need to preserve orthodoxy and avoid heterodoxy and heresy. The Papacy has a central teaching role which is recognised without challenge throughout Latin America.

But Church people in Latin America have witnessed with alarm the historical experience of a largely secularised Europe. There is a common determination not to allow the same thing to happen in Latin America where the new emancipation being worked for by many in the Church may yet bring true independence. If that period arrives in Latin American history, then the Church will not be perceived as having clung to privilege, supported the oligarchies and defended the actions of military dictators. It is the hope of many in Latin America that the role of the Argentinian church in the 1970s will be viewed as an aberration in the history of the latter half of the twentieth century.

There are three chapters in this volume – on Mexico, Cuba and Nicaragua – which reveal the reaction of the Catholic Church to revolution at different phases of the history of the twentieth century. The experience of Nicaragua stands in contrast to the role of the Catholic Church in both the Mexican and Cuban revolutions. In the case of Nicaragua, there has been a conscious effort by Church people to identify openly with the revolutionary process. That has led to sharp divisions within the Catholic Church. Priests have felt obliged to take up ministerial positions in government. That has proved a point of great controversy between the Nicaraguan ecclesiastical authorities and the individuals concerned. But that has not deterred the two Cardenal brothers and Miguel d'Escoto from holding on to their political portfolios even at the expense of having to give up their priestly duties. Nicaragua may prove to be the exception in the history of Latin America. It is a relatively poor country where the political elite has actively sought the direct participation of clergy in government. It is most unlikely that that would happen in any of the larger countries on the continent. But Nicaragua, in this regard, may well prove to be a model for a country like Paraguay. No matter how unusual the practice, the Vatican might be encouraged to keep in mind the contemporary needs of Latin America rather than to have their position coloured by the unhappy experiences of priests in government in twentieth-century Europe. This reverts back to the need for the greatest possible flexibility in pastoral direction from the Vatican rooted in an acceptance of the active leadership role of national hierarchies and the laity.

The mistakes committed by many churchmen in the nineteenth century which lost the support of sizeable sections of the urban classes in industrialised European society will not be repeated in Latin America if the analysis of Jon Sobrino prevails. The pessimism of certain Vatican officials about the preservation of orthodoxy will not stifle justice born of hope and charity in Latin America. 'What is envisaged here', writes Enda McDonagh, 'is a planet-wide movement for the transformation of human relationships from privilege and exploitation by the few into a community of freedom, justice and solidarity.'

NOTES

1. Frances Lannon, *Privilege, Persecution and Prophecy – The Catholic Church in Spain 1875–1975* (Oxford: Clarendon Press, 1987) pp. 170–223, and Dermot Keogh, *Ireland and Europe, 1919–1948* (Dublin: Gill & Macmillan, 1988) chapter 4.
2. José Comblin, *The Church and the National Security State* (Maryknoll, New York: Orbis, 1979).
3. Brian Smith, *Church and Politics in Chile: Challenges to Modern Catholicism* (Princeton, New Jersey: Princeton University Press, 1982) chapter 1.

Pierre Bigo, *The Church and Third World Revolution* (Maryknoll, New York: Orbis, 1977).
Philip Berryman, *The Religious Roots of Rebellion: Christians in the Central American Revolutions* (Maryknoll, New York: Orbis, 1984).
Donal Dorr, *Option for the Poor: A Hundred Years of Social Teaching* (Maryknoll, New York: Orbis, 1983).
Luigi Einaudi, *Changing Context of Revolution in Latin America* (Santa Monica, Ca.: Rand Corporation, 1966).
François Houtart and Emile Pin, *The Church and the Latin American Revolution* (Maryknoll, New York: Orbis, 1965).
Henry Landsberger (ed.), *The Church and Social Change in Latin America* (Indiana: Notre Dame, 1970).

4. Emilio Mignone, *Iglesia y Dictadura – el papel de la iglesia a la luz de sus relaciones con el régimen militar* (Buenos Aires: Ediciones del Pensamiento Nacional, 1986).

Bibliography

Abbott, Walter M. (ed.), *The Documents of Vatican II* (New York: Association Press and America Press; London and Dublin: Geoffrey Chapman, 1966).
Adams, Richard, *Crucifixion by Power. Essays on Guatemala national social structure, 1944–1966* (Austin: University of Texas Press, 1970).
Alonso, Isidro, *La Iglesia en América Latina* (Madrid and Freiburg: Feres, 1964), pp. 214–15, 208–9.
Alves, Rubén, *Christianisme, opium ou libération?* (Paris: Editions du Cerf, 1972).
———, *A Theology of Human Hope* (New York: Corpus, 1969).
Amnesty International, 'Disappearances', A Workbook (New York: 1981).
Assmann, H., *A Practical Theology of Liberation* (London: Search Press, 1975); US title: *Theology for a Nomad Church* (Maryknoll, New York: Orbis, 1975).
Azzi, Riolando, 'Elementos para a História do Catolicismo Popular', in *Revista Eclesiástica Brasileira*, 36 (March 1976) pp. 95–103.
———, 'A Igreja do Brasil na Defesa do Direitos Humanos', in *Revista Eclesiástica Brasileira*, 37 (March 1977) pp. 106–42.
Bailey, David C., *Viva Cristo Rey! The Cristero Rebellion and the Church–State Conflict in Mexico* (Austin: University of Texas Press, 1974).
Beeson, Trevor and Pearce, Jenny, *A Vision of Hope – the Churches and Change in Latin America* (London: Collins, 1984).
Berryman, Philip, 'Latin American Liberation Theology', *Theological Studies* 34 (September 1973) 357–95.
———, 'Popular Catholicism in Latin America', *Cross Currents* 21 (1971) 284–301.
———, *The Religious Roots of Rebellion: Christians in the Central American Revolutions* (Maryknoll, New York: Orbis, 1984).
———, 'What Happened at Puebla', in Daniel H. Levine (ed.), *Churches and Politics in Latin America* (Beverly Hills: Sage, 1980) pp. 55–86.
Bigo, Pierre, *The Church and Third World Revolution* (Maryknoll, New York: Orbis, 1977).
Boff, Clodovis, OSM, 'A influência política das Comunidades Eclesiais de Base (CEBs)', in SEDOC, vols 11–118 (janeiro–fevereiro de 1979) col. 809.
Boff, Leonardo, *Church, Charism and Power, or – Liberation Theology and the Institutional Church* (London: SCM, 1981; New York: Crossroad, 1986).
———, *Jesus Christ Liberator – a Critical Christology for Our Time* (Maryknoll, New York: Orbis, 1976 and 1979).
Bonilla, Victor Daniel, *Servants of God or Masters of Men. The Story of a Capuchin Mission in Amazonia* (Harmondsworth: Penguin, 1972).

Brading, David, *The Origins of Mexican Nationalism*, Cambridge Latin American Miniatures (Cambridge: Centre of Latin American Studies, 1985).
Brockman, James R., *Oscar Romero, Bishop and Martyr* (Maryknoll, New York: Orbis, 1982).
Broderick, Walter, *Camilo Torres* (Garden City, New York: Doubleday, 1975).
Bruneau, Thomas C., 'Basic Christian Communities in Latin America: their nature and significance (especially in Brazil)', in Daniel H. Levine (ed.), *Churches and Politics in Latin America* (Beverly Hills: Sage, 1980) pp. 225–37.
———, 'The Catholic Church and Development in Latin America: the Role of the Christian Base Communities', *World Development* 7 and 8 (1980) 535–44.
———, 'Church and Politics in Brazil: The Genesis of Change', *Journal of Latin American Studies* 17:2 (November 1985) 271–93.
———, *The Church in Brazil: The Politics of Religion* (Austin: University of Texas Press, 1982).
———, *The Political Transformation of the Brazilian Catholic Church* (New York and London: Cambridge University Press, 1974).
———, 'Power and Influence: An Analysis of the Church in Latin America and the Case of Brazil', *Latin American Research Review* 8 (Summer 1973) 25–52.
———, *Religiosity and Politicization in Brazil: the Church in an Authoritarian Regime* (Austin: University of Texas, 1981).
———, and Faucher, Philippe (eds), *Authoritarian Capitalism: Brazil's Contemporary Economic and Political Development* (Boulder, Colorado: Westview Press, 1981).
———, Mooney, Mary and Gabriel, Chester (eds), *The Catholic Church and Religions in Latin America* (Montreal: Centre for Developing Area Studies, 1985).
Cabestrero, Teófilo, *Ministers of God, Ministers of the People – Testimonies of Faith from Nicaragua* (Maryknoll, New York: Orbis, 1980).
———, *Mystic Liberation – a portrait of Bishop Pedro Casaldáliga of Brazil* (Maryknoll, New York: Orbis, 1981).
Calvo, Roberto, 'The Church and the Doctrine of National Security', *Journal of Interamerican Studies and World Affairs* 21:1 (February 1979) 69–88.
Câmara, Helder, *The Church and Colonialism: the Betrayal of the Third World* (Danville, New Jersey: Sheed & Ward, 1969).
Campos, Tomás R., 'La Iglesia y las organizaciones populares en El Salvador', *Estudios Centroamericanos* 359 (1978) 692.
Cardenal, Ernesto, *The Gospel in Solentiname*, 3 vols (Maryknoll, New York: Orbis, 1976, 1978, 1979).
Cardenal, Rodolfo, *Acontecimientos sobresalientes de la Iglesia de Honduras 1900–1962* (Tegucigalpa: 1974).
———, 'La crisis de la Iglesia nicaragüense', *Revista Latinamericano de Teología* 8 (1986).
———, 'En fidelidad al evangelio y al pueblo salvadoreño. El diario

pastoral de Mons. Romero', *Revista Latinamericano de Teología* 4 (1985) and 9 (1986).
———, *Historia de una esperanza. Vida de Rutilio Grande* (San Salvador: Universidad Centroamericano Editores, 1986).
———, *El poder eclesiástico en El Salvador (1871–1931)* (San Salvador: Universidad Centroamericano Editores, 1980).
Carrigan, Ana, *Salvador Witness* (New York: Simon & Schuster, 1984).
Carroll, Denis, *Towards a Story of the Earth* (Dublin: Dominican Publications, 1987).
———, *What is Liberation Theology?* (Cork: Mercier, 1986).
Carvalheira, Dom Marcelo Pinto, 'Momentas Históricas e Desdobramentos da Ação Católica Brasileira', in *Revista Eclesiástica Brasileira*, 43 (March 1983) pp. 10–28.
Cassidy, Sheila, *Audacity to Believe* (London: Collins, 1977).
CEHILA, *História General de la Iglesia en América Latina*, Volúmen 1, Introducción general; V, Mexico; VI Centroamerica; VII Colombia y Venezuela (Mexico and Madrid: Ediciones Sigueme S.A., 1985).
CELEM, *The Church in the Present Day Transformation of Latin America in the Light of the Council*, 2 vols (Bogotá: CELEM, 1970).
Comblin, José, 'The Church in Latin America after Vatican II', LADOC 1–18.
———, *The Church and the National Security State* (Maryknoll, New York: Orbis, 1979).
———, 'Para uma Tipología do Catolicismo no Brasil', in *Revista Eclesiástica Brasileira*, 28 (March 1968) pp. 46–73.
Commission Indépendant sur les Questions Humanitaires, *Disparus* (Paris: Berger-Levrault, 1982).
Costello, Gerald M., *Mission to Latin America – the successes and failure of a twentieth-century crusade* (Maryknoll, New York: Orbis, 1979).
Crahan, Margaret E., 'Religious Freedom in Cuba', *Cuba Review* 5 (September 1975) 22–7.
———, 'Salvation Through Christ or Marx: Religion in Revolutionary Cuba', *Journal of Interamerican Studies and World Affairs* 21 (February 1979) 156–84.
Cruise O'Brien, Conor, *The Siege: Saga of Zionism and Israel* (London: Weidenfeld & Nicolson, 1986).
———, *To Katanga and Back, a UN case history* (London: Hutchinson, 1962).
———, *The United Nations, sacred drama* (London: Hutchinson, 1968).
Davies, J. G., *Christians, Politics and Violent Revolution* (Maryknoll, New York: Orbis, 1976).
de Brucker, José, *Dom Helder Câmara* (London: Collins, 1979).
de Kadt, Emmanuel, *Catholic Radicals in Brazil* (New York and London: Oxford University Press, 1970).
———, 'Church, Society and Development in Latin America', *Journal of Development Studies* 8:1 (October 1971) 23–43.
———, 'Paternalism and Populism: Catholicism in Latin America', *Journal of Contemporary History* 2:4 (October 1967) 89–106.
Della Cava, Ralph, 'Brazilian Messianism and National Institutions: A

Reappraisal of Canudos and Joaseiro', *Hispanic American Historical Review* 48 (1968) 402–20.
————, 'Catholicism and Society in Twentieth-Century Brazil', *Latin American Research Review* 11 (1976) 7–50.
————, *Miracle at Joaseiro* (New York: Columbia University Press, 1970).
Dewart, Leslie, *Christianity and Revolution: The Lesson of Cuba* (New York: Herder & Herder, 1963).
Dodson, Michael, 'The Catholic Church in Contemporary Argentina', in A. Ciria (ed.), *New Perspectives on Modern Argentina* (Bloomington: University of Indiana Latin American Studies Program, 1972) pp. 57–67.
————, 'The Christian Left in Latin American Politics', *Journal of Interamerican Studies and World Affairs* 21 (February 1979) 45–68.
————, 'Liberation Theology and Christian Radicalism in Contemporary Latin America', *Journal of Latin American Studies* 11 (May 1979) 203–22.
————, 'Priests and Perónism: Radical Clergy in Argentine Politics', *Latin American Perspectives* 1 (Fall 1974) 58–72.
————, 'Religious Innovation and the Politics of Argentina: A study of the Movement of Priests for the Third World' (PhD Dissertation, Indiana University, 1973).
————, and Montgomery, Tommie Sue, 'The Churches in the Nicaraguan Revolution', in Thomas Walker (ed.), *Nicaragua in Revolution* (New York: Praeger, 1982) pp. 161–80.
Dorr, Donal, *Option for the Poor – One Hundred Years of Vatican Social Teaching* (Dublin: Gill & Macmillan; Maryknoll, New York: Orbis, 1983).
————, *Spirituality and Justice* (Dublin: Gill & Macmillan, 1985).
Dri, Ruben, *Teología y Dominación* (Buenos Aires: Colección Teológica y Política, Roblanco SRL, 1987).
Dulles, Avery, *Models of the Church* (Garden City, New York: Doubleday, 1974).
Dussel, Enrique, *De Medellín a Puebla: Una década de sangre y esperanza, 1968–1979* (Mexico: Edicol, 1979) pp. 49–82.
————, *Ethics and the Theology of Liberation* (Maryknoll, New York: Orbis, 1979).
————, *Hipótesis para una historia de la iglesia en América Latina* (Barcelona: Editorial Estela, 1967).
————, *A History of the Church in Latin America – colonialism to liberation* (Grand Rapids: Eerdmans, 1981).
————, *History and the Theology of Liberation* (Maryknoll, New York: Orbis, 1976).
————, 'El tercerismo eclesial: táctica política y mecanismo ideológico', in Elsa Támez and Saúl Trinidad (eds), *Capitalismo: Violencia y anti-vida. La opresión de las mayorías y las domesticación de los dioses*, Tomo I (San Jos, Costa Rica: EDUCA, 1978) pp. 315–27.
Eagleson, John (ed.), *Christians and Socialism: Documentation of the Christians for Socialism Movement in Latin America* (Maryknoll, New York: Orbis, 1975).

Eagleson, John, and Scharper, Philip, (eds), *Puebla and Beyond* (Maryknoll, New York: Orbis, 1979).
Eckstein, Susan, 'The Poverty of Revolution' (Thesis, Columbia University, 1972).
——— (ed.), Power and Popular Protest: Latin American Social Movements (Berkeley: University of California Press, 1989).
Einaudi, Luigi, Maullin, Richard, Stepan, Alfred and Fleet, Michael, *Latin American Institutional Development: The Changing Catholic Church* (Santa Monica: RAND Corporation, 1969).
Eisenstadt, S. N., *Tradition, Change and Modernity* (New York: John Wiley & Sons, 1973).
Ellacuría, Ignacio, SJ, *Freedom Made Flesh: the Mission of Christ and His Church* (Maryknoll, New York: Orbis, 1976).
Erdozaín, Plácido, *Archbishop Romero: Martyr of Salvador*, translated by John McFadden and Ruth Warner (Maryknoll, New York: Orbis, 1981).
Esquivel, Adolfo Pérez, *Le Christ au poncho* (Paris: Centurion, 1981).
Floridi, A. and Stiefbold, F., *The Uncertain Alliance: the Catholic Church and Organised Labor in Latin America* (Miami: Center for Advanced International Studies, 1973).
Freire, P., *Pedagogy of the Oppressed* (Harmondsworth: Penguin, 1972; New York: Seabury, 1971).
Frontalini, Daniel and Caiati, Cristina, *El mito de la guerra sucia* (Buenos Aires: Centro de Estudios Legales y Sociales (CELS), 1984).
Geffr, Claude and Gutiérrez, Gustavo (eds), 'Liberation and Faith', *Concilum* (June 1974).
——— and ———, *The Mystical and Political Dimensions of the Christian Faith* (New York: Herder & Herder, 1974).
Gheerbrant, Alain (ed.), *The Rebel Church in Latin America* (Baltimore: Penguin, 1974).
Gibellini, R., *Frontiers of Theology in Latin America* (Maryknoll, New York: Orbis, 1979).
Gilfeather, Katherine Ann, MM, 'Women Religious, the Poor and the Institutional Church in Chile', in Daniel H. Levine (ed.), *Churches and Politics in Latin America* (Beverley Hills: Sage, 1980) pp. 198–224.
Gillespie, Richard, *Soldiers of Perón – Argentina's Montoneros* (Oxford: Clarendon Press, 1982).
Girardi, Guilio, *Chrétiens pour le socialisme* (Paris: Editions du Cerf, 1976).
González, Manuel R., *La Iglesia Mexicana en cifras* (México: Center of Investigation and Social Action, 1969) p. 100.
Gremillion, Joseph (ed.), *The Gospel of Peace and Justice: Catholic Social Teaching Since Pope John* (Maryknoll, New York: Orbis, 1976).
Grubb, Kenneth G., *Religion in Central America* (London: World Dominion Press, 1937).
Gutiérrez, Gustavo, 'Liberation, Theology and Proclamation', in Claude Geffr and Gustavo Gutiérrez (eds), *The Mystical and Political Dimensions of the Christian Faith* (New York: Herder & Herder, 1974).
———, *The Power of the Poor in History* (London: SCM Press, 1983).
Guzmán, E. Jaime, 'The Church in Chile and the Political Debate', in

Pablo Baraona Urzua (ed.), *Chile: A Critical Debate* (Santiago: Institute for General Studies, 1972) pp. 277–309.
Haurion, A., 'Démocratie et forces religieuses', in A. Audibert, A. Bayet, B. E. Brown *et al.*, *La laïcité*, vol. VI (Paris: Presses Universitaires de France, 1960).
Hebblethwaite, Peter, *Christian-Marxist Dialogue and Beyond* (London: Darton, Longman & Todd, 1977).
———, *In the Vatican* (London: Sidgwick & Jackson, 1986).
———, *John XXIII, Pope of the Council* (London: G. Chapman, 1984).
———, *The New Inquisition?* (London: Collins, 1980).
———, *The Runaway Church* (London: Collins, 1975).
———, *Synod Extraordinary* (London: Darton, Longman & Todd, 1986).
———, *The Year of Three Popes* (London: Collins, 1978).
Hermet, Guy, *Les catholiques dans L'Espagne franquiste. Les acteurs du jeu politique*, vol. 1 (Paris: Presses de la Fondation Nationale des Sciences Politiques, 1980).
———, 'Les fonctions politiques des organisations religieuses dans les régimes à pluralisme limité, *Revue Française de Science Politique* 23 (1973) 439–72.
Hollenbach, David, *Claims in Conflict: Retrieving and Renewing the Catholic Human Rights Tradition* (New York: Paulist Press, 1979).
Holleran, Mary, *Church and State in Guatemala* (New York: Columbia University Press, 1949).
Houtart, François (ed.), *Aspects sociologiques du catholicisme américain* (Paris, Ouvrire, 1957) 1 traduction.
———, *El cambio social en América Latina* (Madrid: Feres, 1964).
———, *The Challenge to Change* (New York: Sheed & Ward, 1964) 2 traductions.
———, *Church and Development in Kerala* (Bangalore: Theological Publications in India, 1979).
———, *Church and Development in Sri Lanka* (Colombia: SEDEC, 1980).
———, *The Development Project as a social practice of the Catholic Church in India* (Louvain: 1976).
———, *L'éclatement d'une église* (Paris: Mame, 1969) 7 traductions.
———, *L'église et le Monde* (Paris: Le Cerf, 1962).
———, *Les paroisses de Bruxelles* (Bruxelles: ACH, 1952).
———, *Religion and Development in Asia* (Manilla: Baguio Feres Seminar, 1976).
———, *Religion and Ideology in Sri Lanka* (Bangalore: Hansa, Colombo, PTI, 1974).
——— (ed.), *Religion et modes de production précapitalistes* (Bruxelles: 1980) 2 traductions.
———, *Sociologie et pastorale* (Paris: Fleurus, 1961) 2 traductions.
——— and Lemercinier, G., *Genesis and institutionalisation of the Indian Catholicism* (Louvain-la-Neuve: CRSR, 1981).
——— and ———, *The great Asian religions in their social functions* (Louvain-la-Neuve: CRSR, 1980).

Houtart, François and Lemercinier, G., *Size and Structure of the Catholic Church in India – the indigenization of an exogenous religious institution in a society in transition* (Louvain-la-Neuve: CRSR, 1982).
——— and Pin, E., *L'Église, l'heure de l'Amerique latine* (Paris and Tournai: Casterman, 1964) 3 traductions. English translation: *The Church and the Latin American Revolution* (New York: Sheed & Ward, 1965).
——— and Cp de, M., Grond, L., *Nourrir les hommes* (Bruxelles: CEP, 1965) 2 traductions.
——— and Remy, J., *Église et société en mutation* (Paris: Mame, 1969).
——— and ———, *Milieu urbain et communauté chrétienne* (Paris: Mame, 1968).
——— and ———, *Sacerdoce, autorité et innovation dans l'église* (Paris: Mame, 1970) 1 traduction.
——— and Rousseau, A., *The Church and Revolution* (Maryknoll, New York: Orbis, 1971) 2 traductions.
Illich, Ivan, 'The Powerless Church', in Ivan Illich, *Celebration of Awareness* (New York: Doubleday, 1970) pp. 94–104.
———, 'The Vanishing Clergyman', in Ivan Illich, *Celebration of Awareness* (New York: Doubleday, 1970) pp. 69–94.
Jerez, César, 'Fe, esperanza y amor en una Iglesia que sufre. La Iglesia de Centroamerica después de Puebla', *Diakonia* 15, 59 (1980).
Klaiber, Jeffrey L., *Religion and Revolution in Perú, 1824–1976* (South Bend, Indiana: University of Notre Dame Press, 1977).
Keogh, Dermot (ed.), *Central America, Human Rights and U.S. Foreign Policy* (Cork: Cork University Press, 1985).
——— (ed.), *Romero: El Salvador's Martyr, a study of the tragedy of El Salvador* (Dublin: Dominican Publications, 1981).
Kloppenburg, Bonaventure, OFM, *The People's Church: A Defence of my Church* (Chicago: Franciscan Herald Press, 1978).
Küng, Hans, *The Church* (Garden City, New York: Doubleday, 1976).
———, *Truthfulness: The Future of the Church* (New York: Sheed & Ward, 1968).
Landsberger, Henry A. (ed.), *The Church and Social Change in Latin America* (South Bend, Indiana: University of Notre Dame Press, 1970).
Lane, Dermot (ed.), *Liberation Theology, an Irish Dialogue* (Dublin: Gill & Macmillan, 1976).
Lannon, Frances, *Privilege, Persecution and Prophecy – The Catholic Church in Spain, 1875–1975* (Oxford: Clarendon Press, 1987).
Lernoux, Penny, *Cry of the People. The Struggle for Human Rights in Latin America. The Catholic Church in Conflict with U.S. Policy* (New York: Penguin, 1980, 1982).
Levine, Daniel H., 'Authority in Church and Society: Latin American Models', *Comparative Studies in Society and History* 20: 4 (October 1978) 517–44.
———, 'Church Elites in Venezuela and Colombia: context, background and beliefs', *Latin American Research Review* 14:1 (Spring 1979) 51–79.
——— (ed.), *Churches and Politics in Latin America* (Beverley Hills: Sage, 1980).

Levine, Daniel H., *Conflict and Political Change in Venezuela* (Princeton: Princeton University Press, 1973).
——, 'Continuities in Colombia', *Journal of Latin American Studies* 17:2 (November 1985) 295–317.
——, 'Democracy and the Church in Venezuela', *Journal of Inter-american Studies and World Affairs* 18:1 (February 1976) 3–22.
——, 'Issues in the Study of Culture and Politics: a view from Latin America', *Publius* 4:2 (Spring 1974) 77–104.
——, 'Popular Organizations and the Church: thoughts from Colombia', *Journal of Interamerican Studies and World Affairs* 26 (February 1984) 137–42.
—— (ed.), *Religion and Political Conflict in Latin America* (Chapel Hill: University of North Carolina Press, 1986).
——, 'Religion and Politics: Drawing Lines, Understanding Change', *Latin American Research Review* 20:1 (Winter 1985) 185–201.
——, 'Religion and Politics in Comparative an Historical Perspective', *Comparative Policies* (October 1986).
——, *Religion and Politics in Latin America: the Catholic Church in Venezuela and Columbia* (Princeton: Princeton University Press, 1981).
——, 'Religion and Politics, Politics and Religion: an Introduction', *Journal of Interamerican Studies and World Affairs* 21:1 (February 1979) 5–29.
——, 'Religion and Politics: recent works', *Journal of Interamerican Studies and World Affairs* 16:4 (November 1974) 497–507.
—— 'Religion, Society and Politics: states of the Art', *Latin American Research Review* 16: 3 (Fall 1981) 185–209.
——, 'Urbanisation in Latin America: changing perspectives', *Latin American Research Review* 14: 1 (Spring 1979) 170–83.
——, 'Urbanisation, migrants, and politics in Venezuela', *Journal of Interamerican Studies and World Affairs* 17:3 (August 1975) 358–72.
——, 'Whose Heart Could be So Staunch?', *Christianity and Crisis, 22 July 1985*.
—— and Mainwaring, Scott, 'Religion and Popular Protest in Latin America' in Susan Eckstein (ed.), *Power and Popular Protest: Latin American Social Movements* (Berkeley: University of California Press, 1989).
—— and Wilde, Alexander, 'The Catholic Church, "Politics", and Violence: the Columbian Case', *Review of Politics* 39:2 (April 1977) 220–49.
Lewy, Guenter, *Religion and Revolution* (New York: Oxford University Press, 1974).
McDonagh, Enda, *Between Chaos and New Creation* (Dublin: Gill & Macmillan, 1986).
——, *The Demands of Simple Justice* (Dublin: Gill & Macmillan, 1980).
—— (ed.), *Irish Challenges to Theology* (Dublin: Dominican Publications, 1986).
——, *The Making of Disciples* (Dublin: Gill & Macmillan, 1982).
——, *Social Ethics and the Christian* (Manchester: Manchester University Press, 1978).
MacDonnell, Augusto Conte, Labrune, Noemi and Mignone, Emilio, *El secuestro como método de detención* (Buenos Aires: CELS, 1982).

McGovern, Arthur, *Marxism: An American Christian Perspective* (Maryknoll, New York: Orbis, 1981).
Mainwaring, Scott, 'A JOC e o Surgimento da Igreja na Base, 1958–1970', in *Revista Eclesiástica Brasileira* 43 (March 1983) 29–92.
———, *The Catholic Church and Politics in Brazil, 1916–1985* (Stanford: Stanford University Press, 1986).
Martin, Leonard, CSsR, 'Rumos da Igreja na Brasil: o método de Paradigmas como Instrumento de Análise das mudanças entre Medellín e Puebla' [Thesis] (Pontifícia Universidade Católica do Rio de Janeiro, 1980).
Mecham, J. Lloyd, *Church and State in Latin America* (Chapel Hill: University of North Carolina Press, 1964).
Melville, Thomas and Melville, Marjorie, *Whose Heaven, Whose Earth?* (New York: Alfred A. Knopf, 1971).
Merton, Thomas, *Faith and Violence: Christian Teaching and Christian Practice* (South Bend, Indiana: University of Notre Dame Press, 1968).
Meyer, Jean, *Apocalypse et Révolution au Mexique: La guerre des Cristeros* (Paris: Gallimard-Juillard, 1974).
———, *El Conflicto entre la Iglesia y el Estado* (Mexico: Siglo XXI, 1974).
———, *The Cristero Rebellion – The Mexican People between Church and State 1926–1929* (Cambridge: Cambridge University Press, 1976).
———, *Los Cristeros: sociedad e ideología* (Mexico: Siglo XXI, 1974).
———, *La Cristiada*, 3 vols (Mexico: Siglo XXI, 1973–4).
———, *La Cristiade: l'Église, l'État et le Peuple dans la Révolution Mexicaine* (Paris: Payot, 1975).
———, *La Guerra de los Cristeros* (Mexico: Siglo XXI, 1973).
Mignone, Emilio, 'Les déclarations abusives de disparitions, instrument d'une politique', in *Le refus de l'oublie – La politique de disparition forcée de personnes, Colloque de Paris*, janvier, février 1981 (Paris: Berger-Lévrault, 1982).
———, *Iglesia y Dictadura – El papel de la Iglesia a la luz de sus relaciones con el régimen militar* (Buenos Aires: Ediciones del Pensamiento Nacional, 1986).
———, *Witness to the Truth – The Complicity of Church and Dictatorship in Argentina* (Maryknoll, New York: Orbis, 1988). This is a revised edition of *Iglesia y Dictadura*.
Míguez Bonino, José, *Christians and Marxists: the Mutual Challenge to Revolution* (Grand Rapids: William B. Eerdmans, 1976).
———, *Revolutionary Theology Comes of Age* (London: SPCK, 1975).
Moltmann, Jurgen, *The Crucified God: the Cross of Christ as the Foundation and Criticism of Christian Theology* (New York: Harper & Row, 1974).
Montgomery, Tommie Sue, 'Latin American Evangelicals: Oaxtepec and Beyond', in Daniel H. Levine (ed.), *Churches and Politics in Latin America* (Beverley Hills: Sage, 1980) pp. 87–107.
Moreira-Alves, Marcio, *L'église et la politique au Brésil* (Paris: Editions du Cerf, 1974).
Mousnier, Roland, *Histoire générale des civilisations*, IV, *Les XVIe et XVIIe Siècles* (Paris: Presses Universitaires de France, 1967).

Mutchler, David E., *The Church as political factor in Latin America with particular reference to Colombia and Chile* (New York: Praeger, 1971).
O'Dea, Thomas F., *The Catholic Crisis* (Boston: Beacon, 1968).
———, *The Sociology of Religion* (Englewood Cliffs, NJ: Prentice-Hall, 1966).
O'Halloran, James, *Living Cells – Developing a small Christian Community* (Dublin: Dominican Publications; Maryknoll, New York: Orbis, 1984).
O'Malley, William J., SJ, *The Voice of Blood: Five Christian Martyrs of Our Time* (Maryknoll, New York: Orbis, 1980).
Paoli, Arturo, *Freedom to be Free* (Maryknoll, New York: Orbis, 1927).
Paul VI, Pope, 'Populorum Progressio', 1967, in Joseph Gremillion (ed.), *The Gospel of Peace and Justice: Catholic Social Teaching since Pope John* (Maryknoll, New York: Orbis, 1976) pp. 387–415.
Payne, Stanley G., *Política y sociedad en la España del siglo XX* (Madrid: Akal, 1978).
Paz, Nestor, *My life for my friends: the Guerrilla Journal of Nestor Paz, Christian* (Maryknoll, New York: Orbis, 1975).
Poblete, Renato, 'From Medellín to Puebla: Notes for Reflection', *Journal of Interamerican Studies and World Affairs* 21:1 (February 1979) 31–44.
———, Galilea, Carmen W., and van Dorp, Patricia, *Imagen de la iglesia de hoy y religiosidad de los Chilenos* (Santiago: Centro Bellarmino, 1980).
Pomerlau, Claude, 'The Changing Church in Mexico and its Challenge to the State', *Review of Politics* 43 (1981) 450–559.
Poulat, Emile, *Les cahiers manuscrits de Fourier* (Paris: Editions du Minuit, 1957).
———, *L'église, c'est un monde* (Paris: Editions du Cerf, 1986).
———, *Études sur la tradition française de l'Association Ouvrière* (Paris: Editions du Minuit, 1955). En collaboration.
———, *Histoire, dogme et critique dans la crise moderniste* (Paris: Casterman, 1962, 1979).
———, *Intégrisme et catholicisme intégral* (Paris: Casterman, 1969).
———, *Journal d'un prêtre d'après-demain (1902–1903)* (Paris: Casterman, 1961).
———, *Naissance de prêtres-ouvriers* (Paris: Casterman, 1965).
———, *Priests and Workers. An Anglo-French Discussion* (London: SCM, 1961). En collaboration.
Purcell, Susan K., *The Mexican Profit-Sharing Decision: Politics in an Authoritarian Regime* (Berkeley: University of California Press, 1975).
Pyke, Frederic B. (ed.), *The Conflict between Church and State in Latin America* (New York: Alfred A. Knopf, 1964).
Rahner, Karl, *Shape of the Church to Come* (New York: Seabury Press, 1974).
Ramos, R., *Foundations of Christian Faith: An Introduction to the idea of Christianity* (New York: Seabury Press, 1978).
———, *The Spirit of the Church* (New York: Seabury Press, 1979).
———, Alsonso, I., and Garre, D., *La Iglesia en México Estructuras eclesiásticas* (Freiburg and Bogotá: Feres, 1963).
Read, William R. *el al.*, *Latin American Church Growth* (Grand Rapids: William B. Eerdmans, 1969).

Richard, Pablo, *Mort des chrétientés et naissance de l'église* (Paris: Centre Lebret, 1978).

——, *Origine et développement du mouvement 'Chrétiens pour le Socialisme' Chili, 1970–1973* (Paris: Centre Lebret, 1976).

Roldan, Otto G., *La Iglesia católica mexicana como grupo de presión* (Mexico: UNAM, 1981) Cuadernos de Humanidades, n. 17.

Romero, Oscar, *Romero, Martyr for Liberation* [last two homilies with analysis by Jon Sobrino] (London: CIIR, 1982).

——, *Voice of the Voiceless – the four pastoral letters of Oscar Romero and other statements* (Maryknoll, New York: Orbis, 1985).

——, *La voz de los sin voz; La palabra viva de Monseñor Oscar Arnulfo Romero*, introduction, commentaries and selection of text by R. Cardenal, L. Martin-Baró and Jon Sobrino (San Salvador: Universidad Centroamericano Editores, 1980).

Rosa, Martín de la, 'La Iglesia católica en México: del Vaticano II a la CELAM III', *Cuadernos Políticos* 19 (January–March 1979) 88–104.

Sanders, T. G., *Catholic Innovation in a Changing Latin America* (Cuernavaca: CIDOC, 1969).

——, 'The Chilean Episcopate: an institution in transition', *West Coast South America Series* 15, 3 (New York: American Universities Field Staff, 1968).

——, 'The New Latin American Catholicism', in D. E. Smith (ed.), *Religion and Political Modernisation* (New Haven, Conn.: Yale University Press, 1974) pp. 282–301.

——, 'The Theology of Liberation: Christian Utopianism', *Christianity and Crisis* 33:15 (17 September 1973) 167–73.

—— and Smith, Brian H. 'The Chilean Catholic Church during the Allende and Pinochet regimes', *West Coast South America Series* 23, 1 (New York: American Universities Field Staff, 1976).

Segovia, Rafael, *La politización del niño méxicano* (Mexico: University of Mexico Press, 1975).

——, *The Sacraments Today*, vol. 4, *A Theology for Artisans of a New Humanity* (Maryknoll, New York: Orbis, 1974).

Segundo, J. L., 'Capitalism–Socialism: A Theological Crux', in C. Geffr and G. Gutiérrez (eds), *The Mystical and Political Dimensions of the Christian Faith* (New York: Herder & Herder, 1974) pp. 105–26.

——, *The Community Called Church*, Vol. I, *A Theology for Artisans of a New Humanity* (Maryknoll, New York: Orbis, 1973).

——, *Evolution and Guilt*, Vol. 5, *A Theology for Artisans of a New Humanity* (Maryknoll, New York: Orbis, 1974).

——, *Grace and the Human Condition*, Vol. 2, *A Theology for Artisans of a New Humanity* (Maryknoll, New York: Orbis, 1973).

——, *The Liberation of Theology* (Maryknoll, New York: Orbis, 1976).

——, *Our Idea of God*, Vol. 3 *A Theology for Artisans of a New Humanity* (Maryknoll, New York: Orbis, 1974).

——, *Theology and the Church: A Response to Cardinal Ratzinger and a Warning to the Whole Church* (Minneapolis: Winston Press, 1985).

Simpson, John and Bennett, Jana, *The Disappeared* (London: Sphere Books, 1986).

Smith, Brian H., 'Christians and Marxists in Allende's Chile: Lessons for Western Europe', in Suzanne Berger (ed.), *Religion and Politics in Western Europe* (London: Frank Cass, 1982).

———, *The Church and Politics in Chile: Challenges to Modern Catholicism* (Princeton: Princeton University Press, 1982).

———, 'Churches and Human Rights in Latin America: Recent Trends in the Subcontinent', *Journal of Interamerican Studies and World Affairs* 21 (February 1979) 89–128.

———, 'The Impact of Foreign Church Aid: The Case of Chile', in Gregory Baum and Andrew Greeley (eds), *Communication in the Church* (New York: Seabury Press, 1978).

———, 'Religion and Social Change: Classical Theories and New Formulations in the Context of Recent Developments in Latin America', *Latin American Research Review* 10 (Summer 1975) 3–34.

——— and Rodríguez, José Luis, 'Comparative Working-Class Political Behaviour: Chile, France and Italy', *American Behavioural Scientist* 18 (September–October 1974) 59–96.

Sobrino, Jon, *Christology at the Crossroads*, translated by John Drury (Maryknoll, New York: Orbis, 1978); Spanish edition: *Cristología desde América Latina* (Mexico: Centro de Reflexión Teólogica, 1976).

———, *Romero, Martyr for Liberation* (London: Catholic Institute for Internal Relations, 1982).

———, *The Theology of Liberation*, LADOC Keyhold Series, no. 2 (Washington, DC: United States Catholic Conference, 1974).

———, *The True Church and the Poor* (London: SCM Press, 1984).

———, 'El Vaticano II y la Iglesia en América Latina', in *El Vaticano II, veinte años después* (Madrid: Educiones Cristianidad, 1985).

——— and Pico, Hernández (eds), *Theology of Christian Solidarity* (Maryknoll, New York: Orbis, 1985).

Torres, Camilo, *Father Camilo Torres: Revolutionary Writings* (New York: Harper & Row, 1972).

Torres, Sergio and Eagleson, John (eds), *The Challenge of Basic Christian Communities* (Maryknoll, New York: Orbis, 1981).

——— and Fabella, Virginia, *The Emergent Gospel: Theology from the Underside of History* (Maryknoll, New York: Orbis, 1978).

Turner, Frederick G., *Catholicism and Political Development in Latin America* (Chapel Hill: University of North Carolina Press, 1971).

United Nations Working Group on Forced or Involuntary Disappearances (Commission on Human Rights), *Annual Reports*, 1981–1987 (Geneva: Centre of Human Rights, Palais de Nations, 1981–1987).

United States Catholic Conference, *Basic Christian Communities*, LADOC Keyhold Series, no. 14, Latin American Documentation (Washington, DC: USCC, 1976).

United States Congress (Committee on Foreign Affairs, House of Representatives), *Human Rights and the Phenomenon of Disappearances* (Washington: US Government Printing Office, 1980).

Vallier, Ivan, *Catholicism, Social Control and Modernization in Latin America* (Englewood Cliffs, NJ: Prentice–Hall, 1970).

Vallier, Ivan, 'Comparative Studies of Roman Catholicism: Dioceses as Strategic Units', *Social Compass* 16:2 (1969) 147–84.
——, 'Extraction, Insulation and Re-entry: towards a Theory of Religion Change', in H. Landsberger (ed.), *The Church and Social Change in Latin America* (South Bend, Indiana: University of Notre Dame, 1970) pp. 9–35.
——, 'Radical Priests and the Revolution', in D. Chambers (ed.), *Changing Latin America: New Interpretations of its Politics and Society* (New York: Academy of Political Science, 1972) pp. 15–26.
——, 'Religious Élites: differentiations and developments in Roman Catholicism', in Seymour M. Lipset and A. Solari (eds), *Élites in Latin America* (New York: Oxford University Press, 1967) pp. 190–232.
Vekemans, Roger, *Agonía o resurgimiento. Reflexiones teológicas acerca de la 'contestación' en la iglesia* (Barcelona: Editorial Herder, 1972).
——, *Caesar and God: the Priesthood and Politics* (Maryknoll, New York: Orbis, 1972).
——, 'La iglesia en el proceso de liberación', *Tierra Nueva* 19 (September 1976) 80–6.
——, 'Iglesia y cambio social en América Latina', *Tierra Nueva* 11 (October 1974) 36–64.
——, 'Unidad y pluralismo en la iglesia', *Tierra Nueva* 5 (April 1973) 45–50.
Verbitsky, Horacio, *La última batalla de la tercera guerra mundial* (Buenos Aires: Editorial Legasa, 1984).
Vigil, María López, *Muerte y vida en Morazán. Testimonio de un sacerdote* (San Salvador: Universidad Centroamericano Editores, 1987).
Vives, Cristián, 'La solidaridad: una forma de evangelizar y participar en la iglesia' (Santiago: Centro Bellarmino, 1978) mimeograph.
Whale, John (ed.), *The Man Who Leads the Church* (London: Collins, 1980).
White, Robert A., 'Structural factors in rural development: the church and the peasant in Honduras' (PhD dissertation, Cornell University, 1977).
Wilde, Alexander, 'The Contemporary church: the Political and the Pastoral', in R. Albert Berry, Ronald G. Hellman and Mauricio Solaún (eds), *The Politics of Compromise: Coalition Government in Colombia* (New Brunswick, NJ: Transaction Books, 1980) pp. 207–35.
——, 'The years of change in the Church: Puebla and the Future', *Journal of Interamerican Studies and World Affairs* 21 (August 1979) 299–312.
Ynfante, Jesús, *La prodigiosa aventura del Opus Dei* (Paris: Ruedo Iberico, 1970).

Index